ISBN 979-8-9884558-1-3
90000
9 798988 455813

UPSC

English Grammar and Composition

For UPSC, PSC, State Exams, SSC, RRB, State Boards Bank P.O. and other competitive examinations

Chandan Sukumar Sengupta

UPSC English Grammar

and Composition

For UPSC, PSC, State Exams, SSC, RRB, State Boards Bank P.O.

and other competitive examinations

Chandan Sengupta

Continuing Educatin Series

UPSC English Grammar and Composition

Chandan Sengupta.

ISBN xxx-x-xxxxx-xx-x

In a wider perspective this workbook can be used as a reference material by other fellows. The Question Bank addresses patterns of problems of all possible levels. So there is no specific boundary of distinction of any class or any specific stream of study. Any aspirant remaining engaged in regular studies can have access to this Question Bank. Materials used here were collected from various sources and are also cross checked for finding out specific difficulties. We effectively sortlisted such areas and prepared a revised edition of this volume. This question bank module can also be a helpful companion for aspirants who seek admission in different strams of jobs, services and fellowships for which they have to opt for some examinations duly conducted by UPSC, PSC, SSC, RRB or any other boards of study. This workbook will provide an ample scope to students of high School standard to improve skills related to language and inter—personal communication. Communication process in modern world should be digitally sound also.We aspire for higer scope of progress as students involving in active communication process gains a lot.

Font size of some of the practice papers are kept small for ensuring accommodation of the material of large volume. Students of higher class can explore them with an ease. They may not feel any specific problem while moving through content areas.

Resource Centre: Arabinda Nagar, Bankura, PIN – 722101 (W.B.) Attn: Chandan Sukumar Sengupta

.

This Book is dedicated to fellow aspirants of Continuing Education.

Contents

Foreword

English language users are growing worldwide in a big way. People prefer this language for its wider use and simple rules. English is often classified as a Germanic language because of its shared innovations with other Germanic languages like Dutch, German and Swedish. All these languages developed primarily from proto Germanic stock. Verbs are divided into strong and weak classes. Use of modal verbs is common to all these languages. The period of Early Modern English (1500 to 1700 A.D) was characterised by the Great Vowel Shift, inflectional simplifications and linguistic standardisation. Each shift triggered the subsequent shift in the vowel system. Mid and open vowels were raised and close vowels were finally broken into different types of dipthongs. The Great Vowel Shift also explains the different types of pronunciation as it is recorded in modern English than compared to other languages.

Due to expansion of the British Empire during 18th Century English moved into colonies and got prominence due its wider acceptability among global communities. This language retained its most of the prime position even after attainment of political freedom. All the commonwealth countries maintained a big community of English users. It continued expanding even during the digital age due to the use of English as a base language of Information Technology. Worldwide broadcasting in English made by BBC made this language more popular during the tenure of World War II.

Another standard use of English gained popularity in and around the Non-British zones in the form of American English. Loss of grammatical case is almost complete in modern English. Such case is found only in pronouns, such as he and him, she and her, who and whom. The use of do-support with the verb have is becoming standardised. Regularisation of some irregular forms continues with some sort of slow pace (Example dreamed instead of dreamt). British English also started accepting some sort of changes under the influence of American English to make the language techno-friendly.

According to one of the estimate (2016) 400 million people spoke English as their first language and 1.1 billion accepted it as a secondary language.[1] Almost all the countries and majority of islands got accommodation of English speaking community.[2] The English speaking countries are categorised in three prominent circles: [3] The Inner Circle Countries (having majority of native people speaking English), The Outer Circle (only a small part of community speak English) and Expanding Circle (number of English speaking people increases day by day).

This language can also be considered as pluricentric language as none of the countries or authorities set the standard for using this language. Every country has their own standards and they use such standard for examining skills of the inmigrants as well as job seekers. That is why we have different types of examinations like that of TOEFL for examining the skill of job seekers and inmigrants. Both formal and informal style of this language is now incorporated in the majority of National Curriculum to facilitate the fellow students and to make them fit for such examinations.

This workbook will provide practice materials from traditional as well as informal use of English. One should gain such skill before aspiring for some higher level test. Daily practice is most important in this regard.

Examination is a process through which some of the candidates from a large population are to be selected for fulfilling a particular purpose. Students in general are job seekers, but few of them learn for gaining personal enhancement. They also move on in search of some study materials which can equip them positively so that a considerable ace can be obtained while addressing questions of specific types in examination.

Expectation of parents from their ward resides primarily on the aspect of a gain of high score in examination. They also imply their burden of expectations

[1] "Which countries are best at English as a second language?". World Economic Forum. Archived from the original on 25 November 2016. Retrieved 29 November 2016.
[2] Crystal, David (2003b). The Cambridge Encyclopedia of the English Language (2nd ed.). Cambridge University Press. ISBN 978-0-521-53033-0. Archived from the original on 11 May 2021. Retrieved 4 February 2015.
[3] Svartvik, Jan; Leech, Geoffrey (2006). English – One Tongue, Many Voices. Palgrave Macmillan. ISBN 978-1-4039-1830-7. Retrieved 5 March 2015.

on the fellow student without considering the level of emotions and bands of feelings. Choice factor, wills and wishes of fellow students should be addressed a little so as to ensure their effective participation in the process of examination and evaluation. Fear of examination is generally developed due to the kinds of expectations their parents and other associates imposed upon the ward. It also takes a shape of fear due to the pre-determined idea of the development of agony in the condition if examination results go down. Exam fear itself eats u a considerable part of memory by diverting waves of thinking towards gaining a preparedness which is required to face some sort of adverse situation during the down play duly anticipated by the ward in advance.

How to overcome?

Matter is very simple as well as easy to follow.

1. Prepare a time bound task and maintain the same throughout the academic session.
2. Take support of some standard books on the basis of the types of inputs you want.
3. Consider examination as a part of life as we have to appear periodically all the time up to a prolonged span of our life.
4. Examination also provides us a scope of assessing our own levels of understanding and we should move on through rectification process instead of crying for the performance or score of desired levels duly expected by elders.
5. Examination cannot be considered as any mode of status with which we are to exhibit some superiority on others. It should not be taken as a status symbol or a scale of gradation in society.
6. Examination is not the ultimate state of scaling through which we judge the performance of a student in real life situation.
7. There are lots of other sectors of life for which there is no examination: how pa person is talking; how a person is using words while making some good sentences; the capability of a person to establish and maintain relationship with others; effort of performing a task whenever chance comes; healing others if asked for etc. are some of the hundreds of scaling through which a personality can be judged.
8. Our school system cannot consider all the parameters of scaling to say the level of the personality of a student.
9. There are thousands of cross-academic as well as hybrid faculties available to be opted by students in society. That is why dying for only selected faculty and hunting for money cannot be considered as any brilliant idea.
10. One should have positive mental attitude towards addressing issues and concerns in daily life.
11. Regular study is most important and effective too than compared to intensive study of a short period of time.
12. We always rely upon other non-standard process due to their cheap availability. One should not compromise with quality.
13. Treasure of knowledge never moves towards us, but we have to move towards the treasure of knowledge.
14. There are several sources available in market from which the basic modules required for a specific purpose to be fulfilled can be obtained and also can be worked out for accelerating the regularised study.

Volume of practice material is less important than the strategy with which such volume of practice materials can be used or re-arranged.

Publisher

September 2024

Preface

There are millions of books available in market which can introduce a learner to English language and English grammar. More discussed theme of language learning is the English Grammar. This effort came in focus due to the increasing demand of people from different walks of life regarding the type of workbook which can equip a student in a specific way in terms of the enhancement of language related skills.

This workbook is designed to provide additional study materials to fellow students of High School standards. They equip themselves differently by making them fit for forthcoming examination. Learning by doing is the best way of acquiring such kinds of skills in stipulated time frame.

A language stands upon its rules of grammar and compositions. Similar mechanism is applicable to English also. It has such kinds of sets of rules through which one can aspire for the attainment of a perfectness in writing and expressions.

English as a language is not so difficult for any non-English person. The basic structure of English language is user friendly and is also of a comprehensive type. Modern instruments are also much friendly with this language. Because of this reason and some other, English as a user friendly language is becoming popular day by day. Number of people from non-English community who can read, write and speak English quite fluently are growing in number day by day. They are also taking different roles assigned to them in the cosmopolitan environment.

Non-English learners and aspirants often feel difficulties in pronunciation English words properly with needful tunings. These difficulties often become a serious obstacle while some English people go on trying to establish communication with them. Due to such difficulties also they often become disqualified in proving their capabilities of doing something fruitful.

This workbook and practice manual will provide an ample scope of gaining adequate skill and competence in linguistic communication. Stress is implied in the portions related to grammar and composition of the language so as to enhance the related skills and competences of the fellow learner.

It is also recommended that one should go on practicing related exercises alongside the referral readings for the purpose of gaining proficiency. A discussion on the common mistakes related to the grammar and composition of this language is also included for the purpose of drawing attention of fellow students and aspirants towards the content areas of the communication techniques.

English as a language came to India along with the colonial rule. They people felt it necessary to educate a considerable part of Indian as well as Asian communities in English for ensuring their service lines in the colonies. It was more perfectly pitched in through religious propagations.

People of India accepted the language gladly and started getting adjusted with the cultural bands of English orientation. This West Germanic language is developed from Anglo-Frician dialects.[4] This dialect is brought to Britain during 6th to 7th Century by Anglo-Saxon[5] Migrants. In due course of time this language developed considerably and transformed into the dialect of modern time.[6] Anglo–Saxon dialect was more commonly known as old-English.[7] Near about 400 Latin loan Words[8] were

---

[4] *The Anglo-Frisian languages are the Anglic and Frisian varieties of West Germanic languages. The Northumbrian Language Society also considers Northumbrian a separate Anglic language.*
[5] *The Anglo-Saxon settlement of Britain is the process which changed the language and culture of most of what became England from Romano-British to Germanic. The Germanic-speakers in Britain, themselves of diverse origins, eventually developed a common cultural identity as Anglo-Saxons.*
[6] *Burke, Susan E (1998). ESL: Creating a quality English as a second language program: A guide for churches. Grand Rapids, Michigan: CRC Publications. ISBN 9781562123437.*
[7] *Shore, Thomas William (1906), Origin of the Anglo-Saxon Race - A Study of the Settlement of England and the Tribal Origin of the Old English People (1st ed.), London, pp. 3, 393*

introduced in English alongside the advent of Christianity. During the development Middle English near about 10,000 loan words from French origin[9] entered the English dialect and made it an enriched one. Fully developed English dictionary, the Dictionary of the English Language, was published by Samuel Johnson in 1755. English Grammar by Pristle[10] was an added contribution in the line of development of English Language. In modern time the total English speaking community worldwide may exceed 1.5 billion mark![11] There are several other instances to ascertain the fact regarding the ever increasing popularity of the International Language. It has also secured a prominent position in the international arena as a common dialect that people can opt with an ease.

After becoming assured about the ever increasing popularity of this language we can now imply adequate focus on the development of skills and competence of our fellow students and aspirants through exposing them to the horizon of interactives related to perfect and advanced English dialect. We also expect a timely participation of fellow scholars in this effort. They can continue evaluating their own skills through learning continuity supplemented with self paced evaluations.

Evolution of English Pronoun is another additional advantage of the modern English. Conflated forms of pronouns are also called an objective case. Development of such name is only because it is used only for objects of verbs. Once in old English there was distinct case system for both accusative and dative purposes. Later on such system collapsed into a single system of object (oblique) case having utility for objects of either a verb or a preposition. Studies in English were introduced in different universities during 19th and 20th Century because of its continuous developments in non-European continents. Development of such study was remarkably high in USA during 1970s.[12] It was also due to incorporation of English as another official language in most of the countries in the world.

Different courses in English are meant for different purposes. Studies in English are further accelerated with the advent of Informatics and allied fields. We consider English as a second language (a language study meant for non-English person). Errors in English are mainly observed from the field of syntax error, vocabulary error and error related to punctuations. Rules in English are periodically introduced by different scholars time to time. Not to terminate a sentence by preposition, for an example, was the another rule introduced by *Robert Lowth*[13] .

Chandan Sukumar Sengupta

Author/Publisher

---

[8] *English is a Germanic language, with a grammar and a core vocabulary inherited from Proto-Germanic. However, a significant portion of the English vocabulary comes from Romance and Latinate sources. A portion of these borrowings come directly from Latin,*

[9] *Baugh, Albert and Cable, Thomas. 2002. The History of the English Language. Upper Saddle River, New Jersey: Prentice Hall. pp. 158-178.*

[10] *Joseph Priestley was an English chemist, natural philosopher, separatist theologian, grammarian, multi-subject educator, and liberal political theorist who published over 150 works.*

[11] *Algeo, John. 2010. The Origins and Development of the English Language. Boston, MA: Wadsworth. pp. 182-187.*

[12] *National Center for Education Statistics (January 1993). "120 Years of American Education: A Statistical Portrait" (PDF). National Center for Education Statistics. Retrieved September 12, 2018.*

[13] *Robert Lowth (26 March 1794). A Short Introduction to English Grammar: With Critical Notes. Printed for J.J . Tourneisin – via Internet Archive.*

Key Points

English as a language for any non-english learner is a difficult task. People get afraid of their own limitations and stop interacting. Some of the fellow students put themselves at the side having negligible skill of speaking and interacting. Because of that reason also they seldom find themselves involved in the process of delivering something in writing or speech with any clear apprehension. Use of any uncommon words cannot make any writing beautiful. Writing of any specific type should have a definite pattern which is generally prescribed by some of the international organisations. Writing will reflect the types of thought process through which a writer express feelings, desires, wishes and wills. Writing also reflects the type of personality and the type of knowledge base. Even people express their feelings by carving some symbols for conveying some previously ascertained messages. People in olden times used to write letters in a quite descriptive way. Some of such letters has become the part and parcel of literature. A letter that changed the course of history is written by Albert Einstein. F. D. Roosevelt, President of the United States, White House, Washington, D. C. Sir: Some recent work by E. Fermi and L. Szilard, which has been communicated to me in manuscript, leads me to expect that the element uranium may be turned into a new and important source of energy in the immediate future. Certain aspects of the situation which has arisen seem to call for watchfulness and, if necessary, quick action on the part of the Administration. I believe therefore it is my duty to bring to your attention the following facts and recommendations. In the course of the last four months it has been made probable through the work of Joliot in France as well as Fermi and Szilard in America that it may become possible to set up a nuclear chain reaction in a large mass of uranium, by which vast amounts of power and large quantities of new radium-like elements would be generated. Now it appears almost certain that this could be achieved in the immediate future. it is conceivable —though much less certain—that extremely powerful bombs of a new type may thus be constructed." .... some more paragraphs continued : "Yours very truly, A. Einstein." Another letter drafted by Martin Luther King Jr. from Burminghum Jail is as follows: 16 April 1963 My Dear Fellow Clergymen: While confined here in the Birmingham city jail, I came across your recent statement calling my present activities "unwise and untimely." Seldom do I pause to answer criticism of my work and ideas. If I sought to answer all the criticisms that cross my desk, my secretaries would have little time for anything other than such correspondence in the course of the day, and I would have no time for constructive work. But since I feel that you are men of genuine good will and that your criticisms are sincerely set forth, I want to try to answer your statement in what I hope will be patient and reasonable terms.

Introduction

We will point out some of the basic pre-requisite of using good English while speaking and writing.

Some of the divisions of grammar, as prominently pointed out by different thinkers, are as follows:

There are four great divisions of Grammar, viz.:

a) Orthography, Etymology, Syntax, and Prosody.

b) Orthography treats of letters and the mode of combining them into sets of words.

c) Etymology treats nature of the various classes of words as grouped in the grammar work and the changes they undergo.

d) Syntax treats the connection and arrangement of words to be made perfectly in formation of sentences.

e) The manner of speaking and reading and accommodation of different kinds of verse (Prosody).

f) The three first mentioned concern us most.

g) A distinct sound produced by a single effort of shall, pig, dog [A syllable]. In every set of such distinct sound there must be at least one vowel.

h) A word, having adequate capability of expressing things, works or ideas meaningfully, consists of one syllable or a combination of syllables.

i) The best way to divide words into syllables is to follow, as closely as possible, the divisions made by the organs of speech in properly pronouncing them.

j) There are two distinct types of articles: a or an and the. A or an is called the indefinite article because it does not point put any particular person or thing but indicates the noun in its widest or generalised sense. The points out any particular person, thing or place distinctly.

k) Inflection by which we signify whether the noun is the name of a male, a female, of an inanimate object or something which has no distinction of sex [Gender].

Grammar refers to the way words are used, classified, and structured together to form coherent written or spoken communication. This guide takes a traditional approach to teaching English grammar, breaking the topic into three fundamental elements: Parts of Speech, Inflection, and Syntax. Each of these is a discrete, individual part, but they are all intrinsically linked together in meaning.

The parts of speech are the categories to which different words are assigned, based on their meaning, structure, and function in a definite format of a sentence. We'll look in basic patterns and use of the seven main parts of speech—nouns, pronouns, verbs, adjectives, adverbs, prepositions, and conjunctions—as well as other categories of words that don't easily fit in with the rest, such as particles, determiners, and gerunds.

Inflection: Although the parts of speech provide the building blocks for writing and speaking pattern of English, another very important element in this regard is inflection; the process by which words are changed in form to create new and specific meanings. There are two main categories of inflection: conjugation and declension.

Conjugation refers to the inflection of verbs, while declension refers particularly to the inflection of nouns, pronouns, adjectives, and adverbs. Whenever we change a verb from the present tense to the past tense, for an example, we use conjugation. For making a noun plural to show that there is more than one of it, we use declension.

There are four simple moods,—the Infinitive, the Indicative, the Imperative and the Subjunctive.

The Mood of a verb basically denotes the mode or manner in which it is used in a sentence. Thus if it is used in its widest sense without reference to person or number, time or place, it is in the Infinitive Mood; as "To run."

A verb is used to indicate or declare or ask a simple question or make any direct statement [Indicative Mood]. "The boy likes his book most." Here a direct statement is made concerning the boy. When the verb is used to express a command or entreaty it is in the Imperative Mood as, "Go away." "Give me a penny."

There are different aspects of the Grammar of English language which we come across during the interaction through this workbook. Most prominent ones will be from the daily use of English language to ensure effective communication. Noun, Verbs, Adjectives and Adverbs form open class of Parts of Speech as they readily accept new members in a sentence.[14] Words belonging to similar Parts of Speech exhibit similar syntactical behaviour. Determiners are traditionally classified with adjectives, and have no special place as Parts of Speech in the set of rules. Words having derivational suffixes can be identified as a member of Parts of Speech but general words attain such status only after placing it in a sentence. For an example, run can serve as either a verb or a noun (these cases are regarded as two different lexemes[15]). The lexeme run has some of the common forms runs, ran, runny, runner, and running.

We consider all naming words as Nouns. It is evident from our daily use that many common suffixes form nouns from other nouns or from other types of words, such as -age (as in shrinkage), -hood (as in sisterhood), and so on, although some other nouns are base forms not containing any such suffix (such as cat, grass, eagle, India, France). Pronouns replace a Noun in a sentence and take the role of possessives also (for example: This is his pen.)

English determiners constitute a relatively small class of words and are principally grouped under the head Adjectives. They include the articles "the" and "a[n]"; certain demonstrative and interrogative words such as this, that, and which; possessives such as my and whose (the role of determiner can also be played by noun possessive forms such as John's and the girl's); various quantifying words like all, some, none, scanty, many, various; numerals of ordinal type (first, second, fifth etc.) and numerals of cardinal type (one, two, etc.). There are also many phrases being used in day to day communication (such as a couple of) that can play the role of determiners.

To go through this concept of using determiners in a sentence we rely upon availability of some group of words as determiner. In many contexts, as evident from our daily use, it is required for a noun phrase to be completed with an article or some other determiner. It is not grammatically appropriate to say or write "Cat sat on table."; one must say: " [Our/My/His/A black] cat sat on the table". There exists some common situations in which a complete noun phrase can be formed without a determiner when it refers generally to a whole class or concept (Example: Lions are violent. Dogs are dangerous. Beauty is subjective) and when we speak about a name (Jane, Spain, etc.).

.

---

[14] *Carter, Ronald; McCarthy, Michael (2006), Cambridge Grammar of English: A Comprehensive Guide, Cambridge University Press, p. 984, ISBN 0-521-67439-5*
[15] *In general consideration a lexeme is a unit of lexical meaning that underlies a set of words that are related through inflection. It is a basic abstract unit of meaning, a unit of morphological analysis in linguistics related to English Language that roughly corresponds to a set of forms taken by a single root word.*

1. Popular Phrases

It's a Zoo Out There

Smell a Rat
(feel that something is wrong)
How come the front door is open? Didn't you close it
before we went shopping?
I'm sure I did. I can't understand it.
Frankly, I smell a rat.
Me, too. I'm convinced that something is definitely
wrong here.
We'd better call the police.
Goto the Dogs
(become run-down)
Have you seen their house lately? It's really gone to
the
dogs. It's true that it has become run-down and in
serious
need of repair, but I'm sure that it can be fixed up to
look like new.
I guess with a little carpentry work and some paint it
could look pretty decent.

Fishy
(strange and suspicious)
When the security guard saw a light in the store after
closing hours, it seemed to him that there
was something fishy going on. He called the central
office and explained to his superior that he
thought something strange and suspicious was
occurring.

Take the Bull by the Horns
(take decisive action in a difficult situation)
Julie had always felt that she was missing out on a
lot of fun because of her clumsiness on the
dance floor. She had been putting off taking lessons,
but she finally took the bull by the horns
and went to a professional dance studio for help. She
was tired of feeling left out and acted
decisively to correct the situation.

Horse of a Different Color

(guite a different matter)
Eric likes to play jokes on his friends, but he makes
sure that nobody is hurt by any of his
pranks. A prank that hurts someone is a horse of a
different color! Being playful is one thing,
but hurting someone by one's prank is quite a
different matter.

Let the Cat Out of the Bag
(inform beforehand)
Bob was going to retire from teaching in June, and
the foreign language department was
planning on presenting him with some luggage at his
retirement dinner. He wasn't supposed to
know about it, but someone let the cat out of the bag.
At the dinner Bob acted surprised, even
though someone had told him what he was getting
lief ore the official presentation.

For the Birds
(unlnteresting and meaningless)
They went to a poetry reading, but they got bored
and restless. As far as they were concerned,
it was for the birds! They left during an intermission
because they found the reading totally
uninteresting and meaningless.

Straight From, the Horse's
Mouth,
(from a reliable source)
How did you find out that Jill was engaged? I got the
information from a very reliable source. You mean
Jill
told you so herself? That's right. I got it straight from
the horse's mouth 1

Horse Around
(play around)
Did you hear about Dave's back injury?
No. How did he get hurt?
Well, after the coach left the gym he decided to stay
and
horse around on the parallel bars. He somehow lost
his grip and fell on his back. That's too bad, but he
shouldn't have been aimlessly
playing around on the equipment without proper
supervision.

Cat Got Your Tongue?
(can't talk?)
Come on, Connie! Tell us what you think about our little
ride down the rapids yesterday. Well,uh... Wasn't it exciting? I,uh...
What's the matter? Cat got your tongue? If you must know, I'm keeping quiet because I was
scared out of my wits!

Section Two
The Body Has
Many Uses

Get in Someone's Hair
(bother someone)
Children! Would you please stop making so much noise!
And for heaven's sake, pick up your clothes and toys!
It's hard enough trying to keep this house clean without your throwing your things all over the place! Clara, I know that the children get in your hair, but
you should try not to let it upset you so much.
Listen, Jim. I can't help it. The children bother me and make me very angry when they're so noisy and messy.

Shoot Off One's Mouth,
(express one's opinions loudly)
Jim doesn't play tennis very much, but he's always shooting off his month about how good he
is. Yet he's fooling nobody. Jim is somewhat of a braggart and everyone knows that he gives opinions without knowing all the facts and talks as if he knew everything about the game.

Jump Down Someone's
Throat
(become angry with someone)
That's it, Greg! You'd better not come in after midnight again tonight! I know, dad. You don't have to jump down my throat! I told you that I'd make it home around 11:30.1 don't intend to

be late! Well, you've said that before and in you come at 2:30 in the morning. You can't blame me for getting angry and scolding you. I've got good reason.

Pay Through, the Nose
(pay too high, a price)
At last Mr. Smith came upon the rare stamp he had been seeking at an auction. Since many
other stamp collectors would also be bidding for it, he realized that he would have to pay
through, the nose in order to have it. After considering the increasing value of the stamp, he decided that he would not mind paying such a high price for something so rare.

Tongue-In-Cheek
(not serious)
Why were you teasing Sonia about her new hairdo? She
really took offense at what you said. I didn't mean to offend her. I was simply making a
tongue-in-cheek remark when I said that it was too elaborate for a girl of her young, tender age.
Well, she thought you were serious. She had no idea that
you were just saying that as a joke. I'm really sorry. I suppose I owe her an apology.

Pull Someone's Leg
(fool someone)
Hey, Al. I was invited to be a judge for the Miss America
Beauty Pageant!
Oh, really? Come on, you're pulling my leg! No, honestly. Do you really think that I'm trying to fool you with a ridiculous story? Well, you've told me foolish stories before. I can assure you
that this one is for real.

Play It by Ear
(improvise as one goes along)
Let's go to the movies, agreed?
Sure. And what'll we do after that?
Oh, I don't know. Let's play it by ear.
Well, I would like to have a more definite plan of action.

Don't be like that. It's always more fun not knowing
what to expect and deciding what to do as we go
along.

Stick Out One's Neck
(take a risk)
How come they're asking me to act as their guide
through the jungle?
Evidently they think you're the only one who can
lead them to the lost temple.
That jungle has danger lurking around every corner.
Why should I stick my neck out for them?
They didn't pay me for my services.
They know that you would be taking a great risk and
could possibly get hurt, but you're the
only one with enough knowledge to take them to
their destination. I'm sure you'll be amply
rewarded.

Shake a Leg
(hurry!)
Mary, you always take such a long time to put on
your
makeup. Come on, shake a leg! I'll be finished in a
minute. Be patient. You've got to hurry or
else we won't arrive on time to see the last show.

All Thumbs
(clumsy)
Hey, Bea. Can you help me out? I don't seem to be
able to button up the back of my dress.
Sure. Let's see if I can do it for you.
I guess I'm all thumbs because I'm so nervous. I'm
already late for my date.
Well, I suppose that being so nervous would make
you clumsy and awkward. But don't worry.
I'm sure your date will wait.

Not Have a Leg to Stand On
(to have no good defense for one's opinions
or actions)
Tom maintains that the firm owes him some back
wages for having worked overtime. However,
he won't have a leg to stand on unless he can prove
that he put in all those extra hours. He
doesn't stand a chance of getting his money without
a strong foundation of facts to support

his position.

Get Off Someone's Back
(stop bothering someone)
Hey, John. I'm bored. Come on, let's go out and do
something. Sorry, I'm right in the middle of studying
for a physics exam. I won't be able to make
it tonight. You've been studying for a long time.
Why don't you take a break? Come on! Let's go!
Forget studying for a while!
Look! Get off my back! I can't go anywhere! OK. I'll
stop bothering you only if you promise to
let me know the minute you're finished.

Section Three
That's Not Nice

Drive Someone Up a Wall
(annoy someone greatly)
Wow! What a great set of drums!
Yeah, they're great, but I can't play on them when
my folks are at home. They say I drive them
up a wall with all the loud banging. I get the same
thing at home. My folks tell me that I annoy
them and get them really angry whenever I turn up
the volume on my stereo.

String Someone Along
(lead someone on dishonestly)
Liz had high hopes of marrying Dean. When he ran
off with another woman, she realized that he
was just stringing her along. She had felt very
strongly about him and was really hurt to see
that he was deceiving her and had no intentions of
ever marrying her.

Sell Someone Down the River
(betray someone)
I heard that poor Jud landed up in jail.
Yeah. His so-called girlfriend sold him down the
river and claimed the reward on him.
I can't understand that. I thought she was devoted to
him.
She couldn't have been very devoted to him if she
betrayed him and informed the police
about his hiding place.

That just goes to show you what people will do for money.

Leave Someone High, and Dry
(abandon someone)
Say, Jill. I thought that John was going to help you do the dishes tonight.
So did I. But he left me high and dry. Where did he go? Well, he got a call from some of his pals at work to go bowling, and he left me alone to do all this work without any help at all!

Sell Someone Short
(underestimate someone)
Just because he does not say very much is no reason to sell him abort. Actually, he's a profound thinker and a most talented writer. People tend to underestimate him and not give him the credit he deserves because they think he's shy.

Snow Job
(insincere talk)
The salesman tried to convince a group of investors that the properties he was selling would soon be worth much more money than he was asking. However, no one bought anything from him because they felt he was giving them a snow Job. Wo one was deceived by his insincerity and exaggerated claims about the worth of the properties.

Spill the Beans
(reveal a secret)
Did you know that Harry was going to take Kathy on a Caribbean cruise? Yes, I did. He was planning on surprising her with the tickets for their anniversary, but someone spilled the beans. What a shame! That was supposed to have been a surprise. Yes, it's too bad that someone told her about the trip beforehand and ruined Harry's surprise. That's OK. Her enthusiasm was not dampened in the least!

Feed Someone a Line
(deceive someone)
Mr. Jones had been telling Louise how efficient she was and how much he admired her work at the office. He had promised her a promotion in the near future, but she soon discovered that he was feeding her a line when he passed her by and gave the promotion to someone less capable. Louise was acutely disappointed to find out that Mr. Jones was not telling her the truth, and that he was deceiving her.
39
Section Four
People Do the
Strangest Things

On Ice
(set aside for future use)
We've been working on this sales report for some time now. Don't you think we should take a break for some dinner? Now that you mention it, I am kind of hungry. Let's put the report on ice awhile and grab a bite to eat. That's fine. I'd be happy to stop working on it and set it aside until we get some food. Great! Let's lock up and go.

Shoot the Breeze
(chat informally)
What are you going to be doing this afternoon? Oh, I don't have anything in particular in mind. Why don't you come over to my place? We can listen to some records and shoot the breeze. That sounds OK to me. I'd like to relax listening to music and visit and chat informally until my folks get back from shopping.

Bite the Dust
(go down in defeat)
Andy did exceptionally well in all of the track events, but he bit the dust in the high jump competition. Much to the disappointment of his fans, he went down in defeat, losing to a competitor from the visiting team.

Bend Over Backwards
(try very hard)

When Joan first started teaching she was afraid that
she would have a lot of trouble getting
used to the kids and to the faculty. Her fears turned
out to be unfounded, since everybody bent
over backwards to help her. Everyone tried very hard
to help her feel comfortable and adjust
to the school.

Hit the Hay
(go to bed)
Listen, Kim. We're going to be really busy with
moving tomorrow, and we've got to get an early
start.
I guess you're right. We'll need all the rest we can
get.
What do you say we hit the hay now?
Agreed. Let's go to bed and get a good night's sleep.
It's going to be a long day.

Cough Up
(give unwillingly)
Say, Greg. Did you finally get that computer that
you
wanted so much? Not yet. I needed to raise a couple
of hundred dollars
more.
Is it going to take you a while to raise the money? It
would have taken me forever, but dad said
he'd cough
up the money I need since I'm going to he using the
computer for my school work. Maybe it was difficult
for your dad to give you the
money—but then, he knows that it's for a good
cause.

Jump the Gun
(to be hasty)
Denise was planning on telling her grandparents that
the doctor said she was going to have
twins, but when her dad found out he jumped the
gun and told them before Denise could say a
word. He was so excited that he became hasty and
revealed the news before Denise had a
chance to tell them.

Scratch Someone's Back
(return a favor)

Hey, Bea. I need some help stacking these boxes.
Would you please give me a hand? OK. And
I need some help tidying up the house. How about
your helping me out after that? OK. If you
scratch my back, I'll scratch yours. I know you don't
like doing housework, but I'll help you
with the boxes if you promise to return the favor. No
problem. I'll even do the windows.

Hit the Ceiling
(become very angry)
Don's father hit the celling when he was informed
that his son had been detained by the police
for disorderly conduct. He became violently angry,
since he had often warned his son not to
keep company with that group of boys.

Fork Over
(hand over, give)
Hey, Dan. How come you're looking so sad?
It's nothing, really. I unexpectedly bumped into
Ralph and he asked me to fork over the ten
bucks I owed him.
Did he expect you to pay him back right then and
there? Yes, he did. It was all the money I had,
and I had to hand it over to him. Don't complain.
After all, he did you a favor by lending it to you
in the first place.

Turn Someone Off
(disgust someone)
How was your date with Marty last night?
Well, it started off OK, but he really turned me off
when we went for a snack after the movies.
Did he say or do something to annoy you? Frankly,
he disgusted me when he tried to talk with
his mouth full. I don't blame you. That would have
really bothered me too.

Go Fly a Kite
(go away!)
For the past three hours Jerry had been trying to
convince Linda to go to the art exhibition with
him. She had been refusing all along and finally in
desperation she told him, "Go fly a kite!"
Jerry didn't like to be told to go away in such, a
forceful manner. Nevertheless, he finally

stopped trying to get Linda to attend the exhibition.

Kick the Bucket
(die)
It's been said that the old man knew of a buried
treasure, but lie kicked the bucket before
telling anyone where it was. If the treasure exists, the
old man unfortunately took the secret of
its location with him when he died.

Raise a Stink
(protest strongly)
Listen! Don't try to use any of your sister's clothes
without asking her first. She's liable to raise a
stink if she finds something missing.
I'm sure that there will be no problem. She's
borrowed some of my things before, and I've never
said anything. I really doubt that she will protest
very strongly.

Section Five
Clothes Make the
Man (and Woman)

Wet Blanket
(dull or boring person who spoils the
happiness of others)
James was not invited to go on the outing with the
rest of the group because he's such a wet
blanket. On many previous occasions he has kept
others from enjoying themselves by his
pessimism and lack of enthusiasm. It's
understandable that no one wants him around.

Keep Under One's Hat
(keep something a secret)
Although, the contestants were most anxious to
know who won the prizes in the piano
competition, the judges kept the results under their
hats. They kept the results a secret so
that the formal announcements could be made in
public at the awards ceremony.

Up One's Sleeve
(concealed)
All right, Sara. We know that you're planning
something big for Jean-Paul's birthday. Mind telling

us just what you have up your sleeve?
I wanted to make his birthday a very special event.
Jean-Paul has a sister living in France, and I
sent her an airplane ticket so that she could be here
for his birthday.
Boy! That is something special! We kind of guessed
that you had some concealed plan and
were waiting for the right time to reveal it.
Well, I didn't want to say anything until I was sure
she could come.

Dressed to Kill
(wear one's finest clothing)
The reception for the new Swedish ambassador at
the Jennison's was quite lavish. Naturally,
everybody was dressed to kill. Since it was a formal
occasion, everyone was dressed in their
finest, most elegant clothes.

Give Someone the Slip
(make a getaway)
The police were chasing the thief through the streets
of the city, but he managed to give them
the slip. No wonder. There were so many people
around that the thief managed to escape by
getting lost in the crowds.

Knock Someone's Socks Off
(enthuse and excite)
Hi, John. What's new?
Oh, nothing too much with me, but you ought to see
Al-fredo's new car. It'll knock your socks
off!
So, he finally got that Italian sports car he's been
dreaming about.
He sure did! When you see all the custom features
that it has, you'll get so enthused and
excited you won't know what to do!
Boy, I can hardly wait to go for a ride in it!

Talk Through One's Hat
(make foolish statements)
We were discussing ethnic traditions and customs
with Fred the other day, and he showed just
how little he knew about other cultures.
What do you mean?

Well, he said that as far as he could tell, there wasn't much difference in behavior and
temperament between the English and the Hispanics. It's plain to see that he was talking through, his hat!
True, but Fred thinks he's an authority on everything. It was difficult to convince him that he was
talking ignorantly. He's got a reputation for making foolish, inaccurate statements.

Lose One's Shirt
(lose a great deal of money)
I happened to bump into Doug at lunch yesterday afternoon.
What's new with Doug these days?
He wasn't doing so well. For one thing, he told me he lost his shirt at the races.
Doug has always liked to bet on the horses. I'm not surprised that he lost a great deal of
money.
Yeah. At this rate he'll never have a penny to his name!

In Stitches
(laughing very hard)
Danny was hilarious at the party the other night. He had us all in stitches! I didn't realize that
he was such a comedian.
He's always been funny, but last night he outdid himself. He had us laughing so hard that it
hurt our sides.

Dressed to the Teeth
(dressed elegantly)
Did you see Hilda at the party last night?
Yes, I did. She was really dressed to the teeth!
Well, she had on her finest, most elegant clothing because she was out to make a good impression, on
Bill.

Section Six
When Things
Go Wrong

Lemon
(something defective)
Have you seen Joanne's new car yet?

Yeah. It looks good, but she's had nothing but problems with it.
That's too bad. It sounds like she got a real lemon.
She sure did! No sooner did she drive it home from the dealer's than it proved defective and
started breaking down.

Out of the Woods
(out of danger)
Although Eric was well on his way to recovering from his bout with pneumonia, he was still not
out of the woods. The doctors told him that he would have to take it easy and avoid exposure
to cold, since he was not out of danger and difficulty yet.
Get Up on the Wrong Side of
the Bed
(wake up in a toad mood)
What's the matter with Bernard today? He started shouting from the moment he stepped into
the office. I don't know. He usually doesn't act that way at all.
I guess he got up on the wrong side of the bed. Just because he woke up in a bad mood is
no reason for him to toe so cross and to go around shouting at everybody.
Hopefully he'll relax as the day goes on. Amen!

Out on a Limb
(in a risky position)
The members of the committee realized that their position against expanding the student aid
program was an unpopular one, and that they were going out on a limb by voting against the
program. Nevertheless, their position was justified to a certain extent. Although they knew that
they were placing themselves in a risky position, they felt that other budgetary considerations
were of greater urgency.

Eating Someone
(bothering or worrying someone)
Hey, Alice. What's been eating you lately? Don't you realize how rude and irritable you've
become?
I know. I'm really sorry for the way I've been acting.

Well, why don't you tell me what has been bothering
and upsetting you and maybe we can
work your problem out together.
I'll admit that it would help to talk to someone about
it.

Get the Ax
(toe dismissed, fired)
I feel sorry for Richard. He was feeling quite
depressed when I ran into him. Did he tell you what
was bothering him? Among other things, he
informed me that he got the ax at work. That's
strange. He's always teen a conscientious worker.
I wonder why they dismissed him from his job?
Evidently he had a disagreement on company
policies with one of the top executives.

In the Hole
(in debt)
Unfortunately, Peter had to sell his neighborhood
hardware store. Because of competition from
the bigger stores in the shopping center, he was
going in the hole every month. His store was
small and did not generate enough income to meet
expenses. As a consequence, he was
rapidly losing money and going into debt.

Section Seven
When Things
Go Well
For a Song
(for very little money)
Sara, I picked up the perfect chair for the living
room the other day.
That's wonderful. I know you've been looking for
some time. Where did you finally come across
what you wanted?
I was really quite lucky. I got it for a song at a little
furniture store. I was able to buy it for very
little money because the owners of the store were
right in the middle of their spring liquidation
sale.

Make a Splash.
(be successful and attract attention)
Do you remember Andre and Jack?

Yes, I do. Weren't they working together on some
kind of a novel?
That's right. It was finally published and I
understand that it made quite a splash both
domestically and abroad.
That's great news! They're both talented and
hardworking. It's good to hear that the book was
so successful and attracted such a great deal of
attention.

Have the World by the Tail
(be successful and happy)
Marc finished school at the top of his class and he
was offered an excellent position with an
accounting firm Now he feels that he has the world
by the tail. Everything has been working
out for him lately, and it's no wonder that he's
feeling so successful and happy.

Sitting Pretty
(in a fortunate position)
I heard that Michael and Jennifer got a good price
when
they sold their house. Yes, they did. Now they're
really sitting pretty. As a
matter of fact, they're thinking of going on a long
vacation.
I wish I were in such a fortunate position. I haven't
had a vacation in years.

Feel Like a Million Dollars
(feel wonderful)
I bumped into Nick at the barbershop yesterday. He
looked great, but I noticed that he had a
slight limp when he walked.
I guess you didn't know that he had an operation on
his knee.
No, I didn't. How's he feeling?
He says he's feeling like a million dollars now.
Apparently the pain in his knee is all gone.
It's good that he's feeling so wonderful. It must be a
refreshing change not having to put up
with all that discomfort.

Kick Up One's Heels
(celebrate)

The prerequisites for admission to the Theater Arts
School are quite demanding, and those
students who were finally accepted had reason to
kick up their heels. It was only natural that
those who made it through the exams and interviews
would want to celebrate the occasion by
going out and having a good time.

Bury the Hatchet
(make peace)
Somebody told me that you and Doug had been
quarreling over the construction site of the new
building.
That's true, but we worked out the problem and
decided to bury the hatchet.
Glad to hear that. You guys have always worked
well together.
Well, once we came to the conclusion that we both
had the same goal in mind, we put an end
to our bitter feelings and made peace with each
other.

Paint the Town Red
(carouse and have a good time)
How did you enjoy your vacation to Europe last
summer?
It was marvelous. I'll never forget the time we had
when we were in Rome. There was no end to
things to see and do.
And how was the night life?
Great! We painted the town red the first three nights
we were there.
Didn't that get to be pretty expensive?
I guess so, but we were so excited by all that the city
had to offer that we went out carousing
without thinking about the cost.

Get Away Clean
(escape punishment)
After robbing a neighborhood bank, the robbers sped
off in a waiting car and got away clean. In spite of
all
police efforts to apprehend them, the criminals were
never caught and punished for their crime.

Come Alive
(brighten up and become active)

Up to now the guests at the party had been eating
and making small talk, hut when the rock
band arrived, everyone came alive. When the band
started playing all the latest rock hits,
everybody brightened up and became very active.
84
Section Eight
Do Your Best

Toot One's Own Horn
(boast)
Michael's last novel was a best seller. He has no
need to toot his own horn about his literary
accomplishments. His readers and critics alike will
now become aware of his talent. He won't
have to boast about his skill and success as a writer.

Stick to One's Guns
(maintain one's position)
In spite of the fact that it was inadvisable to have a
controversial figure address the club, the
chairman stuck to his guns and insisted that it would
make good sense to hear the other side
of the question before taking a vote on the issue. He
maintained his opinion and position on
the matter, even though a number of members tried
to make him change his mind.

Get the Ball Rolling
(initiate action)
Look! You've been talking about repairing the roof
for weeks now. Don't you think it's about time
to get the ball rolling?
I know, but I've been busy with other things. I
promise I'll get to it this weekend. The time to
start doing it is right now! According to the weather
report it's supposed to rain tomorrow.

Mind One's P's and Q's
(take care in speech and action)
Listen, Larry. If you want an invitation to Clarissa's
party you'd better mind your P's and Q's. But I
haven't been doing anything to offend her. I'll
tell you one thing. You're going to have to be careful
of what yon say and how yon act around Susan.
Come on! Susan and I are just friends. I

know that, but Clarissa is the jealous type. She's liable
to think that something is going on between the two of you.

Hang On
(persevere)
During the depression years the Smiths had a great deal of trouble with their business, but
somehow or other they were able to hang on. Although they almost lost their store, they
managed to persevere until things got better.

Give It One's Best Shot
(try hard)
Can you do anything about repairing this TV set? I'm not much of an electrician, but I'll give it
my best shot.
Many thanks. I'd be most appreciative. OK. I'll try my hardest to fix it, but I'm not promising that
I'll succeed. At this point, I'll take all the help I can get.

Make Ends Meet
(pay one's bills)
It's almost impossible trying to keep up with the high cost of living.
It's true. Things are so expensive nowadays that it's very difficult to make ends meet.
You know, even with Lucie's salary, our combined income is hardly enough to pay all the
bills.

Get the Jump on Someone
(get the advantage over someone)
Did you have a nice time at the school dance last night?
To tell you the truth, I would have enjoyed myself more if I had been able to go with Teresa
instead of Elena.
Why didn't you ask Teresa in the first place?
I was about to, but Benito got the jump on me.
How did he manage to do that?
He got the advantage over me by telling Teresa that if she went with him, he'd take her out to
dinner and then to the dance in his brand new convertible.

Well, now, she can hardly be blamed for accepting an offer like that!

Pull Strings
(exert influence)
Steven had been unsuccessful in getting tickets for the opening game of the season. However,
he pulled some strings with the manager of the team and got excellent seats. There's no
doubt that he got the tickets only by exerting his influence with a person important enough
to help him get what he wanted.

Spread Oneself Too Thin
(become involved in too many activities)
Although Teresa has always been an excellent student, her marks have been going down lately
because she is spreading herself too thin. Besides spending a great deal of time in afterschool
sports, she got a part-time job as a clerk in a department store. It's only natural that her
grades would suffer. She is becoming involved in so many activities that she cannot
devote the time that it takes to excel in any one of them.

Go to Bat for Someone
(help out and support someone)
Is it true that Don got into some trouble at work last week? Yes, he did. He was reproached for
not turning in his sales reports, but his secretary went to bat for him.
What was she able to do? She helped him out a great deal by admitting that she had
misplaced the reports that he gave her to be typed. So, it was her fault, not his. Bight.

Duck Soup
(easy, effortless)
Can you help me hook up my new stereo equipment? I'm having quite a bit of trouble with all
these connections.
Sure. That's duck soup for me.
Well, with all your experience in electronics, I have no doubt that it will be very easy for you to
do.
No problem. Glad to help out.

Section Nine
You Don't Say

Money Talks
(money can influence people)
We've been waiting for three months to get delivery
on our car, and people who put in their
order after us have already gotten theirs.
Well, money talks. Why don't you try giving the
dealer a little something extra to move things
along?
I know full well that money has the power to
influence people, but I refuse to pay extra for a
service that is owed to me as a client.
If you want to have your car maybe you'd better
reconsider.
Let Sleeping Dogs Lie
(do not agitate a potential source of trouble)
You'd better not say anything to the owner of the
building about painting your apartment. If I
were you I'd let sleeping dogs lie. The last time you
asked him to do some repairs, he raised
your rent.
You're telling me not to make trouble if I don't have
to, but I'm going to risk making him angry,
since I can no longer stand to look at the paint
peeling off the walls.
Shape Up or Ship Out
(behave properly or leave!)
Al had been constantly reprimanded for being
negligent on the job. Finally, in desperation his
supervisor exclaimed, "Shape up or ship out!" Al
admitted that he had not been taking his
work seriously and realized that he should be more
conscientious about his job or he would
be discharged.
If the Shoe Fits, Wear It
(admit the truth)
Joe feels rather badly because he's always being
criticized for his sloppy personal appearance.
With reason. "If the shoe fits, wear it," I always say.
Still, I can't help feeling sorry for the guy. I know
that what people say about him is true, and
that he should admit it. He doesn't seem to want to
improve his appearance. Evidently, he

himself can't see anything wrong with the way he
looks.
Different Strokes For
Different Folks
(everyone has different interests and tastes)
It's hard to understand how Millie and Ron ever got
together. She has always gone in for sailing
and he can't stand to be on water. He enjoys the
opera and she likes jazz.
You know what they say: "Different strokes for
different folks!"
You don't have to tell me that everyone has different
interests and tastes. I still can't figure
out what attracted them to each other in the first
place.
Haven't you heard that opposites attract?
Bark Worse Than One's Bite
(not as bad-tempered as one appears)
On occasion Mr. Hopkins speaks harshly to his
students, especially when they fail to complete
their homework assignment. Nevertheless, they all
know that his bark is worse than his bite.
He threatens to keep them after school and to inform
their parents, but he's not really as badtempered
as he appears.
Eyes Are Bigger Than One's
Stomach
(take more food than one can eat)
Chris, why don't you finish eating that third helping
of dessert?
I guess my eyes were bigger than my stomach when
I said I wanted more.
I'm not surprised. The same thing happens to me.
Sometimes, when I'm really hungry, I'll take
more food than I can possibly eat.
Put One's Money Where
One's Mouth Is
(follow through with a stated intention)
You've been promising to take us to Disneyland for
the past two years. Since the kids are free,
how about putting your money where your mouth is?
You don't have to remind me. I have every intention
of doing exactly what I said I'd do. But
you yourself know that in the past we have been
unable to go because of other financial
obligations. Things have eased up and it looks like
we'll be able to go this year.

The Early Bird Catches the
Worm
(arriving early gives one an advantage)
Marc, the lines for the rock festival are going to be
miles long! If you expect to get tickets for you
and Marika, remember that old saying, "The early
bird eatches the worm."
I guess you're right. Marika is looking forward to the
concert, and I'd hate to disappoint her. I'll
get up real early to get a place at the head of the line.
That way I'll get the tickets I want, for
sure!
People Who Live in Glass
Houses Shouldn't Throw
Stones
(one should not criticize when one is equally at fault)
Janet has often criticized her friend Lois for driving
too fast, yet she herself has had her license
suspended for exceeding the speed limit. Lois once
tried to tell her that people who live in
glass houses shouldn't throw stones, but it didn't do
much good. Janet simply didn't accept
the fact that she should not pass judgment on other
people when she is just as bad as
they are.
All's Well That Ends Well
(a successful outcome is worth the effort)
Hi, Benito. How are things going?
Well, everything's OK now. Remember that teaching
job
for which I applied? Yes, I sure do. Well, I was
finally hired, but I had a bit of a rough time
before I got it. Between all that paperwork and all
those interviews, I'm all worn out. Thank goodness
it's all over. Great! All's well that ends well. After all
that you
went through, I'm happy to hear that things finally
turned out satisfactorily for you. Yes. I'm happy, too.
It was really worth the effort.

Idioms
A
all's well that ends well (a successful outcome
is worth the effort) _______
all thumbs (clumsy) _____
at the end of one's rope (at the limit of one's
ability to cope) _____

B
bark worse than one's bite (not as badtempered
as one appears) _____
bend over backwards (try very hard) _____
bite the bullet (endure in a difficult situation)

_____
bite the dust (go down in defeat) _____
blow it (fail at something) _____
bury the hatchet (make peace) _____
C
cat got your tongue? (can't talk?) _____
come alive (brighten up and become active)

_____
cough up (give unwillingly) _____
D
different strokes for different folks (everyone
has different interests and tastes) _____
dressed to kill (wear one's finest clothing)

_____
dressed to the teeth (dressed elegantly) _____
drive someone up a wall (annoy someone
greatly) _____
duck soup (easy, effortless) _____
E
early bird catches the worm (arriving early
gives one an advantage) _____
eating someone (bothering OF worrying
someone) _____
eyes are bigger than one's stomach (take
more food than one can eat) _____
F
face the music (accept the consequences)_____
feed someone a line (deceive someone) _____
feel like a million dollars (feel wonderful)

_____
fishy (strange and suspicious) __
for a song (for very little money) _____
for the birds (uninteresting and meaningless)

__
fork over (hand over, give) _____
G
get away clean (escape punishment) _____
get In someone's hair (bother someone) _____
get off someone's back (stop bothering
someone) _____
get the ax (be dismissed, fired)_____
get the ball rolling (initiate action) _____

get the jump on someone (get the advantage over someone) _____
get up on the wrong side of the bed (wake up in a bad mood) _____
give it one's best shot (try hard) _____
give someone the slip (make a getaway) _____
go fly a kite (go away!) _____
go to bat for someone (help out and support someone) _____
go to the dogs (become rundown) __

H
hang on (persevere) _____
have the world lay the tall (be successful and happy) _____
hit the celling (become very angry) _____
hit the hay (go to bed) _____ horse around, (play around) __
horse of a different color (quite a different matter) __
hot under the collar (extremely angry) _____

I
If the shoe fits, wear It (admit the truth) _____
in stitches (laughing very hard)_____
in the hole (in debt) _____

J
Jump down someone's throat (become angry with someone) _____
jump the gun (to be hasty) _____

K
keep under one's hat (keep something a secret) _____
kick the bucket (die) _____
kick up one's heels (celebrate) _____
knock someone's socks off (enthuse and excite) _____

L
leave someone high and dry (abandon someone) _____
lemon (something defective) _____
let sleeping dogs lie (do not agitate a potential source of trouble) _____
let the cat out of the bag (inform beforehand) __
lose one's shirt (lose a great deal of money) _____

M

make a splasb (be successful and attract attention) _____
make ends meet (pay one's bills) _____
mind one's P's and Q's (take care in speech and action) _____
money talks (money can influence people) _____

N
not have a leg to stand on (to have no good defense for one's opinion or actions) _____

O
on ice (set aside for future use) _____
on one's last legs (sick and failing) _____
on the line (in danger of being lost) _____
out of the woods (out of danger)_____
out on a limb (in a risky position) _____

P
paint the town red. (carouse and have a good time) _____
pay through the nose (pay too high, a price) _____
people who live in glass houses shouldn't throw stones (one should not criticize when one is equally at fault) _______
play it by ear (improvise as one goes along) _____
pull someone's leg (fool someone) _____
pull strings (exert influence) _______
put one's money where one's mouth is (follow through with a stated intention) _____

R
raise a stink (protest strongly) _____

S
scratch someone's back (return a favor) _____
sell someone down the river (betray someone) _____
sell someone snort (underestimate someone) _____
shake a leg (hurry) _____
shape up or ship out (behave properly or leave!) _____
shoot off one's mouth (express one's opinions loudly) _____
shoot the breeze (chat informally) _____
sitting pretty (in a fortunate position) _____
smell a rat (feel that something is wrong) __
snow job (insincere talk) _____

spill the beans (reveal a secret) ____
spread, oneself too thin (become involved in too many activities) ____
stick out one's neck (take a risk) ____
stick to one's guns (maintain one's position)

____

straight from the horse's mouth (from a reliable source) __
string someone along (lead someone on dishonestly) ____
T
take the trail toy the horns (take decisive action in a difficult situation) __
talk through one's hat (make foolish statements) ____
tongue-in-cheek (not serious) ____
toot one's own horn (boast) ____
turn someone off (disgust someone) ____
U
up one's sleeve (concealed) ____
W
wet blanket (dull or boring person, who spoils the happiness of others) ____

Some Examples

1) A bird in the hand is worth two in the bush- Having something that is certain is much better than taking a risk for more, because chances are you might losing everything.

2) A blessing in disguise- Something good that isn't recognized by first

3) Bull in china shop- One who causes damage

4) A chip on your shoulder- Being upset for something that happened in the past

5) A damp squib- Complete failure

6) A dime A dozen- Anything that is common and easy to get

7) A doubting Thomas- A skeptic who needs physical or personal evidence in order to believe something

8) A drop in the bucket- A very small part of something big or whole

9) A fool and his money are easily parted- It's easy for a foolish person to lose his/ her money

10) A gentleman at large- An unreliable person

11) A green horn- Inexperienced

12) A house divided against itself cannot stand- Everyone involved must unify and function together or it will not work out.

13) A leopard can't change his spots- You cannot change who you are

14) A lost cause- A hopeless case, a person or situation having no hope of positive change.

15) A man of straw- A weak person

16) A mare's nest- A false invention

17) A penny saved is a penny earned- By not spending money, you are saving money (little by little)

18) A picture paints a thousand words- A visual presentation is far more descriptive than words

19) A piece of cake- A task that can be accomplished very easily

20) A slap on the wrist- A very mild punishment

21) A stalking horse- Pretence

22) A steal- Very inexpensive, a bargain

23) A taste of your own medicine- When you are mistreated the same way you mistreat others

24) A toss-up- A result hat is still unclear and can go either way

25) A wolf in sheep's clothing- A dangerous person pretending harmless

26) ABC: Very common knowledge about to- Ready to, just going to

27) Above all- Mainly, especially

28) Above board- Fair and honest

29) According to- In the order of; on the authority of

30) Actions speak louder than words- It's better to actually do something than hust talk about it

31) Add fuel to the fire- Whenever something is done to make a bad situation even worse than it is

32) Against the clock- Rushed and short on time

33) All (day, week, month, year) long- The entire day, week, month, year

34) All along- All the time, from the beginning (without change)

35) All and Sundry- Without making any distinction

36) All bark and no bite- When someone is threatening and/ or aggressive but not willing to engage in a fight

37) All greek to me- Meaningless and incomprehensible like someone who cannot read, speak, or

38) All in all- Considering everything

39) All in the same boat- When everyone is facing the same challenges

40) All of a sudden- Suddenly, without warning (All at once)

41) All right- Acceptable, fine; yes, okay

42) Alpha and omega- First and last letter of Greek alphabet, means beginning and end

43) An arm and a leg- Very expensive, A large amount of money

44) An axe to grind- To have a dispute with someone

45) An eye wash- A pretence

46) An iron hand- By force

47) Apple to my eye- Someone who is cherished above all others

48) As a matter of fact- Really, actually (also: as to)

49) As for- Regarding, concerning (also: as to)

50) As high as a kite- Anything that is high up in the sky

51) As soon as- Just after, when

52) As usual- as is the general case, as is typical

53) At all- To any degree (also: in the least)

54) At heart- Basically, fundamentally

55) At last- Finally, after a long time

56) At least- A minimum of, no fewer (or less) than

57) At odds- In dispute

58) At sixes and seven- Persons who are having different opinions

59) At the drop of a hat- Willing to do something immediately

60) Back and call- At the service

61) Back and forth- In a backward and forward motion

62) Back seat driver- People who criticize from the sidelines, much like someone giving unwanted advice

63) Back to square one- Having to start all over again

64) Back to the drawing board- When an attempt fails and it's time to start all over

65) Bag and baggage- with all goods

66) Baker's dozen- Thirteen

67) Bank on- Depend on, count on

68) Barking up the wrong tree- A mistake made in something you are trying to achieve

69) Bated breath- In anxiety, expectancy

70) Beat a dead horse- To force an issue that has already ended

71) Beating around the bash- Avoiding the main topic, not speaking directly about the issue

72) Bend over backwards- Do whatever it takes to help. Willing to do anything

73) Between a Rock and a Hard place- Stuck between two very bad options

74) Between Scylla and Charybdis- Choice between two unpleasant alternatives

75) Between the cup and the lips- On the point of achievement

76) Bite off more than you can chew- To take on a task that is a way to big

77) Bite your tongue- To avoid talking

78) Black and white- In writing

79) Blood is thicker than water- The family bond is closer than anything else

80) Blow hot and cold- Having no stand, shows favour at one time and unfavour at another

81) Blue moon- A rare event or occurrence

82) Body and soul- Entirely

83) Break a leg- A superstitious way to say 'Good Luck' without saying 'Good Luck',

84) Buy a lemon- To purchase a vehicle that constantly gives problems or stops running after you drive it

85) By & by- Gradually

86) By all means- Certainly, definitely, naturally (also: of course); using any possible way or method

87) By far- By a great margin, clearly

88) By fits and starts- Irregularly

89) By heart- By memorizing

90) By hook or by crook- By any means

91) By leaps and bound- speedily

92) By oneself- Alone, without assistance

93) By the way- Incidentally

94) Call a spade a spade- Straight talks

95) Can't cut the mustard- Someone who isn't adequate enough to compete or participate

96) Cast iron stomach- Someone who has no problems, complications or ill effects with eating anything

97) Cats and bull story- Untrue story

98) Cats and dogs- Heavy rain

99) Charley horse- stiffness in the leg/ A leg cramp

100) Chew someone out- Verbally scold someone

101) Chip on his shoulder- Angry today about something that occurred in the past

102) Chow down- To eat

103) Clear- cut- Clearly stated, definite, apparent

104) Close but no cigar- To be near and almost accomplish a goal, but fall short

105) Close call- A situation involving a narrow escape from danger

106) Cock and bull story- An unbelievable tale, untrue story

107) Come hell or high water- Any difficult situation or obstacle

108) Crack someone up- To make someone laugh

109) Cross your fingers- To hope that something happens the way you want it to

110) Cry wolf- Intentionally raise a false alarm

111) Cup of joe- A cup of coffee

112) Curtain lecture- A reproof by wife to her husband

113) Cut and dried- Ready made form

114) Cut to the chase- Leave out all the unnecessary details and just get to the point

115) Dark horse- One who was previously unknown and is now prominent

116) Day in and day out- Continuously, constantly

117) Dead Ringer- 100 % identical, a duplicate

118) Devil's advocate- Someone who takes a position for the sake of argument without believing in that

119) Dog days of summer- The hottest day of the summer season

120) Don't count your chickens before they hatch- Don't rely on it until you sure of it

121) Don't look a gift horse in the month- When someone gives you a gift, don't be ungrateful

122) Don't pull all your eggs in one basket- Do not pull all your resources in one possibility

123) Doozy- Something outstanding

124) Down to the wire- Something that ends at the last minute or last few seconds

125) Drastic times call for drastic measures- When you are extremely desperate you need to take extremely desperate actions

126) Drink like a fish- To drink very heavily, drinking anything

127) Dry run- Rehearsal

128) Egg on- To urge somebody

129) Eighty six- A certain item is no longer available. Or this idiom can also mean, to throw away

130) Elvis has left the building- The show has come to an end. It's all over

131) Ethnic cleansing- Killing of a certain ethnic or religious group on a massive scale

132) Ever and anon- Now and then

133) Every cloud has a silver lining- Be optimistic, even difficult times will lead to better days

134) Every other (one)- Every second (one), alternate (ones)

135) Everything but the kitchen sink- Almost everything and anything has been included

136) Excuse my French- Please forgive me for cussing

137) Fabian policy- Policy of delaying decisions

138) Face-to-face- Direct, personal; directly, personally (written without hyphens)

139) Fair and wide- Equal opportunity to all

140) Far and wide- Every where

141) Few and far between- Not frequent, unusual, rare

142) Field day- An enjoyable day or circumstance

143) Fifty- fifty- Divided into two equal parts

144) Finding your feet- To become more comfortable in whatever you are doing

145) Finger licking good- To become more comfortable in whatever you are doing

146) Fire and brimstone- A very tasty food or meal

147) Fire and fury- Fearful penalties

148) First and foremost- Extreme enthusiasm

149) Fishy: doubtful- Highest priority

150) Fixed in your ways- Not willing or wanting to change from your normal way of doing something

151) Flash in the pan- Something that shows potential or looks promising in the beginning but fails to deliver

152) Flea market- A swap meet. A place where people gather to buy and sell inexpensive goods

153) Flesh and blood- This idiom can mean living material of which people are made of, or it can refer to human nature

154) Flip the bird- To raise your middle finger at someone

155) Foam at the mouth- To be enraged and show it

156) Fools' Gold- Iron pyrites, a worthless rock that resembles real gold

157) Foot the bill- Bear expenses

158) For good- Permanently, forever

159) For once- This one time, for only one time

160) For sure- Without doubt (also: for certain)

161) For the time being- Temporarily (also: for now)

162) Free and easy- Natural and simple

163) French kiss- An open mouth kiss where tongues touch

164) From now on- From this time into the future

165) From rags to riches- To go from very poor to being very wealthy

166) Fuddy- duddy- An old-fashioned and foolish type of person

167) Full monty- This idiom can mean either, "The whole thing" or "Completely nude"

168) Funny farm- A mental institutional facility

169) Gall and wormwood- Source of irritation

170) Get down to brass tacks- To become serious about something

171) Get over it- To move beyond something that is bothering you

172) Get up on the wrong side of the bed- Someone who is having a horrible day

173) Get your walking papers- Get fired from the job

174) Gird up the loin- To be ready

175) Give and take- Compromise, cooperation between people

176) Give him the slip- To get away from, to escape

177) Give in- Surrender

178) Go down like a lead balloon- To be received badly by an audience

179) Go for broke- To gamble everything you have

180) Go out on a limb- Put yourself in a tough position in order to support someone/ something

181) Go the extra mile- Going above and beyond whatever is required for the task at hand

182) Good Samaritan- Someone who helps others when they are in need, with no discussion for

183) Graveyard shift- Working hours from about 12:00 am to 8.00

184) Great minds think alike- Intelligent people think like each other

185) Green room- The waiting room, especially for those who are about to go on a TV or radio show

186) Gut feeling- A personal intuition you get, especially when feel something may not be right

187) Had better- Should, ought to, be advisable to

188) Hand a gloves- Very intimate friends

189) Hard and fast- Certain

190) Hard of hearing- Partially deaf, not able to hear well

191) Haste makes waste- Quickly doing things results in a poor ending

192) Hat Trick- When one player scores three goals in the same hockey game.

193) Haughty and naughty- Arrogant and naughty

194) Have an axe to grind- To have a dispute with someone

195) Have got- To have, to possess

196) Have got to- Must (also: have to)

197) He lost his head- Angry and overcome by emotions

198) Head and shoulder- Superior

199) Head over heels- Very excited and/ or joyful, especially when in love

200) Heart and soul- With full devotion

201) Hell in a hand basket- Deteriorating and headed for complete disaster

202) Helter Shelter-Here and there

203) Herculean task- A tedious job

204) High five- Slapping palms above each others heads as celebration gesture

205) High on the Hog- Living in luxury

206) Hit below the belt- Contrary the principles of fairness

207) Hit the books- To study, especially for a test or exam

208) Hit the hay- Go to bed or go to sleep

209) Hit the nail on the head- Do something exactly right or say something exactly right

210) Hit the sack- Go to bed or go to sleep

211) Hither and thither- Here and there

212) Hocus Pocus- In general, a term used in magic or trickery

213) Hold your horses- Be patient

214) Hole and corner policy- A secret policy for an evil purpose

215) Hornet's nest- Raise controversy

216) Hue and cry- Great noise

217) Hush money- A bribe

218) Icing on the cake- When you already have it good and get something on top of what you already have

219) Idle hands are the devil's tools- You are more likely to get in trouble if you have nothing to do

220) If it's not one thing, it's another- When one thing goes wrong, then another, and another…

221) Ill at ease- Uncomfortable or worried in a situation

222) In a hurry- Hurried, rushed (also: in a rush)

223) In case- In order to be prepared if the meaning is in order to be prepared if something happens

224) In hand- Under firm control, well managed

225) In like Flynn- To be easily successful, especially when sexual or romantic

226) In no time- Very quickly, rapidly

227) In the bag- To have something secured

228) In the buff- Nude

229) In the heat of the moment- Overwhelmed by what is happening in the moment

230) In the long run- Eventually, after a long period of time

231) In the worst way- Very much, greatly

232) In time to- Before the time necessary to do something

233) In touch- Having contact

234) In vain- Useless, without the desired result

235) In your face- An aggressive and bold confrontation

236) Ins and outs- Full detail

237) Inside out- With the inside facing the outside

238) Intents and purposes- Practically

239) It figures- It seems likely, reasonable, or typical

240) It takes two to tango- A two person conflict where both people are at fault

241) It's a small world- You frequently see the same people in different places

242) It anyone's call- A competition where the outcome is difficult to judge or predict

243) Ivory tower- Imaginary world

244) Ivy league- Since 1954 the Ivy league has been the following universities: Columbia, Brown, Cornell

245) Jaywalk- Crossing the street (from the middle) without using the crosswalk

246) Joshing me- Tricking me

247) Keep an eye on him- You should carefully watch him. Keep an eye on

248) Keep body and soul together- To earn a sufficient amount of money in order to keep yourself alive

249) Keep your chin up- To remain joyful in a tough situation

250) Kick the bucket- Die

251) Kith and kin- Blood relatives

252) Kitty-corner- Diagonally across. Sometimes called Catty- Corner as well

253) Knock on Wood- Knuckle tapping on wood in order to avoid some bad luck

254) Know the ropes- To understand the details

255) Last but not least- An introduction phrase to let the audience know that the last person mentioned is also very important

256) Last straw- The final event in a series of unacceptable actions

257) Latin and Greek- Unable to understand

258) Leave no stone unturned- Make all possible efforts

259) Lend me your ear- To politely ask for someone's full attention

260) Length and breadth- All over

261) Let along- and certainly not (also: not to mention, to say nothing of)

262) Let the cat out of the bag- To share a secret that wasn't suppose to be shared

263) Level playing field- A fair competition where no side has an advantage

264) Life and soul- Main support

265) Like a chicken and its head cut off- To act in a frenzied manner

266) Liquor someone up- To get someone drunk

267) Little by little- Gradually, slowly (also: step by step)

268) Live-wire- Energetic

269) Loaves and fish- Material interests

270) Lock and key- In safe place

271) Long in the tooth- Old people (or horses)

272) Loose cannon- Someone who is unpredictable and can cause damage if not kept in check

273) Make no bones about- To state a fact so there are no doubts or objections

274) Method to my madness- Strange or crazy actions that appear meaningless but in the end are done for a good reason

275) Might and main- With all enthusiasm

276) Milk and water- Weak

277) More or less- Approximately, almost, somewhat, to a certain degree

278) Mumbo Jumbo- Nonsense or meaningless speech

280) Mum's the word- To keep quiet, To say nothing

280) Narrow-minded- Not willing to accept the ideas of others.

***.

2. Error Spotting

Language reflect personality.

-   *Chandan Sengupta*

You can enter the text of the second chapter here.

Some Examples of Error Spotting

I: The condolence messages (a) / received on the (b) / death of Mrs. Gandhi (c)/ speaks highly of her greatness (d) / no error (e).

Explanation

Answer: d. In the above statement the subject is condolence messages which is in plural form. So, the verb should also be in plural form. But the verb here is speaks, which is singular. So we have to use speak instead of speaks. **Thus, answer is (d).**

Eg: They write – plural, he writes – singular.

Sentence should contain Singular subject + singular verb

Plural subject + plural verb

II: He took me to restaurant (a) / and ordered for two cups (b) / of cold coffee (c) / which the waiter brought in an hour (d) / no error (e).

Explanation

In this sentence, after ordered, for cannot be used. Preposition like for, on, to, etc., should not follow transition verbs like moved, ordered, etc., So, remove for from the sentence. **Thus the answer is (b).**

Eg: I moved the chair. (no preposition after moved).

III: I would rather (a) / pay for my education (b) / than financial aid (c)/ no error (d).

Explanation

In the sentence, the part b has noun – education and verb – pay but in part c there is only a noun - aid and no verb. The word rather defines that he can do any one of the above mentioned activities. So both the sentence should have same pattern. **Thus, answer is (c).**

IV: If I would have realised (a) / what a bad driver, you were (b) / I would not have (c) / come with you (d) / no error (e).

Explanation

If + past perfect and I + would have – If conditional. So, I had realised should come in the place of would have realised. **Thus, the answer is (a).**

V: All the woman teachers (a) / are agitated (b) / because of the haughty attitude (c) / of the Principle (d)/ no error (e).

Answer: a

Explanation

In the sentence, "all" is plural form and then "teachers" is also a plural form so instead of woman we should women. **Thus, answer is (a)**

VI: The Chairman had not taken (a) / any decision until (b) / he had studied (c) / the case thoroughly (d) / no error (e).

Answer: a

Explanation

In this sentence, had comes in both the places. But the correct tense is did not take. The past perfect (had not) should follow a simple past tense to maintain its past perfect tense. **Thus, answer is (a)**

VII: Building biogas plant will (a) / help to reduce (b) / the consuming of conventional fuel (c) / such as firewood and kerosene (d) / no error (e).

Explanation

Here the sentence answers for the question what like what will be reduced? The answer is consumption of conventional fuel. So, replace the word consuming with consumption. **Thus, answer is (c).**

VIII: Both the rich (a) / along with the poor (b) / are responsible for a great many vices (c) / with which our country is inflicted (d) / no error (e).

Answer: b

Explanation

This sentence is an example for co relative sentence.

- o   And follows both
- o   Than follows no sooner
- o   When follows hardly
- o   But also follows not only.

So, in this sentence **and** should

replace **along. Thus, answer is (b).**

IX: The six partners (a) / are at daggers drawn (b) / so they do not talk (c) / to each other (d) / no error (e).

Explanation

In this sentence, there are more than 2 persons. So ,use the word one another instead of each other. **Thus, (d) is the correct answer.**

Example 10.

He is almost quite competent (a) / for the post of Manager(b) / so if given a chance (c) / he can show the results (d) / no error (e).

Explanation

It is a superfluous word, that is both contain same meaning.

Eg:

- o   most unique
- o   More better
- o   Almost quite

These words cannot be used together.

So, in this sentence almost is not necessary. **Thus, (a) is the correct answer.**

Rules based on Tenses

Present Tense:-

Simple Present Tense

Simple Present Tense sentences include happening of work in present time.

Subject + 1 st form of Verb

1. Subject (Singular form /third person) + 1st Form of Verb + s/es

Noun Subject is also a third person.

2. Subject(Plural) + 1st Form of Verb

3. For I and You , we will not use 's' and 'es' with Verb.

Example :I study on daily basis.

Present continuous tense

Expresses an action continued at present time.

1. Subject (Singular /third person/He,She,It) + is + (1st Form of Verb + ing) + Object

2. Subject (Plural /You,We,They) + are + (1st Form of Verb + ing) + Object

3. I + am + (1st Form of Verb + ing)

Example:I am reading a novel.

Ram is going office.

We are getting late.

Present perfect tense

An action which happened or completed in the present time

1. Subject (Singular /third person/He,She,It) + has + 3rd Form of Verb + Object

2. Subject (Plural /I,You,We,They) + have + 1st Form of Verb + Object

Example:Divya has gone to school.

He has filled a case.

Past Tense :-

Simple Past Tense

1. Subject (Singular/third person/Plural) + 2nd Form of Verb

2. Different number of subject can not change verb.

Example:I worked on the project last night.

Past continuous tense

1. Subject (Singular /third person/He,She,It) + was + (1st Form of Verb + ing) + Object

2. Subject (Plural /You,We,They) + were + (1st Form of Verb + ing) + Object

Example :

I was reading harry potter last night

Past perfect tense

An action which happened or completed in the past time or usually the two actions which happened or completed one by one in the past time.

1. Subject (Singular /third person/Plural) + had + 3rd Form of Verb + Object

Example:Ramya went to school after she had completed her homework.
I had already heard this news.

Future Tense
Simple future tense
1. Subject (Singular/third person/Plural) + will + 1st Form of Verb
2. I or We + shall + 1st Form of Verb

Example:
We shall go to school tomorrow.
You will read a book.

Future continuous tense
1. I,We + Shall be + (1st Form of Verb + ing) + Object
2. Subject(Other than I,We) + will be + (1st Form of Verb + ing) + Object

Example:We shall be coming to your house.
We will be playing football in evening.

Future perfect tense
1. Subject + will have/shall have + 3rd Form of Verb + Object
2. Wherever you'll see the use of the two sentences in this tense, the action which would be completed first would be in 'Future Perfect Tense' and the action completed after would be in 'Present Simple Tense'.

Example:They will have played the match before the sun sets.
I shall have read my book before you come.

Rule 1.
In Present Indefinite sentences the number and the person of the subject play very important role. If the subject is Singular number third person, affix 's' or 'es' to the verb. If the verb ends in any of the following : ss, o , x, z, sh,ch , add, 'es' instead of 's' with the verb.
Eg: Pass-passes, miss-misses, do – does, mix – mixes, fix – fixes etc.

Rule 2.

When the main verb is in Future Tense, use Present Simple in clauses with if, till, as soon as, when, unless, before, until, even if, in case and as.
Eg:
We shall wait till she arrives.
I shall not go there even if it rains.
Rule 3.
Present Simple Tense must be used instead of Present Continuous Tense with verbs of perception (feel, hear, smell etc.), verbs of cognition (believe, know, think etc.), verbs of emotion (hope, love, hate etc.) which cannot be used normally in continuous form.
Eg:
Incorrect – We are seeing with our eyes. Correct – We see with our eyes.
Incorrect – The water is feeling cold. Correct – The water feels cold.
But these words can be used in progressive form in the following cases.
The Session Judge is hearing our case.
We are thinking of going to London next year.
I am seeing my lawyer today.
I am having some difficulties with this puzzle.
Rule 4.
One must not use adverbs of past time like yesterday, last year, last month, ago, short while ago etc. with Present Perfect Tense.
Eg:
Incorrect – He has completed his book yesterday.
Correct – He completed his book yesterday.
Incorrect – We have met 3 days ago. Correct – We met 3 days ago.
Rule 5.
If two or more actions took place in sequence, we use Simple Past to denote the actions. (Otherwise Past Perfect is used to denote the earlier action). This is usually used with conjunction Before.
Eg:
He switched on the light before he opened the door.
The train started just before I reached the station.
When Rahul reached home, Tina had had her lunch.
Rule 6.
The use of Simple Past Tense with , 'wish' and 'If only' shows unreal Past and present state of things.
Eg:
I wish I were a millionaire! (I am not a millionaire)

I wish I were a queen! (I am not a queen)
If I only knew her! (I don't know her.)
Rule 7.
In the following structure the use of Simple Past denotes unreal past and present time situation.
Eg:
It is time we went home. (It is time for us to go home.)
It is time you finished. (It is time for you to finish.)
Rule 8.
Use of Past Continuous with 'When' and 'While'
When is usually used when one action was completed and another action was going on.
When gives the meaning 'at the time that'.
Eg:
When he arrived, his wife was washing her clothes.
When she went to Banaras, she bought a sari.
While is used to denote a period.
Eg:
While I was teaching, I put through my best.
While I was in Opera, I could enjoy very much.
Rule 9.
Past Perfect is used when we look back on earlier action from a certain point in the past.
Eg:
She had completed her work, before I reached there.
I had started teaching before Manu came to my class.
Rule 10.
The Past Perfect is also used for an action which began before the time of speaking in the Past and which stopped sometime before the time of speaking.
 Eg:
He had served in a bank for twenty years; then he retired and established his business. His children were now well settled.
Rule 11.
Past Perfect Continuous is used when the action began before the time of speaking in the past, and continued up to that time.
Eg:
It is now eight and she was tired because she had been cleaning the house since dawn.
This city has been prosperous since a very long time.
Rule 12.

When two actions are to be taken place on some future time, we use Future Perfect for the action completed first and Present Simple for the action to be completed afterwards.
Eg:
The student will have left the class before the teacher comes.
The Principal will have started before I reach there.
Rule 13.
Future Perfect is also used for such incidents/actions about which we presume that another person had the knowledge of that incident or the action is already completed.
Eg:
You will have heard about Mother Teresa.
He will have read the newspaper so far.
Exercise
1. Adarsh hopes to become(a)/an officer after he complete(b)/his higher education(c)/No error(d)

2. The police have found (a) / who they believe to be (b) / the prime suspect in a murder case (c) / no error (d).

3. Now-a-days he teaches English (a)/ because the teacher of English. (b)/ has gone for a month's leave. (c)/ No Error (d).

4. I will let you know (a)/ as soon as I will get (b)/ any news in this regard. (c)/ No Error (d)

Answers
1. (B) complete should be replaced with completes ,because 1 verb is in future tense

2. (B) believe should be replaced with believed, as 1st part is in past tense.

3. (A)Replace 'he teaches' by 'he is teaching'.

4. (B) replace i will get with i get.

Rules of Noun
Rule 1
The nouns such as – Jury, choir, committee, council, crowd, herd, orchestra, team, government, mob, community, union, club, opposition, firm, flock etc.

are used as collective nouns to denote a group. They are considered to be singular and a singular verb is used with them.
Example
The committee has submitted its report.

Rule 2
The unit of measurement (such as - hour, pound, kilo, mile…etc.) is always used in the singular form in the structure –'Half + a/an + unit of measurement'; as, 'Half a kilo', 'Half an hour'.
Note: The unit of measurement (such as – hour, pound, kilo, mile…etc.) is also used in the singular form in the structure – 'A + half + unit of measurement'; as, 'A half kilo', 'A half hour'.
Example
Only Half an hour left to finish this work.

Rule 3
A plural noun is used after 'one and a half'; as 'One and a half kilos'
While 'A/An + singular noun + and + a half' is used in English Language; as,
'A kilo and a half kilos',
'An hour and a half'.

Rule 4
The structure – 'Numeral Adjectives + plural noun + and + a half' or Numeral Adjectives + and + a half + plural noun is used in the English Language.
Numeral Adjectives: One, two, three, four…..etc. some, all, many, few…..etc. are called Numeral Adjectives; as,
'Two kilos and a half' 'Five hours and a half' 'Two and a half kilos'.

Rule 5
A plural noun is used after 'Cardinal Adjectives except one'. Cardinal Adjectives: One, two, three, four, five, six….etc. are called Cardinal Adjectives; as 'Five kilometres'
Example
I have fifty rupees.

Rule 6

Generally, the plural of a proper noun is not possible. But the plural of a proper noun can be formed (=made) by adding 's' according to need.
Example
There are two Mohans in my class.

Rule 7
These nouns such as – barracks, corps, crossroads, Innings, headquarters, précis, series, species, Issue, offspring, aircraft, craft, swine are used in the same form both in singular and plural.
Example
All the police barrack of Gorakhpur are old.

Rule 8
The structure – 'Noun + preposition + same noun' is always used in the singular. A singular noun is always used before preposition and after a preposition; as'
Example
Village after village has been swept away.

Rule 9
A plural noun or a plural pronoun is used after these phrases – one of, each of, either of, neither of, any one of, a few of, very few of, half of, a lot of, a large number of etc.
Example
One of the boys was innocent.

Rule 10
If we add 's' or 'es' to some Adjectives, they become plural nouns; as'
Example
We have to taste the sweets and bitters of our lives.

Rule 11
Some nouns always remain in plural form. They take plural verb. These nouns have no singular form.
These are -
Assets, alms, amends, annals, archives, ashes ,arrears, athletics, auspices, species, scissors , trousers, pants. clippers, bellows, gallows, fangs, measles, eyeglasses, goggles, belongings, breeches. Bowels , braces ,binoculars, dregs, earnings, entrails, embers ,fetters, fireworks, longings, lees, odds ,outskirts, particulars, proceeds, proceedings ,riches,

remains, shambles, shears, spectacles , surroundings ,tidings ,tactics ,tongs ,vegetables, valuables, wages etc.

Means' — In the sense of income'. Means always takes a plural verb. In the sense way to achieve some end, Means takes a singular verb. When 'a' or 'every' is used before Means', it is singular.

Examples

(a) My means were reduced substantially.

(b) Every means is good if the end is good.

Rule 12

If two adjectives are joined by 'and' and 'The' is used before the first adjectives, A plural noun is used after the second Adjective.

Example

Dr. S.S. Prasad was an examiner of the Patna and Bihar universities.

Incorrect: Dr. S.S. Prasad was an examiner of the Patna and Bihar university.

Rule 13

If two adjectives are joined by 'and' and 'The' used before both Adjectives or each Adjective, A singular noun is used after the second Adjectives.

Example

The first and the second chapter of this book are interesting.

Incorrect: The first and the second chapters of this book are interesting.

Rule 14

Some nouns look plural in form but have singular meaning. Such nouns take singular verb. These are: news, innings, politics, summons, physics, economics, ethics. mechanics, mathematics, measles, mumps, rickets, billiards, draughts, etc.

Rule 15

Some nouns look singular but have plural meaning. Such nouns take plural verbs. These are: cattle, clergy, cavalry, infantry, poultry,peasantry, children, gentry, police etc.

Rule 16

Some nouns are always used in singular . These are uncountable nouns. We should not use article A/An with such nouns. These are -

Scenery, poetry, furniture, advice, information, hair, language. business, mischief, bread, stationery, crockery, luggage, baggage, postage, knowledge, wastage, money, jewellery, breakage etc,

We can not pluralise such nouns by adding `S' or 'es'.

Example It is incorrect to write sceneries, informations, furnitures, hairs.

If hair is used as countable it can be pluralised : e.g., one hair, two hairs.

Example I need three hairs of a black horse.

Rule 17

Some nouns have plural meaning. If a definite numeral adjective is used before them they are not pluralised. e.g., pair, score. Gross , stone ,hundred, dozen, thousand. million. billion. etc.

Otherwise these nouns can well be pluralised: Dozens of women, Hundreds of people, Millions of dollars, Scores of shops. Many pairs of shoes, thousands millions etc.

Rule 18

If a numeral adjective and a fraction are used with a noun, the noun is used with the numeral and the noun will be in singular.

Examples

(a) He gave me one rupee and a half.

(b) She gave me two rupees and a quarter.

Avoid the following structure

Examples

(a) He gave me one and a half rupees. (Incorrect).

(b) She gave rite two and a quarter rupees. (Incorrect)

If the numeral adjective and the fraction refer the multiplication, the noun be placed in the end (after the fraction) and it must be plural.

Examples

(a) Your deposits has grown two and a half times within two years.

(b) My salary has increased three and a quarter times within three years.

Rule 19

Some nouns are known as common gender nouns. They can be used for either sex; Male or Female. These are called dual gender nouns. Such nouns are : teacher, student, child, clerk, candidate. advocate, worker, writer, author, leader, musician, politician, enemy, client, president, person, neighbour etc. When these are used in singular, use third person singular masculine (his) pronoun with them.

Examples

(a) Every candidate should write his (not her) name.

(b) Every person should perform his (not her) duty. Each. either, everyone. everybody, no one, nobody, neither, anybody are also common gender pronouns.

Rule 20

Some nouns are used for specifically for feminine gender only. i.e., blonde, maid, mid wife, coquette, virgin etc.

Now a days nouns 'bachelor' and 'virgin' are being used for masculine and feminine gender as well .

Use of Apostrophe with 's'

(A) You can form the possessive case of a singular noun that does not end in 's' by adding an apostrophe and `s' We should use apostrophe in following situations only

(1) Living things -> Mohan's book

(2) Thing personified; as —> week's holiday

(3) Space time or weight ; as —> a day's leave

(4) Certain dignified objects; as

The court's orders

At duty's call

(5) Familiar phrases; as —

At his wit's end

At a stone's throw

It there are hissing sounds (sounds of sh or s) ending a word, use apostrophe without 's' with such words. e.g., For Jesus' sake, For conscience' sake, The roses' fragrance etc. (It can be noted that if we use apostrophe with s with such words it couldn't be pronounced well)

(B) You can form the possessive case of a plural noun that does not end in 's' by adding an apostrophe and a 's,' as in the following example.

Example The men's cricket team will play as soon as the women's team is finished.

(C) You can form the possessive case of a plural noun that does end in 's' by adding an apostrophe.

Example The concert was interrupted by the 'dogs' barking, the 'ducks' quacking, and the 'babies' squalling.

(D) Do not use apostrophe with possessive pronouns i.e., his, hers, yours, mine, ours, its, theirs etc. Yours faithfully, yours truly, ours garden , his pen, hers purse, theirs room.

(E) Use apostrophe with the last word in following titles.

Examples

(a) Governor-general's instructions.

(b) Commander-in-chiefs orders.

(c) My son-in-law's sister.

(d) Ram and Sons's shop.

(F) Do not use 'Double apostrophe'. Avoid double apostrophe in a sentence.

Example

(a) My wife's secretary's mother has expired. (Incorrect)

The mother of my wife's secretary has expired. (Correct)

(G) Apostrophe with 's' is used with; Anybody/ Nobody / Everybody / Somebody / Anyone / Someone / No one / Everyone.

Example Everyone's concern is no one's concern. If else is used after these words, use apostrophe with else as per following:

Example I can rely on your words, not somebody else's.

Rules of Adjectives

Much / Many :

Many: It refers large quantity of plural countable noun.

Example: There are much cows in the field.(incorrect)

There are many cows in the field.(correct)

Much: It refers large quantity of uncountable material noun.

Example: There are many water in the river.(incorrect)

There are much water in the river.(correct)

Elder / Older:

Elder: It is used for family members only.

" To" is used after elder

Example: Shyam is elder than Sohan. (incorrect)

Shyam is elder to Sohan. (correct)
Older: It is for persons out of family or non-living things.
"Than" is used with older.
Example: I am older to you.(incorrect)
I am older than you.(correct)

Few / a Few / The Few:
Few: It means hardly any or nothing. It is used in negative sense.
Example: There were few members in meeting so the meeting was cancelled.(correct)
There are few rupees in my wallet, I cannot go home.(correct)
A few: It means some or small amount. It is used in positive sense.
Example: A few politician are hard working.(correct)
There are a few students present in the school.(correct)
The few: It means all the amount which is present or remained on said time.
Example: I have read the few books present in library.(correct)
The professor taught the few student that had come.(correct)

Little/A little/the little:
These are used to express quantity of Uncountable Material noun.
Little: This implies "hardly any" or "nothing". It is used in negative sense.
Example: There is little ink in my pen so I cannot write. (correct)
There is little water left in tank, so we cannot bath.(correct)
A little: It means "very small amount ". It is used in positive sense.
Example: There is a little water left in tank, so you can bath.(correct)
The little : It means all the amount , which is available.
Example: I drank the little milk present in the bottle.(correct)

less / fewer:
These are used to express quantity of material

Less: It is used to express the quantity of uncountable material noun.
Example: Not fewer than five litres of oil Is present in tanker.(incorrect)
Not less than five litres of oil is present in the tankers.(correct)
Not fewer than five hundred kilograms of rice present in stock.(incorrect) .
Not less than five hundred kilograms of rice is present in the stock.(correct)
Fewer: It is used to express the quantity of plural countable noun.
Example: Not less than hundrerd students were present last monday.(incorrect)
Not fewer than hundred students were present last Monday.(correct)

Next/ Nearest:
Next: It is used to express order. Example: left, Right etc.
Example: Sita is sitting next to geeta. (correct)
Ram is my next bench classmate. (correct)
Nearest: It is used to express distance.
Example: Sent Paul school is nearest school to my home.(correct)
Ram-lila ground is nearest playground to my school.(correct)

later/ latter:
Later: It is used to express time (in the after).
Example: He came later than me. (correct)
He came latter than me.(incorrect)
Latter: It is used to express order.
Example: Ajay and Amit are brothers but the former is more handsome than later.(incorrect)
Ajay and Amit are brothers but the former is more handsome than latter. (correct)

Kinds of Adjective:

Proper Adjective:
This type of Adjective qualifies proper Noun.
Example: Indian, American, etc.
Virat kohli is an Indian player.
Donald Trump is an American president.

Quantitative Adjective:

This type of Adjective qualifies quantity of material noun.
Example: A great deal of, enough, all, no, some, much etc.
He is kind enough.
All the student are safe.
There is much water in swimming pool.
The baby has drunk much milk.

Demonstrative Adjective:
It qualifies the degree of distance for Noun / Pronoun.
Example: This, That, These, Such, Any etc.
This pen is Blue.
This bike is heavier than car.
Those politicians are good.

Descriptive Adjective:
This kind of Adjective explains the size, characteristic, colour, type of Noun / Pronoun.
Example: Tall, Large, Tiny, Rectangular, Square, Blue, Black, Ugly, Heavy, Dry etc.
I am a tall boy.
He is heavy wrestler.
My playground is triangular.

Distributive Adjective:
It qualifies one object or person between two or more than two person.
Example: Each, Every, either, neither etc.
Neither pen writes well.
Every child goes school.
Either of the Laptop works.

Possessive Adjective:
This kind of Adjective qualifies the possession or relation of noun / pronoun.
Example: Your, My, Our, His, Her etc.
My jacket is red but yours is blue.
That is your car.
This is my college.

Emphasizing Adjective:
This kind of Adjective is used to make special pressure on noun / Pronoun.
Example: Own, Very, Such, Same, Very etc.
I saw her at the Railway station with my own eyes.

This is my own pen.
This is the very thief who has stolen my smart phone.
(very means same to that person who is already known)

Interrogative Adjective:
This kind of adjective is used to make sense of question.
Example: What, How, Where, When etc.
Whose bike is this?
Which book is the best?
What type of laptop do you want to buy?

Numerical adjective:
It qualifies the number of countable noun.
Example: All, Some, No, Many, A good many, A number of etc.
There are many books in the library.
A cow has four legs.
All the students are present in the class.

Note: Enough, All, No, A lot of, Some etc are quantitative and numerical adjective both, but their uses are different. (Will be discussed in rules of adjective topic)

Kinds of Numerical Adjective:
Definite numerical adjective:
Cardinal: One, Two, Three etc.
Ordinal: First, Second, Third etc.
Multiplicative: Single, Double, Triple etc.
Indefinite Numerical Adjective:
Much, many, some, enough, a lot of, several etc.

Exclamatory Adjective:
This kind of adjective is used to express emotion of heart.
Example: What! , How! etc.
What a beautiful day!
What nonsense this is !
What a kind of man he is!
What a nice story is! etc.
Relative Adjective:
This kind of adjective is used to make sense of relation for Noun or Pronoun.
Example: Who, Which, That etc.

This is the laptop that is used for best gaming
experience.
This the singer who sings spiritual songs.

Present / Past participle Adjective:
This kind of Adjective is used where past or present
Participle is needed.
Example: Burning train, flying kite, Singing baby,
Tiring journey, Moving car etc.
I like a flying kite.
Old woman slipped down from the moving train.
I am fond of a tiring journey.

3. Comprehension

Passage 3

Dd

My dad and I both started playing tennis at the same time in 1967. Though I was small for my age, I was fast on my feet and seemed to have an instinct for where my opponent would hit his next shot. At the age of nine, I put on my white shorts and shirt and started playing in tennis tournaments around the New York area. By the time I was 12,1 was No. 7 in the 5 country in the under-12 category. When I was 16,1 won my first national singles title. Then, in 1977, as a chubby faced 18-year old with brown ringlets and a red headband, I came out of nowhere to reach the semifinals at Wimbledon. Though I wouldn't have told a soul back then, that's when I realized I had the potential to be the best tennis player in the world.

10 I worked my way up the ranks and by 1979,1 was world No. 3, hunting down Jimmy Connors and Bjorn Borg. I was winning a lot and I loved it— loved being the lone gunfighter. I won the US Open in both '79 and '80. Then, more and more, the problem became that almost everybody was somebody I shouldn't lose to. There was so much pressure to win in the early rounds of tournaments and make it to the finals. To conquer the pressure, I tried 15 building defences that almost nothing (and nobody) could get through.

But behind my defences were''some very dark places. There was always a devil inside me that I had to fight against. And that devil was fear of failure.

Eventually I had made it to the finals at Wimbledon that year, earning the rematch I'd badly wanted with Borg. Though I'd beaten the great, smooth Swede in last year's US 20 Open, Borg had won Wimbledon an incredible five times in a row, including against me. I got off to a sluggish start. I was tight, over impressed with the occasion. Borg won the first set, 6-4.

As I loosened up, the match turned into a dog fight. I won a tie breaker in the second set, and the third set was going in that direction too. Underneath my nerves and my 25 certainty that I had to play every point to my utmost, a strange idea was starting to materialise: He's not quite as hungry as last year. This match is mine to take, if I can take it. After that, I knew in my bones that I was going to win, and I did. The final score was 4-6, 7-6, 7-6, 6-4. When I beat Borg at the US Open a few months later, I officially replaced him as world 30 No. 1. I had thought that No. 2 was a pretty big deal. But No. 1 was a very strange place indeed—the peak of the mountain, the icy winds blowing around my head.

For four years I was the biggest winner in men's tennis.

Unseen Passage For Class 12 With Answers PDF 2020 - Literary Passages image - 1

Questions:

A. Choose the most appropriate option: (1 x 4 = 4 marks)

(a) The narrator won the match because of his ………………………

skills
determination
consistent practice
all of the above

(b) The top position is called a very strange place because …………………………

of high expectations of the spectators
rivals
happiness of leading others
none of the above

B. Answer the following questions briefly: 1 x 6 = 6

(a) At what age, do you think, John McEnroe started playing tennis?

(b) What two distinctive qualities did the author possess at a tender age?

(c) How did he look when he reached the Wimbledon semi-finals? What did he realise about himself?

(d) What did he try to overcome pressure? Which devil troubled him?

(e) What helped McEnroe to win the match? How did he feel after becoming world No.1?

(f) Discuss the attributes of John McEnroe briefly.

C. Find words in the passage similar in meaning as:
1 x 2 = 2

(a) hidden qualities (lines 5 to 15)

(b) impossible to believe (lines 15 to 25)

Answers:

A.

(a) 2. determination

(b) 4. none of the above

B.

(a) At the age of eight.

(b) (i) fast on his feet

(ii) instinct for where the rival would hit his next shot.

(c) He was a chubby faced 18-year old boy with brown ringlets and a red headband. He realised that he had the hidden talent to be the best tennis player in the world.

(d) He tried building unbreakable defences. The fear of defeat was the devil that troubled him.

(e) His assessment of his opponent that he was not as hungry as last year helped him to win the match. He played every point to the utmost. He was on the peak of the mountain with icy winds blowing around his head.

(f) John McEnroe was a great tennis player. He was hard working, determined and optimistic. He had the art of overcoming pressure.

C.

(a) potential

(b) incredible

Passage 4

As a medium of literary expression, the common language is inadequate. Like the man of letters, the scientist finds it necessary to "give a purer sense to the words of the tribe". But the purity of scientific language is not the same as the purity of literary language. The aim of the scientist is to say only one thing at a time, and to say it unambiguously and with the greatest possible clarity. To achieve this, he simplifies and jargonises. In other words, he uses the vocabulary and syntax of common speech in such a way that each phrase is susceptible to only one interpretation; and when the vocabulary and syntax of common speech are too imprecise for his purpose he invites a new technical language, or jargon specially designed to express the limited meaning with which he is professionally concerned. At its most perfectly pure form, scientific language ceases the matter of words and terms into mathematics.

The literary artist purifies the language of the tribe in a radically different way. The scientist's aim, as we have seen, is to say one thing, and only one thing at a time. This, most emphatically, is not the aim of the literary artist. Human life is lived simultaneously on many levels and has many meanings. Literature is a device for reporting the multifarious facts and expressing their various significance. When the literary artist undertakes to give a pure sense to the words of his tribe, he does so with the express purpose of creating a language capable of conveying, not the single meaning of some particular science, but the multiple significance of human experience, on its most private as well as on its more public levels.

Unseen Passage For Class 12 With Answers PDF 2020 - Literary Passages image - 2

Questions:

A. Choose the most appropriate option: (1 x 4 = 4 marks)

(a) The passage highlights the difference between ....

the language of science and of literature
the language of the tribe and that of a civilised man
jargon and the language of a common man
the central purpose of science and literature
(b) 'Jargon' in the context of the passage means
....

difficult language
technical language
language with limited meaning
mathematical language
B. Answer the following questions briefly: 1 x 6 = 6

(a) What is the purpose of literature according to the writer?
(b) What kind of a language is used in science?
(c) Discuss the similarities between the language of science and that of literature.
(d) What is the objective of a scientist?
(e) How does a literary figure use a language?
(f) Why does a scientist use specific technical words?

C. Find words in the passage similar in meaning as: 1 x 2 = 2

(a) not suffice
(b) side by side

Answers:

A.
(a) 1. the language of science and of literature
(b) 3. language with limited meaning

B.
(a) To report multifarious facts of life.
(b) Precise.
(c) The language of science and that of literature, each in its own way, makes for pure expression.
(d) The objective of a scientist is to be unambiguous.
(e) A literary figure uses a language to convey multiple interpretations.
(f) A scientist uses specific technical words to be intelligible.

C.
(a) inadequate
(b) simultaneously

Passage 5

I wandered lonely as a cloud
That floats on high o'er vales and hills,
When all at once I saw a crowd,
A host of golden daffodils;
Beside the lake, beneath the trees,
Fluttering and dancing in the breeze.
Continuous as the stars that shine
And twinkle on the milky way,
They stretched in never-ending line
Along the margin of a bay:
Ten thousand saw I at a glance,
Tossing their heads in sprightly dance.
The waves beside them danced, but they
Out-did the sparkling leaves in glee;
A poet could not be but gay,
In such a jocund company!
I gazed—and gazed—but little thought
What wealth the show to me had brought:
For oft, when on my couch I lie
In vacant or in pensive mood,
They flash upon that inward eye
Which is the bliss of solitude;
And then my heart with pleasure fills,
And dances with the daffodils.

Questions:
A. Choose the most appropriate option: (1 x 4 = 4 marks)

(a) Poet has compared rows of daffodils with which of the following?

Rows of twinkling stars
Rows of glistening leaves
Rows of milky-way
All of these
(b) Why does the poet become happy after seeing daffodils?

They look beautiful.
They will give fond memories to him.
They shine brilliantly.
They look like twinkling stars.
B. Answer the following questions briefly: 1 x 6 = 6

(a) T in the first line refers to
(b) What does the poet witness there?
(c) How were the daffodils dancing?
(d) When did the poet recall his experience?
(e) Why does the poet feel happy in the end?
(f) What does this poem justify?

C. Find words in the passage similar in meaning as:
1 x 2 = 2

(a) loneliness
(b) joy happiness

Answers:
A.
(a) 1. rows of twinkling stars
(b) 2.they will give fond memories to him
B.
(a) The poet
(b) The poet witness the beauty of nature. He sees daffodils.
(c) The daffodils were tossing their heads and morning from one direction to the other.
(d) The poet recalls his experience in pensive mood.
(e) The poet rejoices because of his sweet experience of witnessing the daffodils dancing under the stars.
(f) This poem justifies Wordsworth's definition of poetry. He said, "Poetry is the spontaneous overflow of powerful feelings recollected in tranquility.

C.
(a) solitude
(b) jocund

Passage 6

I heard a thousand blended notes,
While in a grove I sat reclined,
In that sweet mood when pleasant thoughts
Bring sad thoughts to the mind.

To her fair works did Nature link
The human soul that through me ran;
And much it grieved my heart to think
What man has made of man.
Through primrose tufts, in that green bower,
The periwinkle trailed its wreaths;
And 'tis my faith that every flower
Enjoys the air it breathes.
The birds around me hopped and played,
Their thoughts I cannot measure:—
But the least motion which they made
It seemed a thrill of pleasure.
The budding twigs spread out their fan,
To catch the breezy air;
And I must think, do all I can,
That there was pleasure there.
If this belief from heaven be sent,
If such be Nature's holy plan,
Have I not reason to lament
What man has made of man?

Questions:
A. Choose the most appropriate option: (1 x 4 = 4 marks)

(a) How does the poet feel after seeing nature?

Happy
Sad
Mixed feeling
Philosophical
(b) Which of the following is correct as per the poem?

Pleasure is everywhere.
Pleasure is everywhere except in poet's mind.
Humans do not enjoy nature.
Humans enjoy nature.
B. Answer the following questions briefly: 1 x 6 = 6

(a) Where did the poet hear the melodious music?
(b) Why did the poet feel sad?
(c) What does the poet justify in the last two lines of the first stanza?
(d) How did the birds behave?
(e) Why does the poet feel convinced that "there was pleasure there?

(f) What does the poet think about Nature's plan?

C. Find words in the passage similar in meaning as:
1 x 2 = 2

(a) regret
(b) jumped

Answers:

A.

(a) 3. mixed feeling
(b) 2. pleasure is everywhere except in poet's mind

B.

(a) The poet heard the melodious music in a grove.
(b) The poet felt sad because of man's selfishness and greed.
(c) The poet justifies that pleasant thoughts bring sad thoughts.
(d) The birds enjoyed life by hopping and playing around the poet.
(e) The poet felt convinced that there was pleasure there because he was enjoying in the lap of nature. He saw birds and animals living together happily.
(f) The poet thinks that Nature's plan in divine. It promotes fraternity and happiness.

C.

(a) lament
(b) hopped

Passage 7

Two roads diverged in a yellow wood,
And sorry I could not travel both
And be one traveller, long I stood
And looked down one as far as I could
To where it bent in the undergrowth;
Then took the other, as just as fair,
And having perhaps the better claim,
Because it was grassy and wanted wear;

Though as for that the passing there
Had worn them really about the same,
And both that morning equally lay
In leaves no step had trodden black.
Oh, I kept the first for another day!
Yet knowing how way leads on to way,
I doubted if I should ever come back.
I shall be telling this with a sigh
Somewhere ages and ages hence:
Two roads diverged in a wood, and I
I took the one less travelled by,
And that has made all the difference.

Questions:

A. Choose the most appropriate option: (1 x 4 = 4 marks)

(a) What does the poet mean when he says about another road that it wanted wear?

It was full of grass.
Nobody had used it ever.
It looked cleaner.
It was an intelligent guess.
(b) Why did the poet want to take the less travelled road?

To avoid the bumpy ride of another road
To get lost in the dense forest
In the hope of discovering something new
He liked puzzles

B. Answer the following questions briefly: 1 x 6 = 6

(a) Where was the poet?
(b) Why could the author not travel both roads?
(c) What is the theme of the poem?
(d) Why did the author doubt about coming back?
(e) Which road did he opt for?
(f) What did the poet know about passage?

C. Find words in the passage similar in meaning as:
1 x 2 = 2

(a) separated
(b) a mass of bushes and plants

Answers:

A.

(a) 2. nobody had used it ever
(b) 3. in the hope of discovering something new

B.

(a) The poet was in the forest where two roads diverged.
(b) The author was a single entity. He could not travel both roads at the same time,
(c) The poem is about making choices. Our choices set our destiny.
(d) The poet was pragmatic and practical. He knew that he would not be able to come at that place again as time and tide wait for none.
(e) He opted for the less travelled road.
(f) He knew that passages never come to an end. One passage leads to another.

C.

(a) diverged
(b) undergrowth

Passage 8

Whose woods these are I think I know.
His house is in the village, though;
He will not see me stopping here
To watch his woods fill up with snow.
My little horse must think it queer
To stop without a farmhouse near
Between the woods and frozen lake
The darkest evening of the year.
He gives his harness bells a shake
To ask if there is some mistake.
The only other sound's the sheep
Of easy wind and downy flake.
The woods are lovely, dark and deep,
But I have promises to keep,
And miles to go before I sleep,
And miles to go before I sleep.

Questions:
A. Choose the most appropriate option: (1 x 4 = 4 marks)

(a) Why does the poet stop in between his journey?

To enjoy the slight
To take a break
To recall the owner of the wood
To hear the harness bell
(b) Why the horse may be surprised at the unscheduled stoppage?

It was a very lonely place.
It was the coldest month of the year.
It was approaching darkness during one of the coldest days.
There was risk of bandits.
B. Answer the following questions briefly: 1 x 6 = 6

(a) What did the poet do at last?
(b) What can be said about the weather as described in the poem?
(c) Why is the poet's act called strange here?
(d) What message does the poet want to convey?
(e) Why does the horse feel perturbed?
(f) Which sounds are mentioned in the last stanza?

C. Find words in the passage similar in meaning as: 1 x 2 = 2

(a) strange
(b) falling snow

Answers:

A.

(a) 2. to take a break
(b) 3. it was approaching darkness during one of the coldest days

B.

(a) The poet resumed his onward journey.
(b) The weather described in the poem is not pleasant, it is very cold.

(c) The poet's act seems strange to the horse because there is no farmhouse in the vicinity. It was absurd to stay there.

(d) The poet intends to say that this would is an illusion. We must not get fascinated to the worldly pleasures.

(e) The horse felt perturbed because it was dark and the weather was unpleasant. He did not want his master to stay there.

(f) There sound of the blowing winds and the falling snow.

C.

(a) queer
(b) downy flake

Passage 9

All the world's a stage,
And all the men and women merely players;
They have their exits and their entrances,
And one man in his time plays many parts,
His acts being seven ages.
At first, the infant,
Mewling and puking in the nurse's arms.
Then the whining schoolboy, with his satchel
And shining morning face, creeping like snail
Unwillingly to school.
And then the lover,
Sighing like furnace, with a woeful ballad
Made to his mistress' eyebrow.
Then a soldier,
Full of strange oaths and bearded like the pard,
Jealous in honor, sudden and quick in quarrel,
Seeking the bubble reputation
Even in the cannon's mouth.
And then the justice, '
In fair round belly with good capon lined,
With eyes severe and beard of formal cut,
Full of wise saws and modem instances;
And so he plays his part.
The sixth age shifts
Into the lean and slippered pantaloon,
With spectacles on nose and pouch on side;

His youthful hose, well saved, a world too wide
For his shrunk shank, and his big manly voice,
Turning again toward childish treble, pipes
And whistles in his sound.
Last scene of all,
That ends this strange eventful history,
Is second childishness and mere oblivion,
Sans teeth, sans eyes, sans taste, sans everything.

Questions:
A. Choose the most appropriate option: (1 x 4 = 4 marks)

(a) What have men and women been compared with?

Audience
Actors
Judges
Narrators
(b) What does the poet try to indicate by 'bubble reputation?

Transitory nature of life
Meaningless heroics
Short-lived reputation
All of the above
B. Answer the following questions briefly: 1 x 6 = 6

(a) How has the lover been described here?
(b) How does a school boy behave?
(c) What happens at the sixth stage?
(d) Why is the old age called second childishness?
(e) What do you understand by 'exits' and 'entrances'?
(f) How does a soldier behave?

C. Find words in the passage similar in meaning as: 1 x 2 = 2

(a) complaining peevishly
(b) forgetfulness

Answers:

A.

(a) 2. actors
(b) 4. all of the above

B.

(a) The lover is burning with melancholy.
(b) A school boy reluctantly goes to school.
(c) At the sixth age man becomes weak. His eyesight also becomes weak. He also loses his teeth.
(d) Man becomes forgetful at the old age. He behaves like a child. He needs company. He wants to attract attention as a child does.
(e) 'Exits' means death and 'entrances' means birth.
(f) A soldier is full of pride. He can do anything to safeguard his honour.

C.
(a) whining
(b) oblivion

Passage 10

Too many parents these days can't say no. As a result, they find themselves raising 'children' who respond greedily to the advertisements aimed right at them. Even getting what they want doesn't satisfy some kids; they only want more. Now, a growing number of psychologists, educators and parents think it's time to stop the madness and start teaching kids about what's really important : values like hard work, contentment, honesty and compassion. The struggle to set limits has never been tougher—and the stakes have never been higher. One recent study of adults who were overindulged as children, paints a discouraging picture of their future : when given too much too soon, they grow up to be adults who have difficulty coping with life's disappointments. They also have distorted sense of entitlement that gets in the way of success in the work place and in relationships.

Psychologists say that parents who overindulge their kids, set them up to be more vulnerable to future anxiety and depression. Today's parents themselves raised on values of thrift and self-sacrifice, grew up in a culture where 'no' was a household word.

Today's kids want much more, partly because there is so much more to want. The oldest members of this generation were born in the late 1980s, just as PCs and video games were making their assault' on the family room. They think of MP3 players and flat screen TV as essential utilities, and they have developed strategies to get them. One survey of teenagers found that when they crave for something new, most expect to ask nine times before their parents give in. By every measure, parents are shelling out record amounts. In the heat of this buying blitz, even parents who desperately need to say no find themselves reaching for their credit cards.

Today's parents aren't equipped to deal with the problem. Many of them, raised in the 1960s and 70s, swore they'd act differently from their parents and have closer relationships with their own children. Many even wear the same designer clothes as their kids and listen to the same music. And they work more hours; at the end of a long week, it's tempting to buy peace with 'yes' and not mar precious family time with conflict. Anxiety about the future is another factor. How do well intentioned parents say no to all the sports gear and arts and language lessons they believe will help their kids thrive in an increasingly competitive world? Experts agree: too much love won't spoil a child. Too few limits will.

What parents need to find, is a balance between the advantages of an affluent society and the critical life lessons that come from waiting, saving and working hard to achieve goals. That search for balance has to start early. Children need limits on their behaviour because they feel better and more secure when they live within a secured structure.

Older children learn self-control by watching how others, especially parents act. Learning how to overcome challenges is essential to becoming a successful adult. Few parents ask kids to do chores. They think their kids are already overburdened by social and academic pressures. Every individual can be of service to others, and life has meaning beyond one's own immediate happiness. That means parents eager to teach values have to take a long, hard look at their own.

Unseen Passage For Class 12 With Answers PDF 2020 - Factual and Descriptive Passages image - 1

Questions:

A. Choose the most appropriate option: (1 x 4 = 4 marks)

(a) What do the psychologists, educators and parents want to teach the children?

To teach them about treachery.
To teach them about indiscipline.
To teach them about the values of life like hard work, contentment, honesty and compassion.
None of these
(b) What is essential to become a successful adult?

Learn not to overcome challenges
Learn how to overcome challenges
Nothing is essential.
None of these
(c) Why do children need limits on their behaviour when they live within a secured structure?

They feel more secure and better.
They feel insecure.
They feel bored.
None of these.
(d) What is the drawback of giving children too much too soon?

They fail to cope with life's disappointments when they grow up.
They do not study seriously.
They become quarrelsome when they grow up.
None of these.
B. Answer the following questions briefly: 1 x 6 = 6

(a) What values do parents and teachers want children to learn?
(b) What are the results of giving the children too much too soon?
(c) Why do today's children want more?
(d) What is the balance which the parents need to have in today's world?
(e) What is the necessity to set limits for children?
(f) How do older children learn self-control?

C. Find words in the passage similar in meaning as: 1 x 2 = 2

(a) a feeling of satisfaction (para 1)
(b) valuable (para 3)

Answers:
A.
(a) 3. To teach them about the values of life like hard work, contentment, honesty and compassion
(b) 2. Learn how to overcome challenges
(c) 1. They feel more secure and better.
(d) 1. They fail to cope with life's disappointments when they grow up

B.
(a) Parents and teachers want to inculcate the values of life like honesty, hard work and contentment among children.
(b) When children are given too much too soon, they grow up to be adults who have difficulty in coping with the disappointments of life. Such children may develop distorted sense of entitlement that comes in the way of success in the work place and relationships.
(c) Today's children want much more partly because there is so much more to want. They crave for something new. They consider even luxurious items as essential commodities.
(d) Parents need to find a balance between the advantages of an affluent society and the critical lessons of life that come from waiting, saving and working hard to achieve goals in today's world.
(e) Children need limits on their behaviours because they feel better and more secure when they live within a secured structure.
(f) Older children learn self-control by watching how others, especially parents act.

C.

(a) contentment
(b) precious

Passage 11

If NSYNC singer Lance Bass can't afford the $20 million price tag for a ride into space now, he should try again in, say, a decade.

But within a decade or so, even some of Bass's fans could afford a quick and safe trip to the suborbital edge of space — roughly 50-60 miles above earth, says Frank Seitzen, 5 president of the Space Transport Association.

"I think you're maybe 10 or 12 years away from having companies that are reliable and that can go through that process for $5,000 or $10,000," Seitzen said.

There's a hungry demand from would-be space tourists and a $10 million prize is inspiring designers. The X Prize, created in 1994 to spur the development of new space travel 10 technologies, has attracted at least 21 space vehicle designs from people in five countries. The non-profit X Prize Foundation, founded by a group of donors inspired by the $25,000 Orteig Prize that Charles Lindbergh won in 1927, will give the prize.

Each design team is hoping to develop the first reusable rocket capable of blasting a pilot and two to five passengers to a height of 62 miles. NASA awards astronaut status for 15 flights above 50 miles.

Some design contestants boast that such trips will be available by 2005, although the first few travellers will face $100,000 bills until the market matures.

Despite steep prices and lagging technology, Seitzen and others are convinced that a lucrative travel business awaits. Space Adventures, a travel agency that helped coordinate the first 20 tourist trip to the International Space Station last year by US businessman Dennis Tito, claims it has collected $2 million in deposits from more than 120 would-be suborbital tourists. For client Wally Funk, who has paid her deposit, suborbital travel is a disappointing, yet feasible, alternative to decades of trying to reach space. Funk, a retired aviation safety investigator says, "I would do (a space station trip) in a heartbeat, but I can't because I'm 25 not a millionaire."

Compared to Tito's groundbreaking effort last year, future suborbital flights look easy. Tito was subjected to rigid medical requirements and a gruelling six-month training course in Russia.

But suborbital travellers will need only a few days of training and, pending FAA approval, 30 would have to pass a much lower bar for medical standards.

"We always say that if you can safely ride a rollercoaster, then you are fit for a suborbital flight," says Space Adventures spokeswoman Tereza Predescu.

Four commercial spaceports, which launch rockets into space like airports launch planes, are already licensed to operate by the FAA in Virginia, California, Alaska and Florida, and 35 they are eager to welcome extra business from space tourists, negating the need to catch a ride to Russia.

For those reasons, suborbital travel may represent a $1 billion a year market, according to Space Adventures President and CEO Eric Anderson. Translated, that's 10,000 travellers paying $100,000 each during the first few years of adventure space travel.

Unseen Passage For Class 12 With Answers PDF 2020 - Factual and Descriptive Passages image - 2 Questions:

A. Choose the most appropriate option: (1 x 4 = 4 marks)

(a) Space adventure claims that.....................

it is a lucrative business
it is a business of less profit
people don't want to go to space
none of the above

(b) Some design contestants feel convinced that.....................

space trips will never be made available
space trips are not feasible
space trips are disappointing
space trips will soon be made available

(c) Tito.....................

underwent rigid medical checkups
attended a six month training course

both (i) and (ii)

none of the above

(d) Suborbital travellers will need

two years training course

a few days of training

a lot of money

none of these

B. Answer the following questions briefly: 1 x 6 = 6

(a) Name the first tourist to the International Space Station. What difficulties did he face?

(b) Why is Lance Bass unable to have a ride into space now? What is likely to happen in a decade?

(c) Which two factors are inspiring the designers of new space vehicle—the reusable rocket?

(d) How do you think suborbital tourism is a poor alternative to space travel?

(e) What are the prospects of suborbital travel? Give two examples in support of your answer.

(f) What are the prerequisites for space travelling?

C. Find words in the passage similar in meaning as: 1 x 2 = 2

(a) profitable (lines 15 to 25)

(b) severe, exhausting (lines 25 to 30)

Answers:

A.

(a) 1. it is a lucrative business

(b) 4. space trips will soon be made available

(c) 3. both (i) and (ii)

(d) 2. a few days of training

B.

(a) US businessman Dennis Tito was the first tourist to the International Space Station.

Tito had to undergo rigid medical requirements and a severe six month training course in Russia.

(b) Lance Bass can't afford $20 million for a space ride right now. In a decade, the fare for a space traveller is likely to come down to $10,000 or even $5,000.

(c) (i) a hungry demand from would-be space tourists

(ii) a $10 million prize to the designers

(d) Travellers to space go beyond the orbit of the earth and reach the orbit of the moon. On the other hand, the suborbital tourist will travel in a rocket upto the International Space Station only. Space travel is not possible for everyone, but suborbital tourism is a possible alternative.

(e) Suborbital travel is a lucrative business.

(i) Space Adventures, a travel agency has collected $2 million in deposits from more than 120 would-be suborbital tourists.

(ii) Four commercial space ports are already licensed to operate.

(iii) It is likely to be $1 billion a year market with 10,000 travellers paying $100,000 each dining the first few years of adventure space travel.

(f) The space travellers should be medically fit and they need to get proper training. A man who can ride a roller coaster is fit for space travelling.

C.

(a) lucrative

(b) gruelling

Passage 12

Call it a blessing or a curse of Mother Nature, we have to breathe in over 10,000 litres of air in a day (more than four million litres in a year) to remain alive. By making it essential for life, God has wished that we try to keep the air we breathe clean. Everyone can see the food that is not clean and perhaps refrain from eating it, but one cannot stop breathing even if one can feel the air to be polluted.

Several harmful and noxious substances can contaminate the air we breathe. Generally, much is said and written about outdoor air pollution, most of which is due to vehicular and industrial exhausts.

Given the fact that most of us spend over 90% of our time indoors, it is most important to recognise that the air we breathe in at home or in offices can be polluted. It can be a cause of ill-health. Air pollutants that are generally present in very low concentrations can assume significance in closed ill-ventilated places.

The indoor air pollution can lead to allergic reactions and cause irritation to the skin, the eyes and the nose. But as is logical to assume, the brunt of insult by pollutants is borne by the lungs. It can lead to the development of fresh breathing problems, especially in those who have allergic tendencies, or it can worsen the existing respiratory illnesses like asthma and bronchitis.

There can be several sources of indoor air pollution. Tobacco smoke is one of the most important air pollutants in closed places. "Passive smoking" or environmental tobacco smoke (ETS) pollution can lead to all the harmful effects of tobacco smoking seen in the smokers in their non-smoking companions. ETS as a health hazard has been unequivocally proven and is also getting social recognition now. One can occasionally see signs displaying the all-important message: "Your smoking is injurious to my health" in offices and homes. The children of smoking parents are among the worst affected persons.

The exposure of young children to ETS leads to increased respiratory problems and hospital admissions as compared to non-exposed children. Several studies, including those done at the PGI, have shown an increased risk of lung cancer among women exposed to passive smoking. ETS also worsens the existing lung diseases like asthma and bronchitis.

It may be responsible for the development of asthma in children.

The next most important source of indoor air pollution is the allergens. House dust mites (HDM) are very small insects not visible to the naked eye and are the commonest source of allergy in the house. They are ubiquitous and thrive in a warm and moist atmosphere. They breed very fast and are very difficult to eradicate. Modem houses present ample breeding spaces for them in the form of carpets, curtains, mattresses, pillows, etc.

Exposure to HDM can be prevented by the frequent washing of linen and by encasing the mattresses and pillows in a non-permeable cover. Pets form an important part of life for some of us. But they can add plenty of allergens to our indoor atmosphere. Cats are notorious for doing this. Fine particles from feline fur can remain stuck to the upholstery and carpets for a long time* even after the removal of the animal and lead to the worsening of asthma and skin allergies. Fortunately, owing to religious and social customs cats are not very popular pets in India. Dogs, however, are quite popular and can be as troublesome. Pets should be kept out of the bedrooms and washed frequently. To remove the fur particles one has to use vacuum cleaners as the ordinary broom and mop are not effective.

Moulds, fungi and several other microorganisms thrive in damp conditions and can lead to allergies as well as infections. Humidifiers in the air-conditioning plants provide an ideal environment for certain types of bacteria and have led to major outbreaks of pneumonia. It is important to clean regularly the coolers, air-conditioners and damp areas of the house such as cupboards, lofts, etc to minimise this risk.

Toxic gases can also pollute the indoor environment. Biomass fuels (wood, cowdung, dried plants) and coal, if burned inside, can lead to severe contamination by carbon monoxide (CO): The poor quality of stoves and other cooking or heating appliances that cause incomplete combustion of LPG can also lead to the emission of CO or nitrogen dioxide.

Formaldehyde (a gas) can be released from adhesives that are used for fixing carpets, upholstery and also in making plywood and particleboard.

The gases are very toxic in high concentrations as may be encountered during industrial accidents, but even in very minimal amounts, as may be prevalent in homes and offices, they can cause irritation to the skin or the eyes, rashes, headache, dizziness and nausea. Improving the ventilation is an important preventive measure, besides trying to eliminate the source that may not be always feasible.

Other indoor pollutants are toxic chemicals like cleansing agents, pesticides, paints, solvents and inferior-quality personal-care products, especially aerosols. Very old crumbling pipes, boilers, insulation or false roofing can also be important sources. Asbestos is a hazardous product that can cause cancer in humans.

It is important to realise that the air we breathe at home may not be clean always andwe must try to eliminate the source of pollution. We should give due consideration to ventilation.

Unseen Passage For Class 12 With Answers PDF 2020 - Factual and Descriptive Passages image - 3

Questions:

A. Choose the most appropriate option: (1 x 4 = 4 marks)

(a) The Almighty wants that human beings…………………

should try to breathe clean air
should not pay attention to pollutants
must ignore ETS
should become passive smokers

(b) The toxic gases cause …………………

rashes
headache
dizziness
all of the above

(c) Air conditioning plants become the cause of …………………

allergies
pneumonia
heart attack
infection

(d) Asbestos is a hazardous product because it can

cause cancer in humans
cause respiratory problems
prove fatal to the children
none of these

B. Answer the following questions briefly: 1 x 6 = 6

(a) What is essential for our life? How?
(b) Why should we pay attention to the quality of air we breathe indoor?
(c) Name eight important sources of indoor air pollution.
(d) What do you understand by ETS? How is it harmful? Give two instances.

(e) How can the risk of allergies be minimised?
(f) How can the toxic gases pollute the indoor environment?

C. Find words in the passage similar in meaning as: 1 x 2 = 2

(a) make impure (Para 2)
(b) clearly and unmistakably (Para 5)

Answers:

A.
(a) 1. should try to breathe clean air
(b) 4. all of the above
(c) 2. pneumonia
(d) 1. cause cancer in humans

B.
(a) Air is essential for our life. We have to breathe in over 10,000 litres of air in a day to keep alive.
(b) Most of us spend ninety per cent of our time indoors—in homes or offices. The air we breathe indoors may also be polluted and cause ill health. So, we should pay attention to the quality of air we breathe indoors.
(c) The important sources of indoor air pollution are:
(i) Tobacco smoke
(ii) Animal dusts
(iii) Air conditioners
(iv) Moulds, bacteria
(v) House dust mites
(vi) Cooking and heating
(viii) Asbestos
(vii) Toxic chemicals
(d) ETS stands for Environmental Tobacco Smoke or "passive smoking". It causes all the harms of tobacco smoking to non-smokers, for example, the children of smoking parents suffer from respiratory problems. There is an increased risk of lung cancer among women exposed to passive smoking.
(e) We must first identify the allergen and then prevent exposure to them. Use of vacuum cleaners, exposure to sun, washing linen in warm water and cleaning coolers, air-conditioners etc are some of the important steps to minimise allergies.

(f) The indoor environment becomes polluted when biomass fuels and coal are burnt. They release carbon monoxide and nitrogen dioxide which are detrimental to us.

C.
(a) contaminate
(b) unequivocally

Passage 13

You would have seen an increasing amount of "junk mail" showing up in your e-mail box. The so-called harmless activities of a small number of people are increasingly becoming a serious problem for the Internet.

Spam is the flooding of the Internet with many copies of the same message, in an attempt to force the message on people who would not otherwise choose to receive it.

Spam is basically electronic junk mail or junk newsgroup postings. It is sometimes confused with any unsolicited e-mail. But an old friend may also find your e-mail address on the Net and send you a message but this could hardly be called spam, even though it is unsolicited. Real spam is generally e-mail advertising for some product sent to a 10 mailing list or newsgroup.

In addition to wasting people's time with unwanted e-mail, spam also eats up a lot of network bandwidth. There are many organisations and individuals who have taken it upon themselves to fight spam with a variety of techniques. The problem is that because the Internet is public, there is very little that can be done to prevent spam, just as it is impossible to prevent junk mail.

One of the most recent examples of large-scale spamming was the hoax Ericsson e-mail about a free give away, something most people just cannot resist. The letter begins with a claim that since Nokia is giving away telephones, Ericsson will respond by giving away brand new WAP phone. But the recipient must forward the letter to a minimum of 20 20 people to receive the phone. The letter is signed by Anna Swelund, Executive Promotion Manager for Ericsson Marketing. It was later discovered that there was no such person at Ericsson.

There are numerous instances of these e-mails being used maliciously by someone who has a grudge against an ex-spouse, a public official, a former teacher or someone else with an e-mail address. The person mentioned in the e-mail ends up with thousands of requests from people looking for confirmation that the e-mail—which they actually had nothing to do with—is true.

Spamming works on our own greed to receive freebies. You are instructed by a total stranger (or a well meaning but not very bright friend) to forward a message you know 30 nothing about, except for the fact that maybe a friend passed it along to you and about 90 of their other very close friends.

Very often the victim can receive so many e-mails (and sometimes faxes and phone calls in the more malicious cases) that they have to get a new e-mail box or phone number— thereby ruining established personal and professional communication channels, which was the original intent of the sender.

Most spam is commercial advertising, often for dubious products, get-rich-quick schemes, or quasi-legal services. It costs the sender very little to send—most of the costs are paid for by the recipient or the carriers rather than by the sender.

There are two main types of spam, and they have different effects on internet users. 40 Cancellable Usenet spam is a single message sent to 20 or more Usenet newsgroups. Usenet spam is aimed at "lurkers", people who read newsgroups but rarely or never post and give their address away. Usenet spam robs users of the utility of the newsgroups by overwhelming them with a barrage of advertising or other irrelevant posts. Furthermore, Usenet spam subverts the ability of system administrators and owners to manage the topics they accept on theft1 systems.

E-mail spam targets individual users with direct mail messages. They typically cost users money out-of-pocket to receive. Most of us read or receive our mail through dial-up accounts while the meter is running, so to speak.

There is not much really that can be done to protect yourself except that you can 50 ensure your relative safety by creating internet e-mail accounts like Hotmail or Yahoo which can be easily and frequently changed. Further, these accounts also generally offer the option of blocking senders from whom you get spam and you can also opt to block e-mail which has been copied to more than 20 people.

One can also keep oneself informed about spammers through the Blacklist of Internet Advertisers, a popular report that describes the offending activities of spammers that routinely distribute large mailings via e-mail or post unwelcome advertising on newsgroups. You can also visit www.spam.abuse.net.

Another organisation devoted to countering the destructive effects of spam is MAPS or the Mail Abuse Prevention System. If an offending spammer cannot be shut down, the 60 spammer's ISP may contact MAPS with the subnet addresses allocated to the spammer so those specific addresses may be used instead of the IP address of the entire ISP. The MAPS website at http://mail-abuse.org will yield more useful information on how to counter and control spam.

Unseen Passage For Class 12 With Answers PDF 2020 - Factual and Descriptive Passages image - 4

Questions:

A. Choose the most appropriate option: (1 x 4 = 4 marks)

(a) Email spam victimises ………………

group
individuals
males
females

(b) Usenet spam deprives the users of ………………

the utility of the newsgroups
net facility
actual information
none of the above

(c) Name the organisation that counters the devastating effects of spam ………………

MASP
MAPS
MPAS
MSAP

(d) Who has to pay most of the costs of spam?

senders
receivers
carriers
either (ii) or (iii)

B. Answer the following questions briefly: 1 x 6 = 6

(a) What is spam? What problems are caused to net surfers by spamming?
(b) Give an example of recent large scale spamming.
(c) How does spamming work? Whom does it hit—sender or receiver?
(d) What are the two main types of spams and their effects on Internet users?
(e) How can one protect oneself against spam? Give two options.
(f) Who uses e-mail spam frequently?

C. Find words in the passage similar in meaning as: 1 x 2 = 2

(a) a mischievous trick played on somebody for a joke (lines 10 to 20)
(b) disreputable or risky (lines 31 to 40)

Answers:

A.

(a) 2. individuals
(b) 1. the utility of the newsgroups
(c) 2. MAPS
(d) 4. either (ii) or (iii)

B.

(a) Spamming is basically electronic junk mail or newsgroup posting. It is e-mail advertising for some product sent to a mailing list or group. The internet is flooded with many copies of the same message. The aim is to force the message on people who would not otherwise receive it.

Spamming poses a major inconvenience to net surfers as their accounts get jammed with unwanted junk mail.

(b) The offer of Ericsson to give away WAP phone as Nokia is giving away telephones. It later turned out to be a hoax.

(c) Spamming works on our greed to receive freebies. Sometimes a friend or a total stranger instructs someone to pass a message. It hits the receiver. He receives a large number of e-mails, faxes and phone calls. Most of the costs are paid by the receiver.

(d) The two main types of spams are: Cancellable Usenet spam and e-mail spam. Usenet spam is a single message sent to 20 or more Usenet newsgroups. It sends them a barrage of advertisements or other irrelevant posts and subverts their ability to manage the topics they accept on their system. E-mail spam is aimed at individual users.

(e) (i) By creating internet e-mail accounts like Hotmail or Yahoo and changing them frequently— blocking spammers who send copies to more than 20 persons.

(ii) Consulting Blacklist of Internet Advertisers.

(iii) Mail Abuse Prevention System—The MAPS website at http://mail-abuse-org yields useful information on how to counter and control spam.

(f) The people who are dissatisfied make use of e-mail spam. The advertising agencies do get its benefit.

C.

(a) hoax

(b) dubious

Passage 14

When plastic waste is burnt, a complex weave of toxic chemicals is released. Breaking down polyvinyl chloride (PVC) — used for packaging, toys and coating electrical wires — produces dioxin, an organochlorine which belongs to the family of Persistent Organic Pollutants (POPs). A recent Dioxin Assessment Report brought out by the United States Environment Protection Agency (USEPA) says the risk of getting cancer from dioxin is ten times higher than reported by the agency in 1994.

Yet the Delhi government is giving the green signal to a gasification project which will convert garbage into energy without removing plastic waste. Former transport minister Rajendra Gupta, the promoter of this project, says this is not necessary.

He claims no air pollution will be caused and that the ash produced can be used as manure. An earlier waste-to-energy project set up in Timarpur failed. The new one, built with Australian assistance, will cost ₹ 200 crore. It will generate 25 megawatts of power and gobble 1,000 tonnes of garbage every day.

"Technologies like gasification are a form of incineration," says Madhumita Dutta, central coordinator with Toxics Link, New Delhi. Incineration merely transfers hazardous waste from a solid form to air, water and ash, she points out.

Toxins produced during incineration include acidic gases, heavy metals as well as dioxins and furans. "The 'manure' will be hazardous and a problem to dispose," says Dutta.

Municipal solid waste contains a mix of plastics. Breaking down this waste emits hydrochloric acid which attacks the respiratory system, skin and eyes, resulting in coughing, vomiting and nausea.

Polyethylene generates volatile compounds like formaldehyde and acetaldehyde, both suspected carcinogenic. Breathing styrene from polystyrene can cause leukaemia. Polyurethane is associated with asthma. Dioxin released by PVC is a powerful hormone disrupter and causes birth defects and reproductive problems. There is no threshold dose to prevent it and our bodies have no defence against it.

"Even the best run incinerators in the world have to deal with stringent norms, apart from contaminated filters and ash, making them hugely expensive to operate," says Dutta. In Germany, air pollution devices accounted for two-thirds the cost of incineration. Despite such efforts, the European Dioxin Inventory noted that the input of dioxin into the atmosphere was the highest from incineration.

"India does not have the facility to test dioxin and the cost of setting one up is prohibitively expensive," says Dutta.

Besides, Indian garbage has a low calorific content of about 800 cal/kg, since it has high moisture and requires additional fuel to burn. Toxics Link calculates that the electricity generated from such technology will cost between ₹ 5-7 per unit, which is six times higher than conventional energy. India has chosen a dioxin preventive route and burning of chlorinated plastics is prohibited under Municipal Solid Waste and Biomedical Rules.

Nearly 80 per cent of Indian garbage is recyclable or compostable. Resident associations, the informal sector and the municipal corporation can make Delhi's garbage disappear in a sustainable manner. "Instead, the government promotes end of pipeline solutions," says Dutta.

Unseen Passage For Class 12 With Answers PDF 2020 - Factual and Descriptive Passages image - 5
Questions:
A. Choose the most appropriate option: (1 x 4 = 4 marks)

(a) Dioxine causes ………………..

cancer
heart attack
sickness
hypertension
(b) The gasification process transforms ………………..

energy into garbage
garbage into energy
water into energy
none of the above
(c) Garbage can be converted into energy by ………………..

gasification
gratification
a chemical process
incinators
(d) Indian garbage contains …………………..

low moisture
high moisture
no moisture
none of these
B. Answer the following questions briefly: 1 x 6 = 6

(a) Which toxic chemical is released on burning plastic waste? How is it harmful?
(b) What is the aim of waste-to-energy project? What is likely to happen during incineration?
(c) How will burning plastic adversely impact the health of citizens?
(d) What two arguments are advanced against the use of incinerators?
(e) Why would gasification of waste prove a wasteful luxury in India?
(f) What facts are revealed in the passage pertaining to Indian garbage?

C. Find words in the passage similar in meaning as: 1 x 2 = 2

(a) Waste material
(b) Swallow

Answers:

A.

(a) 1. cancer
(b) 2. garbage into energy
(c) 1. gasification
(d) 2. high moisture

B.

(a) Dioxin, an organochlorine, belonging to the family of Persistent Organic Pollutants (POPs) is produced. It causes cancer.
(b) Converting garbage into energy to produce 25 megawatts of power and swallow 1,000 tonnes of garbage everyday. Incineration simply changes risky waste from solid form to air, water and ash.
(c)
(i) Hydrochloric acid attacks respiratory system, skin and eyes and results in coughing, vomiting and nausea.

(ii) Polyethylene produces volatile carinogens like formaldehyde and acetaldehyde which cause cancer.
(iii) Breathing styrene from polystyrene can cause leukaemia.
(iv) Polyurethane is linked with asthma.
(v) Dioxin disrupts hormones, causes birth defects and reproductive problems.
(d)
(i) Exorbitantly expensive to operate.
(ii) Release of dioxin is highest from incinerators.
(e) Nearly 80% of Indian garbage is recyclable or compostable.
(f) Indian garbage has a^low calorific content of about 800 cal/kg because it has high moisture. It requires additional fuel to bum.

C.

(a) garbage
(b) gobble

Passage 15

The analysis of handwriting has a long history—some say it goes back to Roman times. Modern graphology began early in the 19th century when French churchman Jean Hippolyte Michon created the first graphological "catalogue" examining, for example, where letters fall on the line, their shape and the pressure exerted.
5 Allan Conway, a professional graphologist for 12 years says, "Handwriting says more about you than many chosen words, simply because you cannot hide yourself in your handwriting—it's not really your hand that's writing, but your brain. It's your personality frozen in ink."
Despite public skepticism, graphology plays a covert role in British management. 10 Many companies use it for executive recruitment and analysis. Graphology tells them about the candidates' temperaments, highlighting both weaknesses and strengths. There are about 300 movements on an unlined A4 page of writing and students must find and interpret them all. He also needs to know three things about the writers: their sex, their age and if they are left or right-handed. Then he looks for 16 dominant 15 elements, including the size of the writing, the pressure, the speed and slant of the words, how connected the characters are as well as the form of the connections, the proportions of the "middle zone" (covered by small letters such as "o" and "n") and "upper" and "lower" zones (where letters extend up or down, as with "d" or "p"), and the rhythm and regularity of writing. "But there is one golden rule," Rees says, "No single sign on 20 its own must ever be taken to mean anything."
The principles, according to Conway, are straightforward. The baseline—whether the writing goes straight across the page or slants up and down—helps to determine the writer's state of mind.

A very upward baseline shows a creative, ambitious and outgoing person. A slightly 25 downward one can reveal dissatisfaction or unhappiness though it could simply be a sign of fatigue. "A sharp downward baseline usually indicates serious problems or illness, probably emotional", says Conway, "while a straight one is an excellent sign of emotional stability. An irregular baseline can mean an excitable writer with poor self discipline." The way letters are formed and connected is important: a writer with angular 30 letters, for example, is often persistent and decisive. Arched letters suggest the writer is reluctant to express emotions freely and may appear cold. Where the bottoms of letters are curved like a cup the writer is likely to be open to the world and at ease. And writing with letters threaded—connected together as if by a length of cotton—can indicate speed or laziness. The more connected the letters, the more co-ordinated the patterns of thought. 35 Character size can also be significant. Larger letters tend to suggest vitality, enterprise and self reliance, while small letters can reveal a lack of self-confidence, but are also found in fields of research where concentration and exactness are necessary.
The slant of a person's writing indicates their emotional make-up. Where all the letters 40 are vertical the writer is likely to be some one uncomfortable in groups. For right-handers, left-word slant shows introversion while rightward slant reveals someone outgoing, friendly and ambitious. A

constantly varying slant betrays an unpredictable personality.

The spacing between words points to the writer's organizational abilities: wide spacing suggests individuality, extravagance, self-confidence and sociability.

45 Even the colour of ink a person chooses can be telling. Blue may indicate someone with no desire to be exceptional or pretentious, green likes to impress and red to shock. Brown is often used by people who work in high-security jobs, able to keep secrets, while black shows a demanding or forceful character who wants to make an impression.

Unseen Passage For Class 12 With Answers PDF 2020 - Factual and Descriptive Passages image - 6

Questions:

A. Choose the most appropriate option: (1 x 4 = 4 marks)

(a) The upward baseline proves that the person is.......................

creative
ambitious
outgoing
all of the above

(b) The letters small in size reveal that the writer may be.......................

a researcher
confident
arrogant
humble

(c) The spacing between words reveals.......................

the writer's organisational abilities
the writer's predicament
the writer's grief
the writer's delight

(d) The spacing between words indicates the writer's

forceful character
exceptional talents
organisational abilities
oratorical abilities

B. Answer the following questions briefly: 1 x 6 = 6

(a) What is graphology? How is it more revealing than words?

(b) How is graphology used in British management?

(c) What helps to determine the writer's state of mind and how? Give two examples.

(d) How can we learn one's emotions and patterns of thought through handwriting? Give two examples.

(e) How do slant of words and spacing indicate emotional makeup of a person? Give examples.

(f) How does the colour of ink help us in analysing the personality of the writer?

C. Find words in the passage similar in meaning as: 1 x 2 = 2

(a) prominent, very important (lines 10 to 20)

(b) continuing without interruption (lines 25 to 35)

Answers:

A.

(a) 4. all of the above
(b) 1. a researcher
(c) 1. the writer's organisational abilities
(d) 3. organisational abilities

B.

(a) The scientific analysis and study of handwriting is called graphology. It is more revealing than words because one can't hide oneself in one's handwriting. The hand writes what the brain dictates and freezes the personality in ink.

(b) Companies use it for executive recruitment and analysis of candidates' temperaments, weaknesses and strengths.

(c) Baseline: whether writing is straight or slanted. Examples

(i) upward baseline —> creative, ambitious, sociable person.

(ii) slightly downward baseline —> dissatisfaction, unhappiness or fatigue.

(d) from the way letters are formed and connected; e.g.

(i) angular letters: persistent and decisive nature.

(ii) arched letters: reluctance to express feelings freely, coldness.

(iii) bottom curved life cups: frank, comfortable.

(iv) large letters: vitality, enterprize and self-reliance.

(v) small letters: lack of self-confidence/concentration and exactness in research.

(e) (i) vertical letters: uncomfortable in group.

(ii) leftward slant (right handed person): introvert.

(iii) rightward slant (right handed): friendly and ambitious.

(iv) varying slant: unpredictable personality

(v) wide spacing: extravagance, self-confidence and sociability

(f) A person who opts for blue ink has no desire to be extraordinary. The green colour epitomises status. The red colour is used to shock others. Those who work in high security jobs use the brown ink. Black shows a demanding character.

C.

(a) dominant

(b) persistent

Passage 16

The idea that coffee is bad for heart pops up periodically. It was found that regularly drinking very strong coffee could sharply increase cholesterol levels. Researchers even isolated fatlike chemicals, cafestol and kahweol, responsible for the rise.

It turned out that the European brewing method—boiling water sits on the coffee grounds for several minutes before straining – produces high concentrations of cafestol and kahweol. By contrast, the filter and percolation methods remove all but a trace of these chemicals. Moreover, the studies involved large amounts of coffee—five to six cups a day. Moderate coffee drinkers down only two cups.

Research has also shown that regular, moderate coffee drinking does not dangerously raise blood pressure. And studies have failed to substantiate fears that coffee might trigger abnormal heart rhythms (arrhythmias) in healthy people.

"For heart disease, I think the issue is closed," says Meir Stampfer, an epidemiologist at Harvard who has studied many aspects of coffee and health. "Coffee drinking at reasonable levels is unrelated to heart risk."

Evidence suggests that coffee may help fend off Parkinson's disease. A 30-year study of 8000 Japanese-American men found that avid coffee drinkers had one-fifth the risk of those who didn't drink the brew.

Scientists at Massachusetts General Hospital, USA, found indirect evidence that Caffeine- the habit forming stimulant in coffee – may actually combat Parkinson's disease. The caffeine seemed to protect mice brain cells from depletion of the nerve chemical dopamine – the problem underlying Parkinson's disease in humans. However, these are preliminary findings; human studies have- not consistently supported caffeine's protective role.

The studies on coffee and cancer have focussed on three organs – and are reassuring. You may remember a brief coffee scare in the early 1980s when a single study linked coffee with pancreatic cancer. A false alarm: Many studies since then have shown that the association is either extremely weak or non-existent.

If there's a connection between coffee and bladder cancer, it possibly applies just to coffee junkies. A reanalysis of ten European studies found an increased risk only among people who drank ten or more cups a day. And studies show that coffee seems to have no adverse influence on the risk of colon cancer.

Caffeine is such a powerful stimulant that the International Olympic Committee and the National Collegiate Athletic Association set limits on how much can remain in the blood during competition. In addition to boosting physical endurance, caffeine increases alertness and improves mood. The buzz may come at a price, though. People who drink more than they're used to may become restless and unable to sleep. Moreover, it's possible to become physically dependent on caffeine in days.

The question now arises: how much to drink? Those with heatburn and anxiety may want to see if cutting back coffee improves their condition. For most people, however, there's virtually no risk in consuming up to three normal cups a day. Harvard's Stampfer tries to keep his coffee drinking irregular enough to avoid habituation: "That way, I can get a buzz when I feel like it."

Unseen Passage For Class 12 With Answers PDF 2020 - Factual and Descriptive Passages image - 7

Questions:

A. Choose the most appropriate option: (1 x 4 = 4 marks)

(a) Coffee increases……………………….of those people who regularly drink very strong coffee.

cholesterol
tension
the amount of blood
fats

(b) A person should not drink coffee………………………

less than 10 cups a day
more than ten cups a day
more than three cups a day
none of the above

(c) It has been proved that coffee does not have any adverse effect on the risk of………………………

colon cancer
diabetes
lung cancer
none of the above

(d) Caffeine boosts

physical endurance
mental endurance
positive feelings
none of these

B. Answer the following questions briefly: 1 x 6 = 6

(a) In what respect does coffee harm human heart? How?

(b) What is the finding of latest researches about coffee and human heart?

(c) What problem causes Parkinson's disease? What is the role of coffee in this respect?

(d) Name the three types of cancer listed in the passage.

(e) 'Caffeine is a powerful stimulant'. What are the positive and negative effects of Caffeine?

(f) What do studies reveal about moderate coffee drinkers?

C. Find words in the passage similar in meaning as: 1 x 2 = 2

(a) separated (Para 1)

(b) drug that increases physical or mental activity and alertness (Paras 6, 9)

Answers:

A.

(a) 1. cholesterol
(b) 3. more than three cups a day
(c) 1. colon cancer
(d) 1. physical endurance

B.

(a) Drinking very strong coffee could sharply increase cholesterol levels. Fatlike chemicals— cafestol and kahweol are responsible for the rise.

(b) European brewing method produces high concentrations of cafestol and kahweol. The filter and percolation methods almost remove the chemicals. Regular, moderate drinking of coffee neither raises blood pressure nor causes abnormal heart rhythms.

(c) Depletion of the nerve chemical dopamine in nerve cells causes the disease. Caffeine seemed to protect mice brain cells effectively. Caffeine's protective role for humans is yet to be established.

(d) (i) pancreatic cancer
(ii) bladder cancer
(iii) colon cancer

(e) (i) Advantages : boosts endurance, increases alertness and improves mood.
(ii) Disadvantages : restlessness and sleeplessness on drinking more than usual-possibility of becoming addicts and physically dependent.

(f) Studies reveal about moderate coffee drinkers that it does not dangerously affect their health. They may enjoy three cups of coffee per day without facing any health problem.

C.

(a) isolated
(b) stimulant

Passage 17

Delhi skies were just clear enough last Sunday to let sky-watchers have a ringside view of a close encounter in space: a half-a-mile-wide asteroid buzzing the earth at a distance a little farther than the moon. It was a rare opportunity to watch a close-up of one of these visitors from the asteroid belt between the orbits of Mars and Jupiter who often drop in without notice and cause the world's pulse to quicken.

A two-mile wide tumbling rock from space suddenly became the cynosure of all telescopes last month as astronomers proclaimed it 'the most earth-threatening object' ever detected. Preliminary calculations even suggested it might hit the earth in 2019. That it proved to be a false alarm is another matter. What's important is that such celestial brushes may form part of a countdown to Armageddon.

For every asteroid spotted, several whiz by unnoticed, with some actually passing closer to us than the moon. The number of these Near Earth Objects, or NEOs, far exceeds the known list—a catalogue that needs to be completed before it's too late.

Space agencies have projects to push potential earth-grazers off course. But there's yet to be a comprehensive global space watch programme. Most NEOs slip through unnoticed because of limitations to telescope time, technology and funding. So, it's important for governments not to grudge asteroid hunters the resources they badly need to keep a close watch.

A global asteroid monitoring system of sorts already exists in the form of an assorted group of government and private agencies, along with amateur and professional asteroid researchers. But it has no mechanism to assess the risk factors of NEOs or to determine what, and how much, information should be passed on to the public. As a result, the discoveries of more NEOs do not necessarily lead to a corresponding increase in public awareness of the threat they pose. Newspapers, television and movies aren't of much help either, and a confused public is often left wondering what's fact and what's fiction.

In fact, a kind of 'cry-wolf syndrome' sets in after every sighting, lowering the threat perception in the public mind. If or, more likely, when—there's an asteroid strike, events like Hiroshima and September 11 would pale in comparison. In the cosmic shooting gallery, bruisers larger than a mile across probably have a chance of walloping the earth every 100,000 to 300,000 years, while those 330 feet or larger could score a hit every 1,000 to 2,000 years.

The biggies cause the most concern. If a hunk of stone and metal the size of a 20-storey building hits the earth and sets off a million megaton blast, it'd be like a million city- busting bombs going off simultaneously. Deaths could be counted in millions and most of the flora and fauna would vanish.

Didn't the dinosaurs once think the planet would forever be one big Jurassic Park? The poor beasts never had a space programme and became a smorgasbord for a nasty asteroid. The moral then is to have a space watch programme which includes professional and amateur atronomers maintaining a nightly vigil around the globe. A powerful telescope could be placed outside the earth's orbit to monitor the blind spot created by the sun and rule out unexpected impacts.

In the northern hemisphere, scores of professional astronomers constantly scan the dark skies for tiny points of light and their telltale tracks. But the southern hemisphere is yet to have such sky sentinels whose computers could crunch foot-long numbers to find out if the ultimate destination of any of these shadow mountains in space is Planet Earth.

Unseen Passage For Class 12 With Answers PDF 2020 - Factual and Descriptive Passages image - 8
Questions:
A. Choose the most appropriate option: (1 x 4 = 4 marks)

(a)   The   warning   given   by   the astronomers……………………………..

proved to be a false alarm
was right
did not frighten the people
Proved to be true
(b) Media…………………………..

is useless
often confuses people
enlighten the masses
is insensible
(c)   What   causes   the   most concern……………………………..

biggies
human beings
scientists
none of the above
(d) The northern hemisphere has successfully received the attention of

geographers
professional astronomers
scientists
none of these
B. Answer the following questions briefly: 1 x 6 = 6

(a) Which spectacular event is referred to? Where do the visitors come from and what do they cause?
(b) What became the centre of attraction for all eyes? Why?
(c) Which projects aim at saving the earth? Why do NEOs slip through unnoticed?
(d) Why is global asteroid monitoring system essential? What shortcomings does the existing system suffer from?
(e) Why, do you think, the author mentions dinosaurs?
(f) What does the southern hemisphere lack?

C. Find words in the passage similar in meaning as: 1 x 2 = 2

(a) centre of attraction (para 2)

(b) any set of opinions, events, actions, etc. that are characteristic of a particular condition (para 6)

Answers:

A.

(a) 1. proved to be a false alarm
(b) 2. often confuses people
(c) 1. biggies
(d) 2. professional astronomers

B.

(a) It refers to a close encounter in space: a half-a-mile-wide asteroid flying the earth at a distance a little farther than the moon. The visitors come from the asteroid belt between the orbits of Mars and Jupiter. They cause excitement and tension.
(b) A two-mile wide tumbling rock from space became the centre of attraction for all eyes. It was called 'the most earth-threatening object' ever detected. Though its striking the earth proved a false alarm, such celestial brushes point to the end of the world.
(c) Space agencies have projects to push potential earth-grazers off course. However, some Near Earth Objects (NEOs) slip through unnoticed because technology, telescope, time and funds are limited.
(d) If there is an asteroid strike, Hiroshima and September 11 would pale in comparison. Deaths could be countecf in millions, and most of the flora and fauna would vanish. So global asteroid monitoring system is essential. The present system is an ill- assorted group which has no mechanism to assess the risk factors of NEOs or how much information should be passed on to the public.
(e) The dinosaurs were wiped out by an asteroid strike.
(f) The southern hemisphere has not received the attention of the astronomers yet. It lacks monitoring.

C.

(a) cynosure
(b) syndrome

Passage 18

From the ramparts of the Red Fort for some years now, our prime ministers have been promising the eradication of child labour in hazardous industries.

The truth is, if the government really wanted, child labour in hazardous industries could have been eliminated long time ago; and yes, every Indian child would have been in school by 2003.

The government has failed to eliminate this dehumanisation of childhood. It has also failed to launch compulsory primary education for all, despite the rhetoric. Between 60 and 100 million children are still at work instead of going to school and around 10 million are working in hazardous industries. India has the biggest child population of 380 million in the world, plus the largest number of children who are forced to earn a living.

We have many laws that ban child labour in hazardous industries. According to the Child Labour (Prohibition and Regulation) Act, 1986, the employment of children (below the age of 14) in hazardous occupations has been strictly banned. But each state has different rules regarding the minimum age of employment; this makes implementation of these laws difficult.

Also, there is no ban on child labour in non-hazardous occupations. The Act applies to the organised or factory sector and not to the unorganised or informal sector where most children find employment as cleaners, servants, porters, waiters, among other forms of unskilled work. Thus, child labour continues because the implementation of the existing laws is lax.

There are industries which have a 'special' demand for child labour because of their nimble fingers, high level of concentration and capacity to work hard at abysmally low wages. The carpet industry in UP and Kashmir employs children to make hand-knotted carpets; there are 80,000 child workers in J&K alone. In Kashmir, because of the political unrest, children are forced to work while many schools are shut. Industries like gem¬cutting and polishing, pottery and glass want to remain competitive by employing children.

The truth is that it's poverty which is pushing children into the brutish labour market. We have 260 million people below the poverty line in India, a large number of them are women. Poor, vulnerable parents, especially women-headed families, have no option but to push their little ones in this hard life in hostile conditions, with no human or labour rights.

There is a lobby which argues that there is nothing wrong with children working as long as the environment for work is conducive for learning new skills. But studies have shown that children are made to do boring, repetitive and tedious jobs and are not taught new skills as they grow older. In these hell-holes, like the sweatshops of old, there is no hope.

Children working in hazardous industries are prone to debilitating diseases which can cripple them for life. By sitting in cramped, damp, unhygienic spaces, their limbs become deformed for life. Inside matchstick, fireworks and glass industries, they are victims of bronchial diseases and TB. Their mental and physical development is permanently impaired by long hours of work. Once trapped, they can't get out of the vicious circle of poverty. They remain uneducated and powerless. Finally, in later years, they too are compelled to send their own children to work. Child labour perpetuates its own nightmare.

If the government was at all serious about granting children their rights, an intensive effort ought to have been made to implement the Supreme Court's directive of 1997 which laid down punitive action against employers of child labour (₹ 20,000 per child to be paid by offending employers). Only compulsory primary education can eliminate child labour.

Surely, if 380 million children are given a better life and elementary education, India's human capital would be greatly enhanced. But that needs, as President Abdul Kalam says, a "second vision". Can our political establishment see beyond the haze of shallow realpolitik?

Unseen Passage For Class 12 With Answers PDF 2020 - Factual and Descriptive Passages image - 9

Unseen Passage For Class 12 With Answers PDF 2020 - Factual and Descriptive Passages image - 10

Questions:

A. Choose the most appropriate option: (1 x 4 = 4 marks)

(a) Child labour can be eliminated if
…………………….

compulsory primary education is given to the poor
industries are abolished
industries are established in large numbers
the poor children are sent behind the bars
(b) Poverty …………………….

enhances creativity
encourages child labour
kills people
humiliates human beings
(c) Human capital may be greatly enhanced
…………………….

if child labour is abolished
if children are given employment
if children are educated
all of the above
(d) The state where a large number of children are forced to work because of potential unrest is

Uttar Pradesh
Madhya Pradesh
Kanpur
Kashmir
B. Answer the following questions briefly: 1 x 6 = 6

(a) On what two counts has the government failed in respect of children?
(b) "We have many laws that ban child labour ……………… Even then child labour continues."
What makes implementation of laws difficult?
(c) What forces the children to work in "hazardous' industries? Why do these industries prefer child labour?
(d) What are the adverse effects of "hazardous' industries on children? Give any two.
(e) How can India's human capital be vastly enhanced?
(f) How is poverty responsible for child labour?

C. Find words in the passage similar in meaning as:
1 x 2 = 2

(a) Complete destruction (Para 1)
(b) Putting into practice (Para 3,4)

Answers:

A.

(a) 1. compulsory primaiy education is given to the poor
(b) 2. encourages child labour
(c) 4. all of the above
(d) 4. Kashmir

B.

(a) (i) Eradication of child labour in hazardous industries.
(ii) Providing schooling to every child in India.
(b) (i) Each state has different rules regarding the minimum age of employment.
(ii) The Act does not apply to unorganised or informal sector.
(c) (i) Poverty is the main cause of child labour. 260 million people exist below poverty line in India.
(ii) Child labour is preferred due to their nimble fingers, high level of concentration and capacity to work hard at extremely low wages.
(d) (i) Children become prone to debilitating diseases (which make a person very weak)
(ii) Their limbs become deformed for life.
(iii) They become victims of bronchial diseases and T.B.
(iv) Their mental and physical development is permanently impaired.
(v) They remain uneducated and powerless. (Any two acceptable)
(e) By giving the 380 million children a better quality of life and elementary education, we can greatly enhance India's human capital.
(f) Poverty forces parents to get their children employed in order to get basic things for sustaining life such as food and water.

C.

(a) eradication
(b) implementation

Passage 19

Many of the underdeveloped countries will promote the growth of their economies in one way or the other, no matter whether they receive substantial outside aid in the process or not. The character of that development, however, is likely to be strongly influenced by the types of and amounts of aid available. The outcome is much more likely to be favourable, from the standpoint of the objectives for successful development set up previously, if there is substantial international aid than if there is not.

By substantial aid I mean not only large amounts of technical assistance but also of capital. Initially, the capacity of an underdeveloped country to use capital productively may be surprisingly small, limited by lack of organisation, trained personnel and other social obstacles. At this stage technical assistance is the main need from outside, with comparatively small amounts of capital, much of which may have to be in the form of grants for non-self liquidating projects, in education, health, access to roads in rural areas, and the like, if, at this stage, substantial capital is available from outside to supplement what can be formed internally (and to simulate internal capital formation, for it does that too) the rate of economic growth can be consistently increased, and the strains and frustrations and political risks of the development are likely to be considerably less.

It is possible for underdeveloped economies to modernise themselves with very little capital from outside. Japan imports of capital were small though some of it came at crucial times. The contribution of foreign direct investments to the advancement of technical know-how also was greater than would be indicated merely by the size of the investment. The Soviet Union industrialised its economy with practically no aid from foreign investment capital except for the foreign owned installations confiscated after the revolution, though it imported machinery in the early days on short term or immediate term credits and hired services of foreign experts.

Both Japan and Russia achieved their development in an authoritarian political and social framework. The outcome in both cases from standpoint of the peace in the world and democratic ideals, was highly unfavourable.

In the absence of outside aid, the only way to accumulate capital, is to increase production without taking much of the benefit in more consumption or even while pushing consumption standards down. Where the people are already near the subsistence level this may mean extreme hardship. Somehow the people must be motivated to change their accustomed ways quickly, to work hard and to forgo present consumption so that capital investment can be made.

Unseen Passage For Class 12 With Answers PDF 2020 - Factual and Descriptive Passages image - 11

Questions:

A. Choose the most appropriate option: (1 x 4 = 4 marks)

(a) The passage says that ....

without foreign aid no underdeveloped country can grow.

underdeveloped country must refrain from taking foreign aid.

the economies of the underdeveloped countries are more likely to grow faster with substantial foreign aid than without.

underdeveloped countries are economically backward because their governments have not got their priorities right.

(b) Substantial aid in this context means ....

technical assistance in the form of trained personnel.

capital in the form of bank loans and overdrafts.

large amounts of technical assistance and capital.

a cheap and plentiful supply of labour.

(c) Which of the following points or statements did the writer actually make?

Japan and Russia achieved their development in a democratic framework.

Japan and Russia achieved their development in an authoritarian political and social framework.

Japan and Russia would have developed faster if they had relied on democratic methods.
Japan and Russia are still among the underdeveloped countries of the world.
(d) Accumulation of capital without getting outside and may mean

extreme hardship
more investment
high living standard
low living standard
B. Answer the following questions briefly: 1 x 6 = 6

(a) How does the availability of substantial capital help?
(b) How can a nation accumulate capital if it does not get outside aid?
(c) How did Japan and Russia become developed?
(d) What problems does an underdeveloped country face?
(e) What should an underdeveloped nation do to minimise risk?
(f) What was the contribution of FDI in case of Japan?

C. Find words in the passage similar in meaning as: 1 x 2 = 2

(a) substantial
(b) aid

Answers:

A.

(a) 3. the economies of the underdeveloped countries are more likely to grow faster with substantial foreign aid than without.
(b) 3. large amounts of technical assistance and capital.
(c) 2. Japan and Russia achieved their development in an authoritarian political and social framework.
(d) 1. extreme hardship

B.

(a) The availability of substantial capital gives a nation a great opportunity to develop its infrastructure.
(b) The nation should increase production without taking much of the benefit in more consumption.
(c) Japan and Russia achieved their development in an authoritarian political and social framework.
(d) An underdeveloped country faces the problems of lack of organisation and trained personnel.
(e) The nation should try to increase the economic growth in order to minimise risk.
(f) The contribution of FDI in case of Japan was greater than the technical know-how.

C.

(a) plenty of
(b) assistance

Passage 19

Among the natural resources which can be called upon in national plans for development, possibly the most important is human labour. Since the English language suffers from a certain weakness in its ability to describe groups composed of both male and female members, this is usually described as "manpower".
Without a productive labour force, including effective leadership and intelligent middle management, no amount of foreign assistance or of natural wealth can ensure successful development and modernisation.
The manpower for development during the next quarter century will come from the world's present population of infants, children and adolescents. But we are not sure that they , will be equal to the task. Will they have the health, the education, the skills, the sociocultural attitudes essential for the responsibilities of development?
For far too many of them the answer is no. The reason is basic. A child's most critical years, with regard to physical, intellectual, social and emotional development, are those before he reaches five years of age. During those critical formative years he is

cared for almost exclusively by his mother and in many parts of the world the mother may not have the capacity to raise a superior child. She is incapable of doing so by reason of her own poor health, her ignorance and her lack of status and recognition of social and legal rights, of economic parity of independence. One essential factor has been overlooked or ignored. The forgotten factor is the role of women. Development will be handicapped as long as women remain second-class citizens, uneducated, without any voice in family or community, decisions without legal or economic status, married when they are still practically children, and henceforth producing one baby after another, often to see half of them die before they are of school age.

We can enhance development by improving "women power", by giving women the ' opportunity to develop the&selves. Statistics show that the average family size increases in inverse ratio to the mother's years of education—is lowest among college graduates, highest among those with only primary school training, or no education. Malnutrition is most frequent in large families, and increases in frequency with each additional sibling. The principle seems established that an educated mother has healthier and more intelligent children, and that this is related to the fact that she has fewer children. The tendency of . educated, upper class mothers to have fewer children operates even without access to contraceptive services.

The educational level of women is significant also because it has a direct influence upon their chances of employment, and the number of employed women in a country's total labour force has a direct bearing on both the Gross National Product and the disposable income of the individual family. Disposable income, especially in the hands of women, influences food purchasing and therefore the nutritional status of the family. The fact [that the additional income derives from the paid employment of women provides a logical incentive to restrict the size of the family.

Unseen Passage For Class 12 With Answers PDF 2020 - Factual and Descriptive Passages image - 12 Questions:

A. Choose the most appropriate option: (1 x 4 = 4 marks)

(a) Among the natural resources which can be called upon in national plans for development.....................

the most important is certainly human labour.
the most important is possibly human labour.
the least developed is certainly human labour.
the least developed is undoubtedly human labour.
(b) Without a productive labour force, including effective leadership and intelligent middle management.....................

no productive work is possible.
entrepreneurs will incur heavy losses.
economic development will not keep pace with national movements.
no amount of foreign assistance or of natural wealth can ensure successful development and modernisation.
(c) The manpower development during the next quarter century.....................

will be adversely affected by the threat of war.
will come from the world's present population of infants, children and adolescents.
will be taken care of by the current emphasis on free education for women.
will be adversely affected by the country's economic losses and political instability.
(d) Disposable income in the hands of women strengthen

family bond
nutritional status of the family
spiritual status of the family
none of these
B. Answer the following questions briefly: 1 x 6 = 6

(a) What will be the source of the manpower development during the next quarter century?
(b) During which period is the child growth maximum?
(c) Why can't the first teacher be effective in some of tire regions of India?

(d) What will happen to development if the womenfolk is neglected?
(e) How can we accelerate the rate of progress?
(f) What is the difference between an educated mother and an illiterate mother?

C. Find words in the passage similar in meaning as:
1 x 2 = 2

(a) increase
(b) important

Answers:

A.

(a) 4. the least developed is undoubtedly human labour.
(b) 4. no amount of foreign assistance or of natural wealth can ensure successful development and modernisation.
(c) 1.will be adversely affected by the threat of war.
(d) 2. nutritional status of the family.

B.

(a) The manpower development during the next quarter century will come from the world's present population of infants, children and adolescents.
(b) The child grows maximum before he attains the age of five.
(c) The first teacher remains ineffective because of ignorance, poor health, lack of respect and recognition.
(d) There will be no growth and everything will stagnate.
(e) The rate of progress may be accelerated by educating the womenfolk.
(f) An educated mother does not beget children thoughtlessly but an illiterate mother considers children the blessings of God. Education makes one wise and practical. Those who are uneducated fail to analyse the situation critically.

C.

(a) enhance

(b) significant

Passage 20

While there is no denying that the world loves a winner it is important that you recognise the signs of stress in your behaviour and be healthy enough to enjoy your success. Stress can strike anytime, in a fashion that may leave you unaware of its presence in your life. While a certain amount of pressure is necessary for performance, it is important to be able to recognise your individual threshold. For instance, there are some individuals who accept competition in a healthy fashion. There are others who collapse into weeping wrecks before an exam or on comparing marksheets and finding that their friend has scored better.

It is a body reaction to any demands or changes in its internal and external environment. Whenever there is a change in the external environment such as temperature, pollutants, humidity and working conditions, it leads to stress. In these days of competition when a person makes up his mind to surpass what has been achieved by others, leading to an imbalance between demands and resources, it causes psycho-social stress. It is a part and parcel of everyday life.

Stress has a different meaning depending on the stage of life you're in. The loss of a toy or a reprimand from the parents might create a stress shock in a child. An adolescent who fails an examination may feel as if everything has been lost and life has no further meaning. In an adult, the loss of his or her companion, job or professional failure may appear as if there is nothing more to be achieved.

Such signs appear in the attitude and behaviour of the individual, as muscle tension in various parts of the body, palpitation and high blood pressure, indigestion, hyperacidity and ultimately in self destructive behaviour such as eating and drinking too much, smoking excessively, relying on tranquilisers, trembling, shaking, nervous blinking, dryness of throat and mouth and difficulty in swallowing.

The professional under stress behaves as if he is a perfectionist followed by depression, lethargy and weakness for further work. Periodic mood shifts also indicate the stress status of students, executives and professionals.

In a study sponsored by World Health Organisation and carried out by Harvard School of Public Health, the global burden of diseases and injury indicated that stress diseases and accidents are going to be the major killers in 2020.

The ischaemic heart diseases and neurological depression, both stress diseases, are going to rank first and second in 2020. Road traffic accidents are going to be the third largest killers. These accidents are also an indicator of psycho-social stress in a fast-moving society. Other stress diseases like ulcers, hypertension and neuronal disorders including insomnia have assumed epidemic proportions in modem societies.

A person behaves in different ways in stress but the common ones are flight, fight and flow. Depending upon the nature of stress and capability of the person, the three responses can be elegantly chosen to cope up with the stress so that stress does not damage the system and become distress.

When stress crosses the threshold peculiar to an individual, it deteriorates his/her performance capacity. Frequent jumps over that threshold may result in a syndrome called chronic fatigue in which a person feels lethargic, disinterested and is not easily motivated to achieve anything. This may make the person mentally undecided, confused and accident prone as well. Sudden exposure to un-nerving stress may also result in a loss of memory.

The best technique is self-control. This arises by having faith in oneself, on the usefulness of the job he is doing and on any superpower who would deliver the result of the effort made.

There are many stress modifiers or stress busters. Some of these are diet and massage from naturopathy, food supplements and herbs from herbal medicine hobbies and relaxation techniques, homeopathy and modem medicine. Physical exercise and dance movements are excellent stress modifiers.

Unseen Passage For Class 12 With Answers PDF 2020 - Factual and Descriptive Passages image - 13 Questions:

A. Choose the most appropriate option: (1 x 4 = 4 marks)

(a) The unhealthy competition prevalent in this dog-eat-dog world causes...................

psycho-social stress
political stress
neuro problems
blood pressure

(b) Stress impairs...................

death
hypertension
the performance of an individual
none of the above

(c) The best stress busters are...................

physical exercises
dance movements
both (i) and (ii)
none of the above

(d) Stress leads to

road traffic accidents
neurological depression
hypertension
all of these

B. Answer the following questions briefly: 1 x 6 = 6

(a) What is stress? What factors lead to stress?
(b) Does the age of a person have any impact on stress levels? If yes, then how?
(c) What are the symptoms or signs by which a person can recognise he is under stress?
(d) What are the different diseases a person gets due to stress?
(e) How can a person cope with stress?
(f) What are the disadvantages of chronic fatigue?

C. Find words in the passage similar in meaning as: 1 x 2 = 2

(a) person whose physical or mental health has been seriously damaged. (Para 1)
(b) inactivity; apathy (Para 5)

Answers:

A.

(a) 1.psycho-social stress

(b) 3.the performance of an individual

(c) 3. both (i) and (ii)

(d) 4.all of these

B.

(a) Stress is a reaction of the body to any demands or changes in its internal and external environment. Factors such as imbalance between demands and resources, change in temperature, pollutants, humidity and working conditions lead to stress.

(b) No, stress has a different meaning depending on the stage of life. For a child a re-buke or loss of a toy causes stress. An adolescent may feel tense after failing in the examination. For an adult, loss of job or a dear one causes stress.

(c) (i) Change in the attitude and behaviour

(ii) Muscle tension

(iii) Palpitation, high blood pressure, indigestion and hyperacidity.

(iv) Depression, lethargy, weakness for work.

(d) (i) heart diseases

(ii) neurological depression

(iii) ulcers

(iv) hypertension

(v) insomnia

(vi) injuries due to accidents

(e) (i) Self-control—faith in oneself, usefulness of job and in any super power.

(ii) Use of stress modifiers or stress busters

(f) The chronic fatigue makes one lethargic, disinterested and demotivated.

C.

(a) wreck

(b) lethargy

Passage 21

The children probably don't know, or they don't care, the hugely popular WWF wrestling matches are actually all staged acts. The Hulks, the Undertaker or whatever else they are called—never really punch or kick as hard as they might appear doing on the show. It's all a show, a thrilling show.

So, you can't really blame children for getting hooked. But does that necessarily mean the show is entirely responsible for the beating 12-year-old Subin Kumar got from his WWF-inspired friends? Can viewing or watching violence on TV actually promote aggressive behaviour in children?

Media experts and social scientists have been wrestling with this question for decades 10 and thousands of studies have been done on it. And most of them reached the same conclusion—media violence is responsible for aggressive behaviour in children. Research has found that the more violence children watch on television, the more likely they may act in aggressive ways towards others. Also, they become less sensitive to others' pain and are less likely to help a victim of violence.

A study of violence on Indian television and its impact on children commissioned by UNESCO accused the idiot box of "bombarding young minds with all kinds of violent images, cutting across channels, programmes and viewing times."

Not only studies, but also incidents go to prove that children who watch violent episodes show increased likelihood of behaving aggressively.

20 There have been reports from all over the country of children hurting themselves while trying to ape the superhuman feats of Shaktimaan, the superhero of Indian TV. Then there was the six-year-old child of Lucknow who leapt off the balcony of his second -floor flat trying to imitate a bungee jumping drop shown in a soft drinks commercial. There's no doubt that media is a powerful teacher and contributes greatly to the way we act and behave. In some cases like these, the effects are immediate and in others there is a "sleeper effect", where the results show up much later.

Experts say it's incorrect to blame the media squarely. How would you explain the aggressive behaviour of a child who has never been exposed to television or any other media? So, while there is mounting evidence to link media violence and actual violence, most 30 of it does not prove a direct cause-and-effect relationship. Because no one so far has been able to prove why and how TV effects some people and not the others. "We also have to take into account individual differences and vulnerabilities as human behaviour is a result of many factors," points out Dr Vasantha R. Patri, a counsellor, adding, "violence viewing is only one of the myriad influences on a growing child."

Patri says there exists a population of risk individuals whose anger, aggression and anti-social tendencies are already quite high for whatever reason. Other factors like individual predisposition of the child, parental attitudes and reaction to aggression are probably equally important. In fact, she says that in most cases media is only the fourth most 40 important influence in a child's life—with parents, teachers and peers being the first three. Patri points out that the growing "here-and-now" culture in which kids are getting used to immediate gratification is leading to an intolerant society on the whole. "Children are not taught how to handle failure and conflict," she says. "As a result, they resort to aggression."

But media critics refuse to buy it. They insist the content of media needs to be monitored and care be taken to reduce violence if not remove it. But even if all the gore and violence is completely removed from the media, will it make a significant difference in the aggressive behaviour of children? And then how do you justify the fact that studies have shown that viewing violence on TV also provides an opportunity to discharge the pent-up, 50 aggressive feelings of anger, hostility and frustration.

"The problem is not with the media, but the lack of media education," points out Patri. "No one teaches the children how to assess the reality status of TV programmes." Good parenting, she says, is perhaps the greatest defense against the negative effects of violent images on TV.

Experts say it's time that parents and teachers took a long, hard look at themselves in the mirror. Says Patri, "Most parents treat TV as a baby-sitter when it suits them. And when something goes wrong, they turn around and blame TV for it !"

Unseen Passage For Class 12 With Answers PDF 2020 - Factual and Descriptive Passages image - 14

Questions:

A. Choose the most appropriate option: (1 x 4 = 4 marks)

(a) Violent behaviour is the outcome of..........................

lack of media awareness
lack of sensitivity
increase in population
imperfection

(b) Children fail to understand that the stunts shown on the screen are..........................

real
fake
manipulated
none of the above

(c) Parents consider TV a..........................

babysitter
problem
boon
none of the above

(d) Aggressive behaviour in children can be best handled by

teachers
parents
both teachers and parents
children themselves

B. Answer the following questions briefly: 1 x 6 = 6

(a) Does violence on TV promote children's aggressive behaviour? What is the opinion of media experts and social scientists?
(b) What two points have emerged from research on media violence?
(c) What two incidents are cited to prove the aggressive behaviour of children as an outcome of watching violence on television?
(d) What factors other than violence viewing are important for causing aggressiveness in a child?
(e) How, do you think, can the problem be solved?
(f) How are children becoming impatient?

C. Find words in the passage similar in meaning as:
1 x 2 = 2

(a) exciting (lines 1 to 10)
(b) an extremely large number of something

Answers:

A.

(a) 1. lack of media awareness
(b) 2. fake
(c) 1. babysitter
(d) 3. both teachers and parents

B.

(a) Yes, it does. Most of the media experts and social scientists think that media violence on TV is responsible for actually promoting aggressiveness in children.
(b) (i) The more violence children view on TV, the more aggressively they behave with others.
(ii) They become less sensitive to the pain of others. Hence, they are less likely to help a victim of violence.
(c) (i) Beating that the 12-year-old Subin Kumar got from his WWF inspired friends.
(ii) The six-year-old child of Lucknow who leapt off the balcony of his second-floor flat trying to imitate a bungee jumping drop shown in a soft-drinks commercial.
(d) Other factors are:
(i) individual predisposition of the child
(ii) parental attitudes
(iii) reaction to aggression
(iv) intolerance.
(e) By providing media education and by teaching the children how to assess the reality status of TV programmes. Most parents and teachers have to understand their responsibility in imparting media education to children.
(fl Children of this materialistic age are desirous of getting immediate gratification. It ; makes them impatient.

C.

(a) thrilling
(b) myriad

Passage 22

Mohammed Jamshed Khan replaced the ATM card in his wallet and counted the crisp new notes he'd just withdrawn from the machine. ₹ 6000? "This can't be right!" thought the young Mumbai civil contractor. He counted again. It was indeed ₹ 6000. "All I'd asked for was ? 1200," Khan told his friend Faisal Mukhi who was standing nearby.
"You pressed the wrong buttons, silly," said Mukhi.
"No way!" exclaimed Khan as he pushed his card back in again, keyed in his numeric password and asked for ? 1000. Beep, click……………whirr, beeeep ! Out popped ₹ 5000 and a little transaction slip that read. WITHDRAWAL ₹ 1000.
"Let's try again," said Khan. Card, password, 2-0-0-0………beeeep ! But he got ₹ 10,000. By now it seemed certain that the ATM was giving away 500-rupee notes instead of hundreds. "May be something's wrong with your card," Mukhi told Khan, "let me try mine." Mukhi's balance was low—only ? 1300. He pushed his card in and asked for ? 1000. The machine spat out 5000.
"ATMs (short for automated teller machines) are extremely secure and among the hardest of machines. Look up the Encyclopaedia Britannica for "ATMs" and you'll find it entered under "Locks"—it's virtually impossible to fool an ATM. And the probability of an ATM overpaying is virtually nil. But here they were, two buddies with ? 26000 between them— ₹ 20,800 of it free money.
There were no other customers in sight on that warm July afternoon. And they could have kept on going. Instead, Khan and Mukhi went outside the ATM's enclosure and summoned the guard on duty. "The machine's all mixed up," they told him. The two men then gave the guard a demo: "Look here," said Khan as he inserted his card one last time and hit the buttons, "I'm withdrawing ? 500 but here's 2500!

"Don't let anybody near this place," they told the guard as they hopped into an autorickshaw and sped off with all the money.-

It looked like a daylight robbery—in reverse. For they drove two kilometres, to the nearest branch of the bank that owned the ATM, placed the cash-? 28,500 on the bank manager's desk and complained about their faulty machine.

'We could have lost a real lot that day," says the manager. This is the kind of honesty we can only dream about. A human error made while loading cash in the ATM had caused the problem. Although we could have traced the customers, it might have meant a lot of trouble for us, had they kept our money."

But did either Mohammed Khan or Faisal Mukhi ever think of keeping the money during their moment with the magic machine? "Not once," says Khan. Adds Mukhi: "Never."

Unseen Passage For Class 12 With Answers PDF 2020 - Factual and Descriptive Passages image - 15

Questions:

A. Choose the most appropriate option: (1 x 4 = 4 marks)

(a) The theme of the passage is……………………..

dishonesty
loyalty
honesty
sincerity

(b)   The   passage   proves   the machines…………………….

do not make mistakes
never make mistakes
do make mistakes
all of the above

(c) The manager says that "This is the kind of honesty we can only dream about"because…………

most of the people are corrupt
man is greedy by nature
riches attracts people
all of the above

(d) Khan and Mukhi went outside the ATM's enclosure and summoned the guard on duty to inform him about the

erratic behaviour of ATM
shortage of notes in the ATM machine
suspicious man standing outside the ATM enclosure
none of these

B. Answer the following questions briefly: 1 x 6 = 6

(a) Why was Mohammed Jamshed Khan surprised? How did he express it and to whom?

(b) What efforts did the two friends make to verify the behaviour of the machine?

(c) What do you know about ATM? What was peculiar about this particular ATM?

(d) "It looked like a daylight robbery—in reverse." Substantiate this statement.

(e) How did the manager react to the disclosure?

(f) What did they ask the guard to do?

C. Find words in the passage similar in meaning as: 1 x 2 = 2

(a) slightly stiff
(b) almost

Answers:

A.

(a) 3. honesty
(b) 3. do make mistakes
(c) 4. all of the above
(d) 1. erratic behaviour of ATM

B.

(a) He had asked for ₹ 1200, but the ATM machine gave him ₹ 6000. He counted the money twice. He expressed hi! surprise to his friend Faisal Mukhi who was standing nearby.

(b) Faisal thought Jamshed had pressed wrong buttons. So Khan's ATM card was in-serted again for ₹ 1000. ₹ 5000 popped out. But the transaction slip showed with-drawal as ₹ 1000 only. Two other attempts were made: one with Khan's card and another with Mukhi's. They had inserted cards for ₹ 5200, but got five times the money i.e., ₹ 26,000.

(c) ATM is short for Automated Teller Machine. It is a counting device run by automatic machine. It is quite tough and exact. It is almost impossible to commit an error. This ATM was issuing money five times more.

(d) Here the men were returning the easy money to the rightful owner i.e., the bank. They presented the entire money to the manager.

(e) The manager praised the customers for their dream honesty. A human error while loading cash was responsible for the erratic behaviour of ATM.

(f) They asked the guard not to allow anybody to use the ATM.

C.

(a) crisp

(b) virtually

Short Passages

Question 1. Read the passage below and then choose the best answer to the question.Answer the question based on what is stated or implied in this passage.
Experienced truck drivers often travel in a convoy--a group of trucks that are traveling to the same part of the country. Convoys can help truckers to stay alert.
The author implies that professional long-distance truck drivers may avoid traveling alone because:
A) They might drive too fast.
B) They want to arrive before anyone else.
C) Accidents happen more frequently to lone truck drivers than to car drivers who travel alone.
D) Long-distance travel can cause drowsiness.

Question 2. Read the passage below and then choose the best answer to the question.
One could be struck in awe,if they could relive the earths geological past.Huge beasts such as the dinosaur have never really become extinct. Mothra, a giant caterpillar who later becomes a moth, destroys Tokyo, and stars in the 1962 Japanese film named for him. The famous Japanese cult mothra is born, dies, and reborn regularly on classic movie channels. In Japan Mothra is one of the most popular films ever made. Mothra has survived the creation of more current scary creatures such as giant apes, extraterrestrial beings and swamp creatures. More than 30 years after his creation, Mothra still lives.

The main subject of the passage is:
A) The reasons that fads do not endure
B) The lasting appeal of Mothra
C) The difficulty of marketing good horror movies
D) Old models for creatures are still used because making new monsters is expensive

Question 3. Two underlined sentences are followed by a question or statement. Read the sentences, and then choose which one of the following would be the best answer to the question:
Anxious to ensure that America would depart from European traditions regarding religion and royalty, the early U.S. can be described as a place that focused more on work than on the entertainment offered by spectacle and celebrations offered by the past world. However, national celebrations such as the lighting of the White House Christmas Tree and the ceremonies used to swear in new federal officials give the American people some experiences that are based upon national tradition.

What does the second sentence do?
A) It colludes the meaning of the first sentence.
B) It provides an example of the first sentence.
C) It adds more detail to the first sentence.
D) It offers an exception to the information given in the first sentence.

Question 4. Read the passage below and choose the best answer/option to the question asked below.
The Earth's past climate--including temperature and elements in the atmosphere--has recently been studied by analysing ice samples from Greenland and Antarctica. The air bubbles in the ice have shown that, over the past 160,000 years, there has been a close correlation between changes in the planet's temperature and level of natural greenhouse gases such as carbon dioxide and methane. A recent analysis from a well-known think tank for Greenland showed that at the end of the last glacial period (when the great ice sheets began to retreat to their present position), temperatures in southern part of Greenland rose from 5 to 7 degrees within a span 100 years. Air bubbles are not the only method of determining characteristics of the Earth's ancient climate history. Analysis of dust layers from ancient

volcanic activity is another such method; as is the study of ice cores, which interpret past solar activity that may have affected our climate.

This passage states that:
A) The planet's atmosphere is being destroyed by runaway greenhouse gases.
B) Temperatures in Greenland have been unusually stable over the past 100 years.
C) There are two information's that scientists can use to determine the characteristics of the Earth's early climate.
D) Solar energy is the wave of the future.

Question 5. Read the passages, then choose the best answer to the question or the best completion of the statement.

For the purpose of insurance related works, before video cameras were widely used, home and business owners had to rely only on written reports and photos as a way to document their valuables. This form of documentation was difficult for some insurance policy holders. It was incredibly easy to lose reports in paper format or the reports could be easily tampered with. Because of these possibilities, these insurance inventories were often inaccurate. While videotaping is not an option for every home or business owner, this kind of insurance documentation is helpful for some.

What is the main idea behind the passage?
A) They repeat the same idea.
B) They contradict one another.
C) They compare two forms of written documentation.
D) They present a problem and a solution.

Question 6. Read the sentences, and then choose the best answer to the question or the best completion of the statement.
Public speaking is very different from everyday conversation.
First and foremost of all, speeches are much more structured than a typical informal discussion.

How are these sentences related?

A) The second sentence offers support for the statement made in the first sentence.
B) The second sentence contradicts the statement made in the first sentence.
C) The second sentence which is a contradiction to the first one shows an exception to the first sentence.
D) The second sentence compares two kinds of speeches.

Question 7. Answer the question based on what is stated or implied in these passages.
French physicist Charles Fabry discovered ozone gas in the atmosphere in 1913. At room temperature, ozone is a colourless gas; it condenses to a dark blue liquid at -170 F. At temperatures above the boiling point of water, 212 F, it decomposes. Ozone is all around us. Occasionally After a thunderstorm, or around electrical equipment, ozone is often detected as a sharp odour. Ozone can be used as a strong oxidizing agent, a bleaching agent, and to sterilize drinking water. This gas is also highly reactive. For example, The insulation which is made of rubber around a car's spark plug wires will need to be replaced eventually, due to the small amounts of ozone produced when electricity flows from the engine to the plug.
The meaning behind the passages imply that:
A) Ozone is the major result of pollution.
B) High ozone levels in the atmosphere will cause large numbers of people to buy new car batteries.
C) Ozone has no practical uses for man.
D) Ozone is a natural part of the Earth's atmosphere.

4. Complements

Some verbs have a meaning that is **complete in itself**. Such a verb needs only a subject. When this has been supplied, we have a sentence, for the mere verb, without any additional word or words, is capable of being a predicate.

Birds *fly*.

Fishes *swim*.

The sun *shines*.

The moon *rose*.

The man *scowled*.

The girl *laughed*.

The owls *hooted*.

The clock *ticked*.

Verbs of this kind are sometimes called **complete verbs**, or **verbs of complete predication**.

2. Other verbs are not, by themselves, capable of serving as predicates. Thus,—

The Indians killed ——.

Mr. Harris makes ——.

Tom is ——.

The man seemed ——.

These are not sentences, for the predicate of each is unfinished. The verb requires the addition of a substantive or an adjective to complete its sense.

The Indians killed *deer*.

Mr. Harris makes *shoes*.

Tom is *captain*.

The man seemed *sorry*.

Verbs of this kind are often called **incomplete verbs**, or **verbs of incomplete predication**.

NOTE. The meaning of the verb determines to which of these classes it belongs. Accordingly, the same verb may belong to the first class in some of its senses and to the second in others.

A substantive or adjective added to the predicate verb to complete its meaning is called a complement.

Complements are of four kinds,—the direct object, the predicate objective, the predicate nominative, and the predicate adjective.

In the examples in § 482, *deer* and *shoes* are **direct objects**,—the former denoting the **receiver** of the action, the latter denoting the **product**; *captain* is a **predicate nominative**, denoting the same person as the subject *Tom* (§ 88, 2); *sorry* is a predicate adjective describing the subject *man*.

Complements may, of course, be modified. If they are substantives, they may take adjective modifiers; if adjectives, they may take adverbial modifiers .

For convenience, the definitions of the four kinds of complements are here repeated, with examples.

The Direct Object

Some verbs may be followed by a substantive denoting that which receives the action or is produced by it. These are called transitive verbs. All other verbs are called intransitive. A substantive that completes the meaning of a transitive verb is called its direct object.

> The direct object is often called the **object complement**, or merely the **object of the verb**.

Alfred has broken his *arm*.

Morse invented the electric *telegraph*.

Black foxes command a high *price*.

You have accomplished a *task* of great difficulty.

Have you lost the *dog* which your uncle gave you?

He asked *me* the *news*. [Two direct objects.]

Most of these objects are modified,—*arm* by the possessive *his*; *telegraph* by *the* and *electric*; *price* by *a* and *high*; *task* by the adjective phrase *of great difficulty*; *dog* by *the* and by the adjective clause *which your uncle gave you*.

A noun clause may be used as the direct object of a verb.

You promised *that my coat should be ready to-day*.

The mayor ordered *that the street should be closed for three hours.*
I begged *that my passport might be returned to me.*

Predicates

Verbs of *choosing*, *calling*, *naming*, *making*, and *thinking* may take two objects referring to the same person or thing.
The first of these is the direct object, and the second, which completes the sense of the predicate, is called a predicate objective.
The **predicate objective** is often called the **complementary object** or the **objective attribute**.
The people have elected Chamberlain *governor.*
Peter calls Richard my *shadow.*
The court has appointed you the child's *guardian.*
John thinks himself a *hero.*
An **adjective** may serve as a **predicate objective**. Thus,—
I thought your decision *hasty.*
I call that answer *impertinent.*
The jury found the prisoner *guilty.*
Your letter made him *joyful.*
Care should be taken not to confuse adverbs with adjectives in *-ly* serving as predicate objectives.
You called him *sickly.* [Adjective.]
You called him *early.* [Adverb.]
After the passive, a predicate objective becomes a **predicate nominative.**

Predicate Nominatives

A substantive standing in the predicate, but describing or defining the subject, agrees with the subject in case and is called a predicate nominative .

> A predicate nominative is often called a **subject complement** or an **attribute**.

The predicate nominative is common after *is* and other copulative verbs, and after certain transitive verbs in the passive voice.
Chemistry is a useful *science.*
Boston is the *capital* of Massachusetts.
Jefferson became *President.*
This bird is called a *flamingo.*
Mr. Hale was appointed *secretary.*
Albert has been chosen *captain* of the crew.
You are a *friend* upon whom I can rely.
In most of the examples, the predicate nominative has one or more modifiers. In the first sentence, *science* is modified by the two adjectives *a* and *useful*; in the second, *capital* is modified by the adjective phrase *of Massachusetts*; in the last, *friend* is modified by the adjective clause *upon whom I can rely.*
For the distinction between the **predicate nominative** and the **direct object**.
A **noun clause** may be used as a predicate nominative (§ 386).
My plan is *that the well should be dug to-morrow.*
His intention was *that you should remain here.*
The result is *that he is bankrupt.*
Ruth's fear was *that the door might be locked.*
An **infinitive** may be used as a predicate nominative.
To hear is *to obey.*
My hope was *to reach* the summit before dark.
Their plan was *to undermine* the tower.
My habit is *to rise* early.
The infinitive may have a complement or modifiers. In the second and third examples, it takes an object; in the fourth it is modified by an adverb.

Predicate Adjectives

An adjective in the predicate belonging to a noun or pronoun in the subject is called a predicate adjective. A predicate adjective

completes the meaning of the predicate verb and is therefore a complement.

Like the predicate nominative, the predicate adjective is common after copulative verbs and after certain transitive verbs in the passive voice.

John was *angry*.

My knife is growing *dull*.

This job is becoming tough.

The task seemed very *easy*.

The report proved *false* in every particular.

The boat was thought *unsafe*.

The cover was made perfectly *tight*.

In some of these examples, the predicate adjective has a modifier. In the third, *easy* is modified by the adverb *very*; in the fourth, *false* is modified by the adverbial phrase *in every particular*; in the last, *tight* is modified by *perfectly*.

An **adjective phrase** may be used as a predicate adjective. Thus,—

Richard was *out of health*. [Compare: Richard was *ill*.]

Rachel seemed *in a passion*. [Compare: seemed *angry*.]

This act is *against my interests*. [Compare: is *harmful* to me.]

The adjective phrase may consist of an infinitive with or without the preposition *about* (§ 319).

I was *about to speak*.

This house is *to let*.

I am *to sail* to-morrow.

Modification of Complements

Complements, being either substantives or adjectives, may be modified in various ways.

A **substantive** used as a **complement** may have the same kinds of modifiers that are used with the **subject**.

An **adjective complement** admits only **adverbial modifiers**.

The following sentences illustrate the modifiers of substantive complements:—

Herbert lost *a gold* watch. [The direct object (*watch*) is modified by the adjectives *a* and *gold*.]

The duke built towers *of marble*. [The direct object (*towers*) is modified by the adjective phrase *of marble*.]

My father built *the* house *in which I was born*. [The direct object (*house*) is modified by the adjective *the* and the adjective clause *in which I was born*.]

I saw *a* man *running* across the field. [The direct object (*man*) is modified by the adjective *a* and the participle *running*.]

You have forfeited *your* right *to vote*. [The direct object (*right*) is modified by the possessive pronoun *your* and the infinitive *to vote*.]

I have seen *Henry's* brother. [The direct object (*brother*) is modified by the possessive noun *Henry's*.]

I must ask *my* brother, the *mayor*. [The direct object (*brother*) is modified by the possessive pronoun *my* and the appositive *mayor*.]

The guild has elected Walter *honorary* president. [The predicate objective (*president*) is modified by the adjective *honorary*.]

Her husband is *an old* soldier. [The predicate nominative (*soldier*) is modified by the adjectives *an* and *old*.]

Her sons are veterans *of the Franco-Prussian war*. [The predicate nominative (*veterans*) is modified by the adjective phrase *of the Franco-Prussian war*.]

They are rivals *in business*. [The predicate nominative (*rivals*) is modified by the adjective phrase *in business*.]

The author is Will Jewell, *who was formerly editor of "The Pioneer."* [The predicate nominative (*Will Jewell*) is modified by the adjective clause *who was formerly editor*, etc.]

Baldwin is *the* man *standing* under the tree. [The predicate nominative (*man*) is modified by the adjective *the* and the participle *standing*.]

Your chief fault is *your* inclination *to procrastinate*. [The predicate nominative (*inclination*) is modified by the possessive pronoun *your* and the infinitive *to procrastinate*.]

This man is *Gretchen's* brother. [The predicate nominative (*brother*) is modified by the possessive noun *Gretchen's*.]

The first to fall was *the* bugler, *John Wilson*. [The predicate nominative (*bugler*) is modified by the adjective *the* and the appositive *John Wilson*.]

Adjective clauses are very common as modifiers of substantive complements.

Have you lost the watch *that your cousin gave you?*

This is the very spot *where the temple of Saturn stood.*

The general issued an order *that all non-combatants should be treated well.*

We have abundant proof *that during his stay on the Continent, Bacon did not neglect literary and scientific pursuits.*

An **adjective** used as a complement may be modified by an **adverb**, an **adverbial phrase**, or an **adverbial clause**.

I am *very* sorry *for you.* [*Sorry* is modified by the adverb *very* and the adverbial phrase *for you.*]

Charles seems {*rather* | *very* | *extremely*} angry.

The road is rough {*in places.* | *where they are repairing it.*}

The whole tribe appeared eager *for war.*

He grew envious *of his successful rival.*

Be zealous *in every righteous cause.*

The chief's face looked dark *with passion.*

He was selfish *beyond belief.* [The predicate adjective (*selfish*) is modified by the adverbial phrase *beyond belief.*]

Ellen seemed desirous *that her friends should admire her.*

The secretary appeared unwilling *to resign.*

Modifiers may themselves be modified.

The chief varieties of such modification are illustrated in the following sentences.

> **Adjectives** or **adjective phrases** may be modified by **adverbs** or by words or groups of words used adverbially.

A *very* old man came to the door.

An *exceedingly* dangerous curve lay beyond the bridge.

This *rather* odd proposal interested us.

The quay is *miles* long. [Adverbial objective.]

At least five different amendments have been offered. [*Five* is modified by the adverbial phrase *at least.*]

The general, *wholly* in the dark as to the enemy's intentions, ordered an advance. [The adjective phrase *in the dark* is modified by *wholly.*]

Quite at his ease, John began to speak. [*At his ease* is modified by *quite.*]

Her smile, pathetic *in its weariness*, quickly faded. [The adverbial phrase modifies *pathetic*]

This sleeve is *a good two inches* short. [The phrase modifies *short.*]

> **Possessive nouns** may be modified by adjectives or by possessives.

The poor man's days are numbered.

Honest Tom's face shone with delight.

The faithful animal's head drooped.

My uncle's barn is on fire.

John's brother's name is Reginald.

> **Appositives** may be modified by adjectives or by groups of words used as adjectives.

Joe, *the old* butler, met me at the station.

Sam, *the cunning* rascal, had stolen the oars.

Her mother, a woman *of fashion*, sadly neglected her.

The other, the man *at the table*, laughed rudely.

Ferdinand Oliver, the engineer *who had charge of the construction*, proved incompetent.

Two Englishmen, friends *whom I visited last summer*, are coming to New York in December.

> **Adverbs** or **adverbial phrases** may be modified by adverbs or by words or groups of words used adverbially.

Jane plays *very* well.

Robert spoke *almost* hopefully.

She answered *quite* at random.

I write to him *at least* once *a year*.

An adjective may be modified by an **infinitive** .

Unable *to move*, I suffered torments of anxiety.

The sailors, eager *to reach* the island, plunged into the sea.

Reluctant *to act*, but unwilling *to stand* idle, Burwell was in a pitiful state of indecision.

Adjective and adverbial clauses are very common as modifiers of modifiers.

Geronimo, an old chief *who bore the scars of many battles*, led the attack. [The adjective clause modifies the appositive *chief*.]

The servant, angry *because he had been rebuked*, slammed the door as he went out.

The hunter, confident *that the deer had not heard him*, took deliberate aim.

The fugitive, in a panic *lest he should be overtaken*, made frantic efforts to scale the cliff. [The adverbial clause modifies the adjective phrase *in a panic*.]

5. Paragraph Completion

Set A

In this type, usually a paragraph of two/three line is given and we are asked to identify the statement that would complete the given paragraph.

The Indian Meterological Department (IMD) has come up with dismaying prediction that the southwest monsoon this year will be below normal. If the prognosis holds true, it may mar the prospects of redeeming the rabi crop output losses through bumper harvests in the later kharif season. India's farm sector has certainly acquired a degree of resilience when it comes to monsoon – as reflected in the positive growth numbers in all the weak monsoon years since 2009. However, monsoon rainfall and its distribution still remains crucial.

(a) A poor monsoon and subsequent food inflation might well throw off the Reserve Bank of India's schedule for rate cuts.
(b) The monsoon's behaviour this year seems to bear out the notion that climate change is affecting the Indian monsoon and altering its rainfall calendar.
(c) They impact supplies and prices of most farm commodities, especially coarse cereals, pulses, oilseeds, vegetables, fruit and livestock products, as well as the rural sector demand for consumer goods.
(d) Nevertheless, the first stage monsoon forecast of the IMD should normally be taken with a pinch of salt, as the weather agency's accuracy record on this count is none too inspiring.

Answer (c)

To solve these types of questions following points must be kept in mind.

First of all read the paragraph with full concentration and try to find out the gist of the paragraph.
For e.g. in the above example we are talking about the monsoon and its impact on the farming sector.

The paragraph is left at a particular thread of thought, try to identify that thought and then go to the given options.
For e.g. in the above example the last line asks a question that why monsoon is still important? What will be its effects on the farming sector?
According to the gist of the paragraph and the thought at which it was left, choose the correct option.
For e.g. in the above example option (c) we come to know the impact of monsoon on the farming sector thus option (c) is the correct answer.

Or the other way the same type of question can be asked is:
Which of the following options follows the given sentence?
Cook, 56, said the impact of demonetization has not worked its way through yet and it is "still definitely having some overhang".

(a) Describing India as a "great" market, Cook said Apple will make significant investments in the country going forward.
(b) He further added, "But in the longer term it's a great move and I feel really good about how we are doing there".
(c) He said the iPad and its laptop range Macs did very well in the Indian market.
(d) Apple's CEO said the company established new all-time revenue records in most developed and emerging markets.

Answer (b)

Set B

Which of the following options precedes the given sentence?
_______________________. Both, along with several other tools, are used by the RBI to infuse or suck out liquidity from the market.

(a) RBI has cut the repo rate by 1.50 percent.

(b) Repo rate is the rate at which the banks borrow from the RBI, while CRR refers to quantum of fund to be parked mandatorily with the RBI.

(c) It now remains to be seen how the banks react and when will they start reducing their lending rates.

(d) The rate cut could lead to a very good borrowing environment, particularly for retail customers.

Answer (b)

In these types of questions we need to find out that about which topic the sentence is talking about and then link up the option with the sentence.

For e.g. in the above question we are talking about 2 RBI tools to deal with liquidity and in the options only (b) is talking about 2RBI tools i.e. Repo rate and CRR while in rest of the sentences we are just revolving around the impacts or the steps taken by the RBI.

Set C

Here we need to find the missing sentence.

After demonetization, people rushed to deposit the scrapped notes into their bank accounts.____
______________. In other words, depositors are unable to withdraw as much cash as they deposited. Also, the surge in deposits has not resulted in a corresponding increase in demand of loans.

(a) With restrictions on exchange of old notes and withdrawal of new ones, the banking system has been flushed with deposits.

(b) As a result, banks are forced to lower interest rates on deposit and lending.

(c) For the government, which is the largest borrower, the cost of new borrowings comes down.

(d) The government recalled Rs 500 and Rs 1000 notes on November 8.

Answer (a)

We need to follow the same steps as mentioned above to find the missing sentence. Just find out the main idea, work on the options, try to find what the

options and sentence is saying and you can then easily get the correct answer.

Set D

Ques 1. Normally, falling oil prices would boost global growth. This time, though, matters are less clear cut. The big economic question is whether lower prices reflect weak demand or have been caused by a surge in the supply of crude. If weak demand is the culprit that is worrying: it suggests the oil price is a symptom of weakening growth. If the source of weakness is financial, then cheaper oil may not boost growth all that much: consumers may simply use the gains to pay down their debts. Indeed, in some countries, cheaper oil may even make matters worse by increasing the risk of deflation.

(a) An energy-induced drop in prices, though good for consumer purchasing power, risks reinforcing expectations of lower inflation overall.

(b) The IEA, an oil importers' club, said it expects global demand to rise by just 700,000 barrels a day this year.

(c) On balance, energy consumers win and energy producers and exporting countries lose with falling oil prices.

(d) On the other hand, if plentiful supply is driving prices down, that is potentially better news: cheaper oil should eventually boost spending in the world's biggest economies.

Ques 2. In the annals of computing, nothing has caused as much disappointment as putting ideas on paper. __________. However, with the coming of the inkjet printer it was soon possible to print really high quality images.

(a) For decades, printing computer files was a thankless task for users seeking to reproduce precisely what they saw on their screens.

(b) To start with, thermal inkjets were no match for the costlier laser printers that had just been introduced.

(c) For all its originality the idea behind the inkjet is far from new.

(d) The first inkjet printers were slow, messy machines, but they gradually got better and better.

(e) Designers of printers grew more ambitious and they started to want color, speed and low costs.

Ques 3. _____________________. And they are certainly right. Sunscreen protects your ski n from ultraviolet light rays. Too much ultraviolet is bad for your skin. If you spend a long time outside without any sunscreen on, you might get sunburn because of the ultraviolet rays.

(a) Ultraviolet light can get rid of bacteria in eggs and apple and make them safer to eat

(b) Your parents tell you to wear sunscreen when you're outside in the summer

(c) When we are outdoors, we are exposed to pollens and dust, and other irritants

(d) However, they can also trigger asthma attacks, which are more serious

(e) It seems to be the safest way to make food safer before we buy it

Ques 4. Most Western industrialized nations have an individualistic orientation, which values independence and self-assertiveness. __________. They stress the interdependence of people within the community.

(a) There is no internal evidence to suggest this.

(b) Individuals in collectivist Asian cultures are even less likely to commit such errors.

(c) In contrast, many non-Western cultures have a more collectivist orientation.

(d) This is why Americans tend to use psychological traits to describe themselves.

(e) Actually, situational factors also play quite an important role.

Ques 5. A fax machine works by scanning each outgoing page, turning the image into a series of light and dark dots. This pattern is then translated into audio tones, and sent over regular phone lines. The receiving fax "hears" the tones, pieces the grid together, and prints the total number of dots.---____
_.

(a) He invented a machine capable of receiving signals from a telegraph wire

(b) The idea of fax machines has been around for a long time

(c) They were an easy way to send documents to any phone number

(d) The resulting document is a black and white copy of the original page

(e) Then he finally managed to translate these symbols into images on paper

Answers

Ans 1. d

Ans 2. a

Ans 3. b

Ans 4. b

Ans 5. d

Set E

Ques 1.

1. "Oh my God! What about your Father? Any sign of him?

2. "No Mum, just the trolley. Shall we go out and see if we can find him?

3. No! Whatever happens, we must stay here. It's a trap." Those lights are there to lure us out."

4. "Mum, come quick! The big people have found Dad's shopping trolley and put it on their table next to two huge lights."

a. 2134

b. 4123

c. 4321

d. 1243

Ques 2.

1. "Apparently they've just introduced a second security gate."

2. "Couple of days, what about you?"

3. "Been here long mate?"

4. "Just arrived. Any idea what's causing the queue?

a. 2314
b. 1324
c. 2341
d. 3241

Ques 3.
1. "A treat I think Charlie. We did a trick last time."

2. "There's the front doorbell again Charlie. must be the third time tonight. It'll be more youngsters I expect, out 'Trick or Treating'. Shall I go, or will you?"

3. "OK my sweetheart a treat it shall be. How many would you like?"

4. "I'll go love, you have a rest and finish off your cup of tea. What shall we do this time, trick or treat?"

a. 2143
b. 1324
c. 2413
d. 1234

Ques 4.
1. "Just want to let you know kid, in case you were wondering, that last cake, the chocolate éclair, it's got my name on it. Touch it and I'll have your fingers off!"

2. "Well kid, it's up to you. What's it going to be, cake or fingers?"

3. "Mum, mum, Aunt Sally's dog just said he's gong to bite me. He says the chocolate éclair's his."

4. "Don't be silly dear, little Henry can't talk, he's a dog. Now play nicely with him, there's a darling. And don't feed him any of your cake, Aunt Sally has got him on a strict diet."

a. 1342
b. 2341
c. 1432
d. 2314

Ques 5.
1. "It depends. How heavy are you? 'Cos my Dad says I'm not big enough to lift heavy things."

2. "I'm 14 pounds, give or take a few ounces. If you can't lift me, just drag me to the edge and push me over the side. Please."

3. "No! Don't go. I'm sorry. It's being stranded here on this pier that's making me grumpy. I'm getting a bit short of breath and this sun is starting to dry me out. If you could help me back into the water I'd be extremely grateful."

4. "No need to be rude Mister, I was only asking. My Dad says rude people should be ignored. I wonder if the same goes for rude fish? I think it probably does, I'm off."

a. 1243
b. 4312
c. 3214
d. 2134

Ques 6.
1. "Keep your voice down Billy, he'll hear you."

2. "He won't like that mate. You know what he's like. Nobody ever leaves, not of their own accord anyway. Why don't you just finish your meal. You'll feel better afterwards."

3. "He won't like that mate. You know what he's like. Nobody ever leaves, not of their own accord anyway. Why don't you just finish your meal. You'll feel better afterwards."

4. "I don't care. I'm telling you, things need to change round here, or I'm off."

a. 1243
b. 4231
c. 3214
d. 2143

Ques 7.
1. "Looks like we've found them, sir."

2. "It's a family unit, sir. A female, a male and two young siblings. Our probes indicate that they are the right age and relatively well preserved."

3. "Thank goodness for that Captain. I wasn't looking forward to having to report to the authorities that our mission had failed. What exactly have you got?"

4. "Excellent Captain. How long before we have them securely on board?"

a. 4321
b. 2134
c.1324
d. 1342

Ques 8.
1. "Seems the driver leant out of the car screaming at everyone to get out of his way. Started honking his horn. There was panic. That's when that fiery young lamb, Jake leapt at him and tore off his arm. Blood everywhere."

2. "Not sure mate. Someone says the idiot in the car wouldn't slow down. Seems he hit the old ewe, Matilda. You know, her with the dodgy back legs. She never stood a chance."

3. "Then what? I just heard the screams. That's when I started running."

4. "What's happened Joe?"

a. 1323
b. 4231

c. 1324
d. 1243

Ques 9.
1. "But kids, it's really important. I need all the help I can get and we haven't got much time left. I thought I felt some rain as I was coming in. This could be it."

2. "Noah, leave the children be and stop scaring them. Get back to your boat building and I'll come out and give you a hand after tea. And Noah… please take that silly helmet off, you're going to frighten the neighbours."

3. Dad, leave us alone. We're having fun building dens. We keep telling you, we don't want to help you outside!"

4. "Mum! Dad's being weird again."

a. 3142   b. 4231
c. 1324   d. 1234

Ques 10.
1. "No idea mate. I just process things this end. My job's to make sure you leave your clothes and any other earthly possessions here before you go down the hole. A bloke called Peter will meet you at the bottom and send you on your way."

2. This morning, I think. I remember crossing the road outside my office, hearing the sreech of brakes then nothing. Next thing I know I'm in this queue."

3. "According to my list you should've been knocked down by that lorry yesterday morning not today. Bloody typical of the Grim Reaper, always messing up his timings. Still you're here now. Get you're clothes off, you're next."

4. "But where am I going?"

a. 3214
b. 2341
c. 1243
d. 2413

Answers

1) 4123   2) 3241   3) 2413   4) 1342

5) 4312   6) 2143   7) 1324   8) 4231

9) 3142   10) 2341

Set F

Directions(1-7): Arrange the following sentences to make a coherent paragraph.

A. The tri-junction stretch of the boundary at Sikkim, though contested, has witnessed far fewer tensions than the western sector of the India-China boundary even as India and Bhutan have carried on separate negotiations with China.

B. That the PLA decided to undertake the action just as the year's first group of pilgrims was reaching Nathu La cannot be a coincidence.

C. The warmth that officials reported at the meeting was obviously misleading,

D. In fact, during Chinese President Xi Jinping's visit in 2014, the stretch was opened as an alternative route to Kailash Mansarovar for Indian pilgrims as a confidence-building measure.

E. Moreover, it came only days after Prime Minister Narendra Modi's bilateral meeting with President Xi in Kazakhstan.

F. The boundary stand-off with china at the Doka La tri-junction with Bhutan is by all accounts unprecedented; it demands calmer counsel on all sides.

G. and it is important for India and China to accept that relations have deteriorated steadily since Mr. Xi's 2014 visit.

H. Its action of sending People's Liberation Army construction teams with earth moving equipment to forcibly build a road upsets a carefully preserved peace.

1. Which of the following should be the fifth sentence after rearrangement?

i. B

ii. D

iii. F

iv. A

v. C

2. Which of the following should be the first sentence after rearrangement?

i. B

ii. F

iii. C

iv. A

v. E

3. Which of the following should be the sixth sentence after rearrangement?

i. B

ii. C

iii. E

iv. G

v. F

4. Which of the following should be the fourth sentence after rearrangement?

i. H

ii. F

iii. E

iv. D

v. G

5. Which of the following should be the third sentence after rearrangement?

i. B

ii. D

iii. H

iv. G

v. C

6. Which of the following should be the last sentence after rearrangement?

i. A

ii. G

iii. B

iv. F

v. E

7. Which of the following should be the second sentence after rearrangement?

i. C

ii. A

iii. F

iv. B

v. E

Explanation:

(F, A, H, D, B, E, C, G)

As we all know that first of all we will go through all of these sentences for getting our first sentence and understand the basic meaning of passage and when we read all of these sentences we understand that there are only two sentences (F and A) which can be our first sentence but when we read sentence F we see that in this sentence the passage is something about the boundary of China so it can be our basic sentence.

Now we will find out some pairs of the passage to arrange it easily, when we read sentence A and sentence H we can see that we have an pronoun it which refers China so it should be our first pair and now we have only a single sentence that is incomplete and it is sentence C and we have only one sentence which can be the other part of this sentence and it is sentence Gnow when we read sentence D it says that the stretch was opened as an alternative route to Kailash Mansarovar and when we understand this sentence we can clearly say that another part of this sentence should be sentence B because in this sentence PLA decided the action about the Pilgrim and after this sentence we have only one sentence remaining that is sentence E so it should be our next sentence.

Now we have found three pairs for the passage and these pairs are(A-H),(D-B-E) and (C-G).

Directions(8--14): Arrange the following sentences to make a coherent paragraph.

A. It is not the first such order, an Uttar Pradesh MLA, Umlesh Yadav, was disqualified in 2011 on the same ground, of suppressing expenditure incurred in the publication of paid news.

B. In a typical inquiry into the paid news phenomenon, the newspaper or publication concerned denies that it was paid for publishing the material and insists that it was part of its normal election coverage.

C. However, the EC did not buy his arguments, mainly because it was difficult to believe that he had not seen reports that appeared in his Datia constituency

D. The candidate denies authorising the publication and takes the plea that he or she could not possibly account for something that was not paid for. Mr. Mishra was no exception.

E. The Election Commission's order disqualifying Madhya Pradesh Minister Narottam Mishra for three years is an important step in curbing 'paid news' in the electoral arena.

F. during the campaign for the 2008 Assembly elections, often with his picture and the Bharatiya Janata Party's symbol.

G. The EC has called paid news, a term that refers to propaganda in favour of a candidate masquerading as news reports or articles, a "grave electoral malpractice" on the part of candidates to circumvent expenditure limits.

H. He, in fact, argued that his rivals could be behind the 42 reports that the EC's National Level Committee on Paid News found to be nothing but election advertisements, without any disclaimer.

8. Which of the following should be the seventh sentence after rearrangement?

I. B

II. D

III. C

IV. H

V. A

9. Which of the following should be the fourth sentence after rearrangement?

I. F

II. C

III. E

IV. B

V. G

10. Which of the following should be the sixth sentence after rearrangement?

I. H

II. C

III. D

IV. B

V. A

11. Which of the following should be the second sentence after rearrangement?
I. G
II. A
III. C
IV. F
V. H

12. Which of the following should be the last sentence after rearrangement?
I. D
II. E
III. F
IV. H
V. A

13. Which of the following should be the first sentence after rearrangement?
I. G   II. D   III. H   IV. A
V. E

14. Which of the following should be the fifth sentence after rearrangement?
I. D
II. C
III. A
IV. B
V. F

Explanation
(E, A, G, B, D, H, C, F)
First of all when we solve a parajumble we need to go through all of the given sentences once and when we have done it we can easily find that sentence (1st sentence) in which the main theme has given of the passage in this paragraph we have two sentences that can be our 1st sentence (E or G) but sentence E has the full form of EC so it should be our first sentence.
In sentence E it has given that EC has passed an order to disqualify MP's Minister Narottam Mishra and in sentence A it has given that it is the first order so it can be our second sentence easily.
Now in sentence G we have what EC has called paid news so it can be our next sentence (3rd sentence)
Now we should find those sentences that can be a pair and we can find two pairs easily in this paragraph (D and H), (C and F). In our first pair, we have Mr. Mishra a noun in sentence D and in sentence H we have a pronoun he so it can be a pair easily. In our second pair, we have a word however that is mostly used in a conclusion sentence and in sentence F we have the other part of sentence C so it should be our last pair.
Now we are left with only one sentence (B) and one single place for this sentence place 4th so it can be our 4th sentence.

Set G

Directions: In the following questions, four sentences are given, i.e. (A). (B), (C) and (D). Arrange the sentences to make a meaningful paragraph.

Question 1:
A. However, critics say the scheme is too expensive and question whether the government will be able to support it.
B. Under the National Rural Guarantee Scheme, one member from each of India's 60 million rural households is guaranteed 100 days of work each year.
C. They will receive a minimum wage of 60 rupees ($1.35) or an unemployment allowance if there is no work.
D. The first phase of the programme will cover 200 of the country's poorest and least developed districts.
a) DCAB
b) ACBD
c) CDBA
d) BCDA

Question 2:
A. Already the company has 25 international partners to manufacture and market a host of products ranging from bulk drugs and pharmaceuticals to skin care and cardiac therapy products .
B. This hurry seems to take care of life after 2005,when the product patent regime came into effect.

C. And that seems to be the panacea for growth for the Rs.235 crore Elder Pharmaceuticals .

D. The company is busy entering into alliances as if there is no tomorrow.

a) ADCB

b) DCBA

c) ABDC

d) BDAC

Question 3:

A.   If something is done in the name of modernization, it is considered good, and if it stands in the way of modernization , it is automatically evil.

B. Modernization , as expressed in different terms , is the prosperity of the secondary and tertiary industries.

C. Throughout the entire world, in no matter which country , 'modernization' is the glorious banner under which all people gather.

D. And since these industries are based in the cities , modernization means urbanization.

a) BDAC

b) ABCD

c) CADB

d) CABD

Question 4:

A. Time is our greatest and most precious asset.

B.However , while we are doing that , sometimes we are missing the greatest gift of all- our time to experience our lives.

C.We often spend a great deal of time and energy thinking and worrying about ,or working to earn and pursuing more money.

D.Whether you are rich ,poor, healthy,ill,or just humming along in your life somewhere in between ,we all have 24 hours in each and every day to invest wisely.

a) ACDB

b) DABC

c) ACBD

d) ADCB

Question 5:

A. Nationalists railed against the caste system and wanted to eliminate untouchability.

B.But it was mostly a humanitarian desire to improve a lot of the low castes and to send a clear message to the agrarian high castes that this system is inconsistent with modern society.

C.Sentiment against caste has been gathering among modern Indians for more than a hundred years.

D.It was partly because of caste hindered economic advance.

a) ABCD

b) DCBA

c) CADB

d) CABD

Directions: Read each sentence to find out whether there is any grammatical error in it. The error, if any, Will be in one part of the sentence. If there is no error. Mark (E) i.e. no error as the answer. (Ignore errors of punctuation, if any).

Question 6:

(A.) A dawn-to-dusk hartal called by the Congress-led United Democratic Front (UDF) and BJP to protest against Wednesday's/(B) alleged excessive use of force by the police on Mahija, mother of Jishnu Prannoy, /(C) an engineering college student who died alleged /(D) after being tortured by his college authorities, crippled life across Kerala on Thursday/(E) NO ERROR .

a) A

b) B

c) C

d) D

e) E

Question 7:

(A.) Meanwhile, faced with scathing criticism from different quarters, including those who are sympathetic to the LDF/(B) and the CPI(M) about repeatIng instances of police insensitivity /(C) and highhandedness, Chief Minister Pinarayi Vijayan has called meetings of police /(D) personnel at the range level to discuss the government's law and order priorities/(E) NO ERROR .

a) A

b) B

c) C

d) D

e) E

Question 8:
(A.) As trouble brews and livelihoods suffer over the Supreme Court's ban on retail liquor outlets/(B) and bars between the National and the State highways, practical issues /(C) raised in the courtroom by the Attorney-General, the States and liquor traders about the adverse/(D) impact of a blanket ban have come alive, challenging the rationale of the court's decision/(E) NO ERROR.
a) A
b) B
c) C
d) D
e) E

Question 9:
(A.)The lawyers submitted before the court /(B) that the States must not be put under the guillotine/(C), and effort should be made to /(D) understand the topographical peculiarities of each State/(E) NO ERROR.
a) A
b) B
c) C
d) D
e) E

Question 10:
(A.) While former India captain Sourav Ganguly recently commented that DD was one of the weaker sides/(B) in the competition, Mishra begged to differ./(C) "I personally feel very motivated whenever someone says something like this/.(D) We almost reached the playoffs last year. We have a balanced squad and will try to do better than last year."/(E) NO ERROR.
a) A
b) B
c) C
d) D
e) E

Set H

Answers with Explanation
Ans 1 One can easily get the BC link since 'they' in C refers to the people covered under the National Rural Guarantee Scheme mentioned in B.A logically fits in as the concluding statement since it talks about the criticism and carries the thought further. Thus , we get the BCDA link.Hence ,(4).

Ans 2: DC is a clear link which exists only in option(2)and (4).A cannot be the first sentence of the paragraph . 'That 'in C refers to the company's alliances. Hurry seems to be at trait associated with a company that is fast growing .A records the various products that the company markets and flows from B. So the sequence is DCBA. Hence(2)

Ans 3: C should be the opening sentence because C gives a general opinion and the spread of modernization. The other sentences follow from this hypothesis and try to validate the fact stated in C. A follows from C. The BD link is the most crucial one, with the word' industries' connecting the two. Thus CABD. Hence(4)

Ans 4: The paragraph talks about the importance of time in our lives.Hence, the logical flow of sentences would be ADCB i.e., firstly what is time, secondly how much time do we all have in our lives, then how do we spend most of our time and then how we miss out on the precious time by indulging in wasteful things. Hence(4)

Ans 5: A and C both seem plausible as the opening sentence. The most obvious link in the sentence is the DB link because of the quantifiers 'partly' and 'mostly'.B must follow D and not the other way round because the partial reasoning should be followed by the complete reasoning. This link is present in option (3)- CADB only. Hence(3)

Ans 6: ERROR : "alleged" CORRECT: "allegedly" (C)

Ans 7: ERROR: "repeating " CORRECT : "repeated" (b)

Ans 8: ERROR : " between" CORRECT: "along" (b)

Ans 9: ERROR : "and effort" CORRECT: " and an effort" (c)

Ans 10: NO ERROR

Set I

Set- 1

Directions (Q. 1-5): Read the following sentences, A, B, C, D and E carefully and rearrange them into a coherent paragraph.

(A) External Affairs Minister Sushma Swaraj said she had informed Mr. Jadhav's mother of the order.

(B) India has rarely approached the International Court of Justice (ICJ) in the past, given its hesitation to "internationalise" its bilateral relations, especially when it comes to Pakistan.

(C) A senior official told The Hindu that the Jadhav case required the extreme measure, as "Pakistan had refused to follow any established norm or principle."

(D) The ICJ is a part of the United Nations, and its judgments have binding force and are without appeal for the parties concerned, a press release issued at The Hague on March 09, 2017 said. (The Hague is a city on the North Sea coast of the western Netherlands.)

(E) In a major breakthrough for the Government of India's efforts in the case of Kulbhushan Jadhav, the former naval officer sentenced to death in Pakistan, the Indian government received a stay order from the ICJ at The Hague, in a petition that accused Pakistan of gross violations of international laws.

(1) Which of the following should be the LAST after rearrangement/replacement?
(a) B
(b) E
(c) A
(d) C
(e) D

(2) Which of the following should be the FIRST after rearrangement/replacement?
(a) B
(b) E
(c) A
(d) C
(e) D

(3) Which of the following should be the SECOND after rearrangement/replacement?
(a) B
(b) E
(c) A
(d) C
(e) D

(4) Which of the following should be the FOURTH after rearrangement/replacement?
(a) B
(b) E
(c) A
(d) C
(e) D

(5) Which of the following should be the THIRD after rearrangement/replacement?
(a) B
(b) E
(c) A
(d) C
(e) D

Explanation:
The correct sequence of the sentences is EBCDA.

Opening statement is (E) which tells us about the historic win for the Government of India. It is followed by the statement (B) showing hesitancy of the Government of India in the past for approaching ICJ. Statement (C) follows the statement (B) explaining the reason why the Government approached the ICJ in this particular case and statement (D) follows statement (C) as it describes the press release issued after the judgment. Statement (A) should come at the very end as the final decision has been informed to the mother of Kulbhushan Jadhav by External Affairs Minister.

Set J

Directions (Q. 6-10): Read the following sentences, A, B, C, D and E carefully and rearrange them into a coherent paragraph.

(A) Several boys wearing full sleeve shirts were told that only half-sleeve shirts were allowed in the examination hall.

(B) Left with no choice, the candidates had to "customise" their clothing as per the norms.

(C) Some others wearing shoes had to dump them for the sandals of their parents.

(D) Over 11 lakh Bachelor of Medicine and Bachelor of Surgery (MBBS) and Bachelor of Dental Surgery (BDS) aspirants appeared for the National Eligibility cum Entrance Test (NEET) at over 1,900 centres across the country.

(E) The candidates were also not allowed to carry electronic devices inside the exam centre.

(6) Which of the following should be the LAST after rearrangement/replacement?
(a) B
(b) E
(c) A
(d) C
(e) D

(7) Which of the following should be the FIRST after rearrangement/replacement?
(a) B
(b) E
(c) A
(d) C
(e) D

(8) Which of the following should be the SECOND after rearrangement/replacement?
(a) B
(b) E
(c) A

(d) C
(e) D

(9) Which of the following should be the FOURTH after rearrangement/replacement?
(a) B
(b) E
(c) A
(d) C
(e) D

(10) Which of the following should be the THIRD after rearrangement/replacement?
(a) B
(b) E
(c) A
(d) C
(e) D

Explanation
Opening statement is (D) which states about the NEET Examination. This statement is followed by the inconvenience caused to the aspirants, as reflected in the statement (A). Statements (B) and (C) show how the aspirants managed to abide by the rules and lastly the statement (E) mandatory provision of not allowing the electronic gadgets.

Set K

Direction: Rearrange the following seven sentences to form a meaningful paragraph and then answer the question given below:

A. The court probably had few options but to act in defence of its reputation by holding him guilty of contempt of court — a finding that is unexceptionable.

B. It is singularly unfortunate that the Supreme Court's efforts to discipline Justice C.S. Karnan of the Calcutta High Court has had to end in a six-month prison term for contempt of court.

C. Therefore, it remains a pertinent question whether the court could not have waited for his imminent retirement so that the country is spared the unseemly event of a high court judge being arrested while in office.

D. He had repeatedly sought to pass purported judicial orders in his own cause.

E. With the recalcitrant judge making it a habit to bring the institution into ridicule by his aberrant behaviour,

F. He had not only flung irresponsible charges of corruption against several judges, but also sought to make political capital out of his Dalit identity.

G. His arrest will undoubtedly mark an abysmally low moment in the country's judicial history.

1. Which of the following should be the fourth sentence after rearrangement?
i. E
ii. D
iii. B
iv. C
v. F

2. Which of the following should be the first sentence after rearrangement?
i. G
ii. C
iii. E
iv. B
v. A

3. Which of the following should be the third sentence after rearrangement?
i. F
ii. C
iii. A
iv. D
v. E

4. Which of the following should be the second sentence after rearrangement?
i. E
ii. B
iii. F
iv. G
v. C

5. Which of the following should be the sixth sentence after rearrangement?
i. D
ii. E
iii. F
iv. G
v. A

6. Which of the following should be the fifth sentence after rearrangement?
i. F
ii. C
iii. A
iv. D
v. E

Answers & Solutions

The correct rearrangement is: B, E, A, F, D, G, C

Explanation:

As we can see that there are only two sentences in the paragraph which can be the first sentence and these two sentences are (A and B) so now we need to find out that which can be the first sentence.

Now we should focus on him (pronoun) in sentence A so we can't understand that we are talking about whom and sentence B we have a noun Justice C.S. Karnan so it should be the first sentence.

According to our first sentence Supreme court had to pass the order of C.S. Karnan's prison and now we need to find out why Supreme court had passed it and it has given in the sentence E so our second sentence must be sentence E.

As we can see that there is a (,) in the last of sentence E now we have to connect it with its second part and here in all other three sentences we have pronoun he or his which can't connect with this sentence because they are talking about his behaviour not about him so it will be the sentence A.

Now sentence F says what he had done and sentence D shows that how he takes benefit of being a Dalit hence it can be a pair FD according chronology.

Now we have remaining two sentences in which one sentence has a word therefore, that is used for conclusion and in this sentence therefore is functioning as thus which also mean conclusion.

Set L

Rearrange the following sentences (A), (B), (C), (D), (E) and (F) in the proper sequence to form a meaningful paragraph, the answer the question given below them:

(A) The European Court of Justice said. Advocate Genera Pedro Cruiz Villation declared the legislation as illegal and told the EU's 28 member states to take the necessary steps to withdraw it.

(B) The decision to supper the 2006 Data Retention Directive comes as Europe weighs concerns over electronic snooping in the wake of revelations.

(C) About the United State's systematic surveillance of e-mail and telephone communications.

(D) Europe's top court of Tuesday struck down an EU law forcing telecom operations.

(E) By allowing EU governments to access the data, "the directive interferes in a particularly serious manner with the fundamental rights to respect for private life and to the protection of personal data."

(F) To store private phone and email data for up to two years, deeming it as too invasive despite its usefulness in combating terrorism

Consider the sentences that have been jumbled up and answer the questions that follow:

1) Which of the following is the third sentence of the arrangement?
a) B
b) E
c) C
d) A
e) F

2) Which of the following is the first sentence of the arrangement?
 a) B
b) C
c) E
d) A
e) D

3) Which of the following is the fifth sentence of the arrangement?
a) E
b) D
c) C
d) A
e) F

4) Which of the following is the sixth (last) sentence of the arrangement?
a) E   b) B   c) C   d) A
e) F

5) Which of the following is the fourth sentence of the arrangement?
a) E
b) B
c) C
d) A
e) D

ANSWERS
The correct sequence is: DFEACB

1) 2; E

2) 5; D

3) 3; C

4) 2; B

5) 4; A

Set M

Direction (Q.1 – Q.5): Rearrange the following sentence A , B , C , D , E , F in the proper sequence to form a meaningful paragraph , then answer the questions given below them .

A. Educating children through experiential learning is the new approach to schooling these days.

B. People feel far less reliant on the classroom – plus – teacher model and far more comfortable knowing they simply they have to provide a supportive learning environment.

C. This method also makes the child an independent thinker and an independent decision maker.

D. Unconventional parents opt for this way of educating their children.

E. Some parents prefer to take curriculum on the road , other use the world around them as the curriculum.

F. These parents believe that a child's education is not confined to one classroom , but by experiencing what the text book teaches.

1. Which of the following is the First sentence after rearrangement ?
a. D
b. C
c. E
d. F
e. A

2. Which of the following is the Fourth sentence after rearrangement ?
a. A
b. B
c. E
d. F
e. D

3. Which of the following is the Second sentence after rearrangement ?
a. E
b. D
c. B
d. F
e. A

4. Which of the following is the Third sentence after rearrangement ?
a. B
b. C
c. E
d. F
e. A

5. Which of the following is the Fifth sentence after rearrangement ?

a. D
b. C
c. E
d. F
e. A

6. Which of the following is the Sixth sentence after rearrangement?
a. B
b. D
c. F
d. A
e. C

Answer Key –
1. A
2. B
3. D
4. C
5. E
6. F

Set N

Directions (Ques 1-5): Read the following sentences, A, B, C, D and E carefully and rearrange them into a coherent paragraph.

(A) It was re-discovered by nature enthusiasts K.M. Prabhu Kumar and Tarun Chhabra.

(B) News of the discove-ry was published in May 2017 in Phytotaxa, a journal on botanical taxonomy.

(C) Featuring a distinctive translucent spathe, it was last collected by E. Barnes in 1932 and described by C.E.C Fischer in 1933.

(D) Barely a few hundred cobra lily plants are left in the wild and they can be found only in a small area measuring less than 10 square kilometres in the Nilgiris. (E) The incredibly rare Arisaema translucens, more commonly remembered as the cobra lily, was recently rediscover-ed in the western Nilgiris after 84 years.

(1) Which of the following should be the LAST after rearrangement?
(a) B
(b) E

(c) A

(d) C

(e) D

(2) Which of the following should be the FIRST after rearrangement?

(a) B

(b) A

(c) C

(d) D

(e) E

(3) Which of the following should be the SECOND after rearrangement?

(a) A

(b) B

(c) C

(d) D

(e) E

(4) Which of the following should be the FOURTH after rearrangement?

(a) B

(b) A

(c) D

(d) C

(e) E

(5) Which of the following should be the THIRD after rearrangement?

(a) A

(b) E

(c) B

(d) D

(e) C

Solution : E-A-C-B-D

Opening sentence is (E) which tells about the rediscovery of Cobra lily. Then comes the sentence (A) which tells about the discoverers of Cobra lily. Option (C) gives information about the last discoverers of Cobra lily(Barnes and Fischer). Sentence (D) follows (C) which tells about the present location of Cobra lily. Sentence (B) comes at the last and gives information about the journal in which this discovery was published. Position of (B)

may create confusion(that it comes after (A) but if we put it after (A) then Sentence (C) will get misplaced.

Directions (Ques 6-10): Read the following sentences, A, B, C, D and E carefully and rearrange them into a coherent paragraph.

(A) Tributes to the memory of Raja Ram Mohan Roy have been paid in various parts of the country and they all show how modern Ram Mohan Roy was at the time of his death a hundred years ago.

(B) The secret of this modernity of this great man lies partly in his comprehensive racial outlook and in the intrepid and resolute action that marked his remarkable career touching almost every aspect of life, and partly in the slow progress of events in social and political upheaval for the greater part of the century following his death.

(C) The mere abolition of Sati did not change many aspects of life and Sati was not followed with the same rigour in all parts of the country.

(D) We may prophesy he may probably continue to be equally modern in some respects fifty years hence.

(E) The furtherance of the Brahmo Samaj movement by an advanced party of reformers who succeeded Ram Mohan Roy in the city of Calcutta – seceding from the orthodox fold – prevented no doubt conversions to Christianity on the part of those who desired greater freedom from the trammels of Hindu society.

(6) Which of the following should be the LAST after rearrangement?

(a) A (b) B (c) C (d) D (e) E

(7) Which of the following should be the FIRST after rearrangement?

(a) B (b) A (c) C (d) D (e) E

(8) Which of the following should be the THIRD after rearrangement?

(a) D (b) A (c) B (d) E (e) C

(9) Which of the following should be the FOURTH after rearrangement?

(a) A   (b) B   (c) C   (d) D   (e) E

(10) Which of the following should be the SECOND after rearrangement?

(a) E   (b) D   (c) C   (d) B

Solution: A-D-B-C-E

Opening sentence is (A) which is about the Tributes given to Raja Ram Mohan Roy. Sentence (D) follows (A) which talks about the modernity of Raja Ram Mohan Roy(same as (A)). Option (B) gives possible reasons behind his modernity. Locating sentence (C) may be difficult but it can only come after the initial introduction of Raja Ram Mohan Roy, as he was the pioneer behind this campaign and Brahmo Samaj Movement. Last sentence (E) tells about the reformers who succeeded Ram Mohan Roy.

Set P

Rearrange the following six sentences (A), (B),(C),(D),(E) and (F) in the proper sequence to form a meaningful paragraph; then answers the questions given below them

A)Women outside their home after dusk, or at about any activity other than the domestic chores that gives them social legitimacy — anything that indulges sensual pleasure, such as eating out or watching a film, leave alone something as laden with promiscuous potential as dancing or partying — are considered by many to be less than chaste, and, therefore, fair game for sexual predation.

B)Nirbhaya was neither the first nor the last woman to be brutally assaulted. But the sheer savagery of the assault triggered unprecedented outrage. But mere outrage will not secure women.

C)Much of the focus on this count has been on the physical solutions: helpline numbers to summon emergency teams, better police patrolling and even self-defence lessons for women.

D) These do not address the root problem that lies in social values that subjugate women and their sexuality. Women are deemed virtuous depending on their location in time and space, apart from social class, and how they dress

E)The Supreme Court's Nirbhaya verdict, upholding death for the four accused in jail — one committed suicide and the sixth, a juvenile, was sentenced in 2013 to a three-year term in a juvenile home — will not settle with finality any of the questions that racked society's conscience in the wake of the brutal assault on a young woman on December 16, 2012.

F)These relate to the validity of capital punishment in a humane society, the right punishment for the heinous crime of rape and women's uncertain security in the country.

1. Which of the following sentences should be the SECOND sentence after rearrangement?

a) F
b) E
c) D
d) A
e) B

2. Which of the following sentences should be the FIFTH after rearrangement?

a) B
b) A
c) C
d) F
e) D

3. Which of the following sentences should be the SIXTH(LAST) after rearrangement?

a) E
b) C
c) F
d) A
e) B

4. Which of the following sentences should be the FOURTH after rearrangement?

a) A
b) D

c) C
d) E
e) B

5. Which of the following sentences should be the FIRST after rearrangement?
a) B
b) E
c) D
d) A
e) C

Directions: Read each sentence to find out whether there is any grammatical error in it. The error, if any, Will be in one part of the sentence. If there is no error. Mark (E) i.e. no error as the answer. (Ignore errors of punctuation, if any).

6. It is possible for the government to fund and catalyse the needed R&D (a)/ by contracting in research on the lines of the Defence Advanced Research Projects Agency (b)/, which identifies product and technology requirements (c) / and bids out R&D contracts (d) / NO ERROR (e)

7. So retirement is often an illusion: (a) / it does not materialize in the freedom and happiness one imagined (b) /, and it is dangerous because if you avoid any real challenge (c) / it will leads to a rapid decline in your mental ability for the rest of your life (d) /NO ERROR (e).

8. The success of this latest salvo against bad loans (a) / will depend on the fine print on how the ultimate decision (b) /— whether to take a haircut on a loan and (c) / restructure it or invoke bankruptcy clauses — is arrived at (d) ./ NO ERROR. (e)

9. India has no doubt gained goodwill across the subcontinent through the gesture, (a) /and the moment was neatly captured by the videoconference that followed the launch, showing all SAARC leaders (with the exception of Pakistan's) (b) /together on one screen as they spoke of the benefits they would receive in communication, telemedicine, meteorological forecasting and broadcasting.(c) /The message is equal strong to South Asia's other

benefactor, China, at a time when it is preparing to demonstrate its global clout at the Belt and Road Forum on May 14-15 (d) / NO ERROR (e)

10. There was widespread discontent among voters, particularly among the youth, (a)/with the mainstream political elite; the economy (b) / has been struggling for years; joblessness is high;(c) / there is deepening insecurity among the citizens in general in the wake of multiples terror attacks. (d) / NO ERROR. (e)

Answers:
1) a)F

2) e)D

3) d) A

4) c)C

5) b) E the correct arrangement is : " EFBCDA:

6) (B) ERROR : " CONTRACTING IN " ; RIGHT USAGE : " CONTRACTING OUT "
"CONTRACTING OUT " : to agree by contract to pay someone outside an organization to perform (a job) EXAMPLE : The company contracted out its manufacturing jobs.

7) (C) ERROR : "LEADS " RIGHT USAGE : " LEAD"

8) (E) NO ERROR

9) (D) ERROR : "EQUAL " RIGHT USAGE : "EQUALLY "

10) (D)ERROR : " MULTIPLES RIGHT USAGE : "MULTIPLE"

Set Q

A. It is not the first such order, an Uttar Pradesh MLA, Umlesh Yadav, was disqualified in 2011 on the same ground, of suppressing expenditure incurred in the publication of paid news.

B. In a typical inquiry into the paid news phenomenon, the newspaper or publication concerned denies that it was paid for publishing the material and insists that it was part of its normal election coverage.

C. However, the EC did not buy his arguments, mainly because it was difficult to believe that he had not seen reports that appeared in his Datia constituency

D. The candidate denies authorising the publication and takes the plea that he or she could not possibly account for something that was not paid for. Mr. Mishra was no exception.

E. The Election Commission's order disqualifying Madhya Pradesh Minister Narottam Mishra for three years is an important step in curbing 'paid news' in the electoral arena.

F. during the campaign for the 2008 Assembly elections, often with his picture and the Bharatiya Janata Party's symbol.

G. The EC has called paid news, a term that refers to propaganda in favour of a candidate masquerading as news reports or articles, a "grave electoral malpractice" on the part of candidates to circumvent expenditure limits.

H. He, in fact, argued that his rivals could be behind the 42 reports that the EC's National Level Committee on Paid News found to be nothing but election advertisements, without any disclaimer.

1. Which of the following should be the seventh sentence after rearrangement?
I. B
II. D
III. C
IV. H
V. A

2. Which of the following should be the fourth sentence after rearrangement?
I. F
II. C
III. E
IV. B
V. G

3. Which of the following should be the sixth sentence after rearrangement?
I. H
II. C
III. D
IV. B
V. A

4. Which of the following should be the second sentence after rearrangement?
I. G
II. A
III. C
IV. F
V. H

5. Which of the following should be the last sentence after rearrangement?
I. D
II. E
III. F
IV. H
V. A

6. Which of the following should be the first sentence after rearrangement?
I. G
II. D
III. H
IV. A
V. E

7. Which of the following should be the fifth sentence after rearrangement?
I. D
II. C
III. A
IV. B
V. F
Explanation:
Correct Rearrangement: E, A, G, B, D, H, C, F

First of all when we solve a parajumble we need to go through all of the given sentences once and when we have done it we can easily find that sentence (1st sentence) in which the main theme has given of the passage in this paragraph we have two sentences that can be our 1st sentence (E or G) but sentence E has the full form of EC so it should be our first sentence.

In sentence E it has given that EC has passed an order to disqualify MP's Minister Narottam Mishra and in sentence A it has given that it is the first order so it can be our second sentence easily.

Now in sentence G we have what EC has called paid news so it can be our next sentence (3rd sentence)

Now we should find those sentences that can be a pair and we can find two pairs easily in this paragraph (D and H), (C and F). In our first pair we have Mr. Mishra a noun in sentence D and in sentence H we have a pronoun he so it can be a pair easily. In our second pair we have a word however that is mostly use in a conclusion sentence and in sentence F we have the other part of sentence C so it should be our last pair.

Now we have remained only one sentence (B) and one single place for this sentence place 4th so it can be our 4th sentence.

Set R

Directions(1-7): Arrange the following sentences to make a coherent paragraph.

A. The tri-junction stretch of the boundary at Sikkim, though contested, has witnessed far fewer tensions than the western sector of the India-China boundary even as India and Bhutan have carried on separate negotiations with China.

B. That the PLA decided to undertake the action just as the year's first group of pilgrims was reaching Nathu La cannot be a coincidence.

C. The warmth that officials reported at the meeting was obviously misleading,
D. In fact, during Chinese President Xi Jinping's visit in 2014, the stretch was opened as an alternative route to Kailash Mansarovar for Indian pilgrims as a confidence-building measure.
E. Moreover, it came only days after Prime Minister Narendra Modi's bilateral meeting with President Xi in Kazakhstan.
F. The boundary stand-off with china at the Doka La tri-junction with Bhutan is by all accounts unprecedented; it demands calmer counsel on all sides.
G. and it is important for India and China to accept that relations have deteriorated steadily since Mr. Xi's 2014 visit.
H. Its action of sending People's Liberation Army construction teams with earth moving equipment to forcibly build a road upsets a carefully preserved peace.

1. Which of the following should be the fifth sentence after rearrangement?
i. B
ii. D
iii. F
iv. A
v. C

2. Which of the following should be the first sentence after rearrangement?
i. B
ii. F
iii. C
iv. A
v. E

3. Which of the following should be the sixth sentence after rearrangement?
i. B
ii. C
iii. E
iv. G
v. F

4. Which of the following should be the fourth sentence after rearrangement?

i. H
ii. F
iii. E
iv. D
v. G

5. Which of the following should be the third sentence after rearrangement?

i. B
ii. D
iii. H
iv. G
v. C

6. Which of the following should be the last sentence after rearrangement?

i. A
ii. G
iii. B
iv. F
v. E

7. Which of the following should be the second sentence after rearrangement?

i. C
ii. A
iii. F
iv. B
v. E

Explanation:

(F, A, H, D, B, E, C, G)

As we all know that first of all we will go through all of these sentences for getting our first sentence and understand the basic meaning of passage and when we read all of these sentences we understand that there are only two sentences (F and A) which can be our first sentence but when we read sentence F we see that in this sentence the passage is something about the boundary of China so it can be our basic sentence.

Now we will find out some pairs of the passage to arrange it easily, when we read sentence A and sentence H we can see that we have an pronoun it which refers China so it should be our first pair and now we have only a single sentence that is incomplete and it is sentence C and we have only one sentence which can be the other part of this sentence and it is sentence Gnow when we read sentence D it says that the stretch was opened as an alternative route to Kailash Mansarovar and when we understand this sentence we can clearly say that another part of this sentence should be sentence B because in this sentence PLA decided the action about the Pilgrim and after this sentence we have only one sentence remaining that is sentence E so it should be our next sentence.

Now we have found three pairs for the passage and these pairs are(A-H),(D-B-E) and (C-G).

Directions(8--14): Arrange the following sentences to make a coherent paragraph.

A. It is not the first such order, an Uttar Pradesh MLA, Umlesh Yadav, was disqualified in 2011 on the same ground, of suppressing expenditure incurred in the publication of paid news.

B. In a typical inquiry into the paid news phenomenon, the newspaper or publication concerned denies that it was paid for publishing the material and insists that it was part of its normal election coverage.

C. However, the EC did not buy his arguments, mainly because it was difficult to believe that he had not seen reports that appeared in his Datia constituency

D. The candidate denies authorising the publication and takes the plea that he or she could not possibly account for something that was not paid for. Mr. Mishra was no exception.

E. The Election Commission's order disqualifying Madhya Pradesh Minister Narottam Mishra for three years is an important step in curbing 'paid news' in the electoral arena.

F. during the campaign for the 2008 Assembly elections, often with his picture and the Bharatiya Janata Party's symbol.

G. The EC has called paid news, a term that refers to propaganda in favour of a candidate masquerading as news reports or articles, a "grave electoral malpractice" on the part of candidates to circumvent expenditure limits.

H. He, in fact, argued that his rivals could be behind the 42 reports that the EC's National Level Committee on Paid News found to be nothing but election advertisements, without any disclaimer.

8. Which of the following should be the seventh sentence after rearrangement?
I. B
II. D
III. C
IV. H
V. A

9. Which of the following should be the fourth sentence after rearrangement?
I. F
II. C
III. E
IV. B
V. G

10. Which of the following should be the sixth sentence after rearrangement?
I. H
II. C
III. D
IV. B
V. A

11. Which of the following should be the second sentence after rearrangement?
I. G
II. A
III. C
IV. F
V. H

12. Which of the following should be the last sentence after rearrangement?
I. D
II. E
III. F
IV. H
V. A

13. Which of the following should be the first sentence after rearrangement?

I. G
II. D
III. H
IV. A
V. E

14. Which of the following should be the fifth sentence after rearrangement?
I. D
II. C
III. A
IV. B
V. F

Explanation
(E, A, G, B, D, H, C, F)
First of all when we solve a parajumble we need to go through all of the given sentences once and when we have done it we can easily find that sentence (1st sentence) in which the main theme has given of the passage in this paragraph we have two sentences that can be our 1st sentence (E or G) but sentence E has the full form of EC so it should be our first sentence.
In sentence E it has given that EC has passed an order to disqualify MP's Minister Narottam Mishra and in sentence A it has given that it is the first order so it can be our second sentence easily.
Now in sentence G we have what EC has called paid news so it can be our next sentence (3rd sentence)
Now we should find those sentences that can be a pair and we can find two pairs easily in this paragraph (D and H), (C and F). In our first pair, we have Mr. Mishra a noun in sentence D and in sentence H we have a pronoun he so it can be a pair easily. In our second pair, we have a word however that is mostly used in a conclusion sentence and in sentence F we have the other part of sentence C so it should be our last pair.
Now we are left with only one sentence (B) and one single place for this sentence place 4th so it can be our 4th sentence.

Set S

Rearrange the following six sentences (A), (B), (C), (D), (E) and (F) in the proper sequence to form a meaningful paragraph and then answer the questions given below:

(A) The group desired to enhance the learning experience in schools with an interactive digital medium that can be used within and outside the classrooms.
(B) Then the teacher can act on the downloaded data rather than collect it from each and every student and thereby save his time and effort.
(C) Edutor, decided by the group of engineers, all alumni of the Indian Institute of Technology, when they founded Edutor Technologies in August, 2009.
(D) They can even take tests and submit them digitally using the same tablets and teachers in turn can download the tests using the company's cloud services.
(E) With this desire they created a solution that digitalises the school text books and other learning material so that students no longer need to carry as many books to school and back as before, but can access their study material on their touch screen tablets.
(F) A mechanic works on motors and accountant has his computer. Likewise, if a student has to work on a machine of device, what should it be called?

1) Which of the following sentence should be the FIRST after rearrangement?

a) F   b) D
c) A
d) C   e) E

2) Which of the following sentence should be the THIRD after rearrangement?

a) A   b) B
c) D
d) E   e) F

3) Which of the following sentence should be the SIXTH (LAST) after rearrangement?

a) A   b) F
c) E
d) B   e) D

4) Which of the following sentence should be the FOURTH after rearrangement?

a) A   b) F   c) E
d) B   e) C

5) Which of the following sentence should be the FIFTH after rearrangement?

a) A   b) D   c) C
d) E   e) F

SOLUTION
1) a) - F

2) a) - A

3) d) - B

4) c) - E

5) b) - D

Explanation
Now lets see how to solve this question.

First, read all the sentences and find out the independent sentences. Look at the Sentence (A), it talks about some group, but the question arises which group they are talking about. So this means A will not be the first sentence.

Come to sentence (B), it starts with 'then'. Then is generally used as next in order of time or place. It means there must be some sentence before Sentence (B).

Sentence (C) is talking about Edutor, decided by a group of engineers. This will also be not the first sentence as we do not know about which thing engineers have taken a decision.

Sentence (D) starts with 'They'. Now it's obvious, that we will think about whom they are talking about. So, this will also not be the first sentence.

Look at Sentence (E) - 'With this desire'. Again the question arises which desire. So leave this sentence also as this will also not be the first sentence.

Now, the only option left is the Sentence (F). So this will be the first sentence.

As we came to know about the first sentence, start making pairs of qualifier and qualified sentences.

In the first sentence (F), it is talking about some device and what should it be called? Now observe Sentence (C). In this, a group of engineers has decided the name of the device, Edutor. So, here Sentence (C) is qualifier of Sentence (F).

Now observe Sentence (A). It clarifies about the desire mentioned in Sentence (E). So, here Sentence (E) is qualifier of Sentence (A).

Now only two sentences have left, Sentence (D) and Sentence (B). In sentence (E), it is mentioned about the students and in Sentence (D), they are being used for students who can take tests and submit them digitally. So, Sentence (D) is qualifier of Sentence (E).

As only one option left now, i.e. Sentence (B) is the last sentence of the sequence.

Here is the correct sequence of the sentences:

(F) A mechanic works on motors and accountant has his computer. Likewise, if a student has to work on a machine of device, what should it be called?

(C) Edutor, decided by the group of engineers, all alumni of the Indian Institute of Technology, when they founded Edutor Technologies in August, 2009.

(A) The group desired to enhance the learning experience in schools with an interactive digital medium that can be used within and outside the classrooms.

(E) With this desire they created a solution that digitalises the school text books and other learning material so that students no longer need to carry as many books to school and back as before, but can access their study material on their touch screen tablets.

(D) They can even take tests and submit them digitally using the same tablets and teachers in turn can download the tests using the company's cloud services.

B) Then the teacher can act on the downloaded data rather than collect it from each and every student and thereby save his time and effort.

Though explanation of the solution seems to be long and complicated, but you will find it easy with constant practice. So keep practicing.

Set T

Directions: In the following exercise, the first and last sentence of a paragraph is given as S1 and S6. The remaining sentences of the paragraph are jumbled in various parts, i.e. P, Q, R and S. Rearrange these four parts into a logical order to make a coherent paragraph.

1.

S1: The genesis of service tax emanates from the ongoing structural transformation of the Indian economy.

P: Leading to a steady deterioration in tax-GDP ratio

Q: Despite the growing presence of the services sector in the Indian economy,

R: It remained out of the tax net prior to 1994-95

S: Whereby presently more than one-half of GDP originates from the services sector.

S6: The service tax was introduced in 1994-95 on a select category of services at a low rate of five percent.

a. PRRS

b. SQRP

c. QPSR

d. SQPR

2.

S1: Recently Grameen has taken on a different challenge by setting up operations in the US.

P: Globally, the working microfinance equation consists of borrowing funds cheaply

Q: Money may be tight in the waning recession.

R: And keeping loan defaults and overhead expenses sufficiently low

S: But it is still a nation of 1,00,000 bank branches

S6: Microlenders, including Grameen, do this by charging colossal interest rates – as high as 60% or 70%

a. QSPR

b. RPSQ

c. RQQS

d. PQRS

3.

S1: E-books and e-publishing both has their obvious advantages.

P:. So far with a lot of publishers already showing interest in e-publishing

Q: Also, with the country being the third biggest publisher after the US and UK.

R: Though authors in India have only just begun to realize the immense benefits of digital technology in this field.

S: The potential in this field is immense and the response too has been quite encouraging

S6: E-publishing is a boon for both established and wanna be writers as it is cost effective and cuts down the time.

a. RPSQ

b. QRPS

c. RQPS

d. RQSP

4.

S1: In your home, modern box attached to your computer will look you into wealth of goods and services.

P: People in developed countries like U.S. and Canada have already started using On Line Shopping

Q: As a routine mode of their purchasing goods and services

R:.Not only does it allow you to talk to your friends on the other side of the world.

S: But also allows you to watch a movie, buy airline tickets, pay bills and even get cash.

S6: Internet shoppers still believe that there is no secure and convenient way of paying on the Internet. Consumers are concerned with two main security fears.

a. RSQP

b. SQPR

c. RSPQ

d. PQSR

5.

S1: Arrogant managers can over-evaluate their current performance and competitive position, listen poorly

P: Bureaucratic cultures can smother

Q: That present threats and opportunitiesR: Those who want to respond to shifting conditions.

S: Inwardly focused employees can have difficulty seeing the very forces

S6: The lack of leadership leaves no force inside these organisations to break out of the morass.

a. SQPR

b. SQRP

c. QRSP

d. PQSR

Answers

1. b

2. a

3. d

4. c

5. a

Set U

Directions: In the following exercise, the first and last sentence of a paragraph is given as S1 and S6. The remaining sentences of the paragraph are jumbled in various parts,

i.e. P, Q, R and S. Rearrange these four parts into a logical order to make a coherent paragraph.

1.

S1: In nearly all human populations a majority of individuals can taste the artificially synthesized chemical phenylthiocarbonide (PTC).
P: This polymorphism is observed in non-human primates as well indicates a long evolutionary history which, although obviously not acting on PTC, might reflect evolutionary selection for taste discrimination of other.
Q: More significant bitter substances, such as certain toxic plants.
R: A somewhat more puzzling human polymorphism is the genetic variability in earwax, or cerumen, which is observed in two varieties
S: However, the percentage varies dramatically-- from as low as 60% in India to as high as 95% in Africa.
S6: Among European populations 90% of individuals have a sticky yellow variety rather than a dry, gray one, whereas in northern China these numbers are approximately the reverse.

a. QRPS
b. PSRQ
c. SPQR
d. PQSR

2.

S1: "Reform" in America has been sterile because it can imagine no change except through the extension of this metaphor of a race, wider inclusion of competitors.
P: "A piece of the action," as it were, for the disenfranchised.
Q: America seems not to honor the quiet work that achieves social interdependence and stability
R: There is no attempt to call off the race.
S: Since our only stability is change.
S6: There is, in our legends, no heroism of the office clerk, no stable industrial work force of the people who actually make the system work.

a. PRSQ   b. PRQS   c. RSQP   d. RPSQ

3.

S1. Perhaps the least controversial assertion about the pterosaurs is that they were reptiles.

P: The anatomy of their wings suggests that they did not evolve into the class of birds.
Q: In pterosaurs a greatly elongated fourth finger of each forelimb supported a wing-like membrane
R: Their skulls, pelvises, and hind feet are reptilian.
S: The other fingers were short and reptilian, with sharp claws.
S6: In birds the second finger is the principal strut of the wing, which consists primarily of feathers.

a. QSPR   b. RSPQ   c. RPQS   d. PQRS

4.

S1: In the eighteenth century, Japan's feudal overlords, from the shogun to the humblest samurai, found themselves under financial stress.
P: Commercial efficiency, in turn, had put temptations in the way of buyers
Q: In part, this stress can be attributed to the overlords' failure to adjust to a rapidly expanding economy.
R: Concentration of the samurai in castle-towns had acted as a stimulus to trade.
S: But the stress was also due to factors beyond the overlords' control
S6: Since most samurai had been reduced to idleness by years of peace, encouraged to engage in scholarship and martial exercises or to perform administrative tasks that took little time, it is not surprising that their tastes and habits grew expensive.

a. RPQS   b. QRPS   c. PRSQ   d. QSRP

5.

S1: Most economists in the United States seem captivated by the spell of the free market.
P: In fact, price-fixing is normal in all industrialized societies because the industrial system itself provides, as an effortless consequence of its own development, the price-fixing that it requires.
Q: A price that is determined by the seller or, for that matter, established by anyone other than the aggregate of consumers seems pernicious.

R: Accordingly, it requires a major act of will to think of price-fixing (the determination of prices by the seller) as both "normal" and having a valuable economic function.

S: Consequently, nothing seems good or normal that does not accord with the requirements of the free market

S6: Modern industrial planning requires and rewards great size. Hence, a comparatively small number of large firms will be competing for the same group of consumers.

a. QSRP   b. SQRP   c. PRSQ
d. PQSR

Answers
1. c. SPQR   2. a. PRSQ
3. c. RPQS   4. d. QSRP   5. b. SQRP

Set V

Directions: In each of the following questions, four sentences are given Between the sentences numbered 1 and 6. You are required to arrange the four sentences so that all six together make a logical paragraph

Question 1:
1)The government is considering a proposal to free up foreign direct investment (FDI) policy on retail but only for domestically manufactured goods.
A)Overseas-owned online retailers can only function as marketplaces, or platforms for buyers and vendors, and aren't to sell goods on their own account through an inventory model.
B)The policy under consideration applies tom both offline and online retail and would remove restrictions on companies such as Walmart, India, programme, MakprogrammeTesco Amazon and others when it comes to the sale of things produced in the country.
C)" It has been proposed that FDI restrictions in retail be lifted to the extent of goods manufactuIndia," he said. "The matter will be deliberated by the government in the near future ."

D)Apart from attracting investment in retail, such a policy would also give a big bMac programme, a senior official told.
6)Multi-brand retailers such as Walmart can only own up to 51% of Indian ventures and are subject to other constraints as well.

a)DCBA   b)BCDA
c)BDCA   d)DCAB

Question 2:
1)The current policy allows domestic manufacturers to sell just their own goods through any channel online or offline.
A)Only in the case of food products can locally processed items be sold by anyone through any mode, a policy change made in August last year to give a boost to food processing.
B)They say confining such stores to food product doesn't make business sense.
C)Retailers have been lobbying for similar exceptions to be made for grocery and personal care items as well.
D)Finance minister Arun Jaitley said in his February 1 budget speech that the government is considering further liberalising the FDI policy.More than 90% of FDI is currently through the automatic approval route.
6)Amazon recently submitted a proposal to the government for setting up bricks and mortar stores to sell locally made food products alongside its online platform in India.

a)ACBD   b)CABD
c)DACB   d)BDAC

Question 3:
1)The Reserve Bank of India (RBI) has opposed a pact between the Tata group and NTT Docomo aimed at resolving a two-year-old dispute between the two over the enforcement of a $ 17 billion arbitral award by an international court to the Japanese company.
A)Arguing it amounted to transfer of shares and was hence illegal, dealing a setback to the efforts of the two companies to resolve the dispute which has clouded Indo-Japanese ties.

B)Justice S Murlidhar wanted to know if RBI could oppose the award's enforcement when both parties had agreed to settle and the Tata group was willing to make the payment.

C)During a hearing on Wednesday in the Delhi high court, RBI opposed payment to Docomo that would have followed enforcement of the award,

D)The Indian side has already deposited the amount with the court, which will hear the matter on March 14.

6)"Does the implementation of this award as it reads require a special permission of the RBI"?Justice Muralidhar asked, adding that the ongoing case had international implications.

a)DCBA   b)CABD
c)ADCB   d)BCDA

Direction: select the most appropriate option, out of the five options given, which, in your view, should be grammatically and structurally correct.

Question 4:
a) He said since objections to the enforceability of the award had been withdrawn, it won't be a precedent "as I have not adjudicated on the correctness of the tribunal's ruling".

b)The RBI was also concerned that the Japanese company may pursue enforcement of the award in the US and the UK after six months if it doesn't succeed in India.

c)A new wave of small Japanese investors is scouting in India for early –stage startups they can beat their money on, undeterred by a bearish spell that threatens to upset Tokyo-based Softbank's biggest wagers in the country.

d)This fresh run of capital likely signal a return of confidence in India's startup's ecosystem despite a recent battering of some well-known consumer internet companies, although not without a healthy dose of caution.

e)Unlike SoftBank that invested hundreds of million of dollars in potential blockbusters such as the now struggling Snapdeal, the new investors from Japan are cherry-picking small start-ups with niche technology that can be exported to other Asian markets.

Question 5:
a)Axis bank is withdrawing credit limits it had sanctioned to several merchants at online marketplace Snapdeal.

b)It is among the first few lenders to ringing the bell of alarm over dwindling sales for many retailers on the e-commerce platform, which is struggling to raise fresh capital even as Amazon and Flipkart in one of the World's fastest growing markets for digital commerce.

c)The bank has sent notices to merchants seeking immediate repayment of outstanding loans while informing them of the withdrawal of unavailed credit.

d)In a big step to pump money into rural India and step up infrastructure creation, the government will release half of the Rs. 48000-crore FY2017-18 allocation for the Mahatma Gandhi National Rural Employment Guarantee scheme of states this April.

e)The high premium that English players commanded in the transfer market represents a serious obstacle to Manchester City's plans to fill the team with domestic talent.

Answers

1. C)BDCA   2. A)ACBD
3. b)CABD   4. A
Explanation
b) error: "at" use " in "
c) error:"beat" correct: " bet"
d) error:"signal" correct: "signals"
e) error:"million" replace by "millions"
5. "c"
Explanation
a) error:"at" replace it by "on"
b) error:"ringing" correct: "ring"
d) error: "of" replace by "to"
e) error: "commanded" correct-"command"

Grammar Rules

Set 1

1. Food prices have been … steadily for at least ten years.
a) rising
b) lifting
c) raising
2. I'll have to study hard, … I can pass the exam.
a) so that
b) such
c) in order
3. You … to eat if you are not hungry.
a) needn't
b) haven't
c) don't have
4. We'll dance and … we'll have lunch.
a) straight away
b) so
c) then
5. She has to go to Germany for the next … of the training.
a) step
b) stage
c) point
6. When the meeting had finished, we went … the plan once again.
a) up
b) down
c) over
7. I locked the animals in the cage to … them from getting away.
a) avoid
b) hinder
c) prevent
8. You're … your time trying to persuade her.
a) wasting
b) losing
c) missing

9. Our last cook was better than our … one.
a) latter
b) instant
c) current
10. I am grateful to Mary for being so patient … us.
a) for
b) with
c) at
11. Have you exchanged that lovely car … this?
a) with
b) by
c) for
12. The weather was … the poor harvest.
a) condemned for
b) found fault with for
c) blamed for
13. Olivia is teaching three classes and she is examining at a literature exam tomorrow. …, she is chairing a meeting at the Bright Owl Club.
a) On top of it
b) At top
c) On the top of it
14. I don't see any … in arriving early at the show.
a) cause
b) point
c) reason
15. Your application for a vise was turned … by the consulate.
a) aside
b) over
c) down
16. Shopping malls account for 70 percent of the retail business in this country because they are controlled environments which … concerns about the weather.
a) justify
b) foster
c) eliminate

17. It is … impossible to tell the twins apart.
a) virtually
b) closely
c) extremely
18. The man claimed that he was the … heir to the throne.
a) due
b) correct

c) rightful

19. The rather humid climate in no way … from the beauty of these places.
a) protracts
b) detracts
c) attracts

20. … no need to buy traveller's cheques.
a) It's
b) It has
c) There's

21. Is there … bread for all the sandwiches?
a) enough
b) plenty
c) equal

22. Teaching is not a/an … which pays very well.
a) work
b) post
c) occupation

23. This letter didn't come through the post. It was delivered personally, …
hand.
a) from
b) by
c) with

24. I … do that if I were you.
a) shan't
b) won't
c) wouldn't

25. There was nothing to … her with the burglary until the police found two
gold ring in her car.

a) link
b) place
c) join

26. The manufacturers are advertising a new … of perfume.
a) mark
b) pack
c) brand

27. … my stay in hospital, I lost three kilos.
a) During
b) On
c) In

28. I'm sorry to hear that they have … . They were good friends.
a) dropped out

b) fallen out
c) dropped against

29. Shall I use this … to fry the eggs?
a) dish
b) tin
c) pan

30. She … being given a receipt for the bill she had paid.
a) insisted on
b) demanded
c) asked to

31. These cars historically had two doors but the latest … has four.
a) brand
b) mark
c) model

32. That girl is far ahead … everyone else in the class.
a) of
b) with
c) from

33. She is also interested … art.
a) with
b) in
c) about

34. It's impossible to prevent the boys from quarreling … each other.
a) for
b) with
c) by

35. I'm thinking … looking for a new job in another city.
a) on
b) at
c) of

36. Steve prefers football … tennis.
a) to
b) over
c) than

37. The experience in a psychiatric ward … for the rest of his life.
a) had an influence on him
b) had influence on him
c) had an influence at him

38. If I had known the way to her house, I … her last Monday afternoon.

a) have been visiting
b) had been visiting
c) would have visited
39. He ... that he had been involved in the decision.
a) refused
b) declined
c) denied
40. As brown as ... . This phrase means having a tanned skin after
sunbathing.
a) dust
b) a berry
c) chocolate
41. It's an awful ... your friend couldn't come.
a) shame
b) sorrow
c) shock
42. There is a problem at our TV station. Please do not ... your set.
a) repair

b) change
c) adjust
43. Be careful! The cat may ... you.
a) kick
b) scratch
c) tear
44. They agreed to ... the question of payment.
a) discuss
b) control
c) increase
45. Owing to the bad weather, the garden party was
... .
a) shouted off
b) spoken against
c) called off
46. I am sorry I opened your bag but I ... it for mine.
a) confused
b) imagined
c) mistook
47. The ... of these volunteers for hard work is
remarkable.
a) ability
b) efficiency
c) capacity
48. I like this country, but I wish it ... rain quite so
much.

a) won't
b) didn't
c) hasn't
49. She was so tired that she ... asleep in the chair.
a) fell
b) went
c) became
50. Mike has just taken an examination ...
chemistry.
a) on
b) in
c) for

51. They shouldn't have ... the incident. It wasn't
my fault.
a) accused me of
b) blamed me for
c) blamed me
52. They won't lend you the money without some ...
that you will pay it
back.
a) profit
b) charge
c) guarantee
53. When you come tomorrow why not ... your
brother with you?
a) carry
b) bring
c) fetch
54. After she had broken her leg, Marry could only
go up and down stairs
... .
a) with difficulty
b) in difficulties
c) hardly
55. Who does this laptop belong ... ?
a) for
b) with
c) to
56. All her handbags ... of leather.
a) being made
b) are made
c) had been made
57. John is the perfect person to take on this difficult
job. He's a really hard-
... person and won't stand for any nonsense.
a) ship

b) nosed

c) bargain

58. What does a sabbatical year mean?

a) a miserable year

b) a year in which previously made plans are bound to

c) a year in which one is released from one's normal duties

59. It always … me as odd that she should go to work so late in the day.

a) hit

b) smacked

c) struck

60. I walked away as calmly as I could … they thought I was the thief.

a) in case

b) or else

c) to avoid

61. If it's raining tomorrow, we shall have to … the match till Sunday.

a) cancel

b) put off

c) put away

62. Call in and see our … of spring fashions today.

a) reputation

b) election

c) selection

63. We have no … in our files of your recent letters to the company.

a) record

b) account

c) list

64. When her aunt dies, she … a lot of money.

a) earned

b) inherited

c) paid

65. Give him a telephone number to ring … he gets lost.

a) whether

b) unless

c) in case

66. Her parents never allowed her … .

a) smoking

b) a smoking

c) to smoke

67. Bill is only interested … making money.

a) in

b) about

c) on

68. The boy was very upset by the … of his English examination.

a) failure

b) result

c) effect

69. Their actions caused the rate of inflation to … sharply.

a) lift

b) raise

c) rise

70. They were good friends. I was surprised when they … .

a) fell out

b) fell off

c) fell down

71. I had to leave early … I didn't feel very well.

a) too

b) because

c) also

72. After closing the envelope, the assistant manager … the stamps on firmly.

a) licked

b) stuck

c) struck

73. Don't be so sure … yourself! You might be wrong.

a) on

b) from

c) of

74. This book will prove useful … you.

a) for

b) to

c) on

75. You should not be so sensitive … criticism.

a) to

b) at

c) on

76. I am not familiar … his novels.

a) with

b) about

c) for

77. You should study the college … for full
particulars of enrolment.
a) prospect
b) syllabus
c) prospectus

78. A novel is a form of … which may include many
facts.
a) short story
b) legend
c) fiction

79. The relationship that matters most in the life of a
… is the one between
him and his constituency party, they say.
a) judge
b) politician
c) captain

80. The case of the missing millionaire has become
the … of considerable
interest in the press.
a) focus
b) middle
c) target

81. These people are thought … less friendly than
people from our country.
a) been
b) being
c) to be

82. Would you give this report to Mr. Smith? Sorry,
I can't. He doesn't … .
a) any more work here
b) work any more here
c) work here any longer

83. After hitting her arm, she had a large black … .
a) bruise
b) cut
c) swelling

84. This is not the right … to ask for my help; I am
away on business.
a) situation
b) moment
c) opportunity

85. I hadn't seen him for years, but when I saw him
in the street, I … him at
once.
a) reminded
b) realized

c) remembered

86. The dog was so frightened that it ran … the bed
to hide.
a) along
b) beside
c) under

87. John was unable to … my party as he was ill.
a) visit
b) attend
c) be present

88. Jane bought red shoes to … her red dress.
a) match
b) pair
c) mate

89. We'll have to … the meeting until next month.
a) put down
b) put off
c) put round

90. I am not sure … the black coat is.
a) whom
b) who
c) whose

91. I don't think he'll beat the opponent. He's out of
… .
a) fitness
b) practice
c) play

92. She is a very … person, but she has no sense of
humour.
a) pleasant

b) amusing
c) enjoyable

93. The university arranges a … to Madrid every
year.
a) travel
b) rout
c) trip

94. Beware … these people.
a) from
b) of
c) at

95. If you fail … this attempt, don't count on me for
help.
a) on
b) at
c) in

96. I separated them … each other because they were fighting.
a) of
b) from
c) against
97. I have to leave before six and so … .
a) do you
b) leave you
c) you do
98. There were no lifeboats on the little ship because it was … to be
unsinkable.
a) claimed
b) told
c) believed
99. This church was … by a famous architect.
a) outlined
b) designed
c) produced
100. Mary is plain, but her sister is very … .
a) attractive
b) complex
c) sympathetic

101. Her boyfriend treated her badly. I'm surprised she … it for so long.
a) put off
b) put through
c) put up with
102. The manager … me to open a deposit account.
a) warned
b) approved
c) advised
103. This organization tries to send food to countries where people are
suffering … malnutrition.
a) from
b) for
c) by
104. If they are to understand the notice, the instructions must be … clearer.
a) wrote
b) made
c) done
105. … you like what I want to do or not, you won't make me change my
mind regarding this situation.
a) If
b) When
c) Whether
106. Doctors usually have to study for at least eight years before becoming
fully … .
a) tested
b) proved
c) qualified
107. The weather was pleasant with … a gentle wind to cool us down.
a) just
b) almost
c) nearly
108. I wish you wouldn't … your clothes all over the room.
a) sprawl
b) scatter
c) straggle

109. … she had no money for a bus, Olive had to walk all the way home.
a) As
b) For
c) Thus
110. I didn't want to make up my mind until I had heard her … of the story.
a) angle
b) edge
c) side
111. It's strange that Jane is as … as her mother is beautiful.
a) dull
b) plain
c) raw
112. Since the accident he has been walking with a … .
a) slope
b) lame
c) limp
113. I flew to the island, then … a car for five days and visited most places.
a) charged
b) bought
c) hired
114. In Russia, surgeons have given a man a/an … heart.

a) artificial

b) unreal

c) false

115. The examiners had to … most of the candidates.

a) fire

b) fail

c) fall

116. Our company made a record … last year.

a) benefit

b) wage

c) profit

117. They must economize … fuel.

a) on

b) in

c) with

118. When I understood what she was saying, everything … .

a) fell into the place

b) fell into place

c) fell off the place

119. I had to give a full … of my car when I reported it stolen.

a) detail

b) account

c) description

120. His version of the facts doesn't … with the version I heard from Jane.

a) accord

b) argue

c) amount

121. They have … to accommodate us and the children too.

a) such a small house

b) too small a house

c) a too small house

122. After they had … the carpet, the employees went back to the office.

a) laid

b) lain

c) lied

123. It will … be Christmas again.

a) fast

b) next

c) soon

124. Be careful not to … your coffee on this rug.

a) drip

b) spill

c) filter

125. Mary had to leave her family … when she went abroad to work.

a) at all costs

b) out

c) behind

126. Metal … at high temperatures.

a) grows

b) expands

c) enlarges

127. Because of the poor harvest, cereals prices have … in the last three months.

a) gone up

b) jumped up

c) sprung up

128. I'm … worried about Mary; she always seems to be exhausted.

a) as

b) such

c) so

129. I have difficulty … without glasses.

a) read

b) of reading

c) in reading

130. He arrived rather late. The party was already … .

a) in full swing

b) at full tilt

c) in full bloom

131. My neighbour plays his records … in his flat at night and nobody can get enough sleep.

a) at full tilt

b) at full blast

c) in full cry

132. It's unwise to … in a quarrel between husbands.

a) involve

b) poke

c) interfere

133. I will … the project with other members and see what they think about it.

a) discuss
b) talk
c) explain

134. The poor farmer was very angry … the dogs chasing his sheep.
a) about
b) because
c) with

135. I think she's quite honest … her intentions.
a) about
b) with
c) in

136. I will be waiting … them at the entrance door.
a) on
b) for
c) at

137. It's no use complaining … the cold during winter.
a) of
b) from
c) on

138. Manufacturers are now … of the latest credit restrictions.
a) smelling the rat
b) feeling the pinch
c) cooking the books

139. This music type is an American art form which is now … in Europe
through the efforts of expatriates.
a) foundering
b) waning
c) flourishing

140. She was … disappointed when she learned that she hadn't got the job
she dreamt of.
a) fully
b) highly
c) bitterly

141. They have … the castle and it is now a luxury hotel.
a) undone
b) remade
c) transformed

142. I … so much last night: I feel terrible.
a) shouldn't have eaten

b) mustn't have eaten
c) didn't have to eat

143. The man stole one of the officers' uniforms and managed to escape by
passing himself … as a guard.
a) out
b) off
c) through

144. … we set off in the next minutes, we'll be there on time.
a) In case
b) So long
c) Provided

145. If he drinks any more beer, I don't think he'll be … to football this
afternoon.
a) skilled
b) capable
c) fit

146. My manager's … of my work doesn't matter to me at all.
a) opinion
b) belief
c) meaning

147. The recent … domestic violence is worrying the police.
a) increase in
b) increase of
c) increase about

148. There's … to hurry.
a) no purpose
b) no need
c) impossible

149. The officers … the kidnapper from escaping by blocking all exits.
a) allowed
b) avoided
c) prevented

150. This meat isn't suitable … .
a) the grill
b) for grilling
c) being grilled

151. A bridge is already … over the river.
a) being built
b) erecting
c) been erected

152. The painting is …; the thief will be disappointed.
a) invalid
b) priceless
c) worthless

153. Even though he is thirty-three, he lives … his mother's salary.
a) from
b) at
c) on

154. It should be obvious … you that this problem will be solved.
a) for
b) to
c) at

155. Mike often forgets to do what he has been told and is scolded for being … .
a) rebellious
b) malicious
c) disobedient

156. The house is quite warm. The oil heater gives … .
a) out a good heat
b) off a good heat
c) out good heat

157. In the middle of my trip I stopped … a rest on the river bank.
a) have
b) to have
c) having

158. After ruling that the article had unjustly … the reputation of the
businessman, the judge ordered the magazine to … its libelous statements

in print.
a) praised…publicize
b) injured…retract
c) sullied…communicate

159. When she heard the news she went completely … .
a) fuse
b) thunder
c) spare

160. I won't … those children making a noise in my apartment!

a) have
b) allow
c) let

161. It's great that your father managed to … that man. Somehow he had
deceived many people.
a) see to
b) see through
c) see out

162. My car is much older … than yours.
a) form
b) manufacture
c) model

163. I … in bed all night thinking about it.
a) laid
b) led
c) lay

164. According to the medical doctor, there's absolutely nothing the … with
you.
a) wrong
b) matter
c) problem

165. I looked everywhere but I couldn't find … at all.
a) anyone
b) no one
c) someone

166. It was … a simple question that everyone answered it.
a) much
b) such
c) too

167. I like my eggs soft …, not hard.
a) cooked
b) steamed
c) boiled

168. I was utterly amazed when the train arrived exactly … time.
a) on
b) by
c) in

169. I'd like to take this … of wishing you all the best.
a) chance
b) opportunity

c) occasion

170. Learners of English may fail to .. between unfamiliar sounds.

a) separate

b) differ

c) distinguish

171. … her opinion, English cheese is better than French cheese.

a) To

b) By

c) In

172. Their parents would not ... them to go there for the weekend.

a) agree

b) permit

c) consent

173. Every Sunday the old man's dog goes to the shop to … him a newspaper.

a) carry

b) fetch

c) take

174. It's late! It's time we … .

a) are gone

b) are going

c) were gone

175. I drove around the area for half an hour but I couldn't find a car … .

a) park

b) plan

c) garage

176. The smell was so bad that it … me off my food.

a) took

b) put

c) got

177. Although she hasn't said anything she … to be upset about it.

a) seems

b) acts

c) behaves

178. It's strange: his sister is blonde, … he is very dark.

a) therefore

b) however

c) whereas

179. I very much … that you will come to dinner next Monday.

a) hope

b) want

c) wish

180. Crops are sometimes completely destroyed by … of locusts.

a) bands

b) swarms

c) flocks

181. There's something wrong with my watch: it has … five minutes in the last hour.

a) gained

b) won

c) advanced

182. Keep in mind that if you are … to customers, they'll walk out of the shop.

a) brush

b) rough

c) rude

183. The air in the house felt cold and … after some days of bad weather.

a) wet

b) damp

c) moist

184. Do you want to wait for a table at this restaurant or shall we go … else?

a) anywhere

b) everywhere

c) somewhere

185. Children who use escalators should always be accompanied … an adult.

a) with

b) by

c) beside

186. I took someone else's coat by … .

a) fortune

b) error

c) mistake

187. How long does it … to get home in the morning?

a) take you

b) need you

c) demand

188. It's becoming more and more … that the Government has lost its

confidence.

a) apparent

b) expected

c) anticipated

189. You need a special … to go into this building.

a) agreement

b) allowance

c) permit

190. I don't like her, so I have no intention … speaking to her.

a) about

b) of

c) with

191. I had to drive carefully because the road was icy in several … .

a) places

b) blocks

c) pieces

192. Don't invite him; I can't stand his bad … .

a) mood

b) mind

c) temper

193. Not only … the movie, but she had also read the book.

a) she did see

b) she saw

c) had she seen

194. I had a meeting at work which went … much longer than I expected.

a) in

b) on

c) by

195. Tom … me to take a lawyer to court with me.

a) suggested

b) insisted

c) advised

196. Poor woman! She has so much to cope … .

a) with

b) in

c) by

197. Tim has always gone … strange hobbies like inventing secret codes.

a) by

b) into

c) in for

198. As he is an expert, his opinions would be worth … .

a) to have

b) having

c) of having

199. Nowhere … this room.

a) is as cold as in

b) is it as cold as

c) it is as cold as in

200. There's just something about him that really puts my … up.

a) handle

b) teeth

c) back

201. The explorer walked all the way along the river, from its mouth to its … .

a) cause

b) source

c) well

202. She soon received promotion, for her superiors realised that she was a woman of considerable … .

a) ability

b) future

c) possibility

203. It is … knowledge that they quarrel violently several times a month.

a) complete

b) normal

c) common

204. After his mother died, he was … up by his grandparents.

a) taken

b) brought

c) grown

205. You should do something worthwhile with your time instead of … it!

a) spending

b) using

c) wasting

206. The police have issued … to local citizens to be on the lookout for

thieves.
a) warnings
b) advice
c) information

207. If you require any more … about the event, please telephone us.
a) news
b) fact
c) information

208. Wait … you get at the office before you unpack this.
a) when
b) until
c) after

209. The students … names appear on the list all failed the exam.
a) whose
b) which
c) their

210. When the police appealed for witnesses, many people came … .
a) across
b) on
c) forward

211. Can you give me a rough … of how much it will cost?
a) esteem
b) value
c) estimate

212. I do play billiards, but I … tennis.
a) prefer
b) like
c) would rather

213. The consultant gave me … useful information.
a) one
b) some
c) the

214. One of the … has fallen off the clock.
a) hands
b) pointers
c) arms

215. How old do you have to be … you can drive a car in your country?
a) when

b) since

c) before

216. I'll let you have the book back next Friday without … .
a) miss
b) fail
c) doubt

217. … I ask him for money he owes me, he says he will bring it in a few weeks.
a) However
b) Whatever
c) Whenever

218. I … to inform you that we cannot exchange articles.
a) resent
b) regret
c) sense

219. I am responsible … what has happened.
a) with
b) for
c) by

220. They have to arrange for the … of their furniture accessories.
a) sole
b) sale
c) seal

221. The boy wouldn't go into the sea … his parents went too.
a) unless
b) except
c) but

222. The … part of the week is always busy for Steven.
a) start
b) near
c) early

223. I … to take my neighbour to court if he didn't stop making so much noise.
a) offered

b) suggested
c) threatened

224. It wasn't his … that he was late.
a) blame
b) fault
c) error

225. She sat there with her arms … doing nothing.
a) turned
b) folded
c) twisted

226. Our neighbours … their hedge cut once a year.
a) have
b) do
c) make

227. I could tell she was pleased … the expression on his face.
a) at
b) by
c) for

228. Steve calls himself Steve Milton, but his … surname is Smith.
a) natural
b) current
c) real

229. If you keep trying you might … to do it.
a) succeed
b) manage
c) understand

230. Their child was born in the ambulance … to the hospital.
a) on the way
b) by the way
c) a long way

231. The meeting is now … .
a) on end
b) at the end
c) at an end

232. She promised to write … I never heard from her again.
a) except
b) but
c) because

233. I … to Tim for my bad behaviour.
a) coped
b) excused
c) apologised

234. Ever … she was in school she has wanted to become a medical doctor.
a) since
b) always
c) after

235. The bottle was on the top shelf, out of … .

a) achievement
b) arrival
c) reach

236. Laptops are supposed to … time, but I'm not so sure they do!
a) spare
b) save
c) waste

237. I didn't mean to do it; it was … accident.
a) in
b) on
c) by

238. His speech was …, eliciting thunderous applause.
a) tedious
b) cowardly
c) well-received

239. What does "a wild goose chase" mean?
a) a wild night on the town
b) a search for something that cannot be found
c) a dangerous race in the streets between cars

240. You should have avoided risking …, General!
a) the lives of your soldiers
b) your soldiers' life
c) the life of your soldiers'

241. … goes the train; now we will have to walk!
a) On time
b) There
c) At once

242. Jane is important to him. He wouldn't get … without her.
a) by
b) over
c) round

243. They live in the house … the blue door.
a) which
b) where
c) with

244. I phoned the bank to … how much money I had to pay.
a) control
b) check
c) test

245. His parents give him anything he wants and as a result he's very … .
a) ruined
b) spoilt

c) damaged

246. … I am studying at the best university and I hope to get a job soon.
a) In a moment
b) At present
c) At this instant

247. He is a fast typist but his letters are full of spelling … .
a) mistakes
b) wrongs
c) faults

248. The officers have asked that … who saw the accident should inform
them.
a) one
b) someone
c) anyone

249. If the greengrocer has some tomatoes … buy some?
a) you will
b) would you
c) shall you

Set 2

250. I will offer a small … to anyone who finds my missing cat.
a) reward
b) receipt
c) repayment

251. The party has … to win the elections.
a) achieved
b) managed
c) attained

252. You … do the washing-up: we can do it later.
a) wouldn't
b) daren't
c) needn't

253. They demand higher wages because prices are
… .
a) growing
b) exceeding
c) rising

254. You should be careful when you wash this … blouse.
a) weak
b) feeble
c) sensitive

255. My parents always fall … in front of the TV.
a) asleep
b) sleepy
c) sleeping

256. You can never rely … her to be punctual.
a) of
b) with
c) on

257. Are you interested … rock music?
a) on

b) in
c) of

258. You should reply … his letter.
a) on
b) for
c) to

259. I will certainly act … your advice.
a) with
b) at
c) on

260. as sound as … . This phrase means healthy, in good condition.
a) steel
b) a monkey
c) a bell

261. Buy the … of soap which is now on sale.
a) model
b) brand
c) mark

262. My uncle took … jogging when he retired.
a) up
b) on
c) over

263. There has been a rather worrying … five per cent in our profits last
year.
a) drop in
b) fall in
c) drop of

264. … you hurry, you won't catch the train.
a) Unless

b) Except

c) As

265. The customer … his money back.

a) asked

b) demanded

c) requested

266. I … him to go to the Lost Property office.

a) noticed

b) announced

c) advised

267. I couldn't resist having another slice of pizza even … I was supposed

to be on diet.

a) though

b) however

c) although

268. These old buildings are going to be … soon.

a) laid out

b) run down

c) pulled down

269. … as I like ice-cream, I can't eat any more now.

a) Much

b) Even

c) So

270. You may borrow ten books, provided you show them to … is at the

desk.

a) who

b) whoever

c) whom

271. Is he playing computer games? He's … to be washing the car.

a) hoped

b) supposed

c) expected

272. Mary was angry with me for breaking the windows, but it happened …

accident.

a) by

b) in

c) on

273. The room was crowded with over fifty people … into it.

a) pushed

b) packed

c) stuck

274. Beware of the friends who appear to be enthusiastic … your success.

a) of

b) with

c) about

275. They want to watch the latest movie … TV.

a) in

b) at

c) on

276. … to leave early is rarely granted.

a) Permission

b) Leave

c) Allowance

277. …, my colleagues didn't laugh at me.

a) For my surprise

b) To my surprise

c) As to surprise me

278. If you had gone there, you … my sister.

a) would have met

b) would meet

c) had met

279. She never goes in lifts because she is terrified of … spaces.

a) constricted

b) compressed

c) contained

280. It never … to me that she would be there.

a) recurred

b) occurred

c) contemplated

281. The assistant was … helpful, but Mike felt she could have given him

more information.

a) exactly

b) totally

c) quite

282. The meal was excellent; the steak was particularly … .

a) flavoured

b) tasteful

c) delicious

283. Are there any seats left for this evening's …?

a) opera

b) act

c) performance

284. Having … the table, she called the family for supper.

a) laid

b) spread

c) ordered

285. As I have been ill, I have had no … to discuss the business plan.

a) suitability

b) possibility

c) opportunity

286. Tom … to turn up for the football match.

a) omitted

b) failed

c) stopped

287. The manager's presence was helpful, but he could … us more money.

a) give

b) gave

c) have given

288. There are five lawyers in my town and I have consulted … of them in

turn.

a) every

b) each

c) any

289. The final course was so difficult that I didn't … any progress at all.

a) do

b) create

c) make

290. I'm tired of looking at ancient … .

a) ruins

b) foundations

c) remnants

291. My bike is gone: it must … .

a) have been stolen

b) have stolen

c) be stolen

292. There's a … to her patience.

a) top

b) limit

c) bottom

293. I … hands with the guests.

a) gave

b) nodded

c) shook

294. We had a great … of trouble getting through customs.

a) level

b) lot

c) deal

295. Rose trees need to be … regularly.

a) cut

b) clipped

c) pruned

296. What made you think … such a thing?

a) of

b) on

c) at

297. I would go to the pool if the weather … good.

a) is

b) were

c) has been

298. I rang you up while he … his report.

a) was finishing

b) has been finishing

c) had finished

299. The bus … is 50 cents.

a) cost

b) fare

c) charge

300. Before the invention of refrigeration, the ... of meat was a problem.

a) preservation

b) keeping

c) maintenance

301. Could I have another one? Oh, there doesn't seem to be … .

a) any left

b) some left

c) left any

302. I will go on working on the farm … I can.

a) through

b) during

c) as long as

303. I'll ask Ms. Thompson to … to you as soon as she returns.

a) ring

b) contact

c) speak

304. This new model works by letting light through a small … at the front.
a) leak
b) hole
c) break

305. You will have to … your holiday if you are too ill.
a) cut down
b) call off
c) put aside

306. If you go to the market you might find a … .
a) chance
b) bargain
c) trade

307. The train was ... by three hours because of bad weather.
a) postponed
b) put off
c) delayed

308. My guests didn't leave until 3 a.m.; they … have enjoyed themselves.
a) can't
b) must
c) might

309. She was sitting just ... Steve and John.
a) beside
b) off
c) besides

310. Mary remembered the correct address only … she had posted the letter.
a) since
b) following
c) after

311. I have never … any experience of living in a small village.
a) wished
b) made
c) had

312. I'm very … of cash at the moment.
a) down
b) empty
c) short

313. The … were told to fasten their seat belts.
a) passengers
b) flyers
c) customers

314. There are … trains running today.
a) scarcer
b) fewer
c) little

315. Mary isn't … well with the new manager.
a) going on
b) taking on
c) getting on

316. Has this idea ever occurred … you?
a) at
b) to
c) on

317. I'm … with your stupid ideas.
a) get rid
b) fed over
c) fed up

318. If they had been able … it for you, they would have helped you.
a) to do
b) doing
c) is doing

319. The officers carried out a … search for the missing diplomat.
a) through
b) thoughtful
c) thorough

320. Fitting together the fragments was a … task.
a) minute
b) minuscule
c) painstaking

321. It will … rain later so we should go now.
a) probably
b) likely
c) usually

322. I would have cleaned this mess if I … you were coming.
a) would have known
b) had known
c) have known

323. We have … to meet at the station at 8 o'clock.
a) confirmed
b) combined
c) arranged

324. There is always … traffic in the city centre.
a) full

b) strong
c) heavy

325. He's … to drink too much at parties.
a) adequate
b) apt
c) common
326. We must get there … or other.
a) somehow
b) anyhow
c) anywhere
327. She was left to make all the … for the meeting.
a) procedures
b) provisions
c) arrangements
328. The new girl … type at 45 words per minute.
a) need
b) can
c) dare
329. I'll wait over there until … ready.
a) you are
b) you will be
c) you were
330. You must move your car; … I have to give you a ticket.
a) whether
b) therefore
c) otherwise
331. A manager of a large company is given a big …
.
a) money
b) pay
c) salary
332. Heavy goods delivery vehicles may not carry … of more than fifteen tons.
a) masses
b) sizes
c) loads
333. After they went on strike there was a … of water.
a) shortage

b) drain
c) loss
334. She's entitled to a pension, but she won't dream … retiring yet.

a) on
b) of
c) to
335. Mix the contents … a little water.
a) of
b) with
c) at
336. You can try … if you really need to improve your language skills.
a) listening to BBC
b) listening at BBC
c) to listening to BBC
337. His … of Alexander the Great was acclaimed as one of the best.
a) entertainment
b) portrayal
c) spectacle
338. The army … defeat at the hands of such powerful enemies.
a) bore
b) supported
c) suffered
339. Their accounts were phony. They had been cooking the … for years.
a) books
b) spinner
c) trade
340. Practical … is desirable for candidates.
a) exploit
b) initiative
c) experience
341. The director opened the letter without … to read the address on the envelope.
a) worrying
b) bothering
c) caring

342. Hurry! She's already here. I didn't think she … till tomorrow.
a) was coming
b) is coming
c) is to come
343. If you have any … concerning this report please phone us.
a) requests
b) wishes

c) queries

344. Could you ... exactly what you saw?

a) inform

b) describe

c) point

345. He has brought you a ... of flowers.

a) branch

b) bunch

c) bush

346. The child seems to be incapable ... keeping his room tidy.

a) at

b) with

c) of

347. In the summer I often sleep in the ... air on the terrace.

a) clean

b) clear

c) open

348. This dress ... you perfectly.

a) likes

b) suits

c) matches

349. I bought the phone because the colours ... the colours of the car.

a) match

b) fit

c) suit

350. To promote her so quickly you must have a high ... of her ability.

a) view

b) idea

c) opinion

351. We ... as well go without him.

a) can

b) may

c) just

352. She ... out of the window for a moment and then went on writing.

a) glanced

b) glimpsed

c) regarded

353. You should keep receipts from shops as proof ... purchase.

a) to

b) for

c) of

354. Don't mention it ... my girlfriend, but I paid $80 for this perfume.

a) to

b) at

c) with

355. The child knocked ... the door.

a) on

b) for

c) at

356. You must have ... the examination before Friday.

a) passing

b) entered for

c) sit for

357. They ... for you for more than one hour now.

a) have waited

b) have been waiting

c) wait

358. I would have come home earlier if you ... me.

a) had told

b) have told

c) told

359. Petrol is so expensive ... they use public transport.

a) then

b) thus

c) that

360. There has been some ... in their bilateral relations.

a) destitution

b) deterioration

c) depreciation

361. They take too much ... of his kindness.

a) profit

b) use

c) advantage

362. I can easily ... you up for the night.

a) put

b) take

c) keep

363. My car is very old, but I can't ... to buy a new one.

a) achieve

b) reach

c) afford

364. Two passengers were killed and the other was … injured.
a) hardly
b) severely
c) unusually

365. After ten years the bedroom wallpaper had considerably … .
a) faded
b) mixed
c) lighted

366. My attempt to pass the final exam was … .
a) unmerciful
b) unhelpful
c) unsuccessful

367. She … at the Latin College for French.
a) enlisted

b) inscribed
c) enrolled

368. I admit I suffer from a … of patience with old people.
a) lack
b) limit
c) shortage

369. The building is in good … though it needs to be painted.
a) state
b) condition
c) position

370. I can't be sure I'll be there in time. I … be late.
a) should
b) must
c) may

371. His suit didn't … him properly.
a) meet
b) fit
c) frame

372. She may be quick … understanding, but she's not capable of doing it.
a) at
b) in
c) for

373. We have some important business to attend … .
a) with
b) at
c) to

374. Steve, you should not boast … your success.
a) of
b) with
c) from

375. I'm sorry, I haven't got … change.
a) all
b) any
c) lots

376. An oppressive …, and not the festive mood characterized the mood of the gathering.
a) senility
b) inanity
c) solemnity

377. I think it's … your luck to drive without a license.
a) risking
b) tempting
c) pushing

378. If you looked back far enough, you would see that you are … related to Karl Marx.
a) distantly
b) slightly
c) previously

379. I can't understand it; your handwriting is … .
a) illegible
b) illicit
c) illusive

380. Hello! You … be the new employee.
a) could
b) should
c) must

381. Last year the cereals harvest was disappointing, but this year it looks as if we shall have a better … .
a) crop
b) amount
c) product

382. She was in … of a large number of men.
a) direction
b) leadership
c) charge

383. Tom was born during the last war, which would … him about 50 now.
a) give
b) make

c) calculate

384. The actor never married, choosing to remain …
all his life.
a) separate
b) single
c) individual
385. The consultant showed me … the washing
machine.
a) the working of
b) to work
c) how to use
386. The driver failed to signal his … to turn left.
a) idea
b) purpose
c) intention
387. I wish you wouldn't call her … that name.
a) by
b) with
c) under
388. I had … reached the park when I saw everyone
leaving.
a) quite
b) almost
c) rather
389. She tried to … to see him at least once a week.
a) call up
b) come on
c) drop in
390. No, Kate isn't stupid. …, she's rather clever.
a) Now
b) Currently
c) Actually
391. The Minister resigned as a/an … of the
incident.
a) effect
b) result
c) cause
392. The names of the winners will be … in the next
magazine issue.
a) told

b) informed
c) announced
393. When the clock … twelve, I left.
a) struck
b) beat

c) shot
394. The store is only open … weekday mornings
now.
a) for
b) in
c) on
395. They think he is very good … drawing.
a) at
b) for
c) in
396. Every day thousands of … fly the Atlantic for
negotiations.
a) dealers
b) merchants
c) businessmen
397. Prices continued to rise … the ruling party
became unpopular.
a) on condition that
b) with the result that
c) on the chance that
398. I would help the old lady in her shopping if she
… me.
a) will ask
b) ask
c) asked
399. … for a trip last Friday?
a) Did you go
b) Will you go
c) Have you gone
400. The child was taught that it was … to interrupt.
a) coarse
b) rude
c) crude

401. She was … better than her brother at chess.
a) miles
b) feet
c) inches
402. I often speak to her on my … to work.
a) travel
b) way
c) road
403. The noise prevented me from … to sleep.
a) starting
b) going
c) beginning

404. This horse is famous for … the National race
two times.
a) gaining
b) conquering
c) winning
405. Before starting a new chapter, I'd like to …
what we discussed
yesterday.
a) run up
b) run along
c) run through
406. I think it's time we … on our way.
a) are
b) were
c) will be
407. Would you … taking care of the cat for two
hours?
a) mind
b) matter
c) agree
408. The world record for this event is almost
impossible to … .
a) beat
b) meet
c) compare
409. We've been … with this business partner for
many years.
a) competing

b) shopping
c) dealing
410. She applied for training as a pilot, but they
turned her … .
a) down
b) over
c) back
411. The child wasn't accustomed … by coach.
a) travel
b) to travel
c) to travelling
412. She has left her phone at home. She's always so
… .
a) forgetful
b) forgotten
c) forgetting
413. Newly-… coins always look clean.
a) moulded

b) minted
c) printed
414. I had to go to the library to … some books.
a) give
b) return
c) buy
415. It was such a hot day … the surface of the
material was damaged.
a) as
b) so
c) that
416. She always … out in a crowd because of her
style.
a) stood
b) found
c) looked
417. Please apply … the secretary for this type of
information.
a) for
b) at
c) to

418. Though the concert had been enjoyable, it was
overly … .
a) sublime
b) protracted
c) extensive
419. A skillful …, John adopted a posture of
patience and … toward the
protestors.
a) academician/understanding
b) pundit/tolerance
c) negotiator/compromise
420. Could you give me a rough … of the costs?
a) estimate
b) value
c) correlation
421. There is a … of $2,000 for information leading
to the thief.
a) gift
b) reward
c) prize
422. The manager didn't pay for the meal himself –
he put it on his
company's … account.
a) expense
b) price

c) value

423. I knew her … we were young.

a) until

b) as

c) when

424. I … them run away from the bank.

a) allowed

b) saw

c) felt

425. I only have … days left in Spain.

a) little

b) a few

c) a little

426. She pretended that she agreed with me to avoid … my feelings.

a) hurting

b) to hurt

c) hurt

427. Many fires could be … if new safety standards were introduced.

a) protected

b) excluded

c) prevented

428. My watch stopped so I had no way of knowing the right … .

a) moment

b) time

c) hour

429. He came … an unknown poem while he was searching for something

else.

a) round

b) across

c) off

430. I couldn't beat him at chess; I'm just not in his … .

a) class

b) type

c) set

431. Too much exercise can be harmful but walking is good … you.

a) by

b) with

c) for

432. I find it difficult to talk to her because we have so … in common.

a) few

b) less

c) little

433. His attitude … his parents is very disrespectful.

a) as far as

b) towards

c) as for

434. Surely Anna is not going to drive, … she?

a) does

b) will

c) is

435. You … pay for this. It's free.

a) shouldn't

b) mustn't

c) don't have to

436. A child learns a language best … .

a) when being brought up to it

b) by being brought up to it

c) while being brought into it

437. Urgent discussions will continue … .

a) behind the scenes

b) behind the curtain

c) behind the bars

438. Our house is nothing out of the … .

a) normal

b) usual

c) ordinary

439. "A ladies' man" means:

a) a man most women fall for

b) a man who dresses up like a woman

c) a man who enjoys the company of women

440. The manager warned Kate that the laziness and … could result in her

dismissal.

a) procrastination

b) ambition

c) fortitude

441. The butcher cut some steak and … it up.

a) closed

b) wrapped

c) wound

442. The man … to take a breath test after the incident.

a) denied

b) objected

c) refused

443. I do my best to practise every day … it is difficult sometimes.
a) although
b) also
c) even

444. His arm was so … injured that he couldn't play anymore.
a) deeply
b) badly
c) hardly

445. His home is a … between a palace and a hotel.
a) union
b) link
c) cross

446. The woman … case was described in the article never fully recovered.
a) what
b) whom
c) whose

447. I … put my money there if I didn't consider it was safe.
a) didn't
b) wouldn't
c) hadn't

448. Driving in this city is supposed to be confusing but I didn't find it at …
difficult.
a) all
b) once
c) least

449. I enjoy … but don't like jogging.
a) to swim
b) in swim
c) swimming

450. Would you … the kettle on for some coffee?
a) set
b) put
c) have

451. I suggest … the "meal of the day" rather than fish.
a) to have

b) we have
c) for us having

452. Her father won't … to my marrying Olivia.
a) agree

b) allow
c) approve

453. It was way to hot. I couldn't … it any longer.
a) carry
b) hold
c) stand

454. They had always liked the sea … they moved to the Coast.
a) so
b) since
c) such

455. Just keep .. on him, will you?
a) a look
b) an eye
c) a care

456. By the time you receive this message, I … for China.
a) will leave
b) have left
c) will have left

457. You can depend … me.
a) in
b) of
c) on

458. I invested a lot of money … residential buildings.
a) in
b) for
c) at

459. She is trying to lose weight by … sweets.
a) cutting down at
b) stopping down at
c) cutting down on

460. The terrorist tried to persuade the hostage that he was neither … nor …
. He was just interested in calling attention to his cause.
a) impeccable/sincere
b) antagonistic/vindictive
c) recalcitrant/clandestine

461. The professor was surprised that her English was so … .
a) liquid
b) definite
c) fluent

462. I went to … some pictures by a renowned painter.
a) watch
b) look at
c) see to
463. If it … fine, she shall go out.
a) was
b) were
c) is
464. The idea of a balanced diet is difficult to … in this group.
a) put across
b) take in
c) make over
465. There was a small room into … we all gathered.
a) where
b) that
c) which
466. You … go to dentist's.
a) rather
b) ought to
c) better
467. His speech was interesting at first, but it was … long.
a) so much
b) far too
c) too much
468. The soldier has been on … for twenty-four hours without a break.
a) work

b) job
c) duty
469. When she braked on the icy road, the car … .
a) slid
b) slipped
c) skidded
470. This is the … building in the city.
a) oldest
b) elder
c) elderly
471. You must put your name on this side and then sign on the … side.
a) other
b) under
c) back
472. I will always … our wonderful holidays.

a) reflect
b) remind
c) remember
473. The Prime Minister … his intention to retire.
a) told
b) announced
c) informed
474. As the child walked through the fields, he heard sheep … .
a) braying
b) bleating
c) crying
475. I'm afraid I can't comment … your project yet.
a) about
b) with
c) on
476. Steve was employed … a factory in 2010.
a) in
b) to
c) by

477. It was such a good weather that I decided to go … .
a) fish
b) fishing
c) to fishing
478. I think she … you my regards when you met two days ago.
a) gave
b) has given
c) give
479. Not … did she refuse to speak to me, but she also blamed me for failing.
a) even
b) at all
c) only
480. "To come through flying colours" means:
a) to succeed in one's study
b) to accomplish something with great success
c) to be understood loud and clear
481. I hope she is … to buy some milk.
a) proposed
b) suggested
c) remembered
482. If I were you, I … that gaming PC.
a) would buy

b) will buy
c) am buying
483. The vet decided that he had to operate … the dog.
a) with
b) on
c) at
484. I … like to apologize.
a) could
b) must
c) would
485. Many accidents in the home could be … by taking simple safety measures.

a) protected
b) avoided
c) preserved
486. Try to remember … bring your debit card.
a) me to
b) yourself to
c) to
487. The bride looked … in her dress.
a) beauty
b) lovely
c) handsome
488. We didn't leave for the station until the very … moment.
a) late
b) least
c) last
489. When are you going to give back that book you … me?
a) owe
b) debt
c) lend
490. The poor man was … by a gang last month.
a) murdered
b) destroyed
c) slaughter
491. Each … of the family had to do the washing up.
a) person
b) member
c) individual
492. The woman performs beautifully … the piano.
a) in
b) from

c) on
493. The boy comes … drawing lessons four times a week.
a) to
b) for
c) at

494. She … a coloured thread round her finger so as not to forget about the meeting.
a) rang
b) wound
c) curved
495. You have a new baby?! …!
a) What wonderful news
b) What a wonderful news
c) How wonderful news
496. If my diploma … last week, I would have been able to come sooner.
a) are found
b) were found
c) had been found
497. Old people do not take kindly to having their daily … upset.
a) routine
b) habit
c) custom
498. You were warned never … with those members.
a) to assign
b) to assume
c) to associate
499. If your company wants to attract workers it must … the wages.
a) spread
b) raise
c) rise
500. This computer package is totally … for our need.
a) unsuitable
b) undeniable
c) unspeakable
501. Some people think it is … to use little-known words.
a) clever
b) skilled
c) sensitive

502. He decided to … from the committee.
a) cancel

b) resign
c) prevent
503. Be here at nine o'clock without … .
a) fault
b) late
c) fail
504. The children were … by the cartoons.
a) fascinated
b) fascinating
c) fascination
505. The murderer … escape from the prison.
a) could
b) managed to
c) succeeded in
506. A witness … now been found.
a) was
b) had
c) has
507. She couldn't tell the truth. She had to … a story.
a) invent
b) manage
c) combine
508. She woke up crying because she had … a nightmare.
a) seen
b) dreamt
c) had
509. I hope to get an answer to my final letter by … of post.
a) round
b) return
c) back
510. Didn't it ever … to you that you would be caught?
a) occur
b) enter
c) strike

511. I started early … to avoid the worst of the traffic.
a) so that
b) in so far
c) in order

512. The children threw snowballs at … on their way.
a) themselves
b) each other
c) their own
513. Don't be so sure … yourself.
a) of
b) with
c) on
514. My grandmother buys eggs … the dozen.
a) to
b) for
c) by
515. She's entitled … a pension, but she doesn't want to retire.
a) to
b) on
c) in
516. Before you run … other people, you should consider your own faults.
a) over
b) up
c) down
517. The child won't go to sleep … we leave a light on.
a) except
b) unless
c) but
518. The effectiveness of his work relies … the use of advanced technologies.
a) on
b) by
c) of
519. The minority are suing the government for the return of their … lands.
a) antique

b) ancestral
c) inherited
520. Some species are on the … of becoming extinct.
a) edge
b) side
c) verge
521. One … of my job is that it is near where I live.
a) advantage

b) pleasure

c) preference

522. The little child loved … the old castle.

a) hunting

b) detecting

c) exploring

523. This is a photo of the university I … when I lived in Hamburg.

a) used

b) attended

c) joined

524. It's the first time … here.

a) I have been

b) I was

c) I am coming

525. Many accidents in this town are caused by … driving.

a) harmful

b) careful

c) careless

526. I was delighted when I … to sell my car so quickly.

a) managed

b) could

c) risked

527. It sounds … the situation isn't about to improve.

a) how

b) as if

c) so that

528. This patient … quickly after his illness.

a) recovered

b) covered

c) discovered

529. Caring for her cousin is a … burden for her.

a) sour

b) bitter

c) heavy

530. The manager made a wonderful … .

a) message

b) talk

c) speech

531. There is a fault at our latest TV station. Please don't … your TV set.

a) repair

b) adjust

c) switch

532. The man … going by plane instead of car.

a) suggested

b) agreed

c) convinced

533. Please concentrate … your tasks!

a) with

b) to

c) on

534. Many men do not approve … blood-sports.

a) for

b) of

c) with

535. You must encourage Mary … her efforts.

a) in

b) at

c) with

536. The ball … two or three times before disappearing.

a) leapt

b) bounced

c) hopped

537. It's … helping that man. He will die anyway.

a) good

b) no good

c) not good

538. Would you agree that a man pays less attention … than a woman does?

a) to dress

b) on dress

c) to the dress

539. Our institution can give you the … number of refugees.

a) unclear

b) suggestive

c) approximate

540. As drunk as … . This phrase refers to someone very drunk.

a) a fish

b) a lord

c) a barrel

541. How … you manage to get there so fast?

a) used

b) had

c) did

542. The touristic guide walked so … that most of the people could not
keep up with him.
a) fast
b) quick
c) rapid

543. Membership of the club, … costs $12,000 a year, is only open to
women.
a) what
b) that
c) which

544. The boy swore that he would take … his family's killer.
a) revenge in

b) revenge on
c) revenge at

545. … she wasn't feeling very well, she went to visit her parents as usual.
a) Still
b) Although
c) However

546. That guy has a dishonest … in his character.
a) stripe
b) strip
c) streak

547. Having looked the place …, the strange man went away.
a) down
b) out
c) over

548. I'm selling the building … of the summer.
a) at the end
b) in the end
c) on the end

549. She was complaining … a headache this morning.
a) at
b) from
c) of

Set 3

550. You need to hurry because the … train leaves in five minutes.
a) latter
b) last
c) latest

551. I am not used … spoken to in such a manner.
a) for being
b) to being
c) to be

552. There was a small house standing … hundreds of palm trees near the
beach.
a) in
b) among
c) between

553. As the team were … at the end of the game, he lost the bet.
a) equal
b) fair
c) correct

554. These little stores are always … of people at Christmas time.
a) stuffed
b) busy
c) crowded

555. Their request … me completely by surprise.
a) left
b) made
c) took

556. I have … why the Browns went to live in that country.
a) puzzled
b) surprised
c) wondered

557. You have to be patient … him.
a) for
b) with
c) about

558. Most women never … with violent crimes.
a) get into contact
b) come into contact
c) get in touch

559. I don't think I … this game before.
a) have played
b) will play
c) would play

560. "A City man" refers to:
a) any man with a higher education
b) a man who works in a city, which is a financial power of an area
c) someone who is constantly showing off
561. Is there a bank where I can … these pounds for euros?
a) turn

b) alter
c) exchange
562. The officer said that he saw no … between the murders.
a) joint
b) connection
c) join
563. Drinking is a bad habit, which many people find difficult to … .
a) beat
b) cough
c) break
564. Would you … passing this magazine to him?
a) mind
b) agree
c) want
565. There's … to be frightened of the cat.
a) a fear
b) no need
c) no fear
566. Her boyfriend won't … her drive his car.
a) allow
b) leave
c) let
567. The competitors in the rally had to follow the … laid down by the sponsors.
a) direct
b) route
c) address
568. If only I …play the piano as well as you!
a) might
b) would
c) could
569. It's a great … that the exhibition was cancelled.
a) sorrow
b) sadness
c) pity

570. On our … to Madrid, the car broke down.
a) way
b) road
c) voyage
571. She has adopted two orphans … her own children.
a) except
b) besides
c) in place of
572. I cannot understand how you put … this residential area.
a) out
b) by
c) up with
573. You will have to take things … .
a) like you find them
b) as you find them
c) so as you find them
574. We … to the concert, but we didn't make it.
a) were to have gone
b) would go
c) were gone
575. No one … she was.
a) could be quicker than
b) can be as quick as
c) could be so quick as
576. This computer is cheap, but that one is … .
a) cheaper yet
b) more cheaper
c) even cheaper
577. If the line is busy, don't wait and … .
a) hang on
b) hang up
c) hang down
578. If they … to that event, they would certainly have decided to attend it.
a) will be invited

b) had been invited
c) were invited
579. If I saw Olive, I … her to my party.
a) invite
b) will invite
c) would invite
580. I was very … not to pass the message further.
a) cajoled

b) tempted

c) elicited

581. After the party the dog was allowed to finish off the … sandwiches.

a) left

b) leaving

c) remaining

582. I would much … a reply by the end of the week.

a) appreciate

b) require

c) value

583. When she heard the joke, she burst into loud … .

a) smiles

b) laughter

c) enjoyment

584. I couldn't get used to … to work so early.

a) go

b) going

c) be going

585. … amount of money can buy a true friend.

a) No

b) Never

c) None

586. They should be spending money on a house … than on a car.

a) other

b) better

c) rather

587. I was very … of myself for forgetting that.

a) disgraced

b) ashamed

c) shocked

588. Mary earns a great … of money.

a) quantity

b) level

c) deal

589. He is an expert … coronaviruses.

a) about

b) on

c) in

590. They look exactly the … .

a) alike

b) identical

c) same

591. There was no need to be uneasy … the results.

a) for

b) about

c) on

592. It's impossible to prevent the boys … quarrelling with each other.

a) to

b) in

c) from

593. This bike is inferior … the one I bought last year.

a) to

b) at

c) by

594. Tom plays … the school team.

a) by

b) in

c) on

595. The teacher despairs … ever teaching him anything.

a) of

b) in

c) on

596. Our family is fortunate in having sufficient supplies … the winter.

a) for

b) on

c) to

597. The old man was found guilty … many crimes.

a) from

b) for

c) of

598. … Sam, he can't go alone.

a) As if

b) As for

c) As far as

599. I know nothing about that battle. It was … .

a) behind the times

b) as the same time

c) before my time

600. Many jobs in this area can be directly … to tourism.

a) attributed

b) attracted

c) dedicated

601. When the director went to China on business his … took over all his
duties.
a) officer
b) deputy
c) caretaker

602. She saw the plane crash when its engines … .
a) failed
b) struck
c) held

603. You are going to come to the meeting, …?
a) will you
b) do you
c) aren't you

604. You will not finish that project by tomorrow unless you … some help.
a) get
b) would get
c) will get

605. It's difficult to pay my bills when prices keep … .
a) rising
b) gaining
c) raising

606. After the death of her father, she was brought … by her uncle.
a) round
b) about
c) up

607. Why did the police suspect you? It doesn't make … to me.
a) right
b) sense
c) truth

608. When they heard that their children had crossed the road without
looking, they told them they … do it again.
a) mustn't
b) needn't
c) didn't need to

609. He went to Germany hoping to find a teaching … .
a) work
b) occupation
c) post

610. I can't … what they are doing; it's way too dark down there.
a) look into
b) make out
c) see through

611. This country has … good transport.
a) the
b) a
c) very

612. I'd like you to meet a very good friend of …, Dave.
a) me

b) my
c) mine

613. We travelled to Australia by the most … route.
a) direct
b) unique
c) easy

614. This film is based … a novel.
a) of
b) on
c) in

615. I should be grateful … any advice you can give regarding this
situation.
a) for
b) about
c) with

616. I was shocked … her indifference!
a) on
b) with
c) at

617. The manager has just gone on her … leave. She gets three weeks'
holiday a year.
a) regular
b) annual
c) regular

618. He have … this minute left for the city centre.
a) ever
b) already
c) just

619. To my …, a pandemic is more dangerous than nuclear arms.
a) mind
b) view

c) disbelief

620. They are always … with each other about investments.

a) shouting

b) arguing

c) annoying

621. I took that faulty laptop back to the shop where I'd bought it and asked
the … if they would change it for me.

a) clerk

b) official

c) assistant

622. I … to the cinema last night. I'm so tired now.

a) had not to go

b) shouldn't have gone

c) haven't had to go

623. You will spend at least one year working in this company … you can
find out how things operate here.

a) so that

b) so as to

c) because

624. I can … with most things but I cannot stand lies.

a) put aside

b) put up

c) put off

625. I think she is … her time looking for a job here.

a) losing

b) wasting

c) missing

626. It is a very good idea to be … dressed when you have a business
meeting.

a) finely

b) smartly

c) boldly

627. I was pleased to see how … he looked after his recent COVID-19
illness.

a) well

b) pleasant

c) nice

628. Let's … across this field instead of going by the road.

a) set

b) come

c) cut

629. Tell me … about your holiday in Spain.

a) every

b) much

c) all

630. It's fairly rude to interrupt when someone is …
.

a) talking

b) saying

c) discussing

631. I didn't enjoy the event. No, and … .

a) neither we did

b) we didn't either

c) so didn't we

632. … of the week, I hope I shall have lost another kilo.

a) By the end

b) At the end

c) To the end

633. I reasoned … her, but she would not listen to me.

a) to

b) for

c) with

634. She is responding … treatment and will be cured.

a) on

b) for

c) to

635. Nothing will prevent me … succeeding.

a) on

b) from

c) in

636. Jennifer criticised everything and even ran … his friends.

a) up

b) down

c) into

637. Why did you have … his last tutorial?

a) such difficulties to follow

b) such a difficulty to follow

c) such difficulty in following

638. I was sitting in a famous café … afternoon when I saw her.

a) one
b) in
c) the

639. The … question in this case is whether she was there or not.
a) crucial
b) valuable
c) supreme

640. He's the best employee I've ever had. I couldn't … for a better one.
a) abide
b) average
c) ask

641. You are not allowed … in this room.
a) smoke
b) smoking
c) to smoke

642. I think you'd better … before the manager returns.
a) be gone
b) be going
c) being gone

643. "I … you all", she said, as she left.
a) am hating
b) can hate
c) hate

644. I'm sorry. It's all my …!
a) guilt
b) fault
c) wrong

645. I chose these because they are my … shade of blue.
a) popular
b) favourite
c) fancy

646. I wonder … like to travel by boat.
a) what it is
b) how it is
c) what is it

647. Two other … in their report are worth mentioning.
a) effects
b) points
c) notices

648. Many soldiers were … wounded in the war. They needed a lot of help.

a) hardly
b) seriously
c) utterly

649. She's a luck person. She always seems to fall on her … .
a) ankles
b) legs
c) feet

650. … experience of working in a factory is required.
a) Previous
b) First
c) Initial

651. For a short time after the car crash, I suffered from constant … in my back.
a) hurt
b) pain
c) ache

652. An enormous … of rubbish had built up here.
a) pile
b) hill
c) tower

653. Children can be instructed … swimming at a very early age.
a) with

b) for
c) in

654. Marry will come … home late. Don't wait for her.
a) to
b) into
c) back

655. I was instructed … driving once upon a time.
a) in
b) about
c) at

656. How can you agree … such an idea?
a) with
b) at
c) by

657. It was … to meet you. That's what she said to me.
a) pleasure
b) a pleasure
c) some pleasure

658. Only by shouting loudly … a taxi.
a) she got
b) she's got
c) did she get
659. The lights … out and I was left in the darkness.
a) turned
b) went
c) gave
660. For this meal to be a real success, you … cook the meat for at least
three hours.
a) need
b) ought
c) must
661. It is logical that when factories are … workers tend to lose their jobs.
a) automatic
b) automation
c) automated

662. They are not used … supper so late.
a) to having
b) of having
c) to have
663. Be careful; she has her eyes … you.
a) for
b) at
c) on
664. In spite of the anesthetic, I was fully … during the operation.
a) awake
b) sensitive
c) conscious
665. Today a man was … down the street by my dog.
a) chased
b) hunted
c) sped
666. I don't … to see her again until next month.
a) think
b) expect
c) wait
667. Some drivers, after …, annoy their fellows.
a) passing by
b) taking over
c) overtaking

668. I had … news of what she was doing in London.
a) several
b) little
c) few
669. Now that he is retired, he enjoys … more time watching documentaries.
a) spending
b) to take
c) taking
670. His debt now amounts … $10,000.
a) in
b) with
c) to
671. You demand too much of them; they are not really equal … the project.
a) for
b) to
c) with
672. The student is still dependent … his parents.
a) on
b) from
c) with
673. Will you have … to tell your manager about it?
a) some nerves
b) some nerve
c) the nerve
674. Boys and girls … enjoyed the show.
a) both
b) either
c) alike
675. The reconstruction of the city is now … .
a) well under way
b) well in the way
c) through the way
676. The production goes well now, although there were some … .
a) last straws
b) teething troubles
c) starting problems
677. If I could understand this alphabet, I … the article.
a) read
b) will read

c) would read

678. Please … and see me some time – you are welcome.
a) come to
b) come away
c) come around

679. I could … panic in her voice.
a) desist
b) detect
c) detest

680. Thousands of tourists use the … of footpaths across these hills.
a) network
b) grid
c) circuit

681. The professors … with coronavirus infection one after the other.
a) went down
b) went off
c) went under

682. He agreed to give me $100, … the $300 he had already lent me.
a) extra to
b) surplus to
c) in addition to

683. What do you usually … for delivering things?
a) demand
b) charge
c) cost

684. We chose some attractive … paper for the present.
a) covering
b) wrapping
c) packing

685. It was a beautiful cloth … from velvet.
a) worn
b) threaded
c) woven

686. We have … of time to catch the flight.
a) enough
b) plenty
c) great deal

687. She put the letters into the wrong envelopes … mistake.
a) on

b) with
c) by

688. Mike seems confident but you … never judge by appearances.
a) might
b) should
c) could

689. I couldn't go fishing because it began to … with rain.
a) flow
b) drench
c) pour

690. They … for the same job.
a) chose
b) referred
c) applied

691. The plane was … for over two hours because of fog.
a) delayed
b) landed
c) cancelled

692. She has to be careful which soap she uses, because her skin is … .
a) sensible
b) senseless
c) sensitive

693. The local authorities want people to set … their own businesses.
a) off
b) up
c) in

694. She is quite intelligent but she … common sense.
a) wants
b) fails
c) lacks

695. I wonder who drank all the wine. It … have been Mike because he was out all day.
a) can't
b) could
c) must

696. They are opposed … giving people large pay rises.
a) for
b) to

c) against

697. I will show you the document if I … it.

a) could find

b) will find

c) find

698. Being exhausted, he sent a request asking that his colleagues … their
meeting for one hour.

a) defray

b) defer

c) commence

699. The reporter gave a dramatic … of his adventures.

a) tale

b) saga

c) account

700. Some people are camping for the … of rare species hunting.

a) extinction

b) abolition

c) annihilation

701. I am … in information about this laptop.

a) interested

b) bored

c) concerned

702. They say we're likely to have a … winter.

a) calm

b) smooth

c) mild

703. Do you think Sarah and Tom marry …?

a) lastly

b) at last

c) in the end

704. You should … a lawyer before you sign that contract.

a) check

b) consult

c) counsel

705. "You can take a horse to water, but you can't … it drink!"

a) make

b) compel

c) save

706. The old man is a little bit … in his right ear.

a) disabled

b) deaf

c) dead

707. Some explorers did not survive the terrible … across the mountains.

a) journey

b) step

c) travel

708. Heavy snowfalls have … all flights.

a) omitted

b) delayed

c) postponed

709. The rainstorms … more than three days.

a) went

b) took

c) lasted

710. There will be a … interval for snacks.

a) small

b) short

c) light

711. The play was very long, but there were three …
.

a) rests

b) intervals

c) gaps

712. The jewels were … a lot of money.

a) cost

b) valued

c) worth

713. They had a plan to trick me, but I didn't fall … it.

a) for

b) to

c) at

714. It is unreasonable to demand this … Mary.

a) in

b) at

c) of

715. It took me a long time to get rid … the infection.

a) of

b) against

c) from

716. They differ … each other so much.

a) of

b) with

c) from

717. There is little … in this company.

a) hanging around
b) to hang around
c) hung around
718. I would let her go, if I … all about this mission.
a) know
b) have known
c) knew
719. They were … for smuggling perfumes into the country.
a) judged
b) warned
c) arrested
720. They didn't believe his theory because it didn't seem at all … .
a) feasible
b) plausible
c) creditable
721. … you leave for the airport, you'll miss the flight.
a) Unless

b) However
c) When
722. I haven't met her, but I did once … across her boyfriend.
a) look
b) go
c) come
723. She … her next appointment at the dentist's.
a) erased
b) cancelled
c) wiped
724. Because of the earthquake, the windows … in their frames.
a) rattled
b) slapped
c) shocked
725. I would … go by air than spend two days travelling by car.
a) prefer
b) better
c) rather
726. It's all over between them: she's walked … on him.
a) off
b) away
c) out

727. Our best player got infected and won't be … to play tomorrow.
a) adequate
b) fit
c) proper
728. Sarah spoke so fast I couldn't understand … she was talking about.
a) what
b) which
c) how
729. Mr. Smith is free … you now.
a) see
b) will see
c) to see

730. Everyone felt … for Mr. Brown when he lost his management position.
a) discontent
b) sorry
c) unhappy
731. What … will this decision have on the future of this company?
a) effect
b) result
c) answer
732. This year the trees were … two weeks earlier than usual.
a) in full cry
b) in full bloom
c) at full blast
733. During the last meeting everyone shared … his happiness.
a) in
b) against
c) at
734. The professional climber failed … his attempt.
a) with
b) at
c) in
735. I tried to reason … her, but she was rude to me.
a) on
b) with
c) for
736. Are you aware … the difficulties that lie ahead?
a) by
b) on
c) of

737. It's just an illusion. He's not different …
anyone else.
a) for
b) from
c) on
738. Dave usually goes there … him.
a) with

b) to
c) at
739. Alexia worships the sun and … she spends her
holidays in Greece.
a) yet
b) however
c) accordingly
740. I can't come. I'm tied … at the office.
a) in
b) up
c) down
741. Guests wore … they liked to the party.
a) everything
b) anything
c) nothing
742. The pilot drives so quickly that I am afraid that
one day he will …
someone.
a) crash down
b) turn over
c) knock down
743. Don't worry. This dog is perfectly … .
a) harmless
b) harmful
c) tame
744. One of the main advantages … the new
operating platform is that it is
very simple to use.
a) for
b) of
c) on
745. You'd better set off twenty minutes early …
there is traffic.
a) in case
b) so that
c) as if
746. When I saw Olivia's reaction, I regretted …
told her.
a) to have

b) to having
c) having
747. The shirt I was wearing that day was dirty, but I
don't think anyone …
.
a) watched
b) noticed
c) remarked
748. This is the oldest house … the village.
a) in
b) by
c) to
749. Jane was singing an old rock song, a favourite
of … .
a) her
b) herself
c) hers
750. So … people came to the meeting that they had
to cancel it.
a) a few
b) few
c) little
751. Scientists are still looking for a cure …
COVID-19.
a) for
b) against
c) to
752. Put the salt in the water and let it … before
adding anything else.
a) melt
b) dissolve
c) soften
753. It's too hot for you … this parcel.
a) digging
b) for digging
c) to dig
754. He told Steve … for borrowing his laptop
without permission.
a) on
b) out
c) off

755. In this company, if you interfere … other
people's affairs, you will
regret it.
a) with

b) to
c) about
756. Are you at least partially aware of the difficulties that lie ahead …
you?
a) for
b) of
c) to
757. I left my office after I … the report.
a) had written
b) have written
c) should have written
758. Her medical doctor made her … in bed for two weeks.
a) to stay
b) staying
c) stay
759. As quick as … . This phrase means very quick.
a) cats
b) fire
c) lightning
760. The officers haven't had time to complete the investigation, but they
have concluded … that he committed suicide.
a) tentatively
b) tenuously
c) temporally
761. I'm going to buy a new car; I'm tired … this one.
a) of
b) in
c) with
762. … a personal computer can help you work much faster.
a) To have
b) In having
c) Having

763. I … be delighted to show you the way.
a) might
b) ought to
c) would
764. … the weather, the match went ahead.
a) Owing to
b) In spite of
c) However

765. Melania rang to make an early … at the hairdresser's.
a) order
b) appointment
c) date
766. Adrian was the … in his family.
a) lowest
b) littlest
c) shortest
767. Could you buy a cake please … they come this afternoon?
a) if only
b) in case
c) on account of
768. One … of old public transport is its unreliability.
a) disorder
b) dislike
c) disadvantage
769. Did you know that she is … a baby?
a) expecting
b) hoping
c) waiting
770. The main … to progress is not technical but political.
a) clash
b) obstacle
c) prevention
771. The best rooms in this hotel … the bay.
a) regard

b) overlook
c) view
772. All dogs … be kept on a lead in public.
a) must
b) ought
c) need
773. You should separate the eggs and then beat with a … .
a) whip
b) wick
c) whisk
774. The man was … to steal the laptop when he saw it on the table.
a) dragged
b) tempted
c) brought

775. My parents … me to learn English when I was a child.

a) let

b) heard

c) persuaded

776. I am accustomed … bad weather.

a) to

b) of

c) from

777. She was afraid … mentioning it to her husband.

a) in

b) at

c) of

778. I warned them … the danger.

a) at

b) of

c) in

779. Gold is feared … in price this week.

a) to go up

b) going up

c) to be going up

780. I will ask Jane to come if I … her.

a) saw

b) will see

c) see

781. In the jar there was a … which looked like jam.

a) material

b) solid

c) substance

782. Because his presentation was so confusing, … people understood it.

a) clever

b) few

c) less

783. I am … her to arrive at any moment.

a) expecting

b) waiting

c) hoping

784. You … worry about the bill – I've already paid it.

a) daren't

b) might not

c) needn't

785. I've made an appointment for 11 o'clock. Is that … for you?

a) fit

b) convenient

c) right

786. You look … you've seen a ghost!

a) so that

b) that

c) as if

787. You … blame yourself. It wasn't your fault.

a) daren't

b) won't

c) mustn't

788. I'm … that I didn't pass the examination.

a) deceived

b) despaired

c) disappointed

789. This magazine has … interesting article on space travel.

a) quite an

b) a partly

c) nearly an

790. Your sister is much taller … you.

a) how

b) than

c) from

791. They always quarrel about coffee; she likes it strong, but he wants it …

.

a) small

b) feeble

c) weak

792. Getting divorced was a ... decision for us.

a) firm

b) hard

c) large

793. Mr. Smith was … in a road accident.

a) damaged

b) wronged

c) injured

794. I expected her at eight but she finally … at midnight.

a) came to

b) turned up

c) came off

795. Buses into town run … ten minutes or so.

a) each

b) all

c) every

796. Can you make … what she has written there?
a) for
b) out
c) up for

797. I can't say what his name is though it is … .
a) on the tip of my tongue
b) on top of my tongue
c) on my tongue's tip

798. Whether or not to abolish corporal punishment is still … in political circles.
a) proposal of contention
b) a bone of contention
c) bone of agreement

799. I … a nice watch two days ago.
a) was given
b) have been given
c) would give

800. As bold as … . This phrase means cheeky, impudent.
a) bones
b) a bear
c) brass

801. He was an … writer because he persuaded many people.
a) ordinary
b) influential
c) accurate

802. I … seeing Mary tomorrow so I will give her your message.
a) may be
b) shall be
c) could be

803. The temperature yesterday was about … for this season.
a) average
b) middle
c) moderate

804. Steven swims well and … does his sister.
a) also
b) even
c) so

805. The old man was very … for my help.
a) grateful

b) pleased

c) delighted

806. … it was raining she went out without a raincoat.
a) In spite
b) However
c) Although

807. Your progress will be … in three months' time.
a) valued
b) evaluated
c) counted

808. I don't know why she complains. She doesn't earn as … as I do.
a) less
b) few
c) little

809. The organization will not be … any new members.
a) taking up
b) taking off
c) taking on

810. She can make a delicious … out of almost anything.
a) food
b) meal
c) plate

811. From now on, everything will be … sailing, I hope.
a) plain
b) simple
c) pretty

812. She could hardly … such a generous offer.
a) turn for
b) turn off
c) turn down

813. Tom has made his money by developing a travel … .
a) shop
b) business
c) affair

814. Do you believe … all that nonsense? I honestly don't.
a) in
b) to
c) at

815. I'm not sure … the exact date.
a) with

b) of

c) for

816. She's not capable … bringing up this child.

a) of

b) on

c) for

817. Steven was born … .

a) without wedlock

b) out of a wedlock

c) out of wedlock

818. Although he has travelled extensively, he has never been … .

a) to the Antipodes

b) at Antipodes

c) to Antipodes

819. At that hour, the street was … as people were fast asleep in bed.

a) denuded

b) deserted

c) devastated

820. Artists struggle with the conflict between … their own talent and

knowledge that very few succeed.

a) faith in

b) neglect of

c) dissolution to

821. My house isn't difficult to find. It's … the high school.

a) against

b) beside

c) between

822. A lot of my friends have … smoking in the last year.

a) put off

b) given up

c) held back

823. Please tell me … there is anything special that you would like to eat.

a) which

b) so

c) if

824. I'm making you responsible for this report. Please see … it that it is

finished on time.

a) for

b) into

c) to

825. Olivia suggested … to the cinema together.

a) that we should go

b) us to go

c) we are going

826. It will be mostly cloudy, with … of rain in the west.

a) bursts

b) outbreaks

c) times

827. I … of people who smoke.

a) dislike

b) distrust

c) disapprove

828. Jane bought a new … for the party.

a) dress

b) clothes

c) vest

829. When the organization got a new computer, we had to … a

programming course.

a) do

b) make

c) study

830. This history lesson seemed to go … .

a) over and over

b) on and on

c) off and on

831. I know her by …, but I don't what her name is.

a) sight

b) heart

c) chance

832. The bus burst into … but the driver managed to escape.

a) heat

b) fire

c) flames

833. I know Jane is slow … understanding, but please be patient.

a) to

b) at

c) on

834. I'll be absent … class this week.

a) from

b) at

c) to

835. It gives me ... to introduce her.
a) great pleasure
b) a great pleasure
c) much pleasures
836. They ... in Germany for more than two years now.
a) were staying
b) are staying
c) have been staying
837. Look, I'm not drunk. I am as ... as a judge.
a) calm
b) sober
c) clear
838. The working atmosphere has gone downhill. You have a lot to ... for.
a) agree
b) abide
c) answer

839. That incident happened because of the ... of the employees.
a) infallible
b) negligence
c) diligence
840. "A sore point" means:
a) a very dangerous crossroads
b) a matter that irritates or hurts when it is brought up
c) a blister on a foot
841. She likes to sit there and ... what goes on below.
a) look
b) gaze
c) watch
842. Keep ... the good work!
a) with
b) on
c) up
843. ... he joined the army, Steve had never been abroad.
a) Until
b) Since
c) While
844. If you want to join our club, you must first ... this application form.
a) do up
b) fill in

c) make up
845. I haven't got ... furniture like theirs.
a) some
b) any
c) the

Set 4

846. The librarian went to search for the book in a place ... rare ones were kept.
a) where
b) there
c) that
847. A teacher must ... children to be kind to each other.
a) let

b) force
c) encourage
848. You'll ... a lot of time if you take the car.
a) spend
b) make
c) save
849. They took out a/an ... to that newspaper.
a) inscription
b) subscription
c) conscription
850. The local authorities ... increase taxes soon.
a) may
b) need
c) dare
851. The child hit the vase with his elbow and it ... to the floor.
a) crashed
b) smashed
c) broke
852. I completely ... with what has been said.
a) accept
b) agree
c) approve
853. She lost her homework and she ... do it again.
a) ought
b) needs
c) has to
854. You are not ... to smoke inside.

a) let
b) allowed
c) accepted
855. I believe … this town needs is a new shopping mall.
a) as
b) how
c) what

856. It's still not … that I am going to Madrid tomorrow.
a) certain
b) right
c) exact
857. Even though the old man was often cruel to his dog, it remained
faithful … him.
a) for
b) in
c) to
858. You should encourage your daughter … her efforts.
a) to
b) for
c) in
859. The artists … our town by … .
a) have taken/by surprise
b) have taken/by storm
c) have brought/by storm
860. There is an increasing … to make films portraying love.
a) trend
b) surge
c) tradition
861. I felt sorry … him when he lost his job.
a) with
b) to
c) for
862. It was difficult for me to … what the recommendations I should make.
a) decide
b) realize
c) settle
863. The gorgeous lady walked to the … of the pool and jumped in.
a) extent
b) border

c) side
864. I thought she would like me to buy her a … brown bag.
a) black

b) French
c) new
865. The officer … me the way.
a) said
b) told
c) directed
866. Her boyfriend was sent to prison for … a bank.
a) stealing
b) robbing
c) lending
867. I'm going to stay here … she phones me.
a) for
b) when
c) until
868. You can trust what Daniel says. He's a very … person.
a) trustful
b) profitable
c) reliable
869. Don't worry. I still have one or two … up my sleeve.
a) tricks
b) defenses
c) jokes
870. The Prime Minister got up to … a short speech.
a) tell
b) make
c) hold
871. Mike was an … writer who persuaded many people.
a) influential
b) accurate
c) ordinary
872. If I hadn't done that, I think you … .
a) could die
b) might have died
c) may have died

873. People who live in big cities … to suffer from stress.
a) develop
b) tend

c) lean

874. She has provided … every emergency.

a) to

b) with

c) for

875. There was a note attached … the package.

a) to

b) with

c) on

876. They say Italian is a splendid language … .

a) for singing in

b) to sing in

c) for sing in

877. I saw him … the street.

a) crosses

b) to cross

c) cross

878. Although we have a large number of employees, each one receives … attention when needed.

a) only

b) individual

c) single

879. We negotiated for hours but we weren't able to … at an agreement.

a) agree

b) abide

c) arrive

880. The missing climber appeared at the mountain hut … and kicking.

a) alive

b) hale

c) safe

881. Sarah had had a special … with her aunt ever since her mother died.

a) sense

b) feeling

c) relationship

882. The little boy was so noisy that his mother told him not to be such a …

.

a) trouble

b) nuisance

c) worry

883. I took … football again at the beginning of this month.

a) up

b) with

c) by

884. Would you … the stamps on to the documents?

a) spit

b) suck

c) stick

885. The robber … everyone in the bank lie on the floor.

a) obliged

b) made

c) forced

886. There are … employees who always cause trouble.

a) these

b) that

c) some

887. I am late because my alarm clock … this morning. I'm sorry.

a) came on

b) went off

c) turned on

888. In spite of his protests, Steve … the athlete train two hours a day.

a) made

b) let

c) cause

889. The man was standing … of the diving board, showing off his muscles.

a) by the end

b) on the end

c) in the end

890. I mustn't stop … on this project for another two hours.

a) to work

b) working

c) to have work

891. Would you mind if I … the windows? It's hot in here.

a) did open

b) opened

c) were opening

892. The next time you see Jane, you … apologize.

a) ought to

b) need

c) dare to

893. If she's not back … midnight, I'm going to phone the police.
a) on
b) till
c) by

894. The man … his wife and children and left them to take care of themselves.
a) let
b) spoilt
c) abandoned

895. The customer … on complaining to the manager in person.
a) insisted
b) argued
c) demanded

896. They have a great … for that island because they spent their honeymoon there.
a) feeling
b) affection
c) connection

897. Like her, I hope … something better.
a) to
b) in
c) for

898. I would go to Rome if I … time to do it.
a) have
b) had
c) would have

899. I will play the piano but I'm a little … .
a) out of practice
b) out of use
c) out of turn

900. In this area coal is mined day … night.
a) into
b) after
c) and

901. I had to leave my family … when I went abroad to work.
a) at a loss
b) behind
c) out

902. The author had qualified as a medical doctor but later gave up the …
of medicine.
a) practice
b) procedure
c) prescription

903. It was … . I had to talk quickly to keep warm.
a) fresh
b) mild
c) cold

904. Her novel was more exciting … any she has written.
a) than
b) as
c) to

905. I'm having a party on Sunday. …?
a) Will you come
b) Don't you come
c) Need you come

906. The boy … his head, wondering how he could solve the equation.
a) shaved

b) screwed
c) scratched

907. She swatted some flies on the windows and … the glass.
a) crashed
b) smashed
c) cut

908. She received a e-mail this morning … her a place at university.
a) inviting
b) offering
c) proposing

909. The Browns spent so much money that they're … debt.
a) out of
b) with
c) in

910. … you open the windows, please?
a) Need
b) Will
c) May

911. Will you … what you said? It was rude!
a) take off
b) take up
c) take back

912. Stick this … on the parcel that says "fragile".
a) label

b) sign
c) advice
913. The manager … that the people he works with are very committed.
a) talks
b) says
c) tells
914. The girl learnt to ski on a slope that was not too … .
a) high
b) tall
c) steep

915. The trade … of the company if a bee.
a) mark
b) class
c) brand
916. You will not succeed … working harder on this project.
a) although
b) if
c) without
917. The old lady will never part … her precious possessions.
a) from
b) to
c) with
918. I am grateful … you.
a) to
b) for
c) by
919. They have to work hard for money while the fat … in the city make money doing very little.
a) pack
b) fish
c) cats
920. Youngsters need all the help and … when applying for jobs.
a) incentive
b) stimulation
c) encouragement
921. I'm sorry but I haven't got … change.
a) some
b) lots
c) any

922. Volkswagen is one of the most popular … of car in Germany.
a) makes
b) brands
c) marks
923. I must … shopping tomorrow.
a) to go
b) going
c) go
924. I can't see any … to this complicated problem.
a) result
b) solution
c) reason
925. Yesterday I came … a beautiful old car.
a) across
b) over
c) down
926. I can't find my book anywhere; it has simply … .
a) missed
b) lost
c) vanished
927. Scientists have discovered a close … between smoking and cancer.
a) action
b) connection
c) union
928. He came in quietly … not to wake the children.
a) so as
b) if so
c) as if
929. I decided to … a party to celebrate my promotion.
a) offer
b) give
c) make
930. I have no doubt … the innocence of the accused.
a) over
b) on
c) about
931. Everybody … me for the incident.
a) blamed
b) arrested
c) charged

932. Tomorrow the children are going to see the works … Van Gogh.
a) from
b) of
c) with

933. I consulted my lawyer … the matter and I shall continue.
a) for
b) to
c) on

934. She didn't enjoy … at her aunt's.
a) to stay
b) staying
c) stayed

935. There are … when I have to drive for long distances.
a) times
b) a long time
c) at times

936. … by the rejections of his articles, Daniel … to submit his works to
other publishers.
a) Undaunted/continued
b) Elated/planned
c) Inspired/complied

937. When Mary heard the latest bad news, she hit the … .
a) head
b) bend
c) roof

938. It has been suggested that environment is the … factor in the incidence
of drug addiction.
a) logical
b) conclusive
c) predominant

939. If the door bell … she would rush to answer it.
a) rings
b) rang
c) has rung

940. The five friends all … for the same job.
a) applied
b) referred
c) requested

941. My laptop is out of order, which is a … .
a) hurt
b) harm
c) nuisance

942. We decided to go ahead with the match … the bad weather.
a) unless
b) in spite
c) despite

943. She kept the job … the manager had threatened to sack her.
a) although
b) even
c) unless

944. It takes most people seven to ten days to … from COVID-19.
a) cure
b) recover
c) prevent

945. The building has been left empty for five years; it will be expensive to
… the damage that has been done.
a) fix
b) repair
c) mend

946. The children were … by the noise in the forest.
a) afraid
b) feared
c) frightened

947. No, thanks. I'm trying to … weight.
a) lose
b) rid
c) throw

948. Is there … at all I can do to help you?
a) someone

b) anything
c) no one

949. I'll have to wait until the mechanic … .
a) will come
b) is coming
c) comes

950. … you improve this project, you won't pass the exam.
a) When
b) Unless
c) If

951. We got up early this morning … pack the car for the journey.

a) in order to
b) so that
c) in case
952. I … that a shame!
a) calling
b) might call
c) call
953. When there are people about a deer … for the shelter of the forest.
a) takes
b) makes
c) seeks
954. I am anxious about the … of the negotiations.
a) output
b) outlook
c) outcome
955. We have been corresponding … each other for some years.
a) with
b) to
c) by
956. When questioned about the missing report, he firmly … that he had
ever seen it.
a) defied
b) refused
c) denied

957. Have you ever been introduced to …?
a) royalty
b) the royalty
c) royalties
958. Mary's rung … . I must have said something wrong.
a) off
b) round
c) back
959. The officers set a … to catch them.
a) trap
b) plan
c) device
960. The rise in the flat prices … him to sell his for a large profit.
a) achieved
b) enabled
c) managed

961. She enjoyed the dessert so much that she accepted a second … .
a) load
b) pile
c) helping
962. The little boy put a … against the tree and climbed up.
a) scale
b) grade
c) ladder
963. This is one of the London's most … hotels.
a) well-off
b) luxurious
c) rich
964. Some truck drivers expect everyone else to get … their way.
a) away from
b) off
c) out of
965. It's … long time since I last saw you.
a) such a

b) so
c) too
966. The dentist told me to open my mouth … .
a) broad
b) greatly
c) wide
967. Tom left home more than two hours ago. He … be at the office by
now.
a) can
b) must
c) would
968. I … you wear the blue coat.
a) say
b) suggest
c) encourage
969. When I was in London I went on a few short day … to tourist sights.
a) travels
b) voyages
c) trips
970. The purple curtains began to … after some time in the sun.
a) fade
b) dissolve

c) melt

971. Our new colleague seems calm enough, but he has a very violent … .
a) mood
b) temper
c) stage

972. It's three years … I went to Cambridge.
a) for
b) last
c) since

973. They can only cure Mary … her illness if they operate on her.
a) of
b) on
c) in

974. I believe … taking my time to finish this project.
a) on
b) in
c) with

975. That man is often extremely rude … people.
a) for
b) with
c) to

976. You demand too much … him.
a) of
b) for
c) in

977. The branch gave … and the cat found itself suddenly on the ground.
a) in
b) way
c) back

978. Mira saw her little sister … after the dog.
a) run
b) ran
c) runs

979. If you … Harry, tell him to come and see me.
a) have met
b) meet
c) met

980. Our study … in March if we receive all feedback.
a) is published
b) published
c) will be published

981. I kept the door open by putting a … under it.
a) triangle
b) block
c) wedge

982. … from Sarah, all the employees said they would go.
a) Apart
b) Except
c) Only

983. This cloth … quite thin.
a) touches
b) feels
c) holds

984. The boy says he has got … in his stomach.
a) hurt
b) pains
c) suffering

985. The drivers are complaining that their fares are too … .
a) small
b) little
c) low

986. The terrorist … the pilot to change direction.
a) forced
b) demanded
c) made

987. As soon as the alarm rang everyone walked quickly downstairs, … gathered in the car park.
a) while
b) then
c) before

988. She has a strong … to see her town again.
a) liking
b) feeling
c) desire

989. Don't … your drink on the table. Be careful!
a) spill
b) flood
c) flow

990. This wet weather has lasted for two weeks; … rained every single day.
a) there has
b) it has
c) there was

991. It is a long … from Berlin to Moscow.
a) tour
b) track
c) flight
992. Do you mind not …?
a) to smoke
b) smoke
c) smoking
993. We will have to … sales during the coming
year.
a) expand
b) increase
c) extend
994. The meeting, … I was the guest of honour, was
enjoyable.
a) by which
b) for which
c) at which
995. That's the woman … daughter I nearly kissed
when I was young.
a) whose
b) whom
c) that
996. I am thankful … any advice you could give me.
a) about
b) on
c) for
997. We haven't accused him … anything.
a) by
b) of
c) to
998. The spy surrendered himself … the enemy.
a) in
b) with
c) to
999. This shows continues to … various audiences.
a) enthrall

b) bored
c) catching
1000. The … of supplies and equipment has
hampered the progress of
medical research for a cure.
a) scarcity
b) rationing
c) discontinuance

1001. In this country home ownership has … rapidly
since 1990.
a) raised
b) grown
c) enlarged
1002. Unfortunately, nobody … that airplane crash.
a) lived
b) released
c) survived
1003. We were so late reaching the station that we
… missed the train.
a) almost
b) already
c) soon
1004. The director didn't offer her the job because of
her untidy … .
a) sight
b) presence
c) appearance
1005. You … have seen them yesterday. They're on
holiday.
a) mustn't
b) can't
c) needn't
1006. The mansion has been built on the … of a
lake.
a) border
b) edge
c) front
1007. Her performance was …; everyone was
delighted.
a) faultless
b) unmarked
c) worthless

1008. Please … your bill before you leave the shop.
a) control
b) figure
c) check
1009. I can't even make … where the road is.
a) out
b) up
c) over
1010. I found the articles rather dull; I couldn't read
it … .
a) by the end
b) to the end

c) on the end

1011. She has to work hard to keep the house … and tidy.

a) smooth

b) neat

c) plain

1012. How much have you borrowed … me already? Don't you think that's enough?

a) of

b) from

c) on

1013. This coat will protect you … the cold.

a) from

b) about

c) of

1014. Spies may have a number of … names and documents.

a) false

b) artificial

c) synthetic

1015. They were … after working all day.

a) tired out

b) worn out

c) tired down

1016. If I had known about the problem, I … him to go away.

a) told

b) would tell

c) would have told

1017. You … better be careful not to miss the class.

a) would

b) had

c) should

1018. I hope you don't mind me … so late at night. It's urgent.

a) telephone

b) telephoning

c) to telephone

1019. As cunning as a … . This phrase means very clever, very smart.

a) a fox

b) a leopard

c) an owl

1020. Molecular biology is one of the most interesting scientific … .

a) divisions

b) disciplines

c) matters

1021. Take the bus and get … at Black Lake Road.

a) off

b) down

c) outside

1022. Tom's sister had a baby daughter yesterday and she is his first … .

a) cousin

b) relation

c) niece

1023. Will the company be able to … all their difficulties?

a) overcome

b) dismiss

c) defeat

1024. There was nothing … to eat in the refrigerator.

a) at last

b) at all

c) at least

1025. The professor was angry with them because they kept … talking.

a) up

b) up with

c) on

1026. After going to several interviews, she … to get a job.

a) managed

b) could

c) achieved

1027. If only he … told the police the truth in the first place.

a) has

b) would have

c) had

1028. A small … of students was waiting outside the class.

a) team

b) group

c) gang

1029. Many countries rely on rice as the … food.

a) capital

b) staple

c) winning

1030. Please take your place in the … .

a) queue
b) tail
c) file
1031. I like to sit … the river and fish.
a) beside
b) next
c) along
1032. The poor man fell … in front of a train.
a) in full
b) in full cry
c) full length
1033. Her professor brought her some books … art.
a) on

b) for
c) with
1034. I am thinking of looking … a new job.
a) to
b) for
c) after
1035. I've never been good … math.
a) with
b) at
c) in
1036. It's pointless … .
a) asking her for help
b) to ask help from her
c) to ask her of helping
1037. There is no need for you to shout … .
a) at your top voice
b) on top of your voice
c) at the top of your voice
1038. I … him about it for more than two weeks.
a) am asking
b) have been asking
c) asked
1039. They … their success to hard work.
a) attribute
b) aim
c) angle
1040. Prescribed treatments can … the pain but cannot … the patient.
a) palliate/cure
b) alleviate/infect
c) abate/affect
1041. When the police found my wallet, it was … .
a) vacant

b) empty
c) deserted
1042. It was a sad day when the company closed and the employees were all … .
a) paid back
b) paid up
c) paid off
1043. You will become ill … you stop working so hard.
a) until
b) unless
c) if
1044. The sooner we leave this place, the …!
a) preferable
b) better
c) ideal
1045. The weather seems to be … .
a) clearing up
b) setting up
c) wearing off
1046. After some time you get used to the people's … of life.
a) habit
b) custom
c) way
1047. I can no longer afford the cost of … two cars.
a) operating
b) running
c) managing
1048. A soldier has to learn to carry … orders as soon as they are given.
a) on
b) off
c) out
1049. Too many players refuse to … the referee's decisions.
a) accept
b) allow
c) agree
1050. It's not fair that I … always have to clean the table.
a) should

b) would
c) must

1051. She won't have any problems. She's a very self-... young lady.
a) reliable
b) confident
c) trusting

1052. This summer was so hot that the ... in the woods dried up.
a) bath
b) bowl
c) pond

1053. It's over a year ... I visited the medical doctor.
a) past
b) since
c) when

1054. There's an interesting pc game ... in today's newspaper.
a) advertised
b) informed
c) issued

1055. The lessons usually start ... 8 p.m.
a) with
b) on
c) at

1056. I though you said that you were ... to be in Germany this month.
a) supposed
b) intended
c) assumed

1057. Motorway traffic was ... after a terrible accident.
a) diverged
b) diverted
c) deflected

1058. She is referred to as a/an ... housewife.
a) only
b) sole
c) mere

1059. I wish she ... change her mind so often!
a) shouldn't
b) wouldn't
c) couldn't

1060. The famous woman lived a life thought to be ... even by her contemporaries.
a) exorbitant
b) extraneous
c) extravagant

1061. When I was a child I wanted to ... to play the guitar.
a) know
b) learn
c) discover

1062. I really can't make ... what's happening here.
a) away
b) over
c) out

1063. Mary has put on so much weight that her clothes don't ... her any more.
a) match
b) fit
c) suit

1064. It's amazing what his mother lets him ... away with.
a) get
b) make
c) go

1065. Steve ... to the hospital ten minutes before her birth.
a) was
b) got
c) arrived

1066. The man took the stress to write ... the complete list for us.
a) out
b) through
c) off

1067. ... the papers, the Prime Minister is to give a speech tomorrow.
a) Related to
b) Referring to
c) According to

1068. Clearing the weeds was a much harder ... than they had imagined.
a) deed
b) service
c) task

1069. Be careful! It's a minor road and ... in places.
a) bending
b) wandering
c) winding

1070. My application was ... .

a) turned down
b) let down
c) put down
1071. I am fond of his novels. He is my … author.
a) favourite
b) likely
c) favoured
1072. She studied chemistry at university and … .
a) so did I
b) so I did
c) I did also
1073. Biting one's fingernails is a very bad … .
a) custom
b) habit
c) way
1074. You … be serious about that. I won't do it.
a) mustn't
b) might not
c) can't
1075. He is so keen … learning. He should be encouraged.
a) in

b) on
c) for
1076. Don't blame me … that! It's not my fault.
a) to
b) with
c) for
1077. I don't think she had … me about her problems.
a) tells
b) to tell
c) telling
1078. The judge shouted to counsel on both sides that he would … no argument.
a) hear
b) brook
c) accept
1079. The professor was … out of his job after the scandal.
a) wiped
b) eased
c) wiped
1080. He was unsure that the speech was word … .
a) perfect

b) precise
c) accurate
1081. Mike often … about his expensive car.
a) praises
b) boasts
c) prides
1082. Have you heard? Steven has got married … Susan.
a) to
b) with
c) by
1083. The boy went to bed … very ill.
a) feels
b) having felt
c) feeling

1084. Could you … me fifty dollars? I'll pay you back next Friday.
a) lend
b) take
c) borrow
1085. We hope that one day a cure for cancer will … .
a) find
b) be found
c) been found
1086. We have much pleasure in … the invitation.
a) taking
b) accepting
c) thanking
1087. Tom is a … player. He practises for three hours every morning.
a) keen
b) excited
c) impatient
1088. I had a … that something terrible was going to happen.
a) sense
b) view
c) feeling
1089. If you're trying to lose weight, you should … off fats.
a) eat
b) keep
c) go
1090. Tom decided to … a priest instead of joining the army.

a) train for

b) study for

c) become

1091. Jennifer … drive to the station every day.

a) using to

b) used to

c) had used to

1092. … hard he tries, she never wins at tennis.

a) Wherever

b) Whatever

c) However

1093. When the little boy was hit on the head, he … consciousness.

a) lost

b) fell

c) dropped

1094. The kid got a bad mark because he had … a lot of mistakes in his

homework.

a) done

b) committed

c) made

1095. The student who … in his exams was expelled.

a) cheated

b) tricked

c) deceived

1096. The racing car came round the corner … full speed.

a) for

b) at

c) to

1097. I dreamt … you last night.

a) on

b) in

c) of

1098. He … .

a) set off to a stroll

b) set off on a stroll

c) set down to a stroll

1099. If I can't be back on time, she … her dinner alone.

a) has

b) will have

c) would have

1100. As black as … . This phrase means very dirty.

a) the Ace of Spades

b) ink

c) night

1101. I'm very … in this information.

a) concerned

b) interested

c) surprised

1102. Since his wife died, he has gone to … .

a) fragments

b) bits

c) pieces

1103. I hope that you have read the report and understand … it means.

a) what

b) how

c) that

1104. The crowd's … was amazing.

a) inactive

b) reaction

c) interacted

1105. Sarah met her husband … a computer dating agency.

a) out of

b) from

c) through

1106. As far as I'm …, it's all right to leave now.

a) regarded

b) consulted

c) concerned

1107. There was a serious … of cholera last year.

a) outbreak

b) fallout

c) overflow

1108. The … of the employees led to a series of troubles.

a) sending

b) dismissal

c) parting

1109. She struggled for a time before she … to free herself.

a) managed

b) achieved

c) enabled

1110. She tried to find a good excuse to … the awkward situation.

a) get over for
b) get away
c) get out of
1111. This meat isn't that good; you have to … it for a long time.
a) chew
b) bite
c) swallow
1112. I wear a seat-belt … I have an accident.
a) unless
b) if
c) in case
1113. It takes a while to … in a new house.
a) settle up
b) settle down
c) settle on
1114. More people … football than play it.
a) watch
b) look
c) stare
1115. The conductor told her to get off because she couldn't pay the … .
a) fee
b) fare
c) bill
1116. She is qualified … typing.
a) to
b) at
c) in
1117. We have to … museums and encourage legitimate investors.
a) protect
b) undermine
c) perpetuate

1118. Despite some bad reviews, his importance was not … .
a) diminished
b) distilled
c) embellished
1119. "A French window" means … .
a) a windows with no glass
b) a double glass door that opens on to a garden or balcony
c) a windows that turns out to be too small
1120. Our fortune was … at more than $2 million.
a) judged

b) guessed
c) estimated
1121. To my …, her illness proved not to be as serious as I had feared.
a) anxiety
b) eyes
c) relief
1122. You shouldn't let him treat you like that. You must stand … him.
a) up to
b) by
c) for
1123. This public clock is not as … as it should be.
a) true
b) accurate
c) strict
1124. You … stay at home for another day.
a) had better
b) can better
c) would better
1125. The two cars collided with … loud a crash it woke me.
a) so
b) very
c) such
1126. I … the stolen bike when the insurance money arrived.
a) misplaced

b) displaced
c) replaced
1127. I'm looking forward … you again.
a) to see
b) to seeing
c) seeing
1128. This is a friendly community and everyone … each other very well.
a) gets on with
b) gets up to
c) gets down to
1129. Parking …!
a) stopped
b) prohibited
c) denied
1130. It's a good thing to give at least a two week's … before you leave.
a) time

b) leave

c) notice

1131. More often … not, it rains here in autumn.

a) than

b) if

c) as

1132. Now they are the … of friends.

a) most

b) best

c) nearest

1133. If … I had done it when I had the chance!

a) just

b) then

c) only

1134. She kept the business … for as long as possible.

a) to go

b) going

c) go

1135. This employee is very good .. finding excuses.

a) for

b) in

c) at

1136. … any of these documentaries before?

a) Did you see

b) Have you seen

c) Will you see

1137. Would you mind … these plates a wipe?

a) making

b) giving

c) getting

1138. The lung transplant operation is … complicated.

a) broadly

b) slightly

c) extremely

1139. I … be grateful if you could let me have the details.

a) should

b) ought to

c) might

1140. Do you know … there?

a) whose

b) who's

c) whom

1141. He looks as if he … be her brother.

a) can

b) would

c) could

1142. The little girl is as … as a mouse.

a) quiet

b) small

c) slight

1143. After her absence, she found it difficult to … up with the rest.

a) take

b) catch

c) make

1144. I got to the theatre just … to see the actors entering.

a) in time

b) on time

c) at times

1145. This job … many visits to landlords.

a) concerns

b) offers

c) involves

1146. Do you … my turning the laptop on?

a) want

b) mind

c) object

1147. Jack was not pleased about … called an idiot.

a) was

b) being

c) to be

1148. A hot lemon drink is good … a cold.

a) for

b) with

c) to

1149. I heard a … at the door.

a) lean

b) hit

c) knock

1150. The hotel is … walking distance of the sea.

a) close

b) within

c) inside

1151. The main … of this drink are wine and orange juice.

a) parts

b) ingredients

c) components

1152. Our hands smell … honey soap.
a) of
b) with
c) by
1153. I'm sure she … on 16th February.
a) hasn't come
b) don't come
c) didn't come
1154. If I see John, I … to him.
a) talk
b) would talk
c) will talk
1155. If I get tickets, I … you up.
a) will ring
b) ring
c) could ring
1156. Kate did all the work … her own.
a) by
b) on
c) for
1157. The officers arrested the … criminal.
a) famous
b) renowned
c) notorious
1158. The left faction prospers … the right is losing ground.
a) while
b) until
c) whether
1159. The student took down … quantities of notes.
a) extended
b) detailed
c) copious
1160. Open plains are … of the geography of this country.
a) distinctive

b) specific
c) characteristic
1161. It is a good idea to see your medic for … .
a) a revision
b) a check-up
c) a control
1162. If I had known your address, I … to see you.
a) would come
b) would have come

c) came
1163. Steve has … you some flowers.
a) carried
b) lifted
c) brought
1164. She played an active … in politics.
a) part
b) scene
c) job
1165. Chip-making is a very … work.
a) skilled
b) trained
c) educated
1166. Mary … him of wanting to marry her just for money.
a) cursed
b) accused
c) blamed
1167. It was snowing very … so I took my car.
a) wet
b) badly
c) hard
1168. He was … twenty euros for parking the car illegally.
a) fined
b) punished
c) charged

1169. Do you know what time the train … to Madrid?
a) gets
b) comes
c) reaches
1170. She never turned … at the cinema.
a) out
b) up
c) in
1171. The man … to give the police any more information.
a) objected
b) refused
c) disliked
1172. Can you give me … information about it?
a) any
b) all
c) one
1173. The boy was the only person to … the crash.

a) alive

b) survive

c) cure

1174. I have always been fond … games.

a) with

b) about

c) of

1175. I heard her … to John about holiday plans.

a) talk

b) talked

c) to talk

1176. These sweaters are … by this local firm.

a) well made

b) well-knit

c) well-founded

1177. Many undergraduates think it's east to … a job once they leave
university.

a) collect

b) obtain

c) apply

1178. Brian is sucking up to the manager. I guess he's … for promotion.

a) acting

b) adhering

c) angling

1179. Her poetry is rather vague and … .

a) lucid

b) opaque

c) straightforward

1180. As rich as … . This phrase means extremely rich.

a) honey

b) Croesus

c) nails

1181. I ran … the thief, but I didn't catch him.

a) over

b) after

c) near

1182. Could you … me to take back those books?

a) remind

b) remember

c) memorize

1183. The new play is worth … .

a) to see

b) to seeing

c) seeing

1184. I'm not surprised you failed. You … have worked harder.

a) must

b) would

c) should

1185. … no need to buy a car.

a) You're

b) It has

c) There's

1186. She retired early … ill-health.

a) ahead of

b) in front of

c) on account of

1187. … did I have a sore throat, I also felt quite sick.

a) Not only

b) Also

c) In addition

1188. Do you think you could … me $25?

a) let

b) lend

c) borrow

1189. He is … a lot of money in his new job.

a) having

b) earning

c) gaining

1190. She was … of stealing one of the office laptops.

a) judged

b) charged

c) accused

1191. He tried harder than …, but he failed again.

a) ever

b) never

c) better

1192. Traffic is being … because of the parade.

a) altered

b) converted

c) diverted

1193. Don't blame him … this mess.

a) to

b) for

c) at

1194. Mary often suffers … colds.

a) at

b) on

c) from

1195. My competitor ran so fast I couldn't catch up … him.

a) to

b) from

c) with

1196. She has never done any work. She lives … her mother.

a) on

b) from

c) at

1197. His reports … in its remarks on the issue.

a) pulls no punches

b) pulls no needles

c) puts no punches

1198. My car … in the street.

a) has parked

b) is parked

c) had parked

1199. It's probably that the final price will … .

a) relax

b) evolved

c) escalate

1200. When the old lady tried to walk she had a sharp … in her leg.

a) hurt

b) pain

c) cut

1201. She stood on one leg, … against the wall.

a) leaning

b) stopping

c) staying

1202. … of all of us who are here tonight, thank you.

a) In person

b) On account

c) On behalf

1203. It was a mere …; I didn't mean to hurt them!

a) chance

b) accident

c) error

1204. When I was there my money … .

a) were stolen

b) was stealing

c) was stolen

1205. … to an accident, traffic is moving extremely slowly.

a) Because

b) Since

c) Owing

1206. I need to have a short rest as I … a headache.

a) take

b) have

c) feel

1207. Ducks fly in a definite … .

a) formation

b) formula

c) figure

1208. The police are looking … the matter.

a) up to

b) in on

c) into

1209. She must be … for 80.

a) going by

b) going off

c) getting on

1210. The sky is … so we can go fishing.

a) clean

b) clear

c) open

1211. It tasted so … of lemon. I didn't like it.

a) hardly

b) strongly

c) fully

1212. We are not in the least … about his opinion.

a) concerned

b) interested

c) aware

1213. Whenever you go to the sales, you … your money.

a) miss

b) leave

c) waste

1214. Paris lies … the Seine river.

a) on

b) over

c) at

1215. At the end of the day I watch a little TV … going to bed.

a) then

b) upon

c) before

1216. She decided to … early.

a) retire

b) resign

c) retreat

1217. It's obvious to us that the manager is not responsible … this mistake.

a) for

b) of

c) about

1218. The officer's orders were perfectly … .

a) exercised

b) executed

c) applied

1219. I'm going to get a top job soon. I'm a real high … .

a) cats

b) flier

c) market

1220. The girl takes … her mother.

a) over

b) for

c) after

1221. The … thing about travelling by train is that you can sleep.

a) enjoyed

b) enjoyable

c) enjoyment

1222. I let it ring several times before I … the receiver.

a) raised up

b) picked up

c) took out

1223. I have arranged special insurance to cover medical … .

a) expenses

b) prices

c) money

1224. You will be given an intelligence … during today's interview.

a) fitting

b) proof

c) test

1225. If you hear the baby … please call me.

a) say

b) cry

c) shout

1226. In the last months, a record number of cars … .

a) have been sold

b) have sold

c) had been sold

1227. Tim thought … getting a new job for a long time.

a) at

b) on

c) about

1228. I'm a millionaire … I expect everyone in this club to be a millionaire too.

a) then

b) but

c) and

1229. I'm disgusted … your behaviour!

a) to

b) for

c) at

1230. You forgot to thank her … the present.

a) for

b) on

c) at

1231. She's not fond … dancing.

a) at

b) of

c) on

1232. I was afraid of mentioning it … him.

a) on

b) for

c) to

1233. They have a … future ahead with little comfort and food.

a) grim

b) cruel

c) fierce

1234. Sarah … me all about her new job next Friday.

a) will tell

b) told

c) tells

1235. Mike … for Germany last weekend.

a) has left

b) had left

c) left

1236. I would have bought that PC, if I … money.
a) had have
b) had had
c) have had

1237. As soon as you … to the place, call me.
a) will get
b) has got
c) get

1238. If I had more time, I … some of those studies.
a) will read
b) would read
c) had read

1239. I'd be … to go to China one day.
a) interested
b) fond
c) helpful

1240. The product is a success. We're doing a roaring … in it.
a) ship
b) deal
c) trade

1241. I shouldn't imagine there is … in this organization who can answer
that question.
a) anyone
b) no one
c) somebody

1242. Here they learn how to get … with other people.
a) away
b) along
c) across

1243. Hello. Please put me … to the marketing manager.
a) up
b) over
c) through

1244. … pleasant it is to sit here in the garden!
a) So
b) How
c) What

1245. I'm going to … my suit cleaned.
a) make

b) send
c) have

1246. I'm afraid his writing is becoming more and more … .
a) illegible
b) illiterate
c) eligible

1247. I had to … some trees so that I could extend my herbs plantation.
a) cut
b) cut down
c) cut off

1248. I … rather not go there.
a) would
b) will
c) should

1249. Thank goodness you have come …!
a) finally
b) at the end
c) at last

Set 5

1250. It was an unique car which must have belonged to a … person.
a) plentiful
b) expensive
c) wealthy

1251. I'll give him your message the … I see him.
a) minute
b) soon
c) time

1252. I had a … problem with my laptop.
a) like
b) same
c) similar

1253. She is quite stubborn, so it will be difficult to … her to go.
a) suggest
b) persuade
c) make

1254. In the city park the officer came face … face with the thief.
a) to
b) for
c) by

1255. I can't afford a laptop so we'll just have to do … one.
a) down
b) up with
c) without
1256. I am intent … passing the exam.
a) with
b) to
c) on
1257. … the evening we will meet again.
a) In
b) About
c) On
1258. When I was washing the car, the telephone … .
a) would wing
b) rings
c) rang
1259. The bank is obliged to refuse your application for an extended … .
a) estimate
b) overdraft
c) balance
1260. The delay was brought … by bad weather.
a) up
b) down
c) about
1261. Jane … the office when I arrived.
a) was leaving
b) has left
c) leaves
1262. I will do the work and then send you the … for it.
a) sum
b) note
c) bill
1263. She seems to be … of leaving the house on time. She is always late.
a) unable
b) incapable
c) unaware
1264. She would not … her boyfriend's advice.
a) follow
b) agree
c) want

1265. She has never been too friendly to her colleagues and keeps them at a … .
a) space
b) reserve
c) distance
1266. I … rather go to Spain than Russia for my holiday.
a) would
b) had
c) did
1267. Our organization is a small one with only a few … .
a) employees
b) employs
c) employers
1268. Catching this flight will give us the … to do some shopping.
a) luck
b) occasion
c) opportunity
1269. I've … had time to read the report. I can't give an opinion on it.
a) nearly
b) hardly
c) hard
1270. You … have rushed to the airport. The plane was delayed.
a) needn't
b) mustn't
c) couldn't

1271. They have helped the tourist business … .
a) no end
b) on end
c) at an end
1272. She looked embarrassed … than pleased.
a) apart
b) instead
c) rather
1273. I have been waiting for this day for years, and at … it has come.
a) the end
b) last
c) the finish
1274. This year the company made a … but next year I hope to make a

small profit.
a) loss
b) lose
c) loose
1275. The old man was cruel … his dog.
a) for
b) with
c) to
1276. I expect a great deal … you, Daniel.
a) on
b) from
c) at
1277. Mary is very efficient … her work.
a) on
b) with
c) at
1278. If he … me to do it, I would do so.
a) asks
b) asked
c) has asked
1279. I don't believe that this preposterous plan is …
of our consideration.
a) worthy

b) worth
c) worthless
1280. They say Mary is an excellent manager. She
runs a tight … .
a) deal
b) ship
c) bargain
1281. The gun fell into the river and was … along by
the fast current.
a) caught
b) swept
c) thrown
1282. There is a lot of … when fruit and vegetables
are not sold because
they are scraped.
a) rot
b) ruin
c) waste
1283. Why don't you look it … the dictionary?
a) up
b) at
c) in
1284. Do I have to make that course? No, you … .

a) haven't
b) mustn't
c) needn't
1285. I had no way of making a fire so I had to eat
the meat … .
a) crude
b) rude
c) raw
1286. My plane takes … at 4 p.m.
a) out
b) off
c) up
1287. The child was told to … for being rude.
a) apologize
b) excuse
c) forgive

1288. I'll have to … to you. I don't want him to
hear.
a) whisper
b) shout
c) say
1289. I'll call … you at 7 o'clock.
a) up
b) for
c) in
1290. Try to write the report the way Jane … .
a) puts
b) makes
c) does
1291. The concert was so … that I almost fell asleep.
a) boring
b) bored
c) tired
1292. When he entered the room, Mike looked rather
pale and in … of a
shave.
a) lack
b) need
c) necessity
1293. The traffic lights … to green.
a) removed
b) shone
c) turned
1294. There were people who escaped … prison
camps.
a) from

b) off

c) in

1295. How long have you been working … this project?

a) to

b) in

c) at

1296. I hope she won't … his offer.

a) have Steve up on

b) take Steve up on

c) get Steve up on

1297. After I had discussed my plans with him, I … to work on my project.

a) have started

b) started

c) would start

1298. Absenteeism per employee in our company … out at 7 days per year.

a) averages

b) acts

c) arrives

1299. The storm played … with these houses.

a) down

b) havoc

c) along

1300. If you have a … of cards, I can show you a trick.

a) packet

b) set

c) pack

1301. This is the … of the laptop which was stolen.

a) detail

b) example

c) description

1302. It is … unlikely that the new manager will agree to that.

a) highly

b) mainly

c) greatly

1303. I've grown … to the noise of the trains.

a) familiar

b) accustomed

c) aware

1304. He … me of the first time we met.

a) reminded

b) recalled

c) remained

1305. The noise got … as the bike disappeared into the fog.

a) smaller

b) slighter

c) fainter

1306. … of all colleagues, I would like to wish you a happy retirement.

a) In place

b) On account

c) On behalf

1307. While studying, she depended … her family for money.

a) on

b) of

c) from

1308. Never before … seen such an enormous cake.

a) I had

b) had I

c) I have

1309. I wish she … her phone number before she left.

a) gave

b) would give

c) had given

1310. She always refuses … advice of any kind.

a) accepting

b) to reject

c) to accept

1311. I apologize … keeping you waiting so long.

a) for

b) from

c) with

1312. I appealed … her for help.

a) for

b) by

c) to

1313. The man is responding to treatment and will soon be cured … his illness.

a) from

b) of

c) with

1314. In the sky a … of birds was flying southward.

a) pack

b) swarm
c) flock
1315. A general manager … over all employees.
a) has ultimate authority
b) is an ultimate authority
c) is having ultimate authority
1316. It was … a hot tea that I burnt my mouth.
a) such
b) so
c) so and so
1317. I … to read this book before I found an
interesting review about it.
a) had told
b) was told
c) had been told
1318. As I was … through the newspaper this
morning I saw a picture of
her.
a) staring
b) gazing
c) glancing
1319. Many of his remarks were derogatory and …
lawsuits against him.
a) came upon
b) resulted in
c) assuaged
1320. There is no … that the new policy has been in
any way disastrous.
a) indiscretion
b) indication
c) inducement
1321. When she retired from the job, the manager …
Jane with a symbolic
gift.
a) offered

b) presented
c) pleased
1322. The boat was … without trace during the
storm.
a) crashed
b) vanished
c) lost
1323. … she comes, don't forget to call me.
a) If
b) In case
c) That

1324. He's the …-looking man I have ever met, said
Mary about me.
a) most
b) best
c) well
1325. You can always count … me.
a) in
b) by
c) on
1326. My favourite … is roast chicken.
a) eat
b) dish
c) menu
1327. At seven o'clock, the old man still had some
… to do in the garden.
a) job
b) task
c) work
1328. I … dark chocolate to white chocolate.
a) prefer
b) want
c) like
1329. You can't have this toy back … you promise
to be a good boy.
a) when
b) until
c) while

1330. There was so … noise that I could hardly
understand anything.
a) many
b) much
c) plentiful
1331. If you want to have a cat you must be ready to
look … it for some
time.
a) after
b) at
c) for
1332. She wishes she could … smoking.
a) give away
b) give from
c) give up
1333. The United States … from voting.
a) abstained
b) refused
c) rejected

1334. Don't worry. She always comes … time.
a) in
b) on
c) at
1335. My best friend confessed to me that he had been converted …another religion.
a) on
b) for
c) to
1336. You must have avoided risking …!
a) the life of your soldiers
b) the lives of your soldiers
c) your soldiers' life
1337. Before I decided to buy a plane ticket I … to wife.
a) had talked
b) talked
c) has talked

1338. I'm fed up to the back … with this pandemic.
a) ceiling
b) teeth
c) handle
1339. Given her … the manager's decision, she has no choice but to resign.
a) antipathy towards
b) pretense of
c) support for
1340. I like you because you aren't afraid to tackle … subjects.
a) concurrent
b) consecutive
c) controversial
1341. A crazy driver cut … so suddenly that I had to brake hard.
a) in
b) out
c) by
1342. If she … a little harder, her results would be better now.
a) works
b) worked
c) has worked
1343. The lights … out and we were left in darkness.
a) turned
b) put

c) went
1344. I had no … that the divorce rate was so high.
a) doubt
b) knowledge
c) idea
1345. I don't think he will … the shock of his sister's death.
a) get over
b) get through
c) get by
1346. … he is over seventy, Mr. Smith still goes jogging every day.
a) Despite

b) Unless
c) Although
1347. In today's newspaper it … that a coronavirus cure has been discovered.
a) notices
b) says
c) writes
1348. There is a large park … to the station. You will find an empty space.
a) across
b) close
c) right
1349. Seeing the room, I was … and complained to the manager about it.
a) disgusted
b) ashamed
c) disgusting
1350. … from anything else, he is always late.
a) As well
b) Except
c) Apart
1351. You should keep your dog on a … in this park.
a) lead
b) line
c) link
1352. Margaret has said that she will … the ceremony.
a) engage
b) impart
c) attend

1353. I'm not sure that this is … a good idea after all.
a) as
b) such
c) so

1354. They were unprepared … the news.
a) to
b) at
c) for

1355. The employees have embarked … a new scheme.
a) on
b) with
c) at

1356. What does this drink consist …?
a) with
b) from
c) of

1357. … I had to stand.
a) There's being no seats left
b) There being no seats left
c) There are no seats left

1358. I refused to give up work, … I'd won a big prize.
a) despite
b) however
c) even though

1359. We believe that the latest project will … expectations.
a) undermine
b) succeed
c) surpass

1360. It's distressing to see a kid … in the street.
a) begging
b) pleading
c) imploring

1361. The manager explained that he hoped to … new procedures to save time and money.
a) manufacture
b) control
c) establish

1362. Medicines should be kept out of the … of children.
a) hold
b) reach

c) grasp

1363. The manager … the employees to return to work.
a) ordered
b) insisted
c) suggested

1364. On holiday, I … always on the beach.
a) be
b) were
c) am

1365. Travelling to Moscow … air is quicker than driving.
a) by
b) on
c) over

1366. I'm not going to help you with your project and neither … Steve.
a) isn't
b) is
c) is going to

1367. … is a very good exercise, said the doctor.
a) To swim
b) A swim
c) Swimming

1368. The detective … to open a window at the back of the house.
a) managed
b) forced
c) succeeded

1369. I … going to the concert. It was marvelous.
a) hated
b) wanted
c) enjoyed

1370. She noticed the old lady … to get out of bed.
a) has tried
b) trying
c) tried

1371. Although the town had changed, much of it was still … to me.
a) common
b) relative
c) familiar

1372. If you want to change the item, make sure that you keep the … .
a) ticket

b) bill

c) notice

1373. When are they going to sell that car? Didn't you know? They decided … .

a) not to

b) not to be

c) not

1374. After the officers had questioned him for days, he broke … and confessed.

a) up

b) down

c) out

1375. While studying she was financially dependent … her husband.

a) to

b) of

c) on

1376. Luckily, I remembered … up with diesel.

a) to fill

b) filling

c) filled

1377. I've looked … the phone everywhere, but I can't find it.

a) at

b) on

c) for

1378. This country is well-known for its impressive mountainous … .

a) views

b) scenery

c) scene

1379. If they … to that event, they would attend it.

a) were invited

b) are invited

c) will be invited

1380. I will lend you this book collection next month if I … it.

a) am reading

b) were read

c) finish reading

1381. Our house is … at the corner of a busy street.

a) stood

b) situated

c) stood

1382. If I were you I … go to the doctor.

a) could

b) will

c) would

1383. The new chimney was … than all the trees around it.

a) longer

b) taller

c) deeper

1384. The police officer … me $10 for parking there.

a) fined

b) asked

c) demanded

1385. His mother was very … because he was out so late that night.

a) sorry

b) worried

c) overcome

1386. Take a toothbrush just in … .

a) time

b) order

c) case

1387. The answer … higher employment is a greater production.

a) for

b) with

c) to

1388. We meet for dinner … every Friday.

a) hourly

b) up to date

c) at the same time

1389. On the … to the woods there is a beautiful restaurant.

a) way

b) direction

c) street

1390. We don't have any … sizes in stock.

a) higher

b) larger

c) greater

1391. The patient … to listen to doctor's advice.

a) lacked

b) hindered

c) refused

1392. Children with … diseases should not be allowed to go to school.
a) infectious
b) contact
c) influential

1393. … twenty minutes of the game one player had been sent off.
a) Before
b) Inside
c) Within

1394. It happened … I was asleep.
a) while
b) during
c) for

1395. It's obvious … everyone that she's not responsible for this situation.
a) at
b) from
c) to

1396. His … for the services was a seat in the Cabinet.
a) reward
b) repayment
c) recompense

1397. The documents need … .
a) sorting out
b) sorting off
c) sorting out of

1398. I hope the project … by next month.
a) has been finished
b) had been finished
c) will have been finished

1399. I don't know the answer but I will … around.
a) attend
b) ask
c) accord

1400. I thought the way my cousin behaved was … outrageous.
a) very
b) extremely
c) quite

1401. The only way to clean this is to … it in soap and warm water.
a) polish
b) wash
c) wipe

1402. It's … to rain again today.
a) likely
b) possibly
c) probably

1403. The little girl hasn't … her shyness yet.
a) got under
b) get through
c) get over

1404. The store gave me a 10 per cent … for paying cash.
a) sale
b) discount
c) bargain

1405. My leg was very … after the wasp stung me.
a) swollen
b) wide
c) thick

1406. … I have a beer, please?
a) Must
b) Shall
c) Could

1407. They met yesterday to discuss the … at the factory.
a) closing
b) block
c) strike

1408. I was unable to warn you because my telephone was … .
a) off duty
b) out of order
c) out of work

1409. Don't … her to arrive early.
a) expect
b) judge
c) think

1410. Sometimes I can't … the professor.
a) keep at
b) keep up to
c) keep up with

1411. The car broke … on my way there so I wasn't able to be on time.
a) up
b) down
c) in

1412. He signed the agreement … the General Manager.

a) on behalf of
b) because of
c) on account of
1413. Who is going to pay … this mess?
a) on
b) in
c) for

1414. He is jealous … his older brother.
a) to
b) at
c) of
1415. She might be good … her job, but I can't rely on her.
a) at
b) in
c) on
1416. I felt considerably … after a meal and a rest.
a) renewed
b) refreshed
c) remade
1417. My eldest sister intends to take … skiing next winter.
a) up
b) to
c) away
1418. The bank … planned to escape using a plane.
a) thieves
b) robbers
c) bandits
1419. Which soldier is … this morning?
a) on call
b) on the call
c) at call
1420. Your laziness and … could result in your dismissal.
a) ambition
b) zeal
c) procrastination
1421. Tom is stubborn, so it will be difficult to ... him to go.
a) make
b) suggest
c) persuade
1422. When the time came to … the bill she left.
a) pay

b) pay out
c) pay up
1423. The film … several scenes that might upset some people.
a) admits
b) contains
c) involves
1424. My house is going to be knocked … when the new highway is built.
a) out
b) down
c) away
1425. I returned the laptop to he shop because it was … .
a) mistaken
b) wrong
c) faulty
1426. Can you come here? I … speak to you about something.
a) must
b) can
c) should
1427. I've never had to … such things before.
a) get out of
b) put up with
c) go off with
1428. I don't think I have … eaten something like this before.
a) always
b) rarely
c) ever
1429. We all felt sorry … her.
a) with
b) for
c) about
1430. Which … choose between these two?
a) do your rather
b) would you rather
c) did you rather

1431. Everything was …, just like any other day.
a) normal
b) average
c) common
1432. The mechanic … me $10 for mending my bicycle.
a) asked

b) demanded
c) charged
1433. ... I tell you yesterday not to go there?
a) Hasn't
b) Didn't
c) Haven't
1434. Inflation and its upward ... is worrying.
a) bend
b) stream
c) trend
1435. I apologized for causing so much ... .
a) problem
b) trouble
c) damage
1436. I am ... to come to the meeting.
a) capable
b) excused
c) unable
1437. I suppose I can count ... you for help?
a) on
b) in
c) from
1438. We began by experimenting ... rats.
a) of
b) in
c) on
1439. I bought the land with a ... to building a new office.
a) purpose

b) goal
c) view
1440. In all ... there will never be a third World War.
a) odds
b) probability
c) certainty
1441. The defendant's wife was present at the ... .
a) court
b) hearing
c) law
1442. I don't ... with your decision. It's fine.
a) disagree
b) displease
c) dislike
1443. ... I lock the door?
a) Will

b) Need
c) Shall
1444. My car was badly ... in the accident.
a) hurt
b) damaged
c) broken
1445. Come ... instead of standing on the doorstep.
a) in
b) to
c) by
1446. Everyone in the city ... about the plans for the new road.
a) was concerned
b) took care
c) had concerned
1447. I ... my friends to go camping with me.
a) attracted
b) suggested
c) persuaded

1448. What needs ...?
a) to do
b) to be done
c) to be doing
1449. I ... my family very much when I'm away from home.
a) miss
b) lack
c) long
1450. The ... age of the population is rising.
a) medium
b) general
c) average
1451. You can't get these pills unless you go to the doctor and get a ... .
a) receipt
b) prescription
c) recipe
1452. Driving a bike with faulty brakes is ... quite a risk.
a) taking
b) putting
c) setting
1453. The assistant apologized and said that she didn't have any of them ... yet.
a) in stock

b) in store

c) out of stock

1454. You … have passed that exam. I believe you didn't work hard

enough.

a) must

b) should

c) can

1455. Jennifer hadn't seen her brother for twenty years and … she

recognized him.

a) so

b) despite

c) yet

1456. You … be exhausted after that mission.

a) must

b) can

c) need

1457. These pills are round, so they're easier to … .

a) eat

b) chew

c) swallow

1458. I … myself and left the party. It was late.

a) refused

b) excused

c) thanked

1459. Do you … to go to the meeting?

a) pretend

b) attempt

c) intend

1460. I … the plumber to install an extra radiator.

a) arranged

b) got

c) intend

1461. I'm free this evening. … we go out to dinner?

a) Will

b) Shall

c) Won't

1462. The officer threw the drowning woman a lifebelt in the … of time.

a) nick

b) end

c) quick

1463. Children have to stay … school until 1 p.m.

a) with

b) on

c) at

1464. The management received a lot of … about the service.

a) information

b) advice

c) complaints

1465. It has been raining for five days … now.

a) at an end

b) on end

c) in the end

1466. The opening … of the play took place in camp.

a) stage

b) sight

c) scene

1467. I don't know what to do this Saturday. Perhaps I … at home and so

some work.

a) stay

b) will stay

c) am staying

1468. When you … the Smiths, give them my best wishes.

a) will visit

b) would visit

c) visit

1469. The sign asks people … smoke.

a) not to

b) to not

c) don't

1470. He never became the … of the local chess club, despite his

intelligence.

a) member

b) champion

c) winner

1471. … for Adam, we enjoyed the play very much.

a) Except

b) Apart

c) Aside

1472. Mary is unemployed. She'd feel much happier if she were in … .

a) touch

b) job

c) work

1473. Five meters of this material … at $35.
a) add up
b) fetch down
c) work out
1474. It was difficult to … a date which was
convenient for us.
a) elect
b) arrange
c) organize
1475. There was nothing I could do … leave the car
there.
a) unless
b) but
c) instead of
1476. Did anything emerge … your meeting?
a) from
b) on
c) of
1477. You can't rely … Steve. He's away on holiday
all the time.
a) at
b) on
c) with
1478. The concert began … a new instrumental
song.
a) on
b) in
c) with
1479. When I realized it was three o'clock, I stopped
… a rest.
a) having
b) have
c) had
1480. Are you … to leave?
a) thinking
b) planned
c) about

1481. The soldier … a dangerous mission.
a) undertook
b) agreed
c) entered
1482. What a lovely suit … on!
a) have you
b) you've got
c) have you got

1483. They have just released a new graphic card, …
you must buy.
a) that
b) what
c) which
1484. Because nobody admitted breaking the
windows, the … class was
punished.
a) all
b) whole
c) each
1485. It was a good attempt, but it didn't really come
… .
a) off
b) on
c) away
1486. Your test result is poor, … you have failed.
a) because
b) therefore
c) however
1487. Would you … talking a little bit more quietly?
a) care
b) rather
c) mind
1488. The bank seems to have credited my account
with $500 in … .
a) error
b) fortune
c) accident
1489. I'm sorry but I don't … you at all.
a) agree to

b) disagree to
c) agree with
1490. This wine is cheap but it is very … .
a) drinking
b) drinkable
c) drank
1491. Do you … bringing your laptop? Mine is
broken.
a) mind
b) complain
c) oppose
1492. She has a … temper and often says things,
which she later regrets.
a) warm
b) angry

c) quick

1493. The child says he's sorry … what he did.

a) of

b) for

c) from

1494. I'm satisfied … your project.

a) with

b) to

c) at

1495. She cannot be held responsible … other people's mistakes.

a) by

b) to

c) for

1496. I will ask him to return my book when I … him.

a) see

b) saw

c) will see

1497. My speech may have … you.

a) mistaken

b) misled

c) miscalculated

1498. What she told me was a … of lies.

a) load

b) pack

c) flock

1499. The death penalty was … two years ago in this country.

a) absolved

b) aborted

c) abolished

1500. Stop … yourself. Your work is highly valued.

a) belittling

b) interpreting

c) distinguishing

1501. Food prices have been … steadily for the last two years.

a) lifting

b) rising

c) raising

1502. I'll have to study hard, … I can pass the exam.

a) in order

b) such

c) so that

1503. You … to drink if you don't feel like it.

a) don't have

b) haven't

c) mustn't

1504. We'll play football and … we'll have a drink.

a) then

b) so

c) straight away

1505. She has to go to Berlin for the next … of her training.

a) step

b) stage

c) stand

1506. After the meeting had finished, we went … the project once again.

a) over

b) up

c) on

1507. I locked the bird in a cage to … it from getting away.

a) avoid

b) hinder

c) prevent

1508. You're … your time trying to persuade her.

a) losing

b) wasting

c) missing

1509. Out last cook was better than the … one.

a) former

b) current

c) latter

1510. I am grateful to you for being so patient … me.

a) with

b) at

c) for

1511. Do you mean to say you exchanged that performant laptop … this?

a) for

b) on

c) to

1512. The rain floods were … the poor harvest.

a) accused of

b) blamed for

c) condemned for

1513. I have so many things to get done today. …, I have to finish this

boring project.
a) At top
b) At the top of
c) On top of it
1514. I don't see any … in arriving that early.
a) cause
b) aim
c) point

1515. His application was turned … by the consulate.
a) down
b) out
c) over
1516. This is a controlled environment which … concerns about the weather.
a) foster
b) necessitate
c) eliminate
1517. It is … impossible to tell the twins apart at this age.
a) virtually
b) closely
c) extremely
1518. Thomas claimed that he was the … heir to the throne.
a) due
b) rightful
c) correct
1519. This aspect in no way … from the beauty of the place.
a) protracts
b) attracts
c) detracts
1520. … no need to do it again.
a) There's
b) You're
c) It has
1521. Some colleagues only read the … lines in a newspaper.
a) top
b) head
c) main
1522. You should always check the sell … date of the products you buy.
a) by

b) in
c) off
1523. When the project was completed, the workers were paid … .
a) out
b) over
c) off
1524. The manager was good enough to … our mistakes.
a) overlook
b) overtake
c) overdo
1525. It is … when you misunderstand something.
a) singular
b) attitude
c) embarrassing
1526. Magazines are … to their door every day.
a) taken
b) delivered
c) handed
1527. She expressed her … for all the help.
a) thanking
b) gratitude
c) gratefulness
1528. In … nothing happened at the meeting.
a) short
b) quick
c) briefly
1529. The assembly gave the speaker a standing … .
a) applause
b) support
c) ovation
1530. Local politicians pretend to ignore opinion … .
a) votes
b) polls
c) numbers
1531. Start reading the story from page 20 and then go on until you … the end of the book.
a) arrive
b) touch
c) reach

1532. Make … that you check your ideas carefully.
a) definite

b) sure

c) clear

1533. The purpose of these exercises is to … your knowledge and enhance
it.

a) prone

b) interpret

c) test

1534. A useful way to … your vocabulary is to read more.

a) increase

b) amass

c) gather

1535. You can also read novels so that you can see examples of …
language.

a) automatic

b) axiomatic

c) idiomatic

1536. An important activity is to … your spoken language.

a) train

b) practise

c) exercise

1537. It's very good if you can … the cost of travelling to that country.

a) afford

b) spend

c) expend

1538. Try to … a native speaker to talk to you. I challenge you!

a) influence

b) impress

c) persuade

1539. Play the recording and … everything she said.

a) hold

b) repeat

c) take

1540. It won't be long before you find yourself speaking the language … .

a) fluently

b) frequently

c) flowingly

1541. You have to … a form and send it to my secretary.

a) fill out

b) fill up

c) fill into

1542. We'll have to wait a little longer because I'm sure he will … soon.

a) turn in

b) turn down

c) turn up

1543. Last week I … that perfume you wanted in a boutique.

a) came up

b) came across

c) came into

1544. I have to … a new idea that will enable me to make more money.

a) think up

b) think about

c) think over

1545. I need to find a chemical product that will … the weeds in my garden.

a) keep off

b) keep down

c) keep out

1546. In spring, people feel inclined to … their houses.

a) do over

b) do in

c) do up

1547. It will be necessary to … making a better plan.

a) see about

b) see over

c) see into

1548. It's easy to see from the way the forest is looking that winter has … .

a) set out

b) set in

c) set off

1549. I will always … you darling.

a) stand to

b) stand from

c) stand by

1550. By the way she talks and behaves it's clear that she … her mother.

a) takes after

b) takes to

c) takes back

1551. There's no need to worry. We have … of time.

a) parcels
b) bags
c) sacks

1552. The movie doesn't start at least an hour so I have time to … .
a) kill
b) murder
c) remove

1553. The station isn't far away. We have time to … .
a) save
b) store
c) spare

1554. With time on his … he is likely to get into trouble.
a) feet
b) hands
c) fingers

1555. I told her time and … not to do it.
a) often
b) already
c) again

1556. I like to get to an appointment in … time.
a) best
b) good
c) fine

1557. It's … time she learnt to cook.
a) of
b) in
c) about

1558. I'm not living here for good; just for the time … .
a) being
b) seeing
c) trying

1559. Time … ; it's difficult to believe that I've been here all day.
a) flows
b) flees
c) files

1560. Time will … whether I have made the right decision.
a) say
b) find
c) tell

1561. Our business has lost a lot of orders and is going through a … time.
a) thin
b) slender
c) poor

1562. The trains always arrive … time in this country.
a) for
b) at
c) on

1563. I think they are merely playing … time.
a) at
b) for
c) in

1564. This company is well … the times.
a) behind
b) across
c) under

1565. Her invention proved she was … of her time.
a) before
b) forward
c) ahead

1566. You can tell Tom has hit the … time because of the car he drives.
a) high
b) large
c) big

1567. It's … time you went to the post office.
a) quick
b) high
c) proper

1568. The artists are meant to … time with the conductor.
a) take
b) keep
c) show

1569. If you want to grow your business you must … with the times.
a) move
b) hold
c) follow

1570. The parcel arrived two weeks later and not … time.
a) after
b) for
c) before

1571. Before applying for a job you should be sure that you have the right
paper … .
a) qualities
b) qualifiers
c) qualifications
1572. You should work out the … you have in mind for the ideal employee.
a) picture
b) profile
c) sketch
1573. As soon as the … arrive for the interview it will be your job to show
them around.
a) candidates

b) chosen
c) appliers
1574. The company is doing an advertising campaign with a view to …
new staff.
a) taking
b) recruiting
c) reaching
1575. After you've read the details of the job …
your application.
a) pursue
b) submit
c) undertake
1576. Do you expect her to … with a cost cutting scheme?
a) come over
b) come by
c) come up
1577. You've chosen a good industry to seek employment in because I've
heard that jobs are … there.
a) many
b) frequent
c) plenty
1578. It can be a time … process but it's worth in the end.
a) lasting
b) consuming
c) taking
1579. It's relevant to discuss a candidate's … at previous jobs.

a) deeds
b) doings
c) accomplishments
1580. I can offer you a salary that will be … with the responsibilities.
a) equal
b) level
c) commensurate
1581. He was able to … the cause of her headaches.
a) decide

b) diagnose
c) define
1582. It was beyond my capability and I … the patient to a specialist.
a) referred
b) reduced
c) returned
1583. The doctor reassured Steve that his condition was not … .
a) clear
b) possible
c) serious
1584. The dentist took out of her bag an unusual … but promised her
patient that it wouldn't hurt.
a) utensil
b) instrument
c) control
1585. The prescribed medication has been … .
a) effective
b) effects
c) effecting
1586. If you cancel your … and don't notify the clinic you will be fined.
a) meeting
b) rendezvous
c) appointment
1587. A specialist had to … the extent of her mobility.
a) assess
b) assume
c) accept
1588. The treatment has proved successful but he has to arrange to visit the
doctor's … .
a) always

b) annually

c) usually

1589. It's much easier to ... an illness than to cure it.

a) prevent

b) prepare

c) prefer

1590. We had to write to the previous hospital so as to obtain his ... .

a) writings

b) recordings

c) records

1591. Perhaps you could start by telling me why you've ... .

a) obtained for this job

b) applied for this job

c) asked for this job

1592. Steve likes working in ... .

a) the free air

b) the pure air

c) the open air

1593. Do you like the idea of an office with ...?

a) air control

b) air condition

c) air conditioning

1594. I don't understand what you're ... .

a) on about

b) in about

c) for about

1595. I thought this was ... obvious.

a) pretty

b) mostly

c) clear

1596. To me, ... obvious at all.

a) it can't be

b) it won't be

c) it isn't

1597. I think there must be a mistake. I ... .

a) put it you're Mr. Smith

b) take it you're Mr. Smith

c) place it you're Mr. Smith

1598. I'm afraid it was a case of mistaken ... .

a) personality

b) character

c) identity

1599. You're not after the job of police officer ... .

a) I presume

b) I pretend

c) I preview

1600. I want to be a security guard ... .

a) if you don't care

b) if you don't mind

c) if you don't see

1601. I am writing this e-mail to describe the ... I've been having with this

product.

a) incidents

b) instances

c) problems

1602. I am talking about your latest laptop ... in the January catalogue.

a) deferred

b) considered

c) described

1603. I want to take ... over the name itself this time.

a) issue

b) trouble

c) pains

1604. "Shrewd" to my mind suggests ..., which she doesn't possess.

a) wonderful

b) excellence

c) outstanding

1605. You should have thought it was an essential ... of this system.

a) require

b) requirement

c) requires

1606. Unfortunately, this doesn't ... to your product.

a) concern

b) attribute

c) apply

1607. One day, the lawnmower simply ... over the grass but didn't cut it.

a) walked

b) tripped

c) strode

1608. ..., I was wrong about it.

a) Confessing

b) Admitted

c) Admittedly

1609. I want you to pay me … my money!

a) return

b) again

c) back

1610. I someone to come and repair my laptop at your … .

a) expense

b) expenditure

c) expending

1611. I thought it was … time I called you.

a) at

b) about

c) in

1612. She has at long last … to marry Mike.

a) concerted

b) consented

c) convened

1613. We will be able to make an … man of him.

a) honest

b) honour

c) honestly

1614. I want to ask of you a very important … .

a) favouring

b) favourite

c) favour

1615. Putting it … I am delighted!

a) easily

b) simply

c) fairly

1616. I can … you that the duties are not in any way intricate.

a) assure

b) affirm

c) assert

1617. She is an … supporter.

a) arduous

b) ardent

c) articulate

1618. Why aren't you tying the …?

a) knot

b) rope

c) string

1619. I don't understand why I have to give up my … .

a) latitude

b) scope

c) liberty

1620. I wait for your … as soon as possible.

a) recur

b) respect

c) response

1621. I would like to … this application for the job.

a) deliver

b) submit

c) return

1622. As you can see from my … C.V. I have relevant experience.

a) attached

b) appeared

c) included

1623. This is a … job for someone who has been a manager.

a) stranger

b) unusually

c) peculiar

1624. You should explain the … reason for what you've done.

a) underlying

b) undercover

c) understanding

1625. It's the job of a sales consultant to … the clients into choosing from
the catalogue.

a) push

b) tempt

c) pervade

1626. I'm sure I could easily … all the requirements.

a) fulfill

b) commit

c) completed

1627. She cannot decide whether to have … fruit or tiramisu.

a) picked

b) wet

c) fresh

1628. Make sure you … the one we have most of.

a) decide

b) select

c) effect

1629. I am sure you can … your skills to the new employee.

a) transfer

b) translate

c) transverse

1630. I look forward to … from your company.

a) hear

b) hearing

c) heard

1631. We reached our … after a dramatic journey.

a) destination

b) end

c) aim

1632. She could say that she is having a wonderful time but that would be
… from the truth.

a) distant

b) long

c) far

1633. The airport had a problem because of the industrial … taken by the
baggage handlers.

a) acts

b) action

c) acting

1634. They decided they didn't want to … my case on to the helicopter.

a) lode

b) lead

c) load

1635. Sorry! I was held … for one hour.

a) up

b) by

c) on

1636. As you can … I was tired, hungry and miserable.

a) anticipate

b) think

c) imagine

1637. When I arrived at the motel I had to … my luggage.

a) sort out

b) sort in

c) sort of

1638. She wasn't there any mote. She had simply …

.

a) distorted

b) dislodged

c) disappeared

1639. My first day was spent in local shops … for gifts.

a) finding

b) searching

c) purchasing

1640. The manager greeted us … from ear to ear.

a) streaming

b) screaming

c) beaming

1641. Do you have any idea what this …?

a) means

b) tells

c) says

1642. Apparently, it is an … . So the letters in the word are the first letters
of a group of words.

a) addition

b) anomaly

c) acronym

1643. This acronym … the central building.

a) stands by

b) stands for

c) stands up

1644. The soldier jumped out of a plane 6.000 meters … the river.

a) up

b) higher

c) above

1645. She intended to … across the channel.

a) flee

b) flow

c) fly

1646. The pilot started early in the morning so that he was able to …
commercial flights.

a) avoid

b) evict

c) eject

1647. During the race my supporters … that I reached 220 km/h.

a) attained

b) argued

c) claimed

1648. The fact remains that the terrorist … and managed to escape.

a) survived

b) lived

c) continued

1649. Wilma has created a new … by beating him.

a) recorder

b) record

c) recording

1650. The … is about 30 minutes.

a) duration

b) lasting

c) during

1651. Teaching someone to fly a plane is one of the … experiences you can have.

a) scariest

b) latest

c) cruelest

1652. I'm here to … you in driving a car.

a) learn

b) instruct

c) perform

1653. Be careful when you drive. You can end up in the … .

a) side

b) floor

c) ditch

1654. This is more … if the partner is a member of your family.

a) complicated

b) confused

c) confirmed

1655. The situation between you and your wife could end in … .

a) distance

b) diversion

c) divorce

1656. The secret of being a good teacher is never to lose your temper or your … .

a) brain

b) head

c) idea

1657. She might lose … of the car.

a) break

b) stop

c) control

1658. In my … none of what you've told happened.

a) case

b) example

c) instance

1659. I was proud of them because they all … the exam first time.

a) past

b) passing

c) passed

1660. The only … to me is where she is.

a) confusion

b) mystery

c) intrigue

1661. Those companies find themselves in a … situation.

a) precarious

b) pertinent

c) pretentious

1662. Whenever there is a meeting between them rumours … .

a) abut

b) about

c) abound

1663. They were judged for … the documents.

a) mistaking

b) misfiring

c) mishandling

1664. We want to … the concerns of our borrowers.

a) assert

b) assuage

c) assent

1665. Negotiations will eventually be … .

a) retaken

b) resumed

c) returned

1666. The government tries to convince everyone that it is … of all people.

a) supported

b) supportive

c) supporting

1667. Measures are due to come into … on Friday.

a) force

b) law

c) forcing

1668. Do you know when these laws will be …?

a) rating

b) ratified

c) rated

1669. This is very disappointing for the … car buyer.

a) would-see

b) would-go

c) would-be

1670. I have nothing of … to report.

a) notice

b) noted

c) note

1671. Suppose an … public figure attacked by press and public.

a) embattled

b) engrossed

c) empowered

1672. Any arguments he put up were regarded as a … .

a) cloud

b) fog

c) smokescreen

1673. Her protestations of innocence were wearing a bit … .

a) bare

b) thin

c) scarce

1674. Police forces were determined to … this kind of crime.

a) curb

b) manage

c) restrain

1675. This media trust was … to make publicity about the candidate.

a) picked

b) proposed

c) prompted

1676. Mary spent a lot of time … the press on this subject.

a) briefing

b) training

c) showing

1677. Views … from utter conviction that she was guilty to wild support for her innocence.

a) started

b) ranged

c) began

1678. Even his supporters were beginning to … him.

a) despair

b) destroy

c) desert

1679. New evidence came to … proving she was innocent.

a) light

b) see

c) show

1680. The incident … everything he did for the rest of his life.

a) overlook

b) overcome

c) overshadowed

1681. Such a piece of information cannot be released into the public … .

a) domain

b) domestic

c) dominion

1682. They run the risk of facing a … if they break the official secrets act.

a) back store

b) back strike

c) backlash

1683. There is a … inquiry into specific information.

a) high profile

b) high brow

c) high drama

1684. The more you try to conceal information about an event, the more it fuels … about it.

a) spectacle

b) speculation

c) speculative

1685. You will get … by authorities if you dare reveal this report.

a) rave

b) savaged

c) wild

1686. The officer will … what can be disclosed.

a) sign

b) seal

c) signal

1687. Once the disclosure is … it's her job to analyze the facts.

a) hightailed

b) heightened

c) highlighted

1688. The public can see through the … of a weak argument.

a) clarity

b) clearness

c) transparency

1689. This is likely to … a threat to the safety of the community.

a) start

b) pose

c) place

1690. This small country is a … for troublemakers.

a) heaven

b) location

c) port

1691. Today the government is … plans for a new highway.

a) unveiling

b) opening

c) showing

1692. The plan is about trying to … stealing in the country.

a) kill

b) curb

c) confuse

1693. The new conference system will be … next academic year.

a) introduced

b) welcomed

c) enforced

1694. They should be taught to respect other people's property and … .

a) added

b) additions

c) belongings

1695. She will have to stand up in front of her colleagues and … to being a thief.

a) confess

b) conduce

c) conform

1696. The … said the Prime Minister was sick.

a) spoken person

b) spokesperson

c) speaking person

1697. Last month we had to give an important address to an international …

.

a) assembled

b) assembly

c) assembling

1698. … of the speech she told funny stories.

a) In case

b) Intend

c) Instead

1699. The audience didn't see the funny … of her stories.

a) edge

b) part

c) line

1700. The presenter cannot continue with the news because someone has … the next page.

a) misread

b) mistaken

c) misappropriated

Second set of items

1701. I take my hat … to the new manager for avoiding bankruptcy.

a) to

b) off

c) on

1702. She's not thinking straight. She's talking … her hat.

a) at

b) under

c) up

1703. This is a society wedding where men wear … hats and tails.

a) tall

b) full

c) long

1704. I'd like you to keep this information … your hat.

a) under

b) by

c) over

1705. She decided to throw her hat in the … and become a candidate.

a) circle
b) ring
c) middle
1706. If he wins I'll … my hat.
a) eat
b) consume
c) bite
1707. Steve changes his mind at the … of a hat.
a) jump
b) fall
c) drop
1708. That suit is … hat now.
a) gone
b) late
c) old

1709. I think it would be nice to … round the hat for him.
a) offer
b) hand
c) place
1710. There are so many responsibilities involved that she has to … several
hats.
a) wear
b) take
c) put
1711. A salesperson should … potential customers of the usefulness of a
product.
a) consider
b) confirm
c) convince
1712. You must believe in the product and be … enough to promote it.
a) included
b) indebted
c) inspired
1713. A … customer will return to the same firm and buy again.
a) satisfied
b) interested
c) encouraged
1714. That style of dress was once considered to be a
… .
a) fuss
b) fad

c) fun
1715. We need to … a new product this year.
a) market
b) muster
c) maintain
1716. They watch the supermarkets … for the same clientele.
a) contrasting
b) confusing
c) competing

1717. Weekly meetings were not considered to be … enough.
a) produced
b) productive
c) products
1718. She is able to … facts and figures quickly.
a) consumer
b) consume
c) consuming
1719. On this website customers can … different prices for the same article.
a) continue
b) confer
c) compare
1720. If you want to keep … with the latest developments you have to read
a lot.
a) current
b) currant
c) currents
1721. … every student passed the exam.
a) Near to
b) Next to
c) Nearly
1722. I can look back on my career with great … .
a) satisfied
b) satisfaction
c) satisfactory
1723. The captain, as well as the passengers, … frightened.
a) been
b) were
c) was
1724. Both of these girls … married.
a) are
b) have

c) has

1725. Each learner of a foreign language … a good dictionary.

a) need

b) is

c) needs

1726. Money, nor fame … brought happiness to everybody.

a) has

b) have

c) is

1727. I … at this university before I became an interpreter.

a) taught

b) had taught

c) were taught

1728. The salary of a truck driver is higher … .

a) than a teacher

b) than that of a teacher

c) to compare as a teacher

1729. Professionals expect you to call them when it is necessary … an appointment.

a) cancel

b) to cancel

c) canceled

1730. I have chosen this laptop because of its operation simplicity … its capacity to store information.

a) the same as

b) the same

c) as well as

1731. Many embarrassing situations occur … a misunderstanding.

a) for

b) because

c) because of

1732. This is an extremely cold planet and … .

a) so is Uranus

b) so does Neptune

c) so has Uranus

1733. … when gold was discovered in this area.

a) Because in 1850

b) It was in 1850

c) In 1850 it was

1734. This job has no … .

a) prospector

b) prospects

c) prospective

1735. Frost occurs in valleys … on adjacent hills.

a) more frequently than

b) as frequently than

c) frequently than

1736. The mountain can be … from more than 200 kilometers away.

a) see

b) saw

c) seen

1737. I'd like you … her family.

a) to meet

b) meet

c) meeting

1738. Mr. Smith along with his friends … arriving here tonight.

a) are

b) will

c) were

1739. You must listen very … in order to understand it.

a) care

b) careful

c) carefully

1740. Cold objects emit … hot ones.

a) fewer than infrared rays as

b) fewer infrared rays than

c) as fewer infrared rays

1741. Gunpowder … a mixture of potassium nitrate, charcoal and sulfur.

a) were

b) was

c) is

1742. This city has played a vital role in the industrial … .

a) developing

b) develop

c) development

1743. They … forced to make smaller cars to compete in the market.

a) will

b) are

c) should

1744. Jennifer has … the conditions for entry.
a) satisfied
b) satisfaction
c) satisfactory
1745. The person … was recommended by the manager to replace him is
Marry.
a) whose
b) who
c) which
1746. His fame rested on the breadth of his range, which was … any other
tenor.
a) greater than that of
b) as large as
c) more greater
1747. Words are constantly being invented … new objects and concepts.
a) describe
b) describing
c) to describe
1748. You can't … to learn a foreign language in a month.
a) expect
b) expectant
c) expected
1749. … rain or snow there are always fans at these football games.
a) In spite with
b) Despite of
c) Despite

1750. The prices are … high in urban areas that I can't afford a house.
a) as
b) so as
c) so
1751. To see the church and … pictures of it are two reasons for visiting
this city.
a) taken
b) to take
c) taking
1752. I can't see the … of sitting there all day.
a) attract
b) attractive
c) attractiveness

1753. This product is equal … to none.
a) as
b) to
c) with
1754. These bricks are much harder … that are dried in the sun.
a) those
b) ones
c) than those
1755. Since infection can cause … fever … pain, you must avoid it.
a) both/as well as
b) both/with
c) both/and
1756. Schizophrenia … by genetic predisposition, stress, drugs or
infections.
a) may be triggered
b) may triggered
c) may trigger
1757. They asked us, Olivia and … about it.
a) I
b) me
c) my

1758. She was guilty … racial discrimination.
a) of
b) with
c) for
1759. It is important … it on because it is an expensive coat.
a) of trying
b) try
c) to try
1760. What happened in this city … a reaction from outskirts workers.
a) were
b) was
c) is
1761. The result of the drug experiment was … .
a) satisfactory
b) satisfied
c) satisfaction
1762. A number of … submitted their manuscripts under pseudonyms.
a) novel
b) novelists

c) novels

1763. I require that the secretary … responsible for writing all reports.

a) was

b) been

c) be

1764. Although a medical doctor may be able to diagnose a problem … he

may not be able to find a treatment.

a) perfect

b) perfectly

c) perfection

1765. This law is purely … .

a) prospective

b) prospect

c) prospector

1766. The number of days in a week … seven.

a) is

b) are

c) needs

1767. The nurses will not … you donate blood if you have just had a cold.

a) want

b) need

c) let

1768. This item has two parts: one made up of dust … made up of

electrically charged particles.

a) the other

b) one another

c) each other

1769. There were over fifty boats on the river, … were quire luxurious.

a) many of them

b) many of which

c) many that

1770. Columbus thought that he … the East Indies.

a) had reached

b) has reached

c) had been reached

1771. Most university leavers have the … to go to work.

a) keen

b) keenly

c) keenness

1772. It's good that … objections to the plan haven't happened.

a) expected

b) expectant

c) expect

1773. Many students are afraid … failing an exam.

a) about

b) of

c) to

1774. It is important that the office … your registration.

a) confirms

b) will confirm

c) need confirm

1775. Please state your name, age and … .

a) occupy

b) occupied

c) occupation

1776. Deserts are often formed … surrounding mountain ranges.

a) because

b) in spite of

c) so

1777. … that they settled in this area.

a) It was in 1000

b) That in 1000

c) In 1000 that it was

1778. Staying in a hotel costs … renting a room.

a) twice more than

b) twice as much as

c) as much twice as

1779. When friends insist on … expensive gifts it makes most people

uncomfortable.

a) them to accept

b) they accept

c) their accepting

1780. Do any of these designs … you?

a) attractive

b) attract

c) attractively

1781. These flowers usually smell … .

a) sweet

b) sweetly

c) sweetness

1782. Having … the topic for my essay, I began working on it.
a) chose
b) chosen
c) choose

1783. She is considered the … portrait painter.
a) greeting

b) greatest
c) grander

1784. The detonator for a nuclear device may be made of … .
a) two equipment
b) two equipment pieces
c) two pieces of equipment

1785. An equilateral triangle is a triangle … .
a) that has three sides of equal length
b) it has three sides equally long
c) that have three sides of equal length

1786. Some students are confused … about these exams.
a) about
b) with
c) in

1787. … are found on the surface of the moon.
a) Craters and waterless seas that
b) Craters and waterless seas
c) Since craters and waterless seas

1788. Her … made her cry.
a) fearful
b) fearless
c) fearfulness

1789. … two waves pass a point simultaneously they will have no effect.
a) That
b) If
c) So that

1790. A child in the first grade tends to have … other children in the class.
a) the old like
b) the same as
c) the same age as

1791. I'm very … to succeed.
a) determine
b) determinant
c) determined

1792. This structure is so strong … difficult for anyone to penetrate it.
a) that it is
b) that is
c) and is

1793. I hoped … the game.
a) Brian to win
b) Brian's win
c) Brian would win

1794. This item is … that it's completely damaged.
a) oldest
b) so old
c) such an old

1795. Many Americans … a bowl of cereals every day.
a) are used to eating
b) used to eating
c) use to eat

1796. I will keep you safe … the crowd.
a) on
b) of
c) from

1797. The best form of treatment … mass inoculation.
a) it is
b) is
c) are

1798. I became bored … this work.
a) in
b) with
c) of

1799. We don't require that the students … a thesis in order to graduate.
a) write
b) will write
c) would write

1800. The oxygen of this planet is not … to support life.
a) too sufficient

b) sufficient
c) much sufficient

1801. He supported himself by … taxicabs.
a) driving
b) drive
c) to drive

1802. The kid viewed the … of a week alone without much enthusiasm.
a) prospective
b) prospector
c) prospects

1803. If you have a family history of heart disease you should make yearly
appointments with … doctor.
a) his
b) your
c) yourself

1804. Support for research programs … much less than it was last year.
a) is
b) will
c) being

1805. Here, apartments cost more to rent than they … in other smaller
cities.
a) did
b) will
c) do

1806. This model not only saves time but also … .
a) to save energy
b) saves energy
c) save energy

1807. The government requires that a census be taken every five years …
accurate statistics may be compiled.
a) so that
b) such
c) such that

1808. The main … of economics success is out ability to forecast
indicators.

a) determinant
b) determine
c) determined

1809. Who is responsible … the project?
a) to
b) with
c) for

1810. TV has little … for me.
a) attract
b) attraction
c) attractive

1811. The average life expectancy for people born during that year … 68
years.
a) have been
b) was
c) are

1812. A … mountaineer reached the top of the mountain last week.
a) fearless
b) fearful
c) fearfulness

1813. The flag is … in the morning and taken down at night.
a) risen
b) raised
c) raise

1814. One way to inform the public about this problem is through …
programs on TV.
a) industrial
b) agricultural
c) educational

1815. That book wasn't very … .
a) well written
b) well typed
c) good written

1816. These species can be divided into three groups, two of which …
extinct.

a) is
b) are
c) was

1817. Without alphabetical order dictionaries would be … to use.
a) possible
b) impossible
c) possibility

1818. I was shocked … the news of the accident.
a) from
b) being
c) with

1819. He was awarded the Nobel … for peace.
a) award
b) gift
c) prize

1820. The extent to which an individual is a product of either heredity or environment ... .
a) cannot be proved
b) cannot proved
c) cannot prove
1821. Every country ... a national flag.
a) is
b) have
c) has
1822. Optical fibers ... to deliver laser light.
a) can also use
b) can used
c) can also be used
1823. This project may or may not have been ... by her.
a) make
b) made
c) making
1824. Laptops for sale at ... prices.
a) attractive

b) attraction
c) attractively
1825. Your mistakes are similar ... his.
a) by
b) to
c) with
1826. A team of engineers is often ... .
a) working on one project
b) no one project work
c) work on one project
1827. A vacuum will neither conduct hear nor ... .
a) sound waves are transmitted
b) transmitting sound waves
c) transmit sound waves
1828. To relieve pain cause by burns ... .
a) take immediate steps
b) to take immediate steps
c) taking immediate steps
1829. All cereal grains ... grow on the prairies and plains of this country.
a) excepting rice
b) expect the rice
c) but rice
1830. They are freshmen , ... whom come from countryside.

a) most
b) most of
c) most of the
1831. ... food is as nutritious for a baby as its mother's milk.
a) No
b) Not
c) None
1832. Civil engineers had better ... to use steel supports in this structure.
a) plans
b) to plan
c) plan
1833. Several criminals escaped ... prison yesterday.
a) out
b) for
c) from
1834. The exam results could ... your career.
a) determined
b) determine
c) determination
1835. If the oxygen supply ... replenished by plants, we would soon be dead.
a) wasn't
b) weren't
c) hadn't been
1836. I used to earn ... money.
a) many
b) lot
c) a lot of
1837. The legal implications of euthanasia are so controversial ... it is illegal in most countries.
a) as
b) that
c) since
1838. Understanding lightning might help us ... life itself.
a) understand
b) understood
c) to understanding
1839. These species are particularly ... because of their unusual structures.
a) interest
b) interested

c) interesting

1840. … poetry is enjoyable when it is read aloud.

a) Most

b) Almost

c) Many

1841. It is essential that cancer … diagnosed early.

a) was

b) is

c) be

1842. Products in this shop are … arranged.

a) attract

b) attraction

c) attractively

1843. The battlefield was a … sight.

a) fearsome

b) fear

c) fearless

1844. This plant supports itself even when the original supporting tree is …

longer alive.

a) not

b) no

c) any more

1845. Parents have great … for their children's future.

a) expectant

b) expects

c) expectancies

1846. The consistency of this substance and that of glue … .

a) the same

b) are similar

c) they are alike

1847. The appliances in most homes use alternating current … .

a) instead direct current

b) for direct current instead

c) instead of direct current

1848. When Marry decided to run for another term, the opposition said she

was … .

a) so old

b) too old

c) oldest

1849. This process results in an accumulation of … in porous rocks.

a) the oil

b) oil

c) oils

1850. We discussed the matter calmly and … .

a) reasonably

b) reason

c) reasoned

1851. I saw a sample … their work and it was impressing.

a) on

b) in

c) of

Set 6

1852. It requires that two pieces of identification … .

a) presented

b) must present

c) be presented

1853. Nerve impulses … to the brain.

a) sending sensations

b) send sensations

c) be send sensations

1854. More than one hundred separate nation … are included.

a) counties

b) states

c) continents

1855. … owe much of their success to migration.

a) The bird

b) That birds

c) Birds

1856. I believe … things openly.

a) of discussing

b) for discussing

c) in discussing

1857. People work for many reasons … .

a) besides money

b) beside money

c) money beside

1858. Seals can … .

a) keeps themselves warm

b) keep them warm

c) keep their warm
1859. Liquids flow freely from a container because they have … .
a) no definite shape
b) none definite shape
c) not definite shape
1860. One of hers … was stolen.
a) greatest work
b) greatest works
c) the greatest work
1861. They hoped that the field of transplantation …
.
a) would progress
b) had progressed
c) progressing
1862. We can do this … .
a) efficient more
b) more efficiently
c) most efficient
1863. We are amenable … discipline.
a) at
b) with
c) to
1864. … unknown quantities is the task of algebra.
a) Find
b) To found
c) Finding
1865. I read two volumes but neither book … interesting.
a) was
b) were
c) had been

1866. The path of the sun around the heavens … .
a) is known as the ecliptic
b) known as the ecliptic
c) knowing as the ecliptic
1867. This table is already … .
a) occupy
b) occupied
c) occupation
1868. A man … a woman in so many respects.
a) differs
b) different
c) differs from
1869. The … I'm late is that I missed the flight.
a) reasoned

b) reason
c) reasonable
1870. … have used franchising to extend their sales.
a) Chains restaurants
b) Chain restaurant
c) Chain restaurants
1871. A baby is under parental … .
a) guide
b) guidance
c) guiding
1872. Uranus is … to be seen on a clear night.
a) bright enough
b) brightly enough
c) enough brightly
1873. Before penicillin was discovered, many people had died … .
a) infected with bacteria
b) from infected bacteria
c) from simple bacterial infections
1874. That most natural time units are not simple multiples of each other …
in constructing a calendar.
a) is a primary problem

b) is the primary problem
c) it is a primary problem
1875. The plow is being displaced by new techniques that promise more crops.
a) abundant
b) scarce
c) sparse
1876. 60 percent of the budget is used … the development.
a) supporting
b) supportive
c) to support
1877. The bacteria in milk is destroyed when … to at least 65 Celsius degrees.
a) it is heated
b) it will be heated
c) may be heated
1878. In order for people who spoke different languages to engage in trade … they developed a simplified language.
a) with each another

b) with each the other
c) with each other
1879. There are two … : permanent magnets and electromagnets.
a) kind of magnets
b) kinds of magnets
c) kind magnets
1880. You can't rely … a hotel room.
a) on finding
b) in finding
c) of finding
1881. … doctors do not have a personal physician.
a) A large number
b) A large number of
c) Large number of
1882. There are many beautifully preserved historic buildings … .
a) in this cities

b) in these city
c) in this city
1883. The prime rate is the rate of interest that a bank will charge when it
… money.
a) lends
b) borrows
c) borrowed
1884. The area where a microchip is manufactured must be the …
environment possible.
a) cleaner
b) cleanest
c) most cleanest
1885. Mathematics is … that it is a prerequisite for studying every scientific
discipline.
a) such important field
b) so an important field
c) such an important field
1886. Studies of this kind are unreliable because there … so many
variables.
a) are being
b) are
c) may being
1887. I knew I could rely … them to get the job done.

a) on
b) with
c) in
1888. He founded a military base there and … a fort two years later.
a) had built
b) built
c) might had built
1889. Natural gas often occurs together … petroleum.
a) in
b) along
c) with

1890. There is no limit to the diversity to be … in the people's cultures.
a) found
b) finding
c) find
1891. They were very proud of his …
a) fearlessness
b) fearful
c) fearless
1892. They spend most of … time playing.
a) theirs
b) they're
c) their
1893. They were called Americas according to the … at the time.
a) belief
b) believe
c) believed
1894. … missile was used in the war between America and Iraq.
a) Guided
b) Guidance
c) Guide
1895. This is a device with a sealed metal chamber designed … the changes
in the pressure.
a) read
b) to read
c) to reading
1896. Cotton fiber, like other fibers, … composed of cellulose.
a) is
b) are

c) has

1897. All life depends … chemical reactions with oxygen to produce
energy.
a) to
b) with
c) on

1898. Modern presidents have far … responsibilities than their predecessors
did.
a) greater
b) more great
c) most great

1899. They put a well-… case for increasing the fees.
a) reason
b) reasoned
c) reasonable

1900. Grasshoppers can produce sounds by … their hind legs against heir
wings.
a) rub
b) rubbed
c) rubbing

1901. She was not only a poet but … a successful businesswoman.
a) so well
b) also
c) so

1902. It is an … advice organization.
a) occupy
b) occupation
c) occupational

1903. This is a powerful … of both light and shade.
a) useful
b) useless
c) use

1904. I've succeeded … hold of the telephone number.
a) in getting
b) on getting
c) upon getting

1905. Application fees are waived in cases of economic … like this
pandemic.
a) hard
b) hardship
c) hardware

1906. The elevator … and I had to walk up to ninth floor.
a) stopped functioning
b) exploded
c) spread

1907. Three boys … me and demanded some money.
a) came down to
b) came up to
c) came on to

1908. The secretaries report to the president, give him advice and … him
make decisions.
a) to help
b) helping
c) help

1909. The jury isn't satisfied … the answer.
a) with
b) to
c) of

1910. The satellite … in a fixed position from which it sends radio signals.
a) remain
b) remains
c) remaining

1911. The examiner must have been pleased … my performance.
a) with
b) for
c) in

1912. Being grateful means …
a) fed up with
b) proud of
c) thankful for

1913. That's the … I received!
a) inform
b) information
c) informs

1914. Mary said she … this race.
a) wants to win
b) want to win
c) wanted to win

1915. The thief was … to two years imprisonment.

a) given
b) allowed
c) sentenced

1916. There are some people that think the camel … water in its hump.
a) stores
b) stored
c) has stored

1917. Instead of … about the good news, she seemed quite upset.
a) being excited
b) exciting
c) exciting

1918. Women … to live longer than men.
a) tendency
b) tend
c) tending

1919. I finally finished … at 8 p.m.
a) cooking
b) cooked
c) being cooking

1920. Would you mind not … the radio?
a) turn on
b) turned on
c) turning on

1921. She hoped … to join the private club.
a) inviting
b) to be invited
c) being invited

1922. Many students tend … interest in literature.
a) to lose
b) lose
c) losing

1923. They complained … any sleep.
a) not getting
b) not get
c) about not getting

1924. Mary's perfectly … in her demands.
a) reason
b) reasonable
c) reasoned

1925. It's a plan worth … .
a) doing
b) being done
c) to be done

1926. There are many ways … that.

a) doing
b) to do
c) to be done

1927. Laptop prices continue to show an upward … .
a) tendency
b) tend
c) tendentious

1928. The quality of this photograph is not different … that one.
a) with
b) for
c) from

1929. You should get into the habit of … the news.
a) reading
b) read
c) being read

1930. It's important that you learn how … this tool.
a) using
b) used
c) to use

1931. They will never agree the effects of … the world's first atomic bomb … the World War.
a) drop/to end

b) dropping/to end
c) drop/end

1932. She was unable to speak due to … .
a) fear
b) fearful
c) fearsome

1933. I felt ashamed … his action.
a) to
b) for
c) of

1934. A good schoolboy must know … .
a) how to study effectively
b) to be a good student
c) to study hard

1935. Radioactivity may … future generations.
a) develop
b) create
c) affect

1936.The pilot agreed to land only … the terrorist threatened to kill a passenger.
a) that

b) when
c) which
1937. I was delighted … you've won the first prize.
a) when
b) why
c) that
1938. You are responsible … this error.
a) to
b) on
c) for
1939. They were … to prevent it.
a) powerless
b) power
c) powering

1940. Either my plan or yours … wrong.
a) are
b) is
c) has
1941. She returned the money to the man who … it.
a) had lost
b) loose
c) have lost
1942. The movie didn't … to my expectations.
a) equally
b) give
c) equal
1943. There are two categories … answers you can choose from.
a) about
b) with
c) of
1944. Kids with … faces were waiting for the show to start.
a) expect
b) expectant
c) expected
1945. I want to get … of these items.
a) pant
b) rid
c) chance
1946. These are just some of the ways to increase your … awareness.
a) culture
b) culturally
c) cultural
1947. The guests … dinner by the time I got home.

a) finish
b) finished
c) had finished
1948. Humans express their thoughts by means … word.
a) of
b) in
c) to
1949. The witnesses' accounts were not … with the facts.
a) reliable
b) consistent
c) match
1950. It was not until she had arrived home … remembered her mistake.
a) when she
b) and she
c) that she
1951. Is this car capable … us all the way home?
a) of getting
b) in getting
c) for getting
1952. No one was aware … she had gone.
a) where that
b) of where
c) the place
1953. Mike didn't do well in the class because … .
a) he failed to study
b) he studied bad
c) he was a badly student
1954. They spoke during the … .
a) meet
b) meeting
c) met
1955. You should ask your mentor how to solve this problem … you can't find a solution.
a) because of
b) as long as
c) since
1956. Mrs. Brown will substitute … the history teacher.
a) at
b) on
c) for

Set 7

1957. ... you select reverse hear the car goes backwards.

a) If

b) Unless

c) In spite of

1958. ... I get angry I try to take some deep breaths.

a) Until

b) Whenever

c) Therefore

1959. A ... accident happened yesterday.

a) fearless

b) fearful

c) fearlessness

1960. A small animal needs camouflage to hide itself ... its enemies cannot

find it.

a) so

b) due to

c) so that

1961. I wouldn't give a ... to a young child as a gift.

a) flowers

b) money

c) basket of fruit

1962. Did they ... to that beach when they were in Greece?

a) went

b) go

c) to go

1963. Do you think ... is a good gift for her?

a) money

b) cookies

c) gloves

1964. Her parents gave her some beautiful ... when she finished university.

a) necklace

b) jewelry

c) ring

1965. Theoretically, a comedy is a movie ... you laugh.

a) who makes

b) that makes

c) in that makes

1966. If you cross your fingers they ... that way.

a) stayed

b) won't stay

c) stayed

1967. He's good ... jokes.

a) for telling

b) in telling

c) at telling

1968. I investigate the possibility ... spending a week at the seashore.

a) of

b) on

c) for

1969. What will happen if you ... to loud music?

a) listen

b) listened

c) listening

1970. Huge areas have been ... because of the nuclear incident.

a) restrained

b) evacuated

c) transmitted

1971. Tom was a very unpopular man in that small village. Nobody ... him.

a) liked

b) hated

c) quarreled

1972. The country was in total ... after all those terrorist attacks.

a) confusian

b) confusment

c) confusion

1973. In order to make a good ... at an interview, you should prepare well.

a) impression

b) impressive

c) impressing

1974. When I go fishing for all day I like to get an early ... .

a) start

b) beginning

c) leaving

1975. If these TV series weren't violent, they would not ... in increased violence.

a) contribute

b) give

c) result
1976. … of the passengers were reading.
a) Almost
b) Most
c) Mostly
1977. I was travelling home to … Christmas with
my family.
a) last
b) keep
c) spend
1978. Designing … for actors requires a lot of
creativity.
a) scripts
b) costumes
c) set
1979. The men were found guilty … fraud.
a) with
b) by
c) of
1980. Every house in this neighbour … the same.
a) is
b) has
c) were
1981. What is Mary so nervous …?
a) about
b) for
c) to
1982. Such … statements are likely to provoke
opposition.
a) tendency

b) tend
c) tendentious
1983. Mike was found guilty … from his employer.
a) of stealing
b) in stealing
c) for stealing
1984. We went on our work with an air of … .
a) determine
b) determined
c) determination
1985. He … that if we started at dawn we would be
there by night.
a) reason
b) reasoned
c) reasonable
1986. The patient is getting on … .

a) satisfied
b) satisfaction
c) satisfactorily
1987. My cousin and my sister … engineers.
a) have
b) are
c) was
1988. She answered that question … .
a) fearfully
b) fearful
c) fearless
1989. This planet, … is so big, is the fifth planet
from the sun.
a) who
b) whom
c) which
1990. The students took part in school's activities …
.
a) keen
b) keener
c) keenly

1991. She went to meet me with an air of … .
a) expectancy
b) expectant
c) expect
1992. The telephone … by the time I was born.
a) had already been invent
b) had already been invented
c) had already finished
1993. The army … the enemy's capital.
a) occupation
b) occupied
c) occupational
1994. We objected … to wait so long.
a) with having
b) to having
c) for having
1995. Is Friday the day … not Thursday.
a) when you arrived
b) you'll arrive then
c) on that you arrive
1996. The drought … occurred last year ruined the
crops.
a) that is
b) which it
c) that

1997. This city … the Ghost City attracts many tourists every year.
a) known as
b) is knows as
c) that is known

1998. The shopping mall is advertised as a place … you can find anything.
a) which
b) where
c) in where

1999. She is marrying to a man … .
a) that she hardly knows him

b) whom she hardly knows
c) whose she hardly knows

2000. Men who exercise regularly have greater physical endurance than those … .
a) who doesn't
b) who don't
c) which don't

2001. Is this the city to … you want the package sent?
a) where
b) that
c) which

2002. His latest book is about the people from a small island … for three years.
a) among whom he lived
b) that he lived
c) that he lived among them

2003. By the time he arrived to help, we … moving the furniture.
a) already finished
b) had already finished
c) has already finished

2004. It was hot when I got home, so I … the ventilation system.
a) turned on
b) turn on
c) would turn on

2005. I engaged a … to show me the way.
a) guided
b) guidance
c) guide

2006. By the time the fire fighters arrived, the building … to the ground.
a) burned
b) had burned
c) was burned

2007. I … so much on one outfit.
a) have never spent
b) never have spent
c) was never spent

2008. Two days ago a hornet … me under my arm.
a) was stung
b) had stung
c) stung

2009. Our girl is keen … to art college.
a) in going
b) on going
c) at going

2010. If any of your questions are still … you can call me.
a) unanswered
b) inasnwered
c) answered

2011. I was not happy with the plans … the architect showed me.
a) in that
b) that
c) in which

2012. When I saw that she was having trouble, I … her.
a) was helping
b) help
c) helped

2013. Prior to last year, we … to such a big city.
a) had never been
b) have never been
c) were never

2014. Two years ago I experienced … .
a) how tedious long plane trips can be
b) how can tedious long plane trips be
c) how tedious can long plane trips be

2015. I don't want you … that aspect.
a) mention
b) to mention
c) mentioning

Set 8

2016. If you can't unscrew it, try … it with a hammer.
a) to hit
b) hit
c) hitting

2017. I remember hearing her say the grass needed … two days ago.
a) to cut
b) cutting
c) cut

2018. I advise you to wait before deciding … the job.
a) to accept
b) accepting
c) accept

2019. The lecture was dull and wasn't worth … .
a) listen
b) listening to
c) listened

2020. I couldn't resist asking her why she was trying … meeting me.
a) avoiding
b) avoid
c) to avoid

2021. Did Mary say she … me?
a) would telephone
b) will telephone
c) have telephoned

2022. The … of coming next week is small.
a) possible
b) possibly
c) possibility

2023. There was a nasty … at this crossroad yesterday.
a) happening
b) emergency
c) accident

2024. Some of the passengers were badly … .
a) pained

b) injured
c) hurted

2025. Several … helped to pull people out of the damaged car.

a) audience
b) supporters
c) bystanders

2026. Most of them were found to be suffering from severe … .
a) surprise
b) worry
c) shock

2027. The truck crashed into a car and had completely … it.
a) hit
b) wrecked
c) crashed

2028. The officers took the names and addresses of as many … as possible.
a) suspects
b) viewers
c) witnesses

2029. Injured passengers have the right to claim … .
a) rewards
b) refund
c) compensation

2030. This hat looks … on you.
a) nice
b) well
c) beautifully

2031. I never expected that … find the lost ring.
a) I would
b) I shall
c) I am going to

2032. The car was easy to recognize, … it was easy to find the thieves.
a) because
b) that
c) so

2033. By the end of 2022, they … the building.
a) will finish
b) finish
c) will have finished

2034. The news of his death … the world.
a) astonished
b) announced
c) heard

2035. Select the proper word for: "a multitude of people".
a) large

b) huge crowd

c) small number

2036. Select the proper word for: "Steve has arrived to find his wife in tears".

a) crying

b) panicky

c) confused

2037. People have a … for special occasions.

a) meal

b) festival

c) ceremony

2038. … work is the work that is always done the same way.

a) Manual

b) Routine

c) Mental

2039. To … means to help someone remember something.

a) memorize

b) suggest

c) remind

2040. I … my money because I want it to grow in value.

a) save

b) invest

c) put away

2041. She … to attend the meeting tonight.

a) couldn't

b) shouldn't

c) will not be able

2042. The poor woman has not … .

a) lived lonely

b) lived alone

c) been living lone

2043. The emergency committee has met and … .

a) they have reached a decision

b) it has reached decision

c) its decision reached

2044. Mary's score on last test is the highest in class.

a) She should study

b) She must have studied hard

c) She must have to study hard

2045. The manager requested that … .

a) the employees studied more carefully the problem

b) the problem was more careful studied

c) the employees study the problem more carefully

2046. This county relies on income from fruit crops and … .

a) also Toronto

b) Toronto too

c) so does Toronto

2047. I wanted to serve some wine to my guests. However, … .

a) I didn't have glasses

b) I hadn't glasses

c) I was lacking in glasses

2048. They … to the cemetery.

a) sent faith flowers

b) sent flowers faithfully

c) sent faithfully flowers

2049. The car and the house that you own are your … .

a) area

b) property

c) personal belongings

2050. A … is an object that help you remember a place you have visited.

a) souvenir

b) note

c) memory

2051. If someone commits a …, the police try to catch him.

a) mistake

b) divorce

c) crime

2052. The article contained a lot of … about how much petrol the car used.

a) information

b) news

c) fact

2053. The … crowd moved closer to the barricades.

a) irate

b) irating

c) angrily

2054. We … the validity of her remarks.

a) assisting

b) denied

c) hunted of

2055. Steve … while we watched the movie.

a) withdrew

b) got off

c) napped

2056. Sarah is very stubborn. Find the synonym:

a) patient

b) nice

c) obstinate

2057. They have a full schedule. Find the synonym:

a) busy day

b) project

c) programme of work

2058. Radioactivity causes cancer and affects future generations. Find the

synonym:

a) kill

b) be bad for

c) pollute

2059. They evacuated the area as the enemy advanced. Find the synonym:

a) left (because of danger)

b) bombed

c) attacked

2060. Mary offered a silly excuse. Find the synonym:

a) took

b) gave

c) accepted

2061. It must be … more than $250.

a) cost

b) expensive

c) worth

2062. I wouldn't eat salad … I were starving.

a) unless

b) or

c) provided that

2063. Next year I … this class for five years.

a) teach

b) will teach

c) will have taught

2064. I invited them … the meeting.

a) attend

b) to attend

c) for attending

2065. To call up means:

a) criticize

b) visit

c) telephone

2066. To give up means:

a) to surrender

b) to give all

c) to give a part of

2067. The professor … several words in my article.

a) corrected

b) added

c) cancelled

2068. To check out of a motel is to …

a) register it

b) leave it

c) ask for a room

2069. Children under the age of five … allowed to participate.

a) isn't

b) aren't

c) haven't

2070. Our company often requires that candidates have not only a degree …

.

a) but two years experience

b) but also two-year experience

c) but more years experience

2071. I hope she … to buy some milk.

a) proposed

b) reminded

c) remembered

2072.If I were you I … that suit.

a) would buy

b) will buy

c) am buying

2073. The vet decided that he had to operate … the dog.

a) to

b) on

c) with

2074. I … like to apologize for not being there.

a) might

b) must

c) would

2075.Many accidents in the home could be … .

a) excluded

b) protected

c) avoided

2076. Try to remember … bring your laptop.

a) himself to

b) to

c) yourself

2077. The bride looked … in her wedding dress.

a) pretty

b) lovely

c) handsome

2078. We didn't leave for the station until the very … moment.

a) last

b) latest

c) late

2079. When are you going to give back that money you … me?

a) lend

b) debt

c) owe

2080. These politicians were … by terrorists.

a) destroyed

b) murdered

c) collapsed

2081. Each … of the team had to take it in turns to do the washing up.

a) individual

b) person

c) member

2082. The little girl performs beautifully … the piano.

a) on

b) in

c) at

2083. The tour … about two hours to complete.

a) has

b) takes

c) spends

2084. The airport was temporarily … .

a) stormed

b) delayed

c) closed

2085. You will soon buy a house. …

a) What wonderful news!

b) How wonderful news!

c) What a wonderful news!

2086. If my documents had been found last week, I … to come.

a) would have been able

b) would be able

c) will have been able

2087. The buses are so dirty. … they are never on time.

a) Instead

b) For example

c) In addition

2088. You were warned never … with this extremist group.

a) to assign

b) to associate

c) to assume

2089. If your firm wants to attract workers it must … the pay.

a) raise

b) lower

c) rise

2090. I'm afraid this laptop is totally … for your needs.

a) undeniable

b) unspeakable

c) unsuitable

2091. I regretted my mistake. It was one that I … .

a) hadn't to make

b) shouldn't have made

c) mustn't make

2092. Members of a Parliament are … by the people.

a) represented

b) polled

c) voted

2093. Tom is Sarah's father, so Sarah is Tom's … .

a) daughter

b) niece

c) wife

2094. Her job was so tiring that she felt absolutely … .

a) sharpened

b) shattered

c) scattered

2095. I can sell you some apples but only … .

a) a little

b) little

c) a few

2096. I can't repay you this week. I'm completely … .

a) damaged

b) broken

c) destroyed

2097. I often … money from my parents.

a) borrow

b) lend

c) save

2098. She is said … our country next year.

a) to have visited

b) to be visiting

c) to visit

2099. These students … to Madrid tomorrow.

a) are going

b) have gone

c) will going

2100. Thank you for letting me … your car for a ride.

a) taken

b) taking

c) take

2101. Can you put me … for some days?

a) down

b) away

c) up

2102. Coal is still … in this county.

a) built

b) mined

c) manufactured

2103. The manager's presentation will be … by tomorrow night.

a) ready

b) soon

c) nearly

2104. You certainly wouldn't like … in such bad entourage.

a) to see

b) to be seen

c) to have seen

2105. There isn't … salt on the table.

a) some

b) the

c) any

2106. I tried to call last night you but your line was … .

a) occupied

b) taken

c) engaged

2107. Come to my party … Friday night.

a) the

b) at

c) on

2108. Nobody can fool her. She's never … in.

a) taken

b) giving

c) taking

2109. I will tell you if I … the answer.

a) knew

b) know

c) has known

2110. Are you able to drink something while you …?

a) were whistling

b) whistled

c) whistle

2111. I'll choose another strategy in case it … .

a) happen

b) happens

c) happening

2112. We'll go our if the weather … .

a) improve

b) will improve

c) improves

2113. The food … awful.

a) tastes

b) is tasting

c) have tasted

2114. Your support … a lot now.

a) is meaning

b) meant

c) means

2115. This report … of four parts now.

a) consisted

b) consists

c) is consisting

2116. Where … you found it?

a) has

b) did

c) have

2117. She's just … it on the desk.

a) put

b) putting

c) putted

2118. When I came home, my wife … dinner.

a) already cooked
b) had already cooked
c) was already cooked
2119. They discovered she … it correctly.
a) hasn't done
b) hadn't done
c) didn't do
2120. Mary told me they … on this building project for two years.
a) were working
b) did working
c) had been working
2121. Why … produced now?
a) is it
b) it is
c) is it being
2122. The Moon … round.
a) is
b) could be
c) will be
2123. How long … German?
a) have you been learning
b) did you learn
c) do you learnt
2124. … criticized?
a) Was she ever
b) Has she ever been
c) Did she ever been
2125. It's high time … .
a) you go home
b) you gone home
c) you went home
2126. I'm fond … jogging.
a) at

b) in
c) of
2127. People were amazed … his progress.
a) with
b) at
c) in
2128. I'm not content … my income.
a) with
b) about
c) on
2129. I was absolutely delighted … my new flat.
a) for

b) at
c) in
2130. Don't worry! I strongly believe … .
a) for you
b) you
c) to you
2131. The committee weren't surprised by the approval … your decision.
a) of
b) to
c) on
2132. Mary's under … pressure.
a) a
b) on
c) –
2133. We use to talk on the phone from time … time.
a) to
b) a
c) with
2134. He said: "The method doesn't work.".
a) He said that the method doesn't work
b) He said that hadn't worked
c) He said that the method didn't work

2135. The secretary said: "They have already notified Steve.".
a) She said that they have already notified him
b) She said that they had already notified him
c) She said that Steve was notified
2136. Tim said: "She had forgiven me.".
a) Tim said that she had forgiven him.
b) Tim said that she has forgiven.
c) Tim said that she would have forgiven him.
2137. The assistant manager asked me: "Do you like your job?".
a) She asked me I liked my job.
b) She has asked me I liked my job.
c) She asked me whether I liked my job.
2138. She asked me: "Did they inform John?".
a) She asked me if they informed him.
b) She asked me if they had informed him.
c) She asked me if they have informed him.
2139. My girlfriend asked me: "Where did you do yesterday?".
a) She asked me where I had gone yesterday.
b) She asked me where have I gone yesterday.

c) She asked me where I had gone the day before.

2140. The manager asked me: "What will change?".

a) The manager asked me what would change.

b) The manager asked me what would have changed.

c) The manager asked me what will change.

2141. Mary asked me: "What information will Jane send?".

a) Mary asked me what information Jane would send.

b) Jane asked me what information Mary will send

c) Mary asked me what information Jane will send.

2142. I … well in the exam.

a) made

b) did

c) solved

2143. We were … by her results.

a) amazing

b) amaze

c) amazed

2144. Her husband is so … .

a) irresponsible

b) irresponsibly

c) disresponsible

2145. There are many people who are … in this country.

a) inliterate

b) unliterate

c) illiterate

2146. These details are … .

a) innecessary

b) unnecessary

c) overnecessary

2147. They won at last. They were so … .

a) lucky

b) luckily

c) unlucky

2148. It's … to think so. Most colleagues think so.

a) unnatural

b) innatural

c) natural

2149. Where is the stadium …?

a) situation

b) situating

c) situated

2150. I really can't figure it … . (understand)

a) with

b) out

c) in

2151. The company decided to take … three more employees. (employ)

a) on

b) in

c) about

2152. The woman was taken … . (deceived)

a) about

b) in

c) on

2153. Hang … a second! (wait)

a) up

b) about

c) on

2154. I will do it in spite … .

a) I'm busy

b) mine busy

c) of being busy

2155. She learns German intensively … of having little free time.

a) in spite

b) despite

c) despite in

2156. I'd rather you … it.

a) haven't done

b) don't do

c) didn't do

2157. I'd prefer … everything about her.

a) forget

b) to forget

c) forgetting

2158. This report must … .

a) receive

b) have been received

c) had been received

2159. That day it was … freezing.

a) absolutely

b) very

c) utter

2160. It's … ridiculous.

a) very

b) intense

c) absolutely

2161. Look! They … .

a) are returning
b) return
c) being returning
2162. This thing … us now.
a) concerned
b) concerns
c) is concerning
2163. … she playing the piano professionally?
a) Were
b) Did
c) Was
2164. Choose the right sentence:
a) She has never lied to me. She will lie me again.
b) She never lied. She is truly constant.
c) She never lied. She had always lied.
2165. It has … to enormous problems.
a) leaded
b) lead
c) led

Set 9

2166. I'm afraid I … the details.
a) misheared
b) misheart
c) misheard
2167. The professor … Russian since last year.
a) hasn't being teaching
b) hasn't been teaching
c) hadn't been teaching
2168. … analyzed now?
a) Are their reports
b) Are their reports being
c) Were their reports being

2169. This method … yet.
a) hasn't been verified
b) hasn't verified
c) hasn't being verified
2170. She inform us the decision … .
a) had already been made
b) was already been made
c) has already been made
2171. We came to the conclusion we … .
a) were been informed
b) had been misinformed
c) have been uninformed

2172. When …?
a) had it happened
b) has it being happened
c) did it happen
2173. I … you for ages. How are you?
a) haven't being seen
b) hadn't seen
c) haven't seen
2174. The weather was good. We were walking and talking about future
plans. The sun … brightly.
a) shone
b) shining
c) was shining
2175. It was written that the stadium … .
a) was destroyed
b) had already been destroyed
c) has been destroyed
2176. If she … it much earlier, she would have left that building.
a) had known
b) knew
c) might have known
2177. Sarah … speak English without any mistakes. (it's her desire)
a) has to

b) couldn't
c) must
2178. Kim … to school tomorrow.
a) must go
b) must gone
c) must have gone
2179. They were late … the annual meeting.
a) to
b) for
c) about
2180. I want to congratulate you … passing the final exam.
a) on
b) for
c) with
2181. I heard the most important thing about the mission … the end.
a) for
b) in
c) with

2182. She told him: "I'm so tired".
a) She told him that she was so tired.
b) She told him that she's so tired
c) She told him that she has been so tired
2183. She said: "I have been working on this project for 5 days.".
a) She said that she has been working on this project for 5 days.
b) She said that she's working on that project for 5 days.
c) She said that she had been working on that project for 5 days.
2184. The employee said: "I'll be working more intensively.".
a) He said that he'll be working more intensively.
b) He said that he would be working more intensively.
c) He said that he will being working more intensively.
2185. John said: "I saw her yesterday.".
a) John said that he had seen her yesterday.
b) John said that he had seen her the day before.
c) John said that he has seen her the day before.

2186. She asked me: "Was he irritated?".
a) She asked me if he was irritated.
b) She asked me if he had been irritated.
c) She asked me if he has been irritated.
2187. … my article?
a) Don't you see
b) Haven't you see
c) Couldn't you seen
2188. … this method work?
a) Isn't
b) Doesn't
c) Hadn't
2189. … like our idea?
a) Didn't she not
b) Hasn't she
c) Did she not
2190. … improve his performance?
a) Didn't he
b) Hasn't he
c) Hadn't he
2191. … they join us?
a) Aren't
b) Won't

c) Hadn't
2192. Steve, why are you so …?
a) impatient
b) unpatient
c) ipatient
2193. I totally … of this plan.
a) unapprove
b) approved
c) disapprove
2194. Does this treatment make any …?
a) difference
b) different
c) differenting
2195. It's a very strange way of …, but I like it!
a) thought
b) thinking
c) be thinking
2196. Don't worry! You can share your … with us.
a) thinks
b) thinkings
c) thoughts
2197. It's an … situation.
a) imagine
b) imaginative
c) imaginary
2198. Will this management team be …, too?
a) unefficient
b) inefficient
c) effectively
2199. It's because of their … .
a) disobedience
b) unobedience
c) ilobedience
2200. I checked … at 9 o'clock in the morning at the best hotel.
a) on
b) in
c) within
2201. Today's lesson is … .
a) done
b) gone
c) over
2202. The terrorists wanted to blow … the building but they were arrested.
a) up
b) in

c) at

2203. Samuel owned up … making a mistake.

a) of

b) to

c) about

2204. We'll try to find … all the truth.

a) out

b) over

c) in

2205. I'd rather … at home than go there. It's a pandemic out there.

a) to stay

b) staying

c) stay

2206. This woman might … .

a) be invited

b) has invited

c) have been invited

2207. They may … .

a) accused

b) accusing

c) be accused

2208. Mark … .

a) should have been congratulated

b) should has been congratulated

c) should had been congratulated

2209. Their manager … .

a) could being informed

b) could have been informed

c) could to be informed

2210. I … understand you. Don't worry about it.

a) am

b) do

c) had

2211. I'll prepare for the exam as soon as I … free time.

a) will have

b) would have

c) have

2212. … it right now.

a) He does

b) He did

c) He is doing

2213. It started raining when I … .

a) was jogging

b) were jogging

c) jogged

2214. They … the managers about that problem.

a) didn't consulted

b) weren't consulting

c) being consulted

2215. … it bringing you enough money?

a) Were

b) Was

c) Did

2216. Why … they complaining all the time?

a) was

b) did

c) were

2217. It … five days ago.

a) happened

b) happening

c) had happened

2218. … congratulated me. I'm so happy!

a) He already

b) He has already

c) He had already

2219. The thief hasn't … .

a) shooted

b) shoot

c) shot

2220. My girlfriend … fashionable clothes.

a) wear

b) weared

c) wore

2221. I … Megan for a long time.

a) haven't been seeing

b) haven't seen

c) didn't seen

2222. The detectives found out they … it.

a) already stole

b) stolen

c) had already stolen

2223. What …?

a) has being changing

b) has been changed

c) was being changing

2224. We … next month.

a) meet

b) will meet

c) couldn't meet

2225. I wish I … it two years ago.
a) had bought
b) bought
c) would buy
2226. I wish Mary … the test last month.
a) had passed
b) passed
c) has passed
2227. She's quite confused … the results.
a) by
b) in
c) about
2228. Our marriage ended … divorce.
a) up

b) in
c) about
2229. I'll pay … debit card.
a) by
b) on
c) about
2230. Olivia said: "My work is so boring.".
a) Olivia said that her work is so boring.
b) Olivia said that her work would be so boring.
c) Olivia said that her work was so boring.
2231. The reporter said: "The game will last for two hours.".
a) He said that the game would last for two hours.
b) He said that the game lasts for two hours.
c) He said that the game will last for two hours.
2232. She said: "My brother has been swimming.".
a) She said that her brother had been swimming.
b) She said that her brother was swimming.
c) She said that her brother have been swimming.
2233. I … for your reply.
a) will wait
b) waiting
c) will be waiting
2234. I … this book by December 2020.
a) will be finish
b) will finish
c) will have finished
2235. The manager asked me: "Did you solve the problem?".
a) She asked me if I solved the problem.
b) She asked me if I had solved that problem.
c) She asked me if I was solving the problem.

2236. They asked me: "Will he be in charge of this department?".
a) They asked me if he would be in charge of that department.
b) They asked me if he is in charge of the department.
c) They asked me if he would be in charge of this department.

2237. My wife asked me: "Was it getting more and more expensive?".
a) My wife asked me if it was getting more and more expensive.
b) My wife asked me if it had been getting more and more expensive.
c) My wife asked me if it has been getting more and more expensive.
2238. The teacher asked me: "Have you shown excellent results?".
a) The teacher asked me if you had shown excellent results.
b) The teacher asked me if I had shown excellent results.
c) The teacher asked me if I have shown excellent results.
2239. To my surprise, she asked me: "What are you doing tonight?".
a) She asked me what I was doing tonight.
b) She asked me what have I been doing tonight.
c) She asked me what I was doing that night.
2240. … happy?
a) Hasn't she
b) Isn't she
c) Haven't she
2241. … not return home?
a) Did they
b) Didn't they
c) Weren't they
2242. Are they not meeting …?
a) then
b) when
c) now
2243. Your experience is truly … .
a) amazed
b) amazing
c) been amazed
2244. These instructions are really … .

a) confusing

b) confused

c) confundant

2245. Sarah mostly wears … clothes.

a) unformal

b) deformal

c) informal

2246. Maria wears … clothes.

a) fashion

b) fashioning

c) fashionable

2247. There were … changes in this organization.

a) really

b) real

c) reality

2248. This cancer vaccine has changed our life for ever. It's a real … .

a) break

b) breaking

c) breakthrough

2249. Her remark left me … . I was utterly shocked.

a) speaking

b) speechless

c) speech

2250. She gently took … her dress. (removed)

a) off

b) of

c) about

2251. … the system more thoroughly.

a) You'd better check

b) You had better to check

c) You would better to check

2252. Maria you … better hurry up.

a) would

b) can

c) had

2253. This documentary was worth … .

a) to watch

b) watching

c) been watch

2254. It's no use … now.

a) to cry

b) cried

c) crying

2255. Our team shouldn't … .

a) be divided

b) division

c) divided

2256. It can't … right now.

a) known

b) be known

c) knowing

2257. I'm sorry, but it needed … .

a) to be done

b) to do

c) be done

2258. … you spend on clothes, the more money you have.

a) Less

b) Least

c) The less

2259. The little girl was … terrified.

a) very

b) absolutely

c) absolute

2260. … here I feel satisfied.

a) Working

b) Worked

c) To working

2261. No truly one … it.

a) expected

b) expecting

c) didn't expect

2262. I won't help him unless he … his point of view.

a) change

b) will change

c) changes

2263. I'll fix everything before she … .

a) returns

b) will return

c) will be return

2264. I'll call you as soon as I … back.

a) will get

b) had got

c) get

2265. … a party tonight.

a) Tom is giving

b) Tom gives

c) Tom will given

2266. … this problem.

a) They often mention
b) They are often mentioning
c) They had often mentioning
2267. She … them a request.
a) hadn't send
b) hadn't have
c) wasn't sending
2268. … she leading a new lifestyle after they had broken off?
a) Were
b) Was
c) Had
2269. Choose the correct sentence:
a) Sarah has just remembered it.
b) Sarah has just remembering it.
c) Sarah has just remembered it two days ago.
2270. All of a sudden, the bell … .
a) rung
b) rang
c) ringing

2271. We know you … Russian for many year.
a) teach
b) had been teaching
c) have been teaching
2272. She … this problem with the car for many years.
a) has been having
b) having had
c) has had
2273. We all realized that she … to us.
a) hasn't lied
b) hadn't lied
c) having lied
2274. The child … very professionally now.
a) is taught
b) be teaching
c) is being taught
2275. What … yesterday?
a) had been deleted
b) were deleted
c) has been deleted
2276. We … for half a year.
a) have been dating
b) being dating
c) had dated

2277. By the time I got the letter I … that minor issue.
a) have already solving
b) had already solved
c) had already had solving
2278. The report … yet.
a) wasn't written
b) hasn't been written
c) hadn't been writing
2279. I wish I … another car last year.
a) has found

b) would find
c) had found
2280. It's high time Tim … them all the money.
a) paying
b) paid
c) had paid
2281. I … find a new car.
a) must
b) might can
c) have to had
2282. The managers let her … out.
a) to go
b) go
c) went
2283. I'm fully satisfied … your project. Congrats!
a) about
b) within
c) with
2284. The man said: "She never helps us.".
a) The man said that she never was helping them.
b) The man said she never helped them.
c) The man said she never helped us.
2285. Mark said: "I will be sleeping all night.".
a) Mark said that he would be sleeping all night.
b) Mark said that he will be sleeping all night.
c) Mark said that he would sleep all night.
2286. My girlfriend asked me: "How are you?".
a) She asked me how were you.
b) She asked me how I was.
c) She asked me how I would be.
2287. The thief asked me: "Why did she remain calm?".
a) The thief asked me why she remained calm.
b) The thief asked me why she was remaining calm.
c) The thief asked me why she had remained calm.

2288. The customer asked me: "Why was it a unique offer?".
a) The customer asked me why it had been a unique offer.
b) The customer asked me why had it been a unique offer.
c) The customer asked me why was it a unique offer.
2289. Choose the correct sentence:
a) What are you waiting?
b) What are you waiting for?
c) What are you wait for?
2290. They work … .
a) effective
b) effecting
c) effectively
2291. Your wife sings so … .
a) beautiful
b) beautifully
c) beauty
2292. The professor really likes their … .
a) creativity
b) creative
c) creating
2293. The event was absolutely … .
a) fantasy
b) fantastic
c) fanatic
2294. Why can't she buy … things sometimes?
a) expensive
b) expensively
c) inexpensive
2295. The child has a vivid … .
a) imagination
b) imaginary
c) imagine
2296. Do you think that our … will change after the pandemic?
a) sociable

b) society
c) social
2297. In that area the ground was … .
a) uneven
b) ineven
c) unevenly

2298. Please, calm …! There's nothing to worry about.
a) in
b) over
c) down
2299. Does your laptop often break …?
a) off
b) in
c) down
2300. She really takes care … our child.
a) after
b) of
c) on
2301. We got … trouble during that mission.
a) into
b) on
c) within
2302. They ended up … about the budget.
a) argue
b) arguing
c) arguably
2303. I think they'll call … soon. (visit you)
a) back
b) over
c) round
2304. I would prefer … at home.
a) to stay
b) stay
c) to staying

2305. I have trouble … with this business partner.
a) to deal
b) dealing
c) on dealt
2306. We're supposed … the leaders in this organization.
a) to become
b) become
c) to becoming
2307. The text might … partially.
a) translate
b) translating
c) be translated
2308. I'm sure the employees … more.
a) could have be motivated
b) could have been motivated
c) could have being motivated

2309. Either Mark … John will do it.

a) nor

b) also

c) or

2310. Don't panic. I … see it. It's over there.

a) am

b) are

c) do

2311. We'll stay at home if the weather … .

a) don't improve

b) doesn't improve

c) won't improve

2312. … the trainers asking about that thing?

a) Had

b) Were

c) Have

2313. What … the professor saying about that problem?

a) was

b) has

c) had

2314. Is the following sentence correct? "I was wanting it with all my heart."

a) correct

b) incorrect

2315. Is the following sentence correct? "They were fighting very bravely at that moment."

a) correct

b) incorrect

2316. I … there for a few times.

a) had been

b) had be

c) have been

2317. … all the companies gone bankrupt? I can't believe it!

a) Have

b) Has

c) Having

2318. What things … they said?

a) had have

b) have

c) has had

2319. Have you ever been … the Netherlands?

a) in

b) at

c) to

2320. The lady has … the floor.

a) sweeped

b) sweeping

c) swept

2321. The little girl has … the cats.

a) feeded

b) fed

c) feeding

2322. I … more than enough.

a) sleeped

b) sleeping

c) slept

2323. It was said they … another choice regarding the product.

a) hadn't made

b) haven't made

c) didn't made

2324. These problems … yet.

a) weren't discussed

b) haven't been discussed

c) hadn't been discussed

2325. If she … my advice yesterday, Mary wouldn't be in trouble now.

a) heard

b) had heard

c) have minded

2326. You needn't … about this.

a) worrying

b) be worried

c) worry

2327. They … him about a preliminary result.

a) mustn't have informed

b) mustn't to inform

c) mustn't informing

2328. You … here so early.

a) needn't have come

b) needn't had come

c) needn't be come

2329. I won't let you … so much.

a) to risk

b) risk

c) risking

2330. We are engaged … this project.

a) at

b) for

c) in

2331. It's far … belief.

a) behind

b) beyond

c) beware

2332. The secretary said: "I will read the documents.".

a) The secretary said that she would read the documents.

b) The secretary said that she will read the documents.

c) The secretary said the she would have read the documents.

2333. Steve said: "I will be learning German all day.".

a) Steve said he will be learning German all day.

b) Steve said he would be all day German learning.

c) Steve said he would be learning German all day.

2334. I … this website for three weeks by next month.

a) will had used

b) will have been using

c) will have been used

2335. Susan asked me: "Do you live there?".

a) She asked me if I live there.

b) She asked me if I lived there.

c) She asked me if I would live there.

2336. The teacher asked me: "Are you proud of her?".

a) The teacher asked me if I was proud of her.

b) The teacher asked me if I am proud of her.

c) The teacher asked me if I have been proud of her.

2337. My girlfriend asked me: "Is it a popular resort?".

a) She asked me whether was it a popular resort.

b) She asked me if it had been a popular resort.

c) She asked me if it was a popular resort.

2338. They asked me: "Where do you live?".

a) They asked me where I live.

b) They asked me where I lived.

c) They asked me where I had lived.

2339. The manager asked me: "How will you manage to solve this problem?".

a) The manager asked me how I would manage to solve that problem.

b) The manager asked me how would I manage to solve that problem.

c) The manager asked me how I would manage to solve this problem.

2340. The detective asked me: "Why are they looking for it?".

a) The detective asked me why they are looking for it.

b) The detective asked me why would they be looking for it.

c) The detective asked me why they were looking for it.

2341. … agree with me?

a) Not you

b) Haven't

c) Don't you

2342. … a remarkable achievement?

a) Isn't it

b) Hasn't it

c) Hadn't it

2343. … him?

a) Didn't it interest

b) Didn't it interesting for

c) Hadn't it interesting

2344. This handwriting is totally … .

a) illegible

b) unlegible

c) alegible

2345. We prepared an annual … .

a) reporter

b) report

c) reporting

2346. It's really a matter of … . Let's hope that you'll do better next time.

a) lucky

b) luckily

c) luck

2347. Jessica speaks Russian … . She needs to learn more.

a) unnaturally

b) inaturally

c) unnatural

2348. I feel safe and … now. Thank you!

a) unprotected

b) protective

c) protected

2349. Our world is clearly … .

a) unperfect

b) imperfect

c) aperfect

2350. He … the door using a stolen key.

a) dislocked

b) unlocked

c) locking

2351. The teenager threw … his old clothes. (get rid of)

a) off

b) about

c) away

2352. You'd better … it.

a) not do

b) not doing

c) not to do

2353. I repaired my laptop.

a) myself

b) not myself

c) about myself

2354. … no point in asking her help.

a) There

b) There's

c) This

2355. This report … .

a) must spreading

b) must be spread

c) must be spreaded

2356. Can my perfumes … earlier?

a) deliver

b) delivered

c) be delivered

2357. The officers … .

a) should have been warned

b) should be warn

c) should had been warned

2358. Their mistakes … .

a) should have be correcting

b) should have been corrected

c) should corrected

2359. The book … last month.

a) could have been read

b) could has been read

c) could had been read

2360. The laptop … .

a) could to have sold

b) could had been sold

c) could have been sold

2361. Nobody … remember your mistake.

a) won't

b) will

c) wouldn't

2362. … next Saturday.

a) I work

b) I'm working

c) I'd worked

2363. Honestly, … now.

a) I doubt

b) I doubted

c) I'm doubting

2364. When the bell rang, we … the figures down.

a) was writing

b) had writing

c) were writing

2365. When I … an intricate book, my sister came in.

a) was reading

b) had reading

c) have been reading

2366. I … in that competition.

a) hadn't been participated

b) wasn't participating

c) hasn't been participating

2367. My girlfriend … German.

a) weren't spoken

b) wasn't speaking

c) didn't spoke

2368. … your commander saying it very clearly?

a) Did

b) Had

c) Was

2369. Is the following sentence correct? "The success was depending on me."

a) correct

b) incorrect

2370. … your colleague told you about it?

a) Did

b) Has

c) Had

2371. Where … your sisters seen it?

a) have

b) did

c) were

2372. What thing … the child heard before?

a) have

b) did

c) has

2373. We have … up a new revolutionary program.

a) setted

b) setting

c) set

2374. The evaluation … my strong and weak points.

a) shown

b) showed

c) showing

2375. We … the video system since last week.

a) have been testing

b) had been testing

c) would be testing

2376. … off the computer before she left home?

a) Had she turned

b) Has she turned

c) Did she turned

2377. Choose the correct sentence:

a) The food is cooked at the moment.

b) The food is being cooked at the moment.

c) The food is cooking at the moment.

2378. Choose the correct sentence:

a) Sarah still has problems.

b) Sarah has still having problems.

c) Sarah is still having problems.

2379. When they noticed it we … it.

a) already did

b) had already done

c) have already done

2380. They … us next month.

a) may have visited

b) could have visited

c) may visit

2381. I'm pleased … such amazing results.

a) by

b) on

c) with

2382. Their approach differs … ours.

a) into

b) from

c) of

2383. The marketing assistant disapproves … the decision.

a) of

b) on

c) about

2384. The scientists are … the brink of discovering the truth.

a) in

b) about

c) on

2385. Steve said: "It's what I need.".

a) Steve said that it was what he needed.

b) Steve said that it was what I needed.

c) Steve said that it has been what he needed.

2386. The manager said: "It will remain the same.".

a) The manager said that it will remain the same.

b) The manager said that it would remain the same.

c) The manager said that it would be remaining the same.

2387. Krista said: "I will be waiting for his response.".

a) Krista said that she will wait for his response.

b) Krista said that he would be waiting for her response.

c) Krista said that she would be waiting for his response.

2388. The marketing specialist asked me: "Has it become a real success?".

a) The marketing specialist asked me if it had become a real success.

b) The marketing specialist asked me if it became a real success.

c) The marketing specialist asked me if it has become a real success.

2389. Choose the correct sentence:

a) Was no this treatment effective?

b) Wasn't this treatment effective?

c) Didn't this treatment be effective?

2390. … the latest news shock you?

a) Wasn't

b) Hadn't
c) Didn't
2391. Choose the correct sentence:
a) Will she not come back?
b) Will not she coming back?
c) Won't she be come back?
2392. Who does she agree …?
a) with
b) about
c) within
2393. It was an … town for me.
a) infamiliar
b) unfamiliar
c) ifamiliar
2394. These conclusions are so … .
a) unlogical
b) alogical
c) illogical
2395. My cousin is … . He can't find a job.
a) employed
b) employing
c) unemployed
2396. This thing is … . You don't need it.
a) unnecessary
b) necessary
c) inecessary
2397. It was a very … investment. They lost all their savings.
a) wise
b) unwise
c) wisely

2398. Don't let anybody …! It's a dangerous area.
a) in
b) on
c) about
2399. Please, turn … the TV.
a) about
b) off
c) in
2400. Sorry for interrupting. Please, go … talking!
a) in
b) after
c) on
2401. Sit …, please!
a) down
b) about

c) within
2402. Come …! Hurry up!
a) after
b) on
c) backwards
2403. Today we need to weigh … all the pros and cons.
a) after
b) up
c) on
2404. The student continued learning … of the noise.
a) despite
b) although
c) in spite
2405. She washed her car.
a) itself
b) herself
c) on his own
2406. A new villa can … .
a) be built

b) built
c) building
2407. They mustn't … .
a) punishing
b) be punished
c) had been punished
2408. Might they … by me?
a) be invited
b) invite
c) inviting
2409. She is to … here at four.
a) arriving
b) arrived
c) arrive
2410. No sooner … at the station than the night train left.
a) had I arrive
b) had I arrived
c) arrived had I
2411. While they were having a break, we … negotiations.
a) had been having
b) were having
c) have been having
2412. Where … your sister been?

a) was
b) has
c) will
2413. Choose the correct sentence:
a) We have never been friends. We have almost nothing in common.
b) We never were friends. We have almost nothing in common.
c) We had never been friend. We have almost nothing in common.
2414. His wife has … him and everything is fine between them.
a) forgived
b) forgotten
c) forgiven

2415. They have … me. I will explain it again.
a) misunderstood
b) misunderstand
c) misunderstanding
2416. She … the book because she had enjoyed it a long time ago.
a) reread
b) reading
c) had reread
2417. I … the heating system since last Monday.
a) haven't checked
b) haven't checking
c) didn't check
2418. How long … the institution?
a) have they be controlling
b) have they been controlling
c) had they been controlled
2419. He said he … for two hours.
a) was working
b) has been working
c) had been working
2020. I read they … the assassin.
a) punish
b) be punished
c) had punished
2021. Choose the correct sentence:
a) It has already been said.
b) It was already said.
c) It will already be said.
2422. If I were you, I … choose another team member.

a) will
b) would
c) would have chosen
2423. I … improve my German as soon as possible.
a) must

b) must have
c) must be
2424. This capital is crowded … tourists.
a) of
b) about
c) with
2425. The new colleague is full … innovative ideas.
a) in
b) about
c) of
2426. I'm fed up … this job.
a) with
b) about
c) of
2427. I was impressed … her beauty.
a) of
b) by
c) about
2428. I'm really serious … everything.
a) at
b) of
c) about
2429. I'm so excited … the vaccine news.
a) about
b) in
c) on
2430. I don't know why she is so pessimistic … their future.
a) with
b) about
c) of
2431. It's very nice … you to remember it.
a) to
b) of
c) with

2432. I have just arrived … the airport.
a) in
b) about
c) at
2433. What's the difference … these two laptops?

a) between

b) among

c) of

2434. See you … two months.

a) of

b) with

c) in

2435. Tim said: "I don't teach German.".

a) Tim said that he doesn't teach German.

b) Tim said that he didn't teach German.

c) Tim said that he haven't taught German.

2436. The patient said: "I'm experiencing a strange feeling.".

a) The patient said that he was experiencing a strange feeling.

b) The patient said that he has been experiencing a strange feeling.

c) The patient said that he had been experiencing a strange feeling.

2437. John said: "She has sung a beautiful song.".

a) John said that she has sung a beautiful song.

b) John said that she was singing a beautiful song.

c) John said that she had sung a beautiful song.

2438. We … Russian for an hour by the time she enters the room.

a) are speaking

b) will have been speaking

c) would have been speaking

2439. I … English for five years by next year.

a) will have been teaching

b) will teach

c) will be teaching

2440. They asked me: "Did they destroy that building?".

a) They asked me they had destroyed that building.

b) They asked me if they had destroyed that building.

c) They asked me if they destroyed that building.

2441. The journalist asked me: "Is he accusing her?".

a) The journalist asked me if he had been accusing her.

b) The journalist asked me if he has been accusing her.

c) The journalist asked me if he was accusing her.

2442. My wife asked me: "How long have you been dating with her?".

a) My wife asked me how long I'm dating with her.

b) My wife asked me how long I had been dating with her.

c) My wife asked me how long I was dating with her.

2443. Choose the correct sentence:

a) Doesn't she like this phone?

b) Not she like this phone?

c) Didn't she liked this phone?

2444. Choose the correct sentence:

a) Wasn't it not obvious?

b) Didn't it been obvious?

c) Was it not obvious?

2445. Choose the correct sentence:

a) Who are you talking?

b) Who are you talk to?

c) Who are you talking to?

2446. Choose the correct sentence:

a) Who is this gift for?

b) Whom does this gift for?

c) Who is this gift?

2447. It's the most … song.

a) fame

b) famous

c) famously

2448. What do you know about the world of …?

a) fashion

b) fashionable

c) fashioning

2449. It was a … experiment regarding new treatments.

a) science

b) sciencely

c) scientific

2450. …, what he is saying is true.

a) Actually

b) Recently

c) Actual

2451. Turn … the sound! It's way too loud.

a) up

b) away

c) down

2452. I switched … the laptop.

a) off

b) about

c) away

2453. Sarah showed … at the end of the party.

a) within

b) up

c) beyond

2454. Our plan fell … . We'll try again soon.

a) away

b) through

c) about

2455. Choose the correct sentence:

a) I'm trying to learn German in spite of not having enough free time.

b) I'm trying to learn German in spite to have enough free time.

c) I'm trying to learn German despite of having enough free time.

2456. I … sooner go abroad.

a) had

b) could

c) would

2457. There is no point …, so let's calm down.

a) argue

b) in arguing

c) to argue

2458. The mission … last week.

a) should be cancelled

b) should have been cancelled

c) should cancel

2459. Whatever you say, it … change my life.

a) was

b) has

c) did

2460. Not only … but I also work.

a) I study

b) do I study

c) had I study

2461. Choose the correct sentence:

a) Do you work next Friday?

b) Are you working next Friday?

c) Have you worked next Friday?

2462. Choose the correct sentence:

a) I'm tasting this dish now.

b) I taste the dish now.

c) I've been tasting this dish now.

2463. Choose the correct sentence:

a) She's owing me 300 dollars now.

b) She's been owing me 300 dollars now.

c) She owes me 300 dollars now.

2464. Is the following sentence correct? "I was wanting to help them."

a) correct

b) incorrect

2465. Is the following sentence correct? "Were you knowing all the truth at that moment?"

a) correct

b) incorrect

2466. My old family friend … invited me.

a) will

b) should

c) have

2467. She … brilliant results.

a) showed

b) shown

c) has showing

2468. The manager said he … those employees.

a) hadn't fired

b) doesn't fires

c) will fire

2469. When she noticed me I … the car for two hours.

a) was driving

b) had been driving

c) have been driving

2470. Necessary conditions … now.

a) aren't being provided

b) haven't provided

c) hadn't been provided

2471. Why … to the list?

a) has it adding

b) has it been added

c) had it being added

2472. Don't worry. Your knowledge … enough.

a) are

b) has

c) will be

2473. How long … together?

a) have you being worked

b) have you been working

c) had you been working

2474. She was exhausted. She … hard all morning.

a) had been working
b) had work
c) has been working

2475. If Mary had passed the test, her parents …
much happier.
a) would had been
b) would have been
c) might had been
2476. If only I … more time!
a) have
b) did
c) had
2477. Choose the correct sentence:
a) You don't have to overwork.
b) You don't need be overwork.
c) You didn't needed overwork.
2478. It … much better.
a) would to be
b) would been
c) would have been
2479. This name is familiar … me.
a) to
b) about
c) with
2480. You need to be more polite … your
customers.
a) of
b) to
c) on
2481. He couldn't hear her. She shouted … him
again.
a) to
b) of
c) towards
2482. I agree with you … some extent.
a) of
b) on
c) to
2483. They … this place by ten.
a) will leave

b) will be left
c) will have left
2484. The manager said: "I'm busy now.".
a) The manager said that he was busy now.
b) The manager said that he has been busy then.

c) The manager said that he was busy then.
2485. She asked me: "Do you agree?".
a) She asked me if I agreed.
b) She asked me I agreed
c) She asked me if had I agreed.
2486. My friends asked me: "Where is this place?".
a) My friends asked me where was that place.
b) My friends asked me where that place was.
c) My friends asked me where that place has been.
2487. She asked me: "How are your parents doing?".
a) She asked me how my parents were doing.
b) She asked me how my parents are doing.
c) She asked me how have been doing.
2488. Choose the correct sentence:
a) Won't you hurrying up?
b) Didn't you hurried up?
c) Won't you hurry up?
2489. Choose the correct sentence:
a) Isn't it getting more and more expensive?
b) Is not it getting more and more expensive?
c) Doesn't it getting more and more expensively?
2490. I was … by the latest news regarding the war.
a) shocking
b) shocked
c) shockingly
2491. I was surprised by her … to do something
correctly.
a) inability
b) unability
c) irability

2492. I consider it's … .
a) unprobable
b) improbable
c) aprobable
2493. I felt so … . I wanted to leave that place.
a) comfortable
b) comfy
c) uncomfortable
2494. It happened … because of them.
a) largely
b) large
c) larging
2495. You should think twice. It's a unique … .
a) possibly
b) possibility
c) possible

2496. Wow! This it's the best … .
a) salvation
b) solution
c) solve

2497. The player was fined and … .
a) disqualified
b) qualified
c) unqualifiedly

2498. The little girl likes listening to … music.
a) classic
b) class
c) classical

2499. I've just turned … the laptop. I need to write a report.
a) on
b) up
c) about

2500. We need to think this plan … .
a) away

b) over
c) towards

2501. My parents split … twelve years ago.
a) in
b) against
c) up

2502. We decided to bring … the price of some products.
a) down
b) against
c) amongst

2503. I can't work this problem … .
a) over
b) out
c) beyond

2504. I'd rather … it.
a) didn't say
b) not say
c) not saying

2505. I'd rather … with her.
a) to agree
b) agree
c) agreeing

2506. This goal can't … .
a) achieved
b) be achieving
c) be achieved

2507. This decision may … today.
a) be taken
b) take
c) be token

2508. The truth needed … .
a) be said
b) being say
c) to be said

2509. … friends you have, the better.
a) The more
b) More
c) The less

2510. She felt … exhausted.
a) such
b) absolutely
c) very

2511. Choose the correct sentence:
a) She behaves strangely these days.
b) She had behaved strangely these days.
c) She is behaving strangely these days.

2512. Choose the correct sentence:
a) You are overestimating our abilities now.
b) You overestimate our abilities now.
c) You have overestimated our abilities now.

2513. My superior … me.
a) has being informed
b) was informing
c) informing

2514. … she assisting him that night?
a) Had
b) Did
c) Was

2515. … the detectives experiencing big problems?
a) Were
b) Did
c) Had

2516. Is the following sentence correct? "Was it belonging to you?"
a) correct
b) incorrect

2517. We … Kate.
a) were seen
b) have seen
c) are seen

2518. … the manager understood it?

a) Have
b) Did
c) Has
2519. I have … it completely. I'm sorry!
a) forgot
b) forgetting
c) forgotten
2520. We … those difficulties and everything was fine in the end.
a) overcame
b) overcome
c) overcoming
2521. How long … about it?
a) have you think
b) have you been thinking
c) had you be thinking
2522. I … here for fifteen minutes.
a) have be
b) was
c) have been
2523. … him before they called you?
a) Had you informed
b) Did you inform
c) Have you informed
2524. How about them? … now?
a) Are they trained
b) Are they being trained
c) Have they trained
2525. She understood her friends … her.
a) was using
b) had used
c) have been used
2526. These global opportunities ... today.
a) are considering

b) are considered
c) are being considered
2527. This problem … .
a) has never been mentioned
b) never be mentioned
c) will never mentioning
2528. She would work there if she … a millionaire.
a) is
b) had
c) were
2529. Choose the correct sentence:
a) You don't have prepare these documents today.

b) You didn't have prepare these documents today.
c) You don't have to prepare these documents today.
2530. Tom is rude … her.
a) of
b) to
c) about
2531. I'm familiar … this problem and I'll solve it.
a) to
b) with
c) on
2532. The businessman was so generous … us!
a) of
b) for
c) to
2533. I'll pay … cash.
a) in
b) about
c) on
2534. She always calls me … Mondays.
a) at
b) in
c) on

2535. … instance, it can mean that she likes you.
a) To
b) For
c) With
2536. The girl asked me: "How often do you visit this place?".
a) The girl asked me how often I visited that place.
b) The girl asked me how often I had visited this place.
c) The girl asked me how often you visited that place.
2537. The reporter asked me: "Who was getting richer?".
a) The reporter asked me who had been getting richer.
b) The reporter asked me who was getting richer.
c) The reporter asked me who has got richer.
2538. The journalist asked me: "Why has she become a real star?".
a) The journalist asked me why had she become a real star.
b) The journalist asked me why she had become a real star.

c) The journalist asked me why she was becoming a real star.

Set 10

2539. She asked me: "How long have you been playing football?".
a) She asked me how long I had been playing football.
b) She asked me how long I have played football.
c) She asked me how long had I been playing football.
2540. Choose the correct sentence:
a) Hasn't it lead to lots of problems?
b) Didn't it led to lots of problems?
c) Hasn't it led to lots of problems?
2541. Choose the correct sentence:
a) What are you pointed about?
b) What are you pointing at?
c) What have you been point about?
2542. Why was she so …?
a) frighted
b) frightened
c) frightening
2543. I was … to help him.
a) inable

b) ireable
c) unable
2544. They were … of the threat.
a) unaware
b) disaware
c) inaware
2545. She would like to feel more … .
a) safe
b) saving
c) save
2546. She doesn't know what she wants. She's so …
.
a) decisive
b) undecisive
c) indecisive
2547. You are a very professional … .
a) professor
b) teaching

c) teachers
2548. She experienced a feeling of … .
a) amazing
b) amazement
c) amazed
2549. The level of … is high.
a) competitive
b) competing
c) competition
2550. She's my … .
a) friendship
b) relationship
c) girlfriend
2551. Katherine is a famous … .
a) art
b) artist
c) actor

2552. Her husband is an … man. He's a simple person.
a) ordinary
b) ordinarily
c) ordinal
2553. To our surprise, he turned … at the party.
a) in
b) beyond
c) up
2554. I decided to ask her … .
a) out
b) for
c) about
2555. I burst … laughing.
a) into
b) out
c) away
2556. Choose the correct sentence:
a) My grandmother remembers everything despite being 85.
b) My grandmother remembers everything despite to be 85.
c) My grandmother remembers everything in spite of be 85.
2557. She is known … German professionally.
a) teaching
b) to teach
c) taught
2558. The manager ought to be … .

a) informed
b) informal
c) informing
2559. … a lot, she feels tired.
a) To work
b) Worked
c) Working
2560. The director ought not to be … .
a) interrupt

b) interrupted
c) interrupting
2561. My friend … TV.
a) were watching
b) were being watching
c) was watching
2562. Where … it going on?
a) were
b) have
c) was
2563. What … they looking for in the city?
a) were
b) have
c) was
2564. Is the following sentence correct? "They were overestimating its
power at that moment."
a) correct
b) incorrect
2565. I'm happy! We … a new project.
a) have started
b) had been started
c) will have starting
2566. … these words influenced her?
a) Did
b) Have
c) Might have
2567. Choose the correct sentence:
a) Did you ever hear it?
b) Have you ever heard it?
c) Have you ever be hearing it?
2568. The boy has … a horse.
a) rode
b) riding
c) ridden

2569. I had no other solution. I … them into groups.

a) split
b) splitted
c) splitting
2570. Jane … there for two months.
a) had been working
b) has been working
c) was working
2571. I told him I … Mary.
a) already saw
b) have already seen
c) had already seen
2572. When I came there she … for me for a long time.
a) had been waiting
b) has been waiting
c) was waiting
2573. All the project details … yet.
a) weren't considered
b) haven't been considered
c) hadn't been considered
2574. Choose the correct sentence:
a) Had the losses being covered?
b) Have the losses been covered?
c) Were the losses been covered?
2575. I … Chinese for an hour when she called me.
a) was learning
b) had been learning
c) did learnt
2576. Poor conditions … there. You should avoid that place.
a) provide
b) providing
c) are provided
2577. I wish she … know about it.
a) didn't

b) doesn't
c) wasn't
2578. If she hadn't shown such bad results, her parents … so angry now.
a) wouldn't be
b) wouldn't have been
c) hadn't been
2579. You … insist on it. I won't forget!
a) needn't have
b) didn't need to
c) hadn't need to

2580. He's really worried … his future.

a) in

b) about

c) regard

2581. I'm waiting … my wife.

a) for

b) to

c) on

2582. They blame him … everything.

a) on

b) for

c) about

2583. My cousin is … .

a) on diet

b) in diet

c) on a diet

2584. My wife asked me: "Are you tired?".

a) My wife asked me if I was tired.

b) My wife asked me if I am tired.

c) My wife asked me if I have been tired.

2585. My cousin asked me: "Did Jane enter that university?".

a) My cousin asked me if Jane entered that university.

b) My cousin asked me if Jane have entered that university.

c) My cousin asked me whether Jane had entered that university.

2586. Megan asked me: "Was it getting dark?".

a) Megan asked me if it had been getting dark.

b) Megan asked me if had it ben getting dark.

c) Megan asked me if it was getting darker.

2587. She asked me: "Why were you so serious?".

a) She asked me why you have been so serious.

b) She asked me why I had been so serious.

c) She asked me why I have been so serious.

2588. Choose the correct sentence:

a) Won't you concentrate on the main problem?

b) Not will you concentrate on the main problem?

c) Didn't you concentrated on the main problem?

2589. Choose the correct sentence:

a) Isn't she waited for us?

b) Isn't she waiting for us?

c) Weren't she waiting for us?

2590. The child was … of the dark.

a) terrifying

b) terrified

c) terrifyingly

2591. This is totally … .

a) unacceptable

b) disacceptable

c) inacceptable

2592. She was … to my eyes.

a) unvisible

b) disvisible

c) invisible

2593. It's … that life on other planets exists.

a) indeniable

b) undeniable

c) disdeniable

2594. Suddenly, we were … .

a) inconnected

b) unconnected

c) disconnected

2595. I can't put … with all this injustice.

a) in

b) up

c) about

2596. She made … this story. Don't believe her!

a) up

b) in

c) within

2597. Can you please speak …? I can't hear you well enough.

a) over

b) about

c) up

2598. Tell her to slow …! I'm afraid of her driving style!

a) up

b) away

c) down

2599. When will you stop hanging …? You should do something useful.

a) around

b) off

c) within

2600. Choose the correct sentence:

a) I am used to do it.

b) I used to do it.

c) I have using to do it.

2601. Choose the correct sentence:

a) I'm used to think so about her.
b) I used to think so about her.
c) I had using to think so about her.
2602. You'd better … .
a) don't complain
b) didn't complain
c) not complain

2603. My father repaired his watch.
a) itself
b) himself
c) by itself
2604. These rules … last month.
a) should revise
b) should be revised
c) should have been revised
2605. The strategy … more thoroughly.
a) should been taught
b) should have been thought
c) should had been thought
2606. People were … starving.
a) absolutely
b) utter
c) very
2607. She became … furious after hearing the news.
a) bad
b) extreme
c) absolutely
2608. It's … unbelievable.
a) most
b) absolutely
c) good
2609. By … business you can be more independent.
a) doing
b) done
c) be done
2610. … school, I entered a famous university.
a) To finishing
b) Been finishing
c) Having finished
2611. Choose the correct sentence:
a) Why do you hesitate now?

b) Why have you been hesitating now?
c) Why are you hesitating now?
2612. When I noticed it, they … on the phone.
a) did talking

b) were talking
c) had been talking
2613. Her manager … her of stealing the documents.
a) was accusing
b) did accused
c) have accusing
2614. What … your uncle building there?
a) was
b) did
c) have
2615. Is the following sentence correct? "I was logging in when she entered."
a) incorrect
b) correct
2616. My old friend … said it.
a) did
b) was
c) has
2617. … the experts opened your eyes?
a) Did
b) Have
c) Will
2618. … you visited this place?
a) Has
b) Did
c) Have
2619. I … Jennifer two days ago.
a) saw
b) seen
c) did

2620. She has … many problems lately.
a) having
b) had
c) be having
2621. I … Russian since last month.
a) hadn't learning
b) didn't learnt
c) haven't been learning
2622. How long … correspondence?
a) did you maintained
b) have you been maintaining
c) had you be maintaining
2623. How long … it?
a) had you been wanting
b) have you wanted

c) were you wanted

2624. The girl said she … it for three hours.

a) had been doing

b) has been doing

c) will be doing

2625. He … now by the police.

a) is being controlled

b) is controlled

c) has been controlled

2626. I knew he … her yet.

a) didn't reply

b) hadn't replied

c) hasn't replied

2627. If I had known it, my score … much higher.

a) will be

b) has been

c) would have been

2628. I wish my result … better.

a) could

b) might

c) were

2629. She … her mistakes yesterday.

a) should corrected

b) should have corrected

c) should had corrected

2630. The thief was forced … .

a) to surrender

b) surrender

c) surrendering

2631. The little boy is excellent … maths.

a) in

b) on

c) at

2632. She's annoyed … her boss.

a) about

b) with

c) around

2633. It's very kind … you to help me.

a) of

b) to

c) on

2634. They spend lots of money … food and waste it.

a) for

b) away

c) on

2635. This flat belongs … me.

a) on

b) to

c) of

2636. Steven said: "She has remembered it at last.".

a) Steven said that she had remembered it at last.

b) Steven said that she has remembered it at last.

c) Steven said that she would be remembering it at last.

2637. The boy said: "I will go there anyway.".

a) The boy said that he will go there anyway.

b) The boy said that he would be going there anyway.

c) They boy said that he would go there anyway.

2638. The director said: "She has been working here for all her life.".

a) The director said that she has been working there for all her life.

b) The director said that she had been working there for all her life.

c) The director said that she was working there for all her life.

2639. My partner asked me: "Do you find this idea interesting?".

a) My partner asked me if I found that idea interesting.

b) My partner asked me if I find that idea interesting.

c) My partner asked me if I did found that idea interesting.

2640. My mother asked me: "Are you talking on the phone?".

a) My mother asked me if you were talking on the phone.

b) My mother asked me if I was talking on the phone.

c) My mother asked me if I have been talking on the phone.

2641. Choose the correct sentence:

a) Not it a different method?

b) Didn't it be a different method?

c) Isn't it a different method?

2642. Choose the correct sentence:

a) Weren't you afraid?

b) Didn't you afraid?

c) Were you afraid not?

2643. I will … it clear for you.

a) do
b) make
c) made
2644. It can only lead to his … .
a) unagreement
b) disagreement
c) inagreement
2645. These people are … connected.
a) unseparably

b) diseparably
c) inseparably
2646. This place is … .
a) isafe
b) insafe
c) unsafe
2647. This food is … .
a) inedible
b) unedible
c) disedible
2648. She showed a slight … in her Russian.
a) improvement
b) improving
c) improved
2649. There was a … of clean water.
a) short
b) unshortage
c) shortage
2650. For me, it was a … night.
a) unsleepy
b) sleepless
c) slept
2651. I checked … before midday. I was sorry for leaving.
a) within
b) out
c) about
2652. I'll pick you … in an hour.
a) up
b) about
c) beyond
2653. The marketing assistant handed … the leaflets.
a) about
b) in
c) out

2654. I'd like to point … it's really worth buying.

a) out
b) for
c) about
2655. I … prefer to drop this subject.
a) had
b) can
c) would
2656. Her idea might not … .
a) approved
b) be approved
c) be approving
2657. This report … .
a) could to attach
b) could been attached
c) could have been attached
2658. It may … .
a) to discuss
b) been discuss
c) have been discussed
2659. That problem shouldn't … .
a) have been mentioned
b) been mentioned
c) have mentioned
2660. Neither her mother … her father can help you.
a) or
b) either
c) nor
2661. No one … accused.
a) were
b) wasn't
c) was
2662. We'll discuss the issue after she … .
a) comes back

b) come back
c) will come back
2663. I won't call them unless they … .
a) will apologize
b) apologize
c) would apologize
2664. Choose the correct sentence:
a) What do you do tomorrow?
b) What are you doing tomorrow?
c) What will you done tomorrow?
2665. Choose the correct sentence:
a) I don't recognize you now.
b) I'm not recognizing you now.

c) I didn't recognize you now.

2666. Choose the correct sentence:

a) We are needing it at the moment.

b) We aren't needed it at the moment.

c) We need it at the moment.

2667. Why … your manager following her advice?

a) did

b) was

c) had

2668. Is the following sentence correct? "Her words were sounding

strange."

a) correct

b) incorrect

2669. The trainer … divided us.

a) didn't

b) won't

c) hasn't

2670. … the documents been received by your department?

a) Have

b) Did

c) Will

2671. How long … here?

a) have you being

b) have you been being

c) have you been

2672. I wish I … America last year.

a) visited

b) had visited

c) have visited

2673. Choose the correct sentence:

a) It's high time we visit this place.

b) It's high time we had visited this place.

c) It's high time we visited this place.

2674. You don't have … so early.

a) to get up

b) getting up

c) get up

2675. Choose the correct sentence:

a) You needn't to explaining it again.

b) You don't need to explain it again.

c) You didn't needed to explain it again.

2676. He ought to … the meeting last week.

a) attend

b) been attended

c) have attended

2677. She won't let you … it.

a) do

b) doing

c) to do

2678. Mary's quite good … German.

a) in

b) at

c) about

2679. I'm terrible … dancing.

a) at

b) about

c) in

2680. I was fascinated … that modern technology.

a) with

b) on

c) of

2681. I haven't seen you … ages.

a) from

b) about

c) for

2682. The girl learnt English … herself.

a) on

b) with

c) by

2683. John said: "The professor is explaining these rules.".

a) John said that the professor was explaining those rules.

b) John said that the professor had explained these rules.

c) John said that the professor is explaining these rules.

2684. The professor: "She will correct her mistakes.".

a) The professor said that she'll correct her mistakes.

b) The professor said that she would correct her mistakes.

c) The professor said that she has corrected her mistakes.

2685. She said: "When he arrived I had already prepared everything.".

a) She said that when he arrived she had already prepared everything.

b) She said that when he arrived she has already prepared everything.

c) She said that when he had arrived he had already prepared
everything.
2686. Katherine said: "My parents knew that I had missed that lesson.".
a) Katherine said that her parents had known that she had missed that
lesson.
b) Katherine said that her parents knew that she missed that lesson.
c) Katherine said that her parents have known that she had missed
that lesson.
2687. He said: "They were criticizing her sharply.".
a) He said that they were criticized her sharply.

b) He said that they had been criticizing her sharply.
c) He said that they have criticized her sharply.
2688. She asked me: "Are they ignoring him?".
a) She asked me if they had been ignoring him.
b) She asked me if they were ignoring him.
c) She asked me if they have been ignoring him.
2689. My wife asked me: "What's in the box?".
a) My wife asked me what' in the box.
b) My wife asked me what has been in the box.
c) My wife asked me what was in the box.
2690. The lady asked me: "What kind of job is it?".
a) The lady asked me what kind of job it was.
b) The lady asked me what kind of job was it.
c) The lady asked me what kind of job it has been.
2691. Choose the correct sentence:
a) Who does this business belonging to?
b) Which does this business belong to?
c) Who does this business belong to?
2692. It was a very … situation.
a) embarrassed
b) embarrassing
c) embarrass
2693. We were really … .
a) luckily
b) unlucky
c) inlucky
2694. I appreciate you because your lessons are so
… .
a) informing
b) informed
c) informative

2695. The new colleague is … .
a) unintelligent
b) inintelligent
c) disintelligent

2696. To my surprise, everything was in … .
a) misorder
b) disorder
c) unorder
2697. This power is … .
a) unlegitimate
b) illegitimate
c) dislegitimate
2698. Thieves broke … the bank.
a) into
b) onto
c) away
2699. Would you turn … the sound? I can't hear it.
a) down
b) away
c) up
2700. Get …! I don't want to see you!
a) through
b) out
c) in
2701. Choose the correct sentence:
a) She had better to call him one more time.
b) She'd better call him one more time.
c) She would have better call him one more time.
2702. I'd rather you … it.
a) do
b) done
c) did
2703. I think this meeting must … .
a) be postponed
b) postpone
c) had postponed
2704. This thing can … .
a) sell

b) be selling
c) be sold
2705. They ought not … .
a) to be notified
b) being notified
c) be notified
2706. Choose the correct sentence:

a) Should these laptops to be purchased?

b) Should these laptops have been purchased?

c) Should these laptops had been purchased?

2707. We are … the city in an hour.

a) leave

b) to left

c) to leave

2708. That moment, she was just about … .

a) to panic

b) panicking

c) panic

2709. … known it, he changed his point of view.

a) Being

b) Hading

c) Having

2710. Hardly … some money when he spent it.

a) he had got

b) had he got

c) did he got

2711. I'll inform her in case the price … .

a) doesn't get lower

b) wouldn't get lower

c) won't get lower

2712. Choose the correct sentence:

a) I'm doing it quite frequently.

b) I do it quite frequently.

c) I had being do it quite frequently.

2713. While she was checking her e-mail, I … her project.

a) had checked

b) have checked

c) was checking

2714. The detectives … that crime.

a) weren't investigating

b) hadn't investigating

c) won't being investigated

2715. What … becoming uncontrollable?

a) were

b) did

c) was

2716. Is the following sentence correct? "The project wasn't seeming interesting."

a) correct

b) incorrect

2717. Is the following sentence correct? "She way carrying the baby."

a) correct

b) incorrect

2718. Mary … kept her promise.

a) didn't

b) won't

c) hasn't

2719. I have … a new car.

a) buyed

b) bought

c) buying

2720. When she got to work I … a report for 40 minutes.

a) was making

b) have been making

c) had been making

2721. The dog … today.

a) wasn't been

b) hasn't been

c) didn't been

2722. Choose the correct sentence:

a) It seems strange now.

b) It is seeming strange now.

c) It has been seemed strange now.

2723. I will do it after Mary … .

a) will come back

b) had come back

c) comes back

2724. I know she … it for a long time.

a) has wanted

b) had been wanting

c) has being wanted

2725. The students … for the final exam.

a) wasn't preparing

b) prepared

c) didn't prepared

2726. Choose the correct sentence:

a) They are always being thanked.

b) They are always thanked.

c) They had always being thanked.

2727. If I were you, I … think about it one more time.

a) would

b) will

c) would have

2728. I wish I … 5 apartments.
a) have
b) did had
c) had
2729. You … her one more time.
a) didn't needed criticize
b) hadn't needed criticize
c) needn't have criticized
2730. I worked there … a while, it's true.
a) in

b) for
c) so
2731. They will pay … advance.
a) in
b) about
c) for
2732. This project can be interesting only … theory.
a) at
b) for
c) in
2733. Mr. Brown said: "We were having a great time there.".
a) Mr. Brown said that they had a great time there.
b) Mr. Brown said that they had been having a great time there.
c) Mr. Brown said that they were having a great time there.
2734. I … this project by November.
a) will started
b) will have started
c) will be started
2735. My mother asked me: "Do you enjoy learning English there?".
a) My mother asked me whether I enjoyed learning English there.
b) My mother asked me if I enjoy learning English there.
c) My mother asked me if I have enjoyed learning English there.
2736. The officer asked me: "Did they persuade her to do it?".
a) The officer asked me if they persuaded her to do it.
b) The officer asked me if they had persuaded her to do it.

c) The officer asked me if they did persuaded herself to do it.
2737. The lady asked me: "Will it depend on him?".
a) The lady asked me if it will depend on him.
b) The lady asked me if it would depend on him.
c) The lady asked me if it depended on him.
2738. The policeman asked me: "Who was following her?".
a) The policeman asked me who is following her.
b) The policeman asked me who has been following her.
c) The policeman asked me who had been following her.

2739. Her speech was so … .
a) inspiring
b) inspired
c) disinspiring
2740. I think we … each other.
a) disunderstood
b) misunderstood
c) inunderstood
2741. I think your business partner is … .
a) inreliable
b) disreliable
c) unreliable
2742. It wasn't … that Steve was in the first place.
a) surprising
b) unsurprising
c) dissurprising
2743. They don't know the … state of affairs.
a) actually
b) currently
c) actual
2744. I feel … about this idea.
a) enjoyed
b) enthusiastic
c) enthusiasm
2745. It's a bad result … with her previous achievements.
a) compared
b) comparison
c) comparing
2746. The employees don't like his … .
a) stictment
b) striction
c) strictness

2747. We decided to set ... a company.

a) on

b) away

c) up

2748. I stick ... the idea it can take place.

a) at

b) about

c) to

2749. She burst ... laughter.

a) out

b) into

c) about

2750. Little girls like dressing ... .

a) up

b) away

c) within

2751. Yesterday I got the fence ... .

a) painting

b) painted

c) paint

2752. This book may not ... .

a) be recommended

b) recommending

c) being recommended

2753. It has ... controlled.

a) being

b) be

c) to be

2754. These men shouldn't be ... .

a) trust

b) trusted

c) trusting

2755. May the final report ... tomorrow?

a) be finished

b) finish

c) to finish

2756. It ... beforehand.

a) should has been written

b) should had been written

c) should have been written

2757. Could that outcome ... been predicted?

a) had

b) have

c) did

2758. ... can get rich. Trust me!

a) The poor

b) Poor

c) The poors

2759. This detail is ... minor.

a) absolute

b) absoluting

c) absolutely

2760. The President is ... China next week.

a) to visit

b) visit

c) to visited

2761. Choose the correct sentence:

a) It is seeming to me she's making a terrible mistake now.

b) It seems to me she's making a terrible mistake now.

c) It seems to me she's made a terrible mistake now.

2762. While I was working, she ... a rest.

a) did having

b) has been having

c) was having

2763. ... she thinking about it?

a) Did

b) Was

c) Has

2764. Is the following sentence correct? "They were disagreeing with us."

a) correct

b) incorrect

2765. Choose the correct sentence:

a) I never wanted it. It didn't interest me.

b) I have never wanted it. It hadn't interest me.

c) I had never wanted it. It wouldn't be interest me.

2766. I was ... New York two years ago.

a) to

b) about

c) in

2767. They ... away yesterday.

a) flown

b) flew

c) had flown

2768. I ... this text for an hour.

a) have been translating

b) had translated

c) was translating

2769. ... to work before they got the first call?

a) Did she already got
b) Had she already got
c) Have she already got
2770. Why …?
a) has it being said
b) has it been said
c) did it be saying
2771. Choose the correct sentence:
a) Mary is frequently visiting this place.
b) Mary is frequently being visited this place.
c) Mary frequently visits this place.
2772. Choose the correct sentence:
a) This laptop isn't belonging to me now.
b) This laptop doesn't belong to me now.
c) This laptop didn't belong to me now.
2773. The manager found out some employees …
the money.
a) was stealing

b) had stolen
c) did stolen
2774. By the time she arrived I … for her for 10
minutes.
a) had been waiting
b) had waited
c) did been waiting
2775. … these days?
a) Are they watched
b) Are they being watched
c) Did they be watched
2776. Choose the correct sentence:
a) It's high time we will do it.
b) It's high time we did it.
c) It's high time we had do it.
2777. If your parents hadn't met, you … here now.
a) wouldn't have been
b) wouldn't been
c) wouldn't be
2778. Don't be afraid … this dog!
a) by
b) on
c) of
2779. The motel is suitable … me.
a) for
b) to
c) of
2780. … average, I get 50 dollars a month.

a) On
b) By
c) With
2781. We saw the laptop … TV.
a) in
b) on
c) about

2782. Many people are out … work these days.
a) off
b) away
c) of
2783. What's happening … reality? Can you tell
me?
a) into
b) in
c) of
2784. Tom said: "I really hate it.".
a) Tom said that he is really hating it.
b) Tom said that he did really hate it.
c) Tom said that he really hated it.
2785. She … for you.
a) won't be waiting
b) haven't been waiting
c) didn't be waiting
2786. My mother asked me: "Is she at the station?".
a) My mother asked me whether she was at the
station.
b) My mother asked me if she had been at the
station.
c) My mother asked me whether she is at the station.
2787. Jane asked me: "Are you waiting for him?".
a) Jane asked me if I had been waiting for him.
b) Jane asked me if I was waiting for him.
c) Jane asked me if I have been waiting for him.
2788. The manager asked me: "When are they
free?".
a) The manager asked me when were they free.
b) The manager asked me when they had been free.
c) The manager asked me when they were free.
2789. Kate asked me: "What did you stop doing?".
a) Kate asked me what I had stopped doing.
b) Kate asked me what had I stopped doing.
c) Kate asked me what I stopped doing.
2790. … it a good plan?
a) Isn't

b) Didn't

c) Doesn't

2791. Choose the correct sentence:

a) Will it hurt not your feelings?

b) Won't it hurt your feelings?

c) Wouldn't it hurting your feelings?

2792. Choose the correct sentence:

a) Haven't you be to Madrid?

b) Didn't you been to Madrid?

c) Haven't you been to Madrid?

2793. Her explanation was … .

a) unaccurate

b) inaccurate

c) disaccurate

2794. This speech is … .

a) inappropriate

b) unappropriate

c) disappropriate

2795. You will waste time reading it. This report is … .

a) useful

b) useless

c) uunuseful

2796. She drives so … . I feel safe with her.

a) carelessly

b) carefully

c) carefulness

2797. We were in a … situation.

a) dangerous

b) dangering

c) danger

2798. It's a … example.

a) classical

b) classically

c) classic

2799. The detectives managed to … the truth.

a) incover

b) uncover

c) recover

2800. This is a huge … .

a) misadvantage

b) disadvantage

c) inadvantage

2801. She turned … the TV after a while.

a) on

b) away

c) with

2802. I like working … at the gym.

a) away

b) in

c) out

2803. The team warmed … before the final game.

a) up

b) down

c) in

2804. Choose the correct sentence:

a) She's accustomed to work so much.

b) She's accustomed to being work so much.

c) She's accustomed to working so much.

2805. I have difficulty … English.

a) learn

b) in learnt

c) in learning

2806. She has difficulty … for her new car.

a) pay

b) paying

c) to paying

2807. This phrase mustn't … .

a) be repeated

b) repeat

c) repeating

2808. The problem might not … .

a) to solve

b) be solved

c) to solving

2809. Must it … during today's meeting?

a) mention

b) mentioning

c) be mentioned

2810. Mike's about … .

a) to return

b) returning

c) be returned

2811. Nothing … really difficult.

a) wasn't

b) didn't

c) was

2812. I'll give you this document after you … ready.

a) will be

b) are

c) had been

2813. Choose the correct sentence:

a) She is having two kids now.
b) She has two kids now.
c) She had two kids now.
2814. I … Chinese all day.
a) did learnt
b) had learnt
c) was learning
2815. We … TV at 7 o'clock yesterday evening.
a) were watching
b) did watched
c) had been watching

2816. Is the following sentence correct? "I was supposing it was right."
a) correct
b) incorrect
2817. John … missed the lesson.
a) didn't
b) hasn't
c) wasn't
2818. … they decided what to do?
a) Has
b) Did
c) Have
2819. What … the girl done?
a) would
b) have
c) have be
2820. Choose the correct sentence:
a) We knew it two days ago.
b) We have known it two days ago.
c) We had known it two days ago.
2821. Have you been … Moscow?
a) in
b) about
c) to
2822. She has … away.
a) went
b) gone
c) go
2823. She … me what to do.
a) told
b) asking
c) have asked
2824. The director … it perfectly.
a) known
b) knew

c) did knew

2825. The detective … pieces of information for two months.
a) has collecting
b) has been collecting
c) did collecting
2826. … now?
a) Is it spoilt
b) Is it being spoilt
c) Has it being spoilt
2827. Where … all this time?
a) have you been
b) did you being
c) have you been being
2828. I realized my keys … at home.
a) be left
b) had been left
c) did left
2829. I wouldn't say it if I … you now.
a) had been
b) was
c) were
2830. If only there … a way out!
a) was
b) has been
c) is
2831. Choose the correct sentence:
a) It's time for you say it.
b) It's time you said it.
c) It's time you had said it.
2832. As I have no choice, I … overwork.
a) have to
b) could
c) might
2833. I know she … win.
a) could to

b) did to
c) had to
2834. I'm disappointed … the results.
a) for
b) on
c) about
2835. The kid was absent … school.
a) from
b) at

c) in

2836. She's suspicious … her new manager.

a) in

b) of

c) with

2837. My grandfather is brilliant … chess.

a) in

b) with

c) at

2838. Jane is enthusiastic … this idea.

a) about

b) in

c) on

2839. It's very cruel … her to say such terrible things.

a) to

b) on

c) of

2840. It's very generous … you to give me this perfume.

a) to

b) of

c) with

2841. I … for the exam all day tomorrow.

a) will be preparing

b) would be preparing

c) will be prepared

2842. The secretary asked me: "Was this time convenient?".

a) The secretary asked me if that time had been convenient.

b) The secretary asked me if that time was convenient.

c) The secretary asked if that time was convenient for me.

2843. The customer asked me: "How much money does it cost?".

a) The customer asked me how much money did it cost.

b) The customer asked me how much money it had cost.

c) The customer asked me how much money it cost.

2844. She asked me: "How busy is the manager?".

a) She asked me how busy the manager was.

b) She asked me how busy was the manager.

c) She asked me how busy the manager had been.

2845. She asked me: "How much will it cost?".

a) She asked me how much will it cost.

b) She asked me how much it would cost.

c) She asked me how much did it cost.

2846. Choose the correct sentence:

a) Wasn't it a waste of time?

b) Wasn't it being a waste of time?

c) Didn't it be a waste of time?

2847. This approach is … .

a) imperfect

b) disperfect

c) unperfect

2848. What a … woman!

a) beautifully

b) beauty

c) beautiful

2849. I … like your YouTube channel.

a) real

b) really

c) reality

2850. … as it may seem, they won.

a) Incredible

b) Incredibly

c) Credible

2851. I'd like to get a good … .

a) educate

b) educational

c) education

2852. Her result was so … . It was a surprise.

a) unpredictable

b) predicting

c) predictable

2853. This mechanism is still … .

a) inknown

b) unknown

c) unknowingly

2854. This perfume was sold … . It was a real success.

a) out

b) in

c) about

2855. Choose the correct sentence:

a) They will never let you down!

b) They would never be let you down!

c) They will never let down you!

2856. These scenarios might not … .

a) be compare
b) comparing
c) be compared
2857. Can it …?
a) checking
b) be checked
c) being check
2858. I'm sorry but it had … .
a) to be said
b) be said
c) be saying

2859. The sooner, … .
a) better
b) the better
c) the best
2860. I … think so!
a) am
b) being
c) do
2861. We'll start reading the project as soon as she … .
a) arrives
b) will arrive
c) be arrived
2862. Some customers … refused to accept it.
a) would
b) be
c) have
2863. How … you done it?
a) has
b) did
c) have
2864. Choose the correct sentence:
a) I hadn't seen it yet.
b) I haven't seen it yet.
c) I didn't see it yet.
2865. Choose the correct sentence:
a) I have never met her.
b) I didn't never meet her.
c) I hadn't ever meet her.
2866. Choose the correct sentence:
a) I never did it in my childhood.
b) I never would done it in my childhood.
c) I never had did it in my childhood.
2867. It … more money than you think.
a) costed

b) costing
c) cost
2868. She has … her old car.
a) sold
b) sell
c) been sold
2869. My mother has … her finger.
a) cutted
b) cut
c) be cut
2870. The water was … .
a) frozen
b) freeze
c) freezed
2871. I … here since last year.
a) have live
b) have been living
c) had been living
2872. When I returned she … for about 2 hours.
a) had been sleeping
b) was sleeping
c) has been sleeping
2873. This project … now.
a) is discussed
b) has been discussing
c) is being discussed
2874. Those islands … now.
a) aren't attacked
b) aren't being attacked
c) haven't being attacked
2875. … 3000 dollars been paid?
a) Had
b) Have
c) Did

2876. I wish she … two hour ago.
a) came
b) had come
c) did come
2877. I think you … me tomorrow.
a) could help
b) helped
c) could been helping
2878. We'll be forced … with them.
a) agree
b) agreeing

c) to agree

2879. Megan is unaware … some possible threats.

a) about

b) on

c) of

2880. What's … the agenda for today?

a) on

b) in

c) about

2881. I went there … air.

a) by

b) with

c) among

2882. The family was … the verge of despair.

a) in

b) on

c) about

2883. They were out … sight.

a) from

b) with

c) of

2884. We'll see one another … Christmas. I promise!

a) on

b) at

c) in

2885. The student said: "It's really interesting.".

a) The student said that it's really interesting.

b) The student said that it has been really interesting.

c) The student said that it was really interesting.

2886. The marketing manager said: "It isn't the right choice.".

a) The marketing manager said it wasn't the right choice.

b) The marketing manager said that it isn't the right choice.

c) The marketing manager said it hasn't been the right choice.

2887. My cousin said: "We were there last year.".

a) My cousin said that they had been there last year.

b) My cousin said that they had been there the year before.

c) My cousin said that they have been there the year before.

2888. She asked me: "Why do you think so?".

a) She asked me why you thought so.

b) She asked me why I had thought so.

c) She asked me why I thought so.

2889. She asked me: "What time do you usually get up?".

a) She asked me what time I get usually up.

b) She asked me what time I usually got up.

c) She asked me what time I am usually getting up.

2890. The new employee asked me: "How did he create such a positive atmosphere?".

a) The new employee asked me how he had created such a positive atmosphere.

b) The new employee asked me how he created such a positive atmosphere.

c) The new employee asked me how has he created such a positive atmosphere.

2891. Choose the correct sentence:

a) Am not I the best professor?

b) Am I not the best professor?

c) Have I not being the best professor?

Set 11

2892. … you gain some experience during that months?

a) Wasn't

b) Didn't

c) Hadn't

2893. Who is she jealous …?

a) with

b) on

c) of

2894. I can't … away with money.

a) make

b) do

c) find

2895. You look really … .

a) worried

b) worrying

c) worry

2896. The 2019 pandemic was … .

a) avoidable

b) inavoidable

c) disavoidable
2897. Keep in mind that the … is different.
a) really
b) reality
c) real
2898. I felt there so … . I wanted to live there.
a) comfortable
b) uncomfortable
c) discomfortable
2899. It's … . There is only 1 per cent that you will win.
a) probable
b) improbable
c) disprobable
2900. Why is she so …?
a) unsincere

b) dissincere
c) insincere
2901. Her answers were … .
a) indefinite
b) undefinite
c) definitely
2902. The price went … suddenly.
a) wrong
b) up
c) away
2903. The kid grew … of his clothes.
a) out
b) off
c) behind
2904. She looks … her parents.
a) of
b) with
c) after
2905. She nodded … during the meeting.
a) out
b) in
c) off
2906. Choose the correct sentence:
a) Let's put off it.
b) Let's putting it off.
c) Let's put it off.
2907. I'd rather … them.
a) didn't compare
b) not compare
c) nor comparing

2908. She's supposed … that job.
a) to get
b) be got
c) get
2909. … often disagree with it.
a) The olds
b) Olds
c) The old
2910. It was … unimaginable that she would die.
a) over
b) absolutely
c) utter
2911. My wife … at 7 o'clock yesterday morning.
a) has been cooking
b) was cooking
c) had been cooking
2912. Is the following sentence correct? "I was owning a flat that time."
a) correct
b) incorrect
2913. Your plan … a tremendous success.
a) has been
b) had been
c) did be
2914. Steven … repaired his apartment.
a) hadn't
b) didn't
c) hasn't
2915. How … this book helped you?
a) has
b) did
c) had
2916. How long … it?
a) did you discussed
b) have you been discussing
c) would you being discussing
2917. This path … now.
a) isn't being chosen
b) isn't chosen
c) didn't be chosen

2918. Choose the correct sentence:
a) They are sometimes being helped.
b) They had sometimes been help.
c) They are sometimes helped.
2919. Her room … yet.

a) hasn't been decorated

b) wasn't decorated

c) didn't be decorated

2920. If it …, I'll stay at home.

a) won't stop raining

b) doesn't stop raining

c) hadn't stopped raining

2921. When I came back, she … a letter.

a) was writing

b) has been writing

c) had been writing

2922. When I called my girlfriend she … a shower for 5 minutes.

a) was taking

b) has been taking

c) had been taking

2923. The money … there.

a) aren't

b) isn't

c) didn't

2924. I knew the truth … yet.

a) hadn't been discovered

b) wasn't discovered

c) hasn't been discovered

2925. If they had caught him, they … him to prison.

a) would sent

b) would have sent

c) would had sent

2926. You don't need … .

a) say it

b) saying it

c) to say it

2927. The spy … her to do it during their conversation which took place several weeks ago.

a) might not persuade

b) might not have persuaded

c) didn't have persuaded

2928. Mark is addicted … smoking.

a) of

b) to

c) with

2929. What's your attitude … this method?

a) to

b) of

c) on

2930. Do you really believe in love … first sight?

a) with

b) to

c) at

2931. The members chose it … random.

a) for

b) at

c) in

2932. She said: "I'm talking on the phone.".

a) She said that she was talking on the phone.

b) She said that I'm talking on the phone.

c) She said that she has been talking on the phone.

2933. The financial advisor said: "It will be bringing him money all year.".

a) The financial advisor said that it would be bringing him money all year.

b) The financial advisor said that it will be bringing him money all year.

c) The financial advisor said that it might be bringing him money all year.

2934. The girl asked me: "How old is your father?".

a) The girl asked me how old was my father.

b) The girl asked me how old my father had been.

c) The girl asked me how old my father was.

2935. Choose the correct sentence:

a) Weren't the presentations really boring?

b) Didn't the presentations been really boring?

c) Haven't the presentations being really boring?

2936. Choose the correct sentence:

a) What is he keen about?

b) What is he keen on?

c) What is he keen with?

2937. What are you accustomed …?

a) for

b) in

c) to

2938. The little boy is … in science.

a) interesting

b) interested

c) interest

2939. It was a … experience for her.

a) frightened

b) frightening

c) frighten
2940. This time is … .
a) disconvenient
b) inconvenient
c) unconvenient
2941. Maria is a very … woman.
a) unpractical
b) dispractical
c) impractical
2942. We were clearly in … .
a) danger

b) dangerous
c) dangering
2943. My best friend is a … person. I like his recommendations.
a) impractical
b) practical
c) dispractical
2944. This process is … . It will never stop.
a) ending
b) endless
c) endlessly
2945. We live … together.
a) happily
b) happiness
c) happy
2946. What's the … of Moscow?
a) populated
b) populating
c) population
2947. So? What are you …?
a) choice
b) choosing
c) chosen
2948. What's your …?
a) choice
b) choosing
c) chosen
2949. Hold … a second! I have something to tell you.
a) by
b) with
c) on
2950. Milton passed … last year.
a) out
b) away

c) in

2951. You bought a new flat. Have you already moved …?
a) out
b) with
c) in
2952. You … better stay there with your parents.
a) would
b) had
c) could
2953. I'd rather you … your sister.
a) didn't criticize
b) won't criticize
c) hadn't criticize
2954. These rules must … .
a) being follow
b) be followed
c) following
2955. This problem can't … .
a) foresee
b) be foresee
c) be foreseen
2956. Should the roof …?
a) be repaired
b) repaired
c) repairing
2957. … have lots of problems.
a) Unemployed
b) The unemployed
c) The employing
2958. We … to leave the party in ten minutes.
a) must
b) would
c) are
2959. They are due … at 20.
a) to arrive

b) arriving
c) to arrived
2960. She is due … the city at 10.
a) leaving
b) to leave
c) to left
2961. She'll buy a new laptop as soon as she … enough money for it.
a) will have

b) has

c) had

2962. Choose the correct sentence:

a) I'm flying tonight.

b) I fly tonight.

c) I will be fly tonight.

2963. Choose the correct sentence:

a) My wife's having a bath then.

b) My wife has a bath now.

c) My wife is having a bath now.

2964. His colleagues … him.

a) were criticizing

b) have criticizing

c) did criticizing

2965. … the companies getting richer?

a) Had

b) Did

c) Were

2966. How … the policy changing?

a) was

b) did

c) had

2967. Is the following sentence correct? "Mike was blaming her."

a) correct

b) incorrect

2968. Why … your partners changed their decision?

a) did

b) have

c) had

2969. This place has … several changes.

a) undergone

b) underwent

c) undergo

2970. The dog … a hole in the ground.

a) have dug

b) dugged

c) dug

2971. Her words … me.

a) misleaded

b) misled

c) misleading

2972. I knew he … the exam.

a) hadn't failed

b) hasn't failed

c) didn't failed

2973. The employees … now.

a) aren't controlled

b) aren't being controlled

c) didn't be controlled

2974. Her knowledge … .

a) has already been tested

b) have already been tested

c) had already been tested

2975. Choose the correct sentence:

a) We see each other rarely.

b) We are seeing each other rarely.

c) We did seeing each other rarely.

2976. If only I … speak Russian better!

a) can

b) couldn't

c) could

2977. She … something inappropriate last week.

a) may have said

b) may had said

c) may being said

2978. Mary's certain … her success.

a) with

b) on

c) about

2979. Why are they so rude … him?

a) of

b) to

c) with

2980. She was born … 25 July.

a) on

b) in

c) at

2981. Tom said: "I will achieve my aim this week.".

a) Tom said that he will achieve his aim this week.

b) Tom said that he would be achieving his aim that week.

c) Tom said that he would achieve his aim that week.

2982. Olivia asked me: "Will you join us?".

a) Olivia asked me if I would join them.

b) Olivia asked me if you would join us.

c) Olivia asked me if would I join us.

2983. The woman asked me: "Will it definitely happen?".

a) The woman asked me if it would definitely happen.

b) The woman asked me if it will definitely happen.

c) The woman asked me if it would be happening definitely.
2984. My business partner asked me: "Have they already invested their
money?".
a) My business partner asked me if they already invested their
money.
b) My business partner asked me if they had already invested their
money.

c) My business partner asked me if had they been investing already
their money.
2985. She asked me: "Have you been working here for more than two
years?".
a) She asked me if I had been working there for more than two years.
b) She asked me if I had been worked there for more than two years.
c) She asked me if I have been working there for more than two
years.
2986. She asked me: "Have you been teaching German for more than 3
years?".
a) She asked me if you have been teaching German for more than 3
years.
b) She asked me if I had been teaching German for more than 3
years.
c) She asked me if I had taught German for more than 3 years.
2987. The officer asked me: "When did she leave the city?".
a) The officer asked me when she left the city.
b) The officer asked me when she have left the city.
c) The officer asked me when she had left the city.
2988. She asked me: "What's happened there?".
a) She asked me what happened there.
b) She asked me what had happened there.
c) She asked me what did happened there.
2989. He asked me: "What has influenced her most of all?".

a) He asked me what influenced her most of all.
b) He asked me what has been influenced her most of all.
c) He asked me what had influenced her most of all.
2990. Choose the correct sentence:
a) Did she notice it not?
b) Didn't she notice it?
c) Hadn't she notice it?
2991. Choose the correct sentence:
a) Aren't you searching for a better car?
b) Didn't you searched for a better car?
c) Hadn't you been searched for a better car?

2992. Why do you consider it's an … word?
a) insulted
b) insulting
c) insult
2993. This laptop offer seems … .
a) unattractive
b) inattractive
c) disattractive
2994. That was so … for you.
a) inusual
b) unusual
c) disusual
2995. It's … to do this kind of things.
a) infair
b) disfair
c) unfair
2996. Not surprisingly, she has had so many accidents. She drives so … .
a) carefully
b) carelessly
c) careful
2997. The new colleague can't hide her … .
a) incompetence
b) uncompetence
c) discompetence
2998. Don't worry! I won't let you … .
a) off
b) away
c) down
2999. The officers clamped … on illegal protesters.
a) down
b) with
c) up
3000. You'd better … about it anymore.

a) not to think

b) not thinking

c) not think

3001. I'd rather you … with him.

a) not argue

b) won't argue

c) didn't argue

3002. I … prefer to keep this secret.

a) would

b) had

c) better

3003. I'd sooner … another model.

a) to buy

b) buy

c) buying

3004. It's no use … about it now.

a) to talk

b) talking

c) be talked

3005. She has difficulty … the exam.

a) passing

b) to passing

c) pass

3006. He can speak either German … Chinese.

a) nor

b) neither

c) or

3007. My wife is either at home … at work.

a) or

b) nor

c) neither

3008. His ideas are … brilliant.

a) utter

b) good

c) completely

3009. I was … amazed at her beauty.

a) utterly

b) intense

c) complete

3010. All students … this vaccine.

a) to take

b) are to take

c) are to taking

3011. We will go there in case Jane … us.

a) will join

b) joining

c) joins

3012. Choose the correct sentence:

a) I'm typing the letter now.

b) I have been typing the letter now.

c) I type the letter now.

3013. They … behaving strangely.

a) hadn't

b) weren't

c) didn't

3014. This employee … effectively.

a) hadn't be working

b) haven't been worked

c) wasn't working

3015. … the students making too many mistakes?

a) Were

b) Had

c) Did

3016. … she already returned?

a) Did

b) Had

c) Has

3017. What … your business partner decided?

a) did

b) has

c) had

3018. Choose the correct sentence:

a) I never visited this place.

b) I've never visited this place.

c) I had never visited this place.

3019. He has … about it many times.

a) think

b) thinking

c) thought

3020. I … it for the first time.

a) heard

b) heared

c) hearing

3021. My car … down.

a) breaked

b) broken

c) broke

3022. He … the town two days ago.

a) leaved

b) left

c) leaving

3023. They … for such a long time.
a) haven't been complaining
b) hadn't been complaining
c) didn't been complained
3024. I … in this place for more than 3 hours.
a) been
b) had been
c) have been
3025. The child's mistakes … now.
a) didn't been correcting
b) aren't being corrected
c) aren't correcting

3026. … now?
a) Is this thing being mentioned
b) Does this thing mention
c) Was this thing be mentioned
3027. Choose the correct sentence:
a) It has usually checked.
b) It is being usually checked.
c) It is usually checked.
3028. The students said she … the text by heart.
a) had already learnt
b) already learnt
c) did already learnt
3029. I wish I … it yesterday.
a) knew
b) knowing
c) had known
3030. I … finish the document by 5.
a) might to
b) have to
c) could to
3031. I'm sure … our mutual success.
a) in
b) on
c) about
3032. I'm aware … this specific danger.
a) of
b) about
c) on
3033. She's looking … a new job. She really wants
to find it.
a) to
b) in
c) for
3034. Why are you laughing … her?

a) on

b) at

c) with

3035. This house is for … .
a) sales
b) selling
c) sale
3036. I said it … the beginning.
a) in
b) at
c) on
3037. The professor said: "She has failed her last
exam.".
a) The professor said that she has been failing her
last exam.
b) The professor said that she had failed her last
exam.
c) The professor said that she failed her last exam.
3038. My girlfriend told me: "I have been extremely
busy this week.".
a) My girlfriend told me that she had been extremely
busy that week.
b) My girlfriend told me that she has been extremely
busy that week.
c) my girlfriend told me that she was extremely busy
that week.
3039. Mark said: "I want to see her today.".
a) Mark said that he wanted to see her today.
b) Mark said that he wanted to see her that day.
c) Mark said the he has wanted to see her today.
3040. The lady asked me: "Has he sent her all the
money?".
a) The lady asked me if he would send her all the
money.
b) The lady asked me if he has sent her all the
money.
c) The lady asked me if he had sent her all the
money.
3041. The detective asked me: "What did she teach
there?".
a) The detective asked me what I had taught there.
b) The detective asked me what she had taught there.
c) The detective asked me what have she taught
there.
3042. She asked me: "How was the party?".
a) She asked me how the party had been.

b) She asked me how had been the party.

c) She asked me how have the party been.

3043. My girlfriend asked me: "What are you doing now?".

a) My girlfriend asked me what I was doing now.

b) My girlfriend asked me what I was doing then.

c) My girlfriend asked me what I have been doing then.

3044. Choose the correct sentence:

a) Didn't you learnt English yesterday?

b) Didn't you learn English yesterday?

c) Hadn't you learn English yesterday?

3045. Choose the correct sentence:

a) Do they not providing all the necessary conditions?

b) Haven't they providing all the necessary conditions?

c) Are they not providing all the necessary conditions?

3046. She … badly in the exam.

a) made

b) did

c) could

3047. What made you feel so …?

a) frustrated

b) frustrating

c) frustrate

3048. I felt so … .

a) surprising

b) surprised

c) surprise

3049. This chair is so … .

a) uncomfortable

b) discomfortable

c) incomfortable

3050. What does he …?

a) prefering

b) preference

c) prefer

3051. Jennifer is so … . I always try to follow her advice.

a) unwise

b) wise

c) wisely

3052. I put … two proposals.

a) into

b) of

c) forward

3053. She dropped … school.

a) out of

b) away

c) within

3054. It's no use … .

a) to complain

b) complaining

c) to complaining

3055. There is no point … for it. It's lost!

a) in looking

b) looked

c) of looked

3056. I have difficulty … time for my hobbies.

a) to find

b) found

c) finding

3057. They might … .

a) be attack

b) be attacked

c) be attacking

3058. The soldiers must … more intensively.

a) be trained

b) training

c) trained

3059. I find you … gorgeous.

a) complete

b) absolutely

c) utter

3060. … my project, I went out.

a) Having finished

b) Hading finished

c) To finish

3061. Choose the right sentence:

a) They accuse him now.

b) They are accusing him now.

c) They had accusing him now.

3062. My wife … all night.

a) had been working

b) did working

c) was working

3063. … they using the right vaccine technique?

a) Were

b) Did

c) Had

3064. Is the following sentence correct? "She was wishing us good luck."

a) correct

b) incorrect

3065. You … achieved so much lately.

a) had

b) have

c) did

3066. The boat … sunk.

a) hasn't

b) didn't

c) couldn't had

3067. … your girlfriend changed her mind?

a) Did

b) Can

c) Has

3068. … your director paid her all the money?

a) Has

b) Did

c) Has been

3069. … the weather got worse?

a) Have

b) Did

c) Has

3070. Choose the correct sentence:

a) She just checked it.

b) She had just checked it.

c) She has just checked it.

3071. Choose the correct sentence:

a) I was there many times.

b) I have been there many times.

c) I did be there many times.

3072. Choose the correct sentence:

a) We achieved a lot this month and it's not over.

b) We had achieved a lot this month and it's not over.

c) We have achieved a lot this month and it's not over.

3073. I have … in the end.

a) winning

b) won

c) been won

3074. I read they … him in the end.

a) were arrested

b) had arrested

c) would be arrested

3075. He remembered he … there yet.

a) wasn't

b) haven't be

c) hadn't been

3076. This food … now.

a) isn't eaten

b) isn't being eaten

c) couldn't be eaten

3077. Why … now?

a) is she being ignored

b) has she be ignored

c) had she be ignored

3078. The truth …. .

a) hadn't been revealed

b) hasn't been revealed

c) didn't be revealed

3079. What information …?

a) have been found

b) could being founded

c) has been found

3080. I … about that when I was a boy.

a) have never thought

b) never thought

c) didn't never think

3081. Looking back, this aspect … .

a) was never mentioned

b) has never be mentioning

c) would never being mentioning

3082. I … it during our last meeting.

a) wouldn't being said

b) wouldn't have said

c) wouldn't had said

3083. Brian won't be allowed … there until midnight.

a) stay

b) to stay

c) staying

3084. She's hopeless … foreign languages.

a) in

b) for

c) at

3085. I'm engaged … her.

a) to

b) in

c) on

3086. I was shocked … that accident.
a) with
b) by
c) on
3087. Listen … me!
a) to
b) about
c) with
3088. I feel … drinking a coffee.
a) like
b) how
c) about
3089. She reacted … it in a strange way.
a) on
b) about
c) to
3090. Don't worry! We're out … danger.
a) from
b) of
c) without
3091. She said: "Steve always tries to lead.".
a) She said that Steve always had tried to lead.
b) She said that Steve always tried to lead.
c) She said that Steve always trying to lead.
3092. John said: "I have never been there.".
a) John said that I have never been there.
b) John said that he had never been there.
c) John said that he would never be there.
3093. He said: "When Mary returned I had already done it.".
a) He said that when Mary had returned he had already done it.
b) He said that when Mary had returned I had already done it.
c) He said that when Mary returned he have already done it.
3094. She asked me: "Were the boys famous?".
a) She asked me if the boys were famous.

b) She asked me if the boys would be famous.
c) She asked me if the boys had been famous.
3095. She asked me: "Was she reading a book all day?".
a) She asked me if she had been reading a book all day.
b) She asked me if she was reading a book all day.

c) She asked me if she would be reading a book all day.
3096. Olivia asked me: "Have you been waiting for me for a long time?".
a) Olivia asked me if you had been waiting for me for a long time.
b) Olivia asked me if I had been waiting for her for a long time.
c) Olivia asked me if I had being waited for her for a long time.
3097. The professor asked me: "What things were interesting?".
a) The professor asked me what things had been interesting.
b) The professor asked me what things have been interested.
c) The professor asked me what things would be interested.
3098. My manager asked me: "Who will you inform?".
a) My manager asked me who you would inform.
b) My manager asked me who I would inform.
c) My manager asked me who I am going to be informed.
3099. The advisor asked me: "What was becoming real?".
a) The advisor asked me what was becoming real.
b) The advisor asked me what had been becoming real.
c) The advisor asked me what would be becoming real.
3100. The teacher asked me: "Who has already completed the project?".
a) The teacher asked me who already completed the project.
b) The teacher asked me who completed the project.
c) The teacher asked me who had already completed the project.

Set 12

3101. Choose the correct sentence:
a) Didn't you found out the truth?
b) Haven't you found out the truth?
c) Haven't you founded out the truth?

3102. Why is she so ...?
a) inorganized
b) unorganzied
c) disorganized

Set 13

3103. The vaccine can have an ... effect.
a) indirect
b) undirect
c) disdirect
3104. Of course we aren't ... .
a) inmortal
b) immortal
c) amortal
3105. The sun went ... and a new day was
beginning.
a) up
b) down
c) with
3106. They broke ... and stole more than 1 million
dollars.
a) with
b) in
c) down
3107. They went ... the rules.
a) for
b) without
c) against
3108. The group must ... .
a) divided
b) be divided
c) dividing
3109. Should this be ... down?
a) written
b) wrote
c) writing
3110. The document ... two days ago.
a) had written
b) has been written
c) had to be written
3111. We ... it at 10 o'clock yesterday.
a) were discussing

b) have being discussed
c) had being discussed
3112. The guests ... Russian.

a) didn't spoken
b) weren't speaking
c) hadn't speaking
3113. ... it becoming a success?
a) Had
b) Did
c) Was
3114. Is the following sentence correct? "Were you
hearing her well?"
a) correct
b) incorrect
3115. The ship has ... .
a) sunk
b) sinking
c) being sink
3116. What ... now?
a) is delivered
b) is being delivered
c) is delivering
3117. This question ... yet.
a) hasn't asked
b) hasn't been asked
c) wasn't been asked
3118. Listen! The young lady ... now.
a) sings
b) is singing
c) singed
3119. I ... for you for one hour.
a) have been waiting
b) waiting
c) did waited
3120. It ... now.
a) is checked

b) checking
c) is being checked
3121. I wish I ... the city last night.
a) had left
b) leaving
c) left
3122. If only she ... another way!
a) choosing
b) had chosen
c) has choosing
3123. If she had kept her word, she ... my wife now.
a) would have been
b) could have been

c) would be

3124. She's envious … her manager.

a) to

b) of

c) with

3125. She apologized … everything.

a) for

b) on

c) in

3126. I went to Turkey … business.

a) in

b) on

c) with

3127. The commander said: "They have trained professionally.".

a) The commander said that they have trained professionally.

b) The commander said that they had trained professionally.

c) The commander said that they be training professionally.

3128. My aunt told me: "He will be staying with them.".

a) My aunt told me that he would stay with them.

b) My aunt told me that he would be staying with them.

c) My aunt told me that he will be staying with them.

3129. I … English for 15 years by next year.

a) will be learning

b) would be learning

c) will have been learning

3130. I … this report for two hours by the time the director gets to work.

a) have been making

b) will have been making

c) would be making

3131. I … German with her for six months by next year.

a) will have been speaking

b) will spoken

c) would be spoken

3132. The investigator asked me: "Was it happening there?".

a) The investigator asked me if it was happening there.

b) The investigator asked me if it has been happening there.

c) The investigator asked me if it had been happening there.

3133. Choose the correct sentence:

a) Is she not sincerely with you?

b) Isn't she sincere with you?

c) Didn't she be sincere with you?

3134. … she share your point of view?

a) Didn't

b) Hasn't

c) Doesn't

3135. Choose the correct sentence:

a) Didn't he worry about that?

b) Hasn't he worrying about that?

c) Hadn't he worrying about that?

3136. Choose the correct sentence:

a) Will not you train more intensively?

b) Won't you train more intensively?

c) Didn't you trained more intensively?

3137. Choose the correct sentence:

a) Are they not working on their mistakes?

b) Are they no worked on their mistakes?

c) Hadn't they been worked on their mistakes?

3138. Choose the correct sentence:

a) Didn't she apologized?

b) Hasn't she apologized?

c) Hadn't she be apologizing?

3139. Choose the correct sentence:

a) What are you talking?

b) What are you talking about?

c) What are you talk about?

3140. Choose the correct sentence:

a) Where are you from?

b) Didn't you been from?

c) Where from are you?

3141. Choose the correct sentence:

a) What are you interested?

b) Didn't you been interested?

c) What are you interested in?

3142. She … a purchase.

a) did

b) made

c) done

3143. These girls are … .

a) inemployed

b) unemployed

c) disemployed

3144. The scientists achieved international … .

a) famous

b) faming

c) fame

3145. I … agree with you on this matter.

a) utter

b) complete

c) absolutely

3146. It doesn't meet these … standards.

a) educational

b) education

c) educating

3147. It cost … 200 euros.

a) approximate

b) approximation

c) approximately

3148. This goal is … . It's impossible to achieve it.

a) achievable

b) achieving

c) unachievable

3149. I bumped … her near the shopping center.

a) into

b) with

c) about

3150. I hope we can count … your expertise.

a) in

b) on

c) with

3151. This report should … one more time.

a) check

b) be checked

c) checking

3152. Following this discovery, she should … .

a) be awarded

b) awarding

c) awarded

3153. The costs ought to … .

a) minimizing

b) be minimize

c) be minimized

3154. The most suitable candidate might … been missed.

a) had

b) have

c) having

3155. Her knowledge may … .

a) check

b) have been checked

c) been checking

3156. They may … yesterday.

a) have been examined

b) be examined

c) been examining

3157. … can't afford this car.

a) Poor

b) The poors

c) The poor

3158. They say that the more you pay, … quality you get.

a) better

b) the better

c) the best

3159. … discussed it, we signed a new contract.

a) Having

b) Being

c) Hading

3160. In no way … it.

a) will I do

b) do I will

c) will do I

3161. Stay with us unless your brother … .

a) return

b) returns

c) will return

3162. Choose the correct sentence:

a) We are meeting two times a week.

b) We were meet two times a week.

c) We meet two times a week.

3163. Choose the correct sentence:

a) It's getting hot today.

b) It gets hot today.

c) It has get hot today.

3164. Brian … encouraging us.

a) wasn't

b) didn't

c) hadn't

3165. Is the following sentence correct? "They were needing much more money."

a) correct

b) incorrect

3166. Is the following sentence correct? "She was signing the contract

when I came in."

a) correct

b) incorrect

3167. I see you … laughed at her.

a) didn't

b) weren't

c) haven't

3168. Her parents have … her do that.

a) letting

b) let

c) letted

3169. They … thoroughly now.

a) are examined

b) are being examined

c) are be examining

3170. Their report … yet.

a) hasn't been read

b) weren't read

c) hasn't read

3171. The kids wish there … only happiness in the world.

a) is

b) had

c) was

3172. If only I … about that problem earlier!

a) had known

b) didn't know

c) have known

3173. She … her boyfriend yesterday.

a) may not see

b) may not have seen

c) may didn't see

3174. We … them.

a) didn't need to warn

b) need not warned

c) did needed not warn

3175. This professor is very patient … his students.

a) about

b) on

c) with

3176. It's rude … them to push him.

a) to

b) of

c) on

3177. She said: "The baby is crying.".

a) She said that the baby is crying.

b) She said that the baby was crying

c) She said that the baby has been crying.

3178. The officer said: "The negotiations will be peaceful.".

a) The officer said that the negotiations would be peaceful.

b) The officer said that the negotiations would being peaceful.

c) The officer said that the negotiations will being peaceful.

3179. Steven said: "We'll talk about everything soon.".

a) Steven said that they would talk about everything soon.

b) Steven said that they'll talk about everything soon.

c) Steven said that they would be talking about everything soon.

3180. She asked me: "Do you see it?".

a) She asked me if I saw it.

b) She asked me if I see it.

c) She asked me if I did seen it.

3181. The manager asked me: "Was it the best offer?".

a) The manager asked me whether had it been the best offer.

b) The manager asked me if had it be the best offer.

c) The manager asked me if it had been the best offer.

3182. The customer asked me: "Have you already installed the program?".

a) The customer asked me if I have already installed that program.

b) The customer asked me if I had already installed that program.

c) The customer asked me if I installed the program.

3183. My girlfriend asked me: "Why is it becoming more and more

expensive?".

a) She asked me why it is becoming more and more expensive.

b) She asked me why it would become more and more expensive.

c) She asked me why it was becoming more and more expensive.

3184. Jane asked me: "What has changed?".

a) Jane asked me what had changed.

b) Jane asked me what had had changed.

c) Jane asked me what would have changed.

3185. My wife asked me: "How long have you been waiting for me?".

a) My wife asked me how long I had been waiting for me.

b) My wife asked me how long I had been waiting for her.

c) My wife asked me how long had I been waited for her.

3186. The security advisor asked me: "How long have you been using this website?".

a) The security advisor asked me how long I was using that website.

b) The security advisor asked me how long I did being used that website.

c) The security advisor asked me how long I had been using that website.

3187. Choose the correct sentence:

a) You didn't understood?

b) Don't you understand?

c) Didn't you understood?

3188. Choose the correct sentence:

a) Doesn't she trust you?

b) Didn't she trusted you?

c) Haven't she trusting you?

3189. Choose the correct sentence:

a) Weren't they luckily?

b) Weren't they lucky?

c) Weren't they lucking?

3190. ... it a rush hour?

a) Didn't

b) Haven't

c) Wasn't

3191. It was a ... idea.

a) fascinating

b) fascinated

c) fascinate

3192. I was ... with her reply.

a) insatisfied

b) dissatisfied

c) asatisfied

3193. This offer is so bad! It's really ... .

a) unattractive

b) attractive

c) inattractive

3194. We reached ... in the end. We started cooperating.

a) a disagreement

b) an agreement

c) a conclusive

3195. She's fond of ... .

a) artist

b) actress

c) art

3196. I was ... by his speech.

a) impressive

b) impressed

c) impressing

3197. Dave is his ... relative.

a) distance

b) distantly

c) distant

3198. The poor woman came ... against so many difficulties.

a) up

b) on

c) with

3199. Let's get ... to business.

a) down

b) at

c) within

3200. Choose the correct sentence:

a) I used to be done it.

b) I am used to doing it.

c) I had used to be done it.

3201. Choose the correct sentence:

a) She used to getting up early.

b) She is used to getting up early.

c) She is using to getting up early.

3202. I would sooner ... than play.

a) study

b) studying

c) to study

3203. I … sooner do it by myself.

a) had

b) should

c) would

3204. I'd rather you … him this information.

a) not tell

b) no telling

c) didn't tell

3205. The result may … .

a) have predict

b) be predicted

c) be predicting

3206. This misunderstanding could … .

a) have been avoided

b) had been avoided

c) have avoided

3207. You neither win … lose.

a) or

b) nor

c) either

3208. It was … hilarious.

a) absolutely

b) complete

c) utter

3209. … poor she lives in a small flat.

a) Be

b) To be

c) Being

3210. … stopped there, he asked her a question.

a) To

b) Hading

c) Having

3211. No one … against it.

a) isn't

b) hadn't

c) is

3212. Choose the correct sentence:

a) We meet this evening.

b) We are meeting this evening.

c) We have meeting this evening.

3213. Choose the correct sentence:

a) Listen! The girl is crying.

b) Listen! The girl cries.

c) Listen! The girl has crying.

3214. Choose the correct sentence:

a) They ignore Mary now.

b) They are ignoring Mary now.

c) They have ignored Mary now.

3215. It stopped raining when we … .

a) were eating

b) eaten

c) have been eating

3216. I know they disturbed you when you … .

a) was working

b) were working

c) have been working

3217. Is the following sentence correct? "I was preferring the first way."

a) correct

b) incorrect

3218. Choose the correct sentence:

a) Did you never done it?

b) Hadn't you never done it?

c) Have you ever done it?

3219. Choose the correct sentence:

a) We didn't get her answer yet.

b) We haven't got her answer yet.

c) We hadn't get her answer yet.

3220. She has … the door.

a) hitting

b) hitted

c) hit

3221. I see you … for the exam since Sunday.

a) haven't been preparing

b) haven't preparing

c) haven't prepare

3222. How long … him?

a) have you been knowing

b) had you known

c) have you known

3223. … when he came back?

a) Had she finished cooking

b) Have she finished cooking

c) Hadn't she finishing cooking

3224. It … now.

a) is checked

b) is being checked

c) have been checking

3225. Choose the correct sentence:

a) The goods have been sold.

b) The goods have sold.
c) The good had be sold.
3226. The kids … football when the professor arrived.
a) was playing
b) were playing
c) have been playing
3227. The meeting … by the time I arrived.
a) already started
b) has already started
c) had already started
3228. When I joined that club she … his member for two years.
a) had been
b) have been
c) had been being
3229. It was said it … .
a) was already announced
b) had already been announced
c) have already be announce
3230. If I had one more chance, I … show much better results.
a) will

b) would
c) would had
3231. If she … another man, her parents would have criticized her sharply.
a) married
b) have marry
c) had married
3232. Choose the correct sentence:
a) It's high time the truth about the pandemic was discovered.
b) It's high time we discover the truth about the pandemic.
c) It's high time the truth about the pandemic would be discovered.
3233. I'm accustomed … it.
a) for
b) on
c) to
3234. She's keen … classical music.
a) on
b) of
c) in
3235. She's sensitive … criticism.

a) for
b) to
c) about
3236. I was amused … her manners.
a) at
b) on
c) in
3237. The kid is allergic … nuts.
a) with
b) to
c) about
3238. I understood everything … once.
a) for
b) in
c) at

3239. Don't take everything … granted!
a) on
b) for
c) at
3240. John said: "When she called me I was working.".
a) John said that when she had called him he had been working.
b) John said that when she called him he was working.
c) John said that when she would call him he would be working.
3241. Kate said: "I was learning English all day.".
a) Kate said that she had been learning English all day.
b) Kate said that she has been learning English all day.
c) Kate said that she was learning English all day.
3242. Jennifer said: "I have been watching his channel for more than a year.".
a) Jennifer said that she has been watched his channel for more than a year.
b) Jennifer said that she was watching his channel for more than a year.
c) Jennifer said that she had been watching his channel for more than a year.
3243. My wife asked me: "Where is it happening?".

a) My wife asked me where it was happening.
b) My wife asked me where was it happening.
c) My wife asked me where had it happened.
3244. The detective asked me: "What things were happening there?".
a) The detective asked me what things were happening there.
b) The detective asked me what things had been happening there.
c) The detective asked me what things have been happening there.
3245. Choose the correct sentence:
a) What are you thinking?
b) What are you thinking about?
c) What have you thinking about?
3246. This function is … .
a) unactive

b) inactive
c) disasctive
3247. The results are … .
a) uncredible
b) discredible
c) incredible
3248. You can't … know it.
a) possibly
b) possible
c) impossible
3249. She feels … . She needs someone's help.
a) protected
b) protective
c) unprotected
3250. It's an … remark.
a) unrelevant
b) irrelevant
c) disrelevant
3251. Cheer …! Why are you so depressed?
a) down
b) up
c) again
3252. After some months she gave up … tennis.
a) play
b) playing
c) played
3253. Choose the correct sentence:
a) They called it off.
b) They called off it.

c) They had been calling it off.
3254. I'd rather you … with your boss.
a) not compete
b) not competing
c) didn't compete

3255. I … my car washed.
a) had have
b) having
c) got
3256. He is expected … .
a) to win
b) win
c) winning
3257. His question … .
a) had answered
b) had to be answered
c) had answering
3258. This interview … .
a) might already recorded
b) might have already been recorded
c) might had already be recording
3259. The artist must … .
a) have been inspired by her fans
b) have inspired by her fans
c) had be inspiring by her fans
3260. She's just about … herself to the committee.
a) introducing
b) introduce
c) to introduce
3261. The professor … those students.
a) hasn't been compared
b) wasn't comparing
c) hadn't be comparing
3262. What … your parents doing there?
a) did
b) were
c) had
3263. Mary … to convince him.
a) was trying

b) trying
c) has be trying
3264. Your child … enough yesterday.
a) eaten
b) has eaten
c) ate

3265. The man has … it at last.
a) founded
b) finded
c) found
3266. I have … him some money.
a) lent
b) lend
c) lended
3267. After receiving the treatment I … much better.
a) feeling
b) felt
c) had felt
3268. My wife has … back.
a) came
b) coming
c) come
3269. You … it brilliantly. Congrats!
a) did
b) has
c) done
3270. The dog … me yesterday.
a) bitted
b) bit
c) has bitten
3271. How long … for this competition?
a) has you be preparing
b) did you be preparing
c) have you been preparing

3272. … it when he came?
a) Has she already done
b) Did she already do
c) Had she already doing
3273. … the building by the time the police arrived?
a) Had they left
b) Have they left
c) Did they left
3274. Your brother … with murder now.
a) is charged
b) is being charged
c) has being charged
3275. Choose the correct sentence:
a) She currently works on this project.
b) She is currently working on this project.
c) She has currently being worked on this project.
3276. My sister … to Italy.
a) had been

b) was
c) has been
3277. I wish I … one more chance.
a) had had
b) have had
c) would had
3278. She needn't … it.
a) mentioning
b) mentioned
c) mention
3279. I'm ready … a change.
a) to
b) for
c) with
3280. The final decision depends … him.
a) on

b) from
c) about
3281. This mission plan can lead … big problems.
a) for
b) about
c) to
3282. What's the reason … doing it?
a) to
b) for
c) in
3283. We're … debt.
a) on
b) with
c) in
3284. The marketing specialist said: "My idea is brilliant.".
a) The marketing specialist said that his idea was brilliant.
b) The marketing specialist said that his idea had been brilliant.
c) The marketing specialist said that my idea was brilliant.
3285. She said: "When I saw him he was walking in the park.".
a) She said that when she had seen him he had been walking in the park.
b) She said that when she had seen him he would be walking in the park.

c) She said that when she has seen him he was walking in the park.

3286. John said: "I have been waiting for you for such a long time.".

a) John said that he was waiting for me for such a long time.

b) John said that he had been waiting for me for such a long time.

c) John said that he was waiting for me for such a long time.

3287. My wife asked me: "Did you decline their offer?".

a) My wife asked me if you had declined their offer.

b) My wife asked me if I would decline their offer.

c) My wife asked me if I had declined their offer.

3288. The professor asked me: "Have you already guessed the right

answer?".

a) The professor asked me if I had already guessed the right answer.

b) The professor asked me if you were already guessing the right

answer.

c) The professor asked me if I would already be guessing the right

answer.

3289. The examiner asked me: "Have you been learning Russian

intensively for the last three months?".

a) The examiner asked me whether I had been learning Russian

intensively for the previous three months.

b) The examiner asked me if I have been learning Russian

intensively for the last three months.

c) The examiner asked me if I had learnt Russian intensively for the

last three months.

3290. The mentor asked me: "Why has she already known everything?".

a) The mentor asked me why she has already known everything.

b) The mentor asked me why she had already known everything.

c) The mentor asked me why she was already knowing everything.

3291. Choose the correct sentence:

a) Aren't you satisfied with her answer?

b) Hadn't you being satisfied with her answer?

c) Weren't you be satisfied with her answer?

3292. Choose the correct sentence:

a) Who is this document?

b) Who was this document about?

c) Who is this document for?

3293. How are you going to … a living in that country?

a) do

b) make

c) had

3294. They were … with the exams.

a) bored

b) boring

c) bore

3295. I was … by their presentation.

a) inspiring

b) inspire

c) inspired

3296. It's an … situation.

a) unsane

b) insane

c) insanely

3297. I'm for … methods.

a) traditional

b) tradition

c) traditionally

3298. She … so unexpectedly.

a) disappeared

b) unappeared

c) inappeared

3299. This step is … . It's the only right way.

a) unnecessary

b) necessary

c) necessarily

3300. These exercises will … your body.

a) strength

b) strengthing

c) strengthen

3301. The woman felt so … .

a) insecure

b) securing

c) asecure

3302. The detectives will look … the crime.

a) in
b) with
c) into
3303. My wife often shows … . She likes attracting other people's attention.
a) off
b) in
c) about

3304. … no use doing it.
a) How's
b) There's
c) What's
3305. There is no point … it again.
a) to check
b) about check
c) in checking
3306. I have difficulty … for this exam.
a) to prepare
b) preparing
c) prepared
3307. This competitor is expected … .
a) to lose
b) losing
c) lose
3308. It should … .
a) be say
b) be said
c) being said
3309. These conditions should … .
a) be provided
b) providing
c) provide
3310. The more practice, … .
a) better
b) the best
c) the better
3311. She won't change unless her parents … to her.
a) talk
b) will talk
c) had talked
3312. When his mother arrived, he … .
a) has been sleeping

b) would be sleeping
c) was still sleeping
3313. … the manager explaining it?

a) Had
b) Was
c) Did
3314. Is the following sentence correct? "What was she wanting?"
a) correct
b) incorrect
3315. Is the following sentence correct? "The girls were commenting."
a) correct
b) incorrect
3316. Is the following sentence correct? "I was parking there."
a) correct
b) incorrect
3317. Is the following sentence correct? "Brian was having a rest."
a) correct
b) incorrect
3318. Choose the correct sentence:
a) I was never to China.
b) I've never been to China.
c) I'd never been to China.
3319. You brother has … the last place.
a) be taken
b) been taken
c) taken
3320. Olivia … it for six years.
a) had been doing
b) has been doing
c) would be done
3321. … her since you finished university?
a) Have you known
b) Have you been knowing
c) Did you known

3322. Choose the correct sentence:
a) Did it ever been controlled?
b) Had it ever being controlled?
c) Has it ever been controlled?
3323. Her mistakes … .
a) did be spotted
b) have been spotted
c) had being spotted
3324. I observed that his mistakes … yet.
a) weren't corrected
b) didn't be correct

c) hadn't been corrected

3325. I … it two months ago.

a) have done

b) done

c) did

3326. How long … there?

a) are you staying

b) have you been staying

c) did you being stay

3327. My sister … Russian for three years.

a) has been learning

b) had been learning

c) did learning

3328. Choose the correct sentence:

a) It is currently monitored.

b) It had currently be monitored.

c) It is currently being monitored.

3329. I found out that some things … .

a) had been stolen

b) were stolen

c) did be stolen

3330. The students is frightened … her words.

a) of

b) with

c) on

Set 14

3331. She's ashamed … her poor skills.

a) by

b) on

c) of

3332. This text was translated from Russian … German.

a) into

b) with

c) on

3333. Why is he staring … her?

a) on

b) at

c) to

3334. I'm working here … the time being.

a) for

b) at

c) in

3335. The analyst said: "The situation isn't getting better.".

a) The analyst said that the situation isn't getting better.

b) The analyst said that the situation wasn't getting better.

c) The analyst said that the situation wouldn't get better.

3336. The manager said: "They were discussing it.".

a) The manager said that they had been discussing it.

b) The manager said that they were discussing it.

c) The manager said that they would be discussing it.

3337. The secretary asked me: "Did he apologize for it?".

a) The secretary asked me if he apologized for it.

b) The secretary asked me if he has apologized for it.

c) The secretary asked me if he had apologized for it.

3338. Mary asked me: "Has she already introduced him?".

a) Mary asked me if she had already introduced him.

b) Mary asked me if she already introduced him.

c) Mary asked me if she would already introduce him.

3339. Kate asked me: "What time do you usually get up?".

a) Kate asked me what time did I usually get up.

b) Kate asked me what time had I usually got up.

c) Kate asked me what time I usually got up.

3340. The manager asked me: "Who was responsible for it?".

a) The manager asked me who had been responsible for it.

b) The manager asked me who was responsible for it.

c) The manager asked me who has be responsible for it.

3341. The girl asked me: "How often will you go to the gym?".

a) The girl asked me how often I will go to the gym.

b) The girl asked me how often I would go to the gym.

c) The girl asked me how often I used to go to the gym.

3342. My neighbour asked me: "Why were you doing it all night?".

a) My neighbour asked me why you had been doing it all night.
b) My neighbour asked me why I had been doing it all night.
c) My neighbour asked me why have I been doing it all night.
3343. Choose the correct sentence:
a) Hadn't it improve your English?
b) Doesn't it improve your English?
c) Haven't it improving your English?
3344. … she trust you?
a) Doesn't
b) Isn't
c) Hadn't
3345. … she lose control?
a) Wasn't
b) Hadn't
c) Didn't
3346. Choose the correct answer:
a) Hasn't Dave become a rich man?
b) Didn't Dave became a rich man?
c) Hadn't Dave been became a rich man?
3347. …, it ruined all our hopes.
a) Luck

b) Iluckily
c) Unluckily
3348. Maria feels so … . Something bad must have happened to her.
a) unhappy
b) unhappily
c) happily
3349. This … isn't enough to enter our organization.
a) unknown
b) knowledge
c) knowing
3350. He's an … person. He's so special!
a) ordinarily
b) ordinary
c) extraordinary
3351. Her father ran … when she was a small kid.
a) off
b) in
c) out
3352. We'll sort … this problem quite easily.
a) in
b) about

c) out
3353. I can't get rid … my headache.
a) on
b) of
c) out
3354. She always stands … in a crowd.
a) within
b) out
c) about
3355. We broke … all the relations.
a) off
b) out
c) to

3356. You … better change your mind.
a) can
b) had
c) would
3357. I … my hair cut.
a) can
b) should
c) had
3358. This thing can be … .
a) proved
b) proving
c) prove
3359. The team shouldn't … .
a) divide
b) be divided
c) diving
3360. It's … fantastic what you've done.
a) completely
b) utter
c) such a
3361. We won't go there in case she … buy a ticket.
a) won't
b) doesn't
c) wouldn't
3362. How … it changing?
a) did
b) have
c) was
3363. It … an effect on me.
a) won't have
b) hadn't have
c) wouldn't had
3364. The police … suspected Mary.

a) have

b) has

c) did

3365. They … broken the law. I guarantee.

a) didn't

b) haven't

c) won't

3366. The customer … responded.

a) won't

b) didn't

c) hasn't

3367. She … the money.

a) withdrew

b) withdrawed

c) withdraw

3368. She realized she … inappropriate words.

a) was used

b) had used

c) did used

3369. They … now.

a) be criticized

b) are criticize

c) are being criticized

3370. What … now?

a) is being said

b) has being said

c) does been said

3371. Who … about this situation?

a) did been warned

b) has been warned

c) would being warned

3372. How long … this movie?

a) did you watched

b) hadn't you watch

c) have you been watching

3373. Jennifer confessed she … him all the truth.

a) didn't told

b) won't tell

c) hadn't told

3374. I wish I … a better job.

a) had

b) would had

c) have

3375. I … be in best shape because it's my desire to be so.

a) must

b) have to

c) had to

3376. I … to finish this report today.

a) have to

b) had to

c) would have

3377. The professor told me: "We'll support her.".

a) The professor told me that they will support her.

b) The professor told me that they would support her.

c) The professor told me that they would be supporting her.

3378. I … my final exam by December.

a) will completed

b) will be completing

c) will have completed

3379. We … for two hours by the time they arrive.

a) will have been talking

b) will had been talked

c) will had been talking

3380. The assistant asked me: "Will you compare their results?".

a) The assistant asked me whether I would compare their results.

b) The assistant asked me if I will compare their results.

c) The assistant asked me if I would be comparing their results.

3381. The professor asked me: "Have you been learning Russian for three years?".

a) The professor asked me if you had been learning Russian for three

years.

b) The professor asked me if I had been learning Russian for three

years.

c) The professor asked me if I have learnt Russian for three years.

3382. My cousin asked me: "How was your trip?".

a) My cousin asked me how my trip was.

b) My cousin asked me how my trip had been.

c) My cousin asked me how my trip would be.

3383. What does Jane insist …?

a) of

b) with

c) on

3384. Her colleagues … her.

a) disrespect

b) inrespect

c) arespect

3385. He's my … .

a) competition

b) competitive

c) competitor

3386. The coronavirus can't be cured … .

a) traditional

b) traditionally

c) tradition

3387. She improved her Chinese only … .

a) unsignificantly

b) insignificantly

c) dissignificantly

3388. We lead an … lifestyle.

a) inhealthy

b) dishealthy

c) unhealthy

3389. They are very … to him.

a) unkind

b) inkind

c) rekind

3390. Brian dozed ... during the lecture.

a) down

b) in

c) off

3391. Choose the correct sentence:

a) Get out it your head!

b) Get it out of your head!

c) Get out of your head it!

3392. Choose the correct sentence:

a) I'm accustomed to staying at home all day.

b) I'm accustomed to stay at home all day.

c) I'm accustom to staying at home all day.

3393. I'd rather … cycling than play computer games.

a) going

b) gone

c) go

3394. I'd rather … a little bit.

a) wait

b) waiting

c) to wait

3395. She's supposed … the first place.

a) take

b) to take

c) to have take

3396. Are we supposed … there on time?

a) arrive

b) arriving

c) to arrive

3397. These risk factors should … .

a) minimize

b) minimizing

c) be minimized

3398. This subject shouldn't … at university.

a) teach

b) be taught

c) teaching

3399. They mustn't … .

a) punished

b) punishing

c) be punished

3400. …, the better.

a) The shorter

b) Shorter

c) The shortest

Answers

1.a 2.a 3.c 4.c 5.b 6.c 7.c 8.a 9.c 10.b

11.c 12.c 13.a 14.b 15.c 16.c 17.a 18.c 19.b 20.c

21.a 22.c 23.b 24.c 25.a 26.c 27.a 28.b 29.c 30.a

31.c 32.a 33.b 34.b 35.c 36.a 37.a 38.c 39.c 40.b

41.a 42.c 43.b 44.a 45.c 46.c 47.c 48.b 49.a 50.b

51.b 52.c 53.b 54.a 55.c 56.b 57.b 58.c 59.c 60.a

61.b 62.c 63.a 64.b 65.c 66.c 67.a 68.b 69.c 70.a

71.b 72.b 73.c 74.b 75.a 76.a 77.c 78.c 79.b 80.a

81.c 82.c 83.a 84.b 85.c 86.c 87.b 88.a 89.b 90.c

91.b 92.a 93.c 94.b 95.c 96.b 97.a 98.c 99.b 100.a

101.c 102.c 103.a 104.b 105.c 106.c 107.a 108.b 109.a

110.c 111.b 112.c 113.c 114.a 115.b 116.c 117.a 118.b

119.c 120.a 121.b 122.a 123.c 124.b 125.c 126.b 127.a

128.c 129.c 130.a 131.b 132.c 133.a 134.a 135.c 136.b

137.a 138.b 139.c 140.c 141.c 142.a 143.b 144.c 145.c

146.a 147.a 148.b 149.c 150.b 151.a 152.c 153.c 154.b

155.c 156.a 157.b 158.b 159.c 160.a 161.b 162.c 163.c

164.b 165.a 166.b 167.c 168.a 169.b 170.c 171.c 172.b

173.b 174.c 175.a 176.b 177.a 178.c 179.a 180.b 181.a

182.c 183.b 184.c 185.b 186.c 187.a 188.a 189.c 190.b

191.a 192.c 193.c 194.b 195.c 196.a 197.c 198.b 199.a

200.c 201.b 202.a 203.c 204.b 205.c 206.a 207.c 208.b

209.a 210.c 211.c 212.a 213.b 214.a 215.c 216.b 217.c

218.b 219.b 220.b 221.a 222.c 223.c 224.b 225.c 226.a

227.b 228.c 229.b 230.a 231.c 232.b 233.c 234.a 235.c

236.b 237.c 238.c 239.b 240.a 241.b 242.a 243.c 244.b

245.b 246.b 247.a 248.c 249.b 250.a 251.b 252.c 253.c

254.c 255.a 256.c 257.b 258.c 259.c 260.c 261.b 262.a

263.c 264.a 265.b 266.c 267.a 268.c 269.a 270.b 271.b

272.a 273.b 274.c 275.c 276.a 277.b 278.a 279.c 280.b

281.c 282.c 283.c 284.a 285.c 286.b 287.c 288.b 289.c

290.a 291.a 292.b 293.c 294.c 295.c 296.a 297.b 298.a

299.b 300.a 301.a 302.c 303.c 304.b 305.b 306.b 307.c

308.b 309.a 310.c 311.c 312.c 313.a 314.b 315.c 316.b

317.c 318.a 319.c 320.c 321.a 322.b 323.c 324.c 325.b

326.a 327.c 328.b 329.a 330.c 331.c 332.c 333.a 334.b

335.b 336.a 337.b 338.c 339.a 340.c 341.b 342.a 343.c

344.b 345.b 346.c 347.c 348.b 349.a 350.c 351.b 352.a

353.c 354.a 355.c 356.b 357.b 358.a 359.c 360.b 361.c

362.a 363.c 364.b 365.a 366.c 367.c 368.a 369.b 370.c

371.b 372.a 373.c 374.a 375.b 376.c 377.c 378.a 379.a

380.c 381.a 382.c 383.b 384.b 385.c 386.c 387.a 388.b

389.c 390.c 391.b 392.c 393.a 394.c 395.a 396.c 397.b

398.c 399.a 400.b 401.a 402.b 403.b 404.c 405.c 406.b

407.a 408.a 409.c 410.a 411.c 412.a 413.b 414.b 415.c

416.a 417.c 418.b 419.c 420.a 421.b 422.a 423.c 424.b

425.b 426.a 427.c 428.b 429.b 430.a 431.c 432.c 433.b

434.c 435.c 436.b 437.a 438.c 439.c 440.a 441.b 442.c

443.a 444.b 445.c 446.c 447.b 448.a 449.c 450.b 451.b

452.a 453.c 454.a 455.b 456.c 457.c 458.a 459.c 460.b

461.c 462.b 463.c 464.a 465.c 466.b 467.b 468.c 469.c

470.a 471.a 472.c 473.b 474.b 475.c 476.a 477.b 478.a

479.c 480.b 481.c 482.a 483.b 484.c 485.b 486.c 487.b

488.c 489.a 490.a 491.b 492.c 493.a 494.b 495.a 496.c

497.a 498.c 499.b 500.a 501.a 502.b 503.c 504.a 505.b

506.c 507.a 508.c 509.b 510.a 511.c 512.b 513.a 514.c

515.a 516.c 517.b 518.a 519.b 520.c 521.a 522.c 523.b

524.a 525.c 526.a 527.b 528.a 529.c 530.c 531.b 532.a

533.c 534.b 535.a 536.b 537.b 538.a 539.c 540.a 541.c

542.a 543.c 544.b 545.b 546.c 547.c 548.a 549.c 550.b

551.b 552.b 553.a 554.c 555.c 556.c 557.b 558.b 559.a

560.b 561.c 562.b 563.c 564.a 565.b 566.c 567.b 568.c

569.c 570.a 571.b 572.c 573.b 574.a 575.a 576.c 577.b

578.b 579.c 580.b 581.c 582.a 583.b 584.b 585.a 586.c

587.b 588.c 589.b 590.c 591.b 592.c 593.a 594.b 595.a

596.a 597.c 598.b 599.c 600.a 601.b 602.a 603.c 604.a

605.a 606.c 607.b 608.a 609.c 610.b 611.c 612.c 613.a

614.b 615.a 616.c 617.b 618.c 619.a 620.b 621.c 622.b

623.a 624.b 625.b 626.b 627.a 628.c 629.c 630.a 631.b

632.a 633.c 634.c 635.b 636.b 637.c 638.a 639.a 640.c

641.c 642.a 643.c 644.b 645.b 646.a 647.b 648.b 649.c

650.a 651.b 652.a 653.c 654.c 655.a 656.a 657.b 658.c

659.b 660.c 661.c 662.a 663.c 664.c 665.a 666.b 667.c

668.b 669.a 670.c 671.b 672.a 673.c 674.c 675.a 676.b

677.c 678.c 679.b 680.a 681.a 682.c 683.b 684.b 685.c

686.b 687.c 688.b 689.c 690.c 691.a 692.c 693.b 694.c

695.a 696.b 697.c 698.b 699.c 700.b 701.a 702.c 703.c

704.b 705.a 706.b 707.a 708.b 709.c 710.b 711.b 712.c

713.a 714.c 715.a 716.c 717.a 718.c 719.c 720.b 721.a

722.c 723.b 724.a 725.c 726.c 727.b 728.a 729.c 730.b

731.a 732.b 733.a 734.c 735.b 736.c 737.b 738.a 739.c

740.b 741.b 742.c 743.a 744.b 745.a 746.c 747.b 748.a

749.c 750.b 751.a 752.b 753.c 754.c 755.a 756.b 757.a

758.c 759.c 760.a 761.a 762.c 763.c 764.b 765.b 766.c

767.b 768.c 769.a 770.b 771.b 772.a 773.c 774.b 775.c

776.a 777.c 778.b 779.a 780.c 781.c 782.b 783.a 784.c

785.b 786.c 787.c 788.c 789.a 790.b 791.c 792.b 793.c

794.b 795.c 796.b 797.a 798.b 799.a 800.c 801.b 802.b

803.a 804.c 805.a 806.c 807.b 808.c 809.c 810.b 811.a

812.c 813.b 814.a 815.b 816.a 817.c 818.a 819.b 820.a

821.b 822.b 823.c 824.c 825.a 826.b 827.c 828.a 829.a

830.b 831.a 832.c 833.b 834.a 835.a 836.c 837.b 838.c

839.b 840.b 841.c 842.c 843.a 844.b 845.b 846.a 847.c

848.c 849.b 850.a 851.a 852.b 853.c 854.b 855.c 856.a

857.c 858.c 859.b 860.a 861.c 862.a 863.c 864.c 865.b

866.b 867.c 868.c 869.a 870.b 871.a 872.b 873.b 874.c

875.a 876.b 877.c 878.b 879.c 880.a 881.c 882.b 883.a

884.c 885.b 886.c 887.b 888.a 889.b 890.b 891.b 892.a

893.c 894.c 895.a 896.b 897.c 898.b 899.a 900.c 901.b

902.a 903.c 904.a 905.a 906.c 907.b 908.b 909.c 910.b

911.c 912.a 913.b 914.c 915.a 916.c 917.c 918.a 919.c

920.c 921.c 922.a 923.c 924.b 925.a 926.c 927.b 928.a

929.b 930.c 931.a 932.b 933.c 934.b 935.a 936.a 937.c

938.c 939.b 940.a 941.c 942.c 943.a 944.b 945.b 946.c

947.a 948.b 949.c 950.b 951.a 952.c 953.b 954.c 955.a

956.c 957.a 958.a 959.a 960.b 961.c 962.c 963.b 964.c

965.a 966.c 967.b 968.b 969.c 970.a 971.b 972.c 973.a

974.b 975.c 976.a 977.b 978.a 979.b 980.c 981.c 982.a

983.b 984.b 985.c 986.a 987.b 988.c 989.a 990.b 991.c

992.c 993.b 994.c 995.a 996.c 997.b 998.c 999.a 1000.a

1001.b 1002.c 1003.a 1004.c 1005.b 1006.b 1007.a 1008.c 1009.a

1010.b 1011.b 1012.b 1013.a 1014.a 1015.a 1016.c 1017.b 1018.b

1019.a 1020.b 1021.a 1022.c 1023.a 1024.b 1025.c 1026.a 1027.c

1028.b 1029.b 1030.a 1031.a 1032.c 1033.a 1034.b 1035.b 1036.a

1037.c 1038.b 1039.a 1040.a 1041.b 1042.c 1043.b 1044.b 1045.a

1046.c 1047.b 1048.c 1049.a 1050.a 1051.b 1052.c 1053.b 1054.a

1055.c 1056.a 1057.b 1058.c 1059.b 1060.c 1061.b 1062.c 1063.b

1064.a 1065.b 1066.a 1067.c 1068.c 1069.c 1070.a 1071.a 1072.a

1073.b 1074.c 1075.b 1076.c 1077.b 1078.b 1079.b 1080.a 1081.b

1082.a 1083.c 1084.a 1085.b 1086.b 1087.a 1088.c 1089.b 1090.c

1091.b 1092.c 1093.a 1094.c 1095.a 1096.b 1097.c 1098.b 1099.b

1100.a 1101.b 1102.c 1103.a 1104.b 1105.c 1106.c 1107.a 1108.b

1109.a 1110.c 1111.a 1112.c 1113.b 1114.a 1115.b 1116.c 1117.a

1118.a 1119.b 1120.c 1121.c 1122.a 1123.b 1124.a 1125.a 1126.c

1127.b 1128.a 1129.b 1130.c 1131.a 1132.b 1133.c 1134.b 1135.c

1136.b 1137.b 1138.c 1139.a 1140.b 1141.c 1142.a 1143.b 1144.a

1145.c 1146.b 1147.b 1148.a 1149.c 1150.b 1151.b 1152.a 1153.c

1154.c 1155.a 1156.b 1157.c 1158.a 1159.c 1160.c 1161.b 1162.b

1163.c 1164.a 1165.a 1166.b 1167.c 1168.a 1169.a 1170.b 1171.b

1172.a 1173.b 1174.c 1175.a 1176.a 1177.b 1178.c 1179.b 1180.b

1181.b 1182.a 1183.c 1184.c 1185.c 1186.c 1187.a 1188.b 1189.b

1190.c 1191.a 1192.c 1193.b 1194.c 1195.c 1196.a 1197.a 1198.b

1199.c 1200.b 1201.a 1202.c 1203.b 1204.c 1205.c 1206.b 1207.a

1208.c 1209.c 1210.b 1211.b 1212.a 1213.c 1214.a 1215.c 1216.a

1217.a 1218.b 1219.b 1220.c 1221.b 1222.b 1223.a 1224.c 1225.b

1226.a 1227.c 1228.c 1229.c 1230.a 1231.b 1232.c 1233.a 1234.a

1235.c 1236.b 1237.c 1238.b 1239.a 1240.c 1241.a 1242.b 1243.c

1244.b 1245.c 1246.a 1247.b 1248.a 1249.c 1250.c 1251.a 1252.c

1253.b 1254.a 1255.c 1256.c 1257.a 1258.c 1259.b 1260.c 1261.a

1262.c 1263.b 1264.a 1265.c 1266.a 1267.a 1268.c 1269.b 1270.a

1271.a 1272.c 1273.b 1274.a 1275.c 1276.b 1277.c 1278.b 1279.a

1280.b 1281.b 1282.c 1283.a 1284.c 1285.c 1286.b 1287.a 1288.a

1289.b 1290.c 1291.a 1292.b 1293.c 1294.a 1295.c 1296.b 1297.b

1298.a 1299.b 1300.c 1301.c 1302.a 1303.b 1304.a 1305.c 1306.c

1307.a 1308.b 1309.c 1310.c 1311.a 1312.c 1313.b 1314.c 1315.a

1316.a 1317.c 1318.c 1319.b 1320.b 1321.b 1322.c 1323.a 1324.b

1325.c 1326.b 1327.c 1328.a 1329.b 1330.b 1331.a 1332.c 1333.a

1334.b 1335.c 1336.b 1337.a 1338.b 1339.a 1340.c 1341.a 1342.b

1343.c 1344.c 1345.a 1346.c 1347.b 1348.b 1349.a 1350.c 1351.a

1352.c 1353.b 1354.c 1355.a 1356.c 1357.b 1358.c 1359.c 1360.a

1361.c 1362.b 1363.a 1364.c 1365.a 1366.b 1367.c 1368.a 1369.c

1370.b 1371.c 1372.c 1373.a 1374.b 1375.c 1376.a
1377.c 1378.b
1379.a 1380.c 1381.b 1382.c 1383.b 1384.a 1385.b
1386.c 1387.c
1388.c 1389.a 1390.b 1391.c 1392.a 1393.c 1394.a
1395.c 1396.a
1397.a 1398.c 1399.b 1400.c 1401.b 1402.a 1403.c
1404.b 1405.a
1406.c 1407.c 1408.b 1409.a 1410.c 1411.b 1412.a
1413.c 1414.c
1415.a 1416.b 1417.a 1418.b 1419.a 1420.c 1421.c
1422.a 1423.b
1424.b 1425.c 1426.a 1427.b 1428.c 1429.b 1430.b
1431.a 1432.c
1433.b 1434.c 1435.b 1436.c 1437.a 1438.c 1439.c
1440.b 1441.b
1442.a 1443.c 1444.b 1445.a 1446.a 1447.c 1448.b
1449.a 1450.c
1451.b 1452.a 1453.a 1454.b 1455.c 1456.a 1457.c
1458.b 1459.c
1460.b 1461.b 1462.a 1463.c 1464.c 1465.b 1466.c
1467.b 1468.c
1469.a 1470.b 1471.a 1472.c 1473.c 1474.b 1475.b
1476.a 1477.b

1478.c 1479.a 1480.c 1481.a 1482.b 1483.c 1484.b
1485.a 1486.b
1487.c 1488.a 1489.c 1490.b 1491.a 1492.c 1493.b
1494.a 1495.c
1496.a 1497.b 1498.b 1499.c 1500.a 1501.b 1502.c
1503.a 1504.a
1505.b 1506.a 1507.c 1508.b 1509.b 1510.a 1511.a
1512.b 1513.c
1514.c 1515.a 1516.c 1517.a 1518.b 1519.c 1520.a
1521.b 1522.a
1523.c 1524.a 1525.c 1526.b 1527.b 1528.a 1529.c
1530.b 1531.c
1532.b 1533.c 1534.a 1535.c 1536.b 1537.a 1538.c
1539.b 1540.a
1541.a 1542.c 1543.b 1544.a 1545.b 1546.c 1547.a
1548.b 1549.c
1550.a 1551.b 1552.a 1553.c 1554.b 1555.c 1556.b
1557.c 1558.a
1559.b 1560.c 1561.a 1562.c 1563.b 1564.a 1565.c
1566.c 1567.b
1568.b 1569.a 1570.c 1571.c 1572.b 1573.a 1574.b
1575.b 1576.c

1577.c 1578.b 1579.c 1580.c 1581.b 1582.a 1583.c
1584.b 1585.a
1586.c 1587.a 1588.b 1589.a 1590.c 1591.b 1592.c
1593.c 1594.a
1595.a 1596.c 1597.b 1598.c 1599.a 1600.b 1601.c
1602.c 1603.a
1604.b 1605.b 1606.c 1607.b 1608.c 1609.c 1610.a
1611.b 1612.b
1613.a 1614.c 1615.b 1616.a 1617.b 1618.a 1619.c
1620.c 1621.b
1622.a 1623.c 1624.a 1625.b 1626.a 1627.c 1628.b
1629.a 1630.b
1631.a 1632.c 1633.b 1634.c 1635.a 1636.c 1637.a
1638.c 1639.b
1640.c 1641.a 1642.c 1643.b 1644.c 1645.c 1646.a
1647.c 1648.a
1649.b 1650.a 1651.a 1652.b 1653.c 1654.a 1655.c
1656.b 1657.c
1658.a 1659.c 1660.b 1661.a 1662.c 1663.c 1664.b
1665.b 1666.b
1667.a 1668.b 1669.c 1670.c 1671.a 1672.c 1673.b
1674.a 1675.c
1676.a 1677.b 1678.c 1679.a 1680.c 1681.a 1682.c
1683.a 1684.b
1685.b 1686.c 1687.c 1688.c 1689.b 1690.a 1691.a
1692.b 1693.a
1694.c 1695.a 1696.b 1697.b 1698.c 1699.c 1700.c
1701.b 1702.a
1703.c 1704.a 1705.b 1706.a 1707.c 1708.c 1709.b
1710.a 1711.c
1712.c 1713.a 1714.b 1715.a 1716.c 1717.b 1718.b
1719.c 1720.a
1721.c 1722.b 1723.c 1724.a 1725.c 1726.a 1727.b
1728.b 1729.b
1730.c 1731.c 1732.a 1733.b 1734.b 1735.a 1736.c
1737.a 1738.a
1739.c 1740.b 1741.c 1742.c 1743.b 1744.a 1745.b
1746.a 1747.c
1748.a 1749.c 1750.c 1751.b 1752.c 1753.b 1754.c
1755.c 1756.a
1757.b 1758.a 1759.c 1760.b 1761.a 1762.b 1763.c
1764.b 1765.a
1766.a 1767.c 1768.a 1769.b 1770.a 1771.c 1772.a
1773.b 1774.a
1775.c 1776.a 1777.a 1778.b 1779.c 1780.b 1781.a
1782.b 1783.b

1784.c 1785.a 1786.a 1787.b 1788.c 1789.b 1790.c 1791.c 1792.a

1793.c 1794.b 1795.a 1796.c 1797.b 1798.b 1799.a 1800.b 1801.a

1802.c 1803.b 1804.a 1805.c 1806.b 1807.a 1808.a 1809.c 1810.b

1811.b 1812.a 1813.b 1814.c 1815.a 1816.b 1817.b 1818.c 1819.c

1820.a 1821.c 1822.c 1823.b 1824.a 1825.b 1826.a 1827.c 1828.a

1829.c 1830.b 1831.a 1832.c 1833.c 1834.b 1835.b 1836.c 1837.b

1838.a 1839.c 1840.a 1841.c 1842.c 1843.a 1844.b 1845.c 1846.b

1847.c 1848.b 1849.b 1850.a 1851.c 1852.c 1853.b 1854.b 1855.c

1856.c 1857.a 1858.a 1859.a 1860.b 1861.a 1862.b 1863.c 1864.c

1865.a 1866.a 1867.b 1868.c 1869.b 1870.c 1871.b 1872.a 1873.c

1874.b 1875.a 1876.c 1877.a 1878.c 1879.b 1880.a 1881.b 1882.c

1883.a 1884.b 1885.c 1886.b 1887.a 1888.b 1889.c 1890.a 1891.a

1892.c 1893.a 1894.a 1895.b 1896.a 1897.c 1898.a 1899.b 1900.c

1901.b 1902.c 1903.c 1904.a 1905.b 1906.a 1907.b 1908.c 1909.a

1910.b 1911.a 1912.c 1913.b 1914.c 1915.c 1916.a 1917.a 1918.b

1919.a 1920.c 1921.b 1922.a 1923.c 1924.b 1925.a 1926.b 1927.a

1928.c 1929.a 1930.c 1931.b 1932.a 1933.c 1934.a 1935.c 1936.b

1937.c 1938.c 1939.a 1940.b 1941.a 1942.c 1943.c 1944.b 1945.b

1946.c 1947.c 1948.a 1949.b 1950.c 1951.a 1952.b 1953.a 1954.b

1955.c 1956.c 1957.a 1958.b 1959.b 1960.c 1961.c 1962.b 1963.a

1964.b 1965.b 1966.b 1967.c 1968.a 1969.a 1970.b 1971.a 1972.c

1973.a 1974.b 1975.c 1976.b 1977.c 1978.b 1979.c 1980.a 1981.a

1982.c 1983.a 1984.c 1985.b 1986.c 1987.b 1988.a 1989.c 1990.c

1991.a 1992.b 1993.b 1994.b 1995.a 1996.c 1997.a 1998.b 1999.b

2000.b 2001.c 2002.a 2003.b 2004.a 2005.c 2006.b 2007.a 2008.c

2009.b 2010.a 2011.b 2012.c 2013.a 2014.a 2015.b 2016.c 2017.b

2018.a 2019.b 2020.c 2021.a 2022.c 2023.c 2024.b 2025.c 2026.c

2027.b 2028.c 2029.c 2030.a 2031.c 2032.c 2033.c 2034.a 2035.b

2036.a 2037.c 2038.b 2039.c 2040.b 2041.c 2042.b 2043.a 2044.b

2045.c 2046.c 2047.a 2048.b 2049.b 2050.a 2051.c 2052.a 2053.a

2054.b 2055.c 2056.c 2057.c 2058.b 2059.a 2060.b 2061.c 2062.a

2063.c 2064.b 2065.c 2066.a 2067.a 2068.b 2069.b 2070.b 2071.c

2072.a 2073.b 2074.c 2075.c 2076.b 2077.b 2078.a 2079.c 2080.b

2081.c 2082.a 2083.b 2084.c 2085.a 2086.a 2087.c 2088.b 2089.a

2090.c 2091.b 2092.c 2093.a 2094.b 2095.c 2096.b 2097.a 2098.b

2099.a 2100.c 2101.c 2102.b 2103.a 2104.b 2105.c 2106.c 2107.c

2108.a 2109.b 2110.c 2111.b 2112.c 2113.a 2114.c 2115.b 2116.c

2117.a 2118.b 2119.b 2120.c 2121.c 2122.a 2123.a 2124.b 2125.c

2126.c 2127.b 2128.a 2129.b 2130.b 2131.a 2132.c 2133.a 2134.c

2135.b 2136.a 2137.c 2138.b 2139.c 2140.a 2141.a 2142.b 2143.c

2144.a 2145.c 2146.b 2147.a 2148.c 2149.c 2150.b 2151.a 2152.b

2153.c 2154.c 2155.a 2156.c 2157.b 2158.b 2159.a 2160.c 2161.a

2162.b 2163.c 2164.b 2165.c 2166.c 2167.b 2168.b 2169.a 2170.a

2171.b 2172.c 2173.c 2174.c 2175.b 2176.a 2177.c 2178.a 2179.b

2180.a 2181.b 2182.a 2183.c 2184.b 2185.b 2186.b 2187.a 2188.b

2189.c 2190.a 2191.b 2192.a 2193.c 2194.a 2195.b 2196.c 2197.c

2198.b 2199.a 2200.b 2201.c 2202.a 2203.b 2204.a 2205.c 2206.a

2207.c 2208.a 2209.b 2210.b 2211.c 2212.c 2213.a 2214.b 2215.b

2216.c 2217.a 2218.b 2219.c 2220.c 2221.b 2222.c 2223.b 2224.b

2225.a 2226.a 2227.c 2228.b 2229.a 2230.c 2231.a 2232.a 2233.c

2234.c 2235.b 2236.a 2237.b 2238.b 2239.c 2240.b 2241.a 2242.c

2243.b 2244.a 2245.c 2246.c 2247.b 2248.c 2249.b 2250.a 2251.a

2252.c 2253.b 2254.c 2255.a 2256.b 2257.a 2258.c 2259.b 2260.a

2261.a 2262.c 2263.a 2264.c 2265.a 2266.a 2267.c 2268.b 2269.a

2270.b 2271.c 2272.c 2273.b 2274.c 2275.c 2276.a 2277.b 2278.b

2279.c 2280.b 2281.a 2282.b 2283.c 2284.b 2285.a 2286.b 2287.c

2288.a 2289.b 2290.c 2291.b 2292.a 2293.b 2294.c 2295.a 2296.b

2297.a 2298.c 2299.c 2300.b 2301.a 2302.b 2303.c 2304.a 2305.b

2306.a 2307.c 2308.b 2309.c 2310.c 2311.b 2312.b 2313.a 2314.b

2315.a 2316.c 2317.a 2318.b 2319.c 2320.c 2321.b 2322.c 2323.a

2324.b 2325.b 2326.c 2327.a 2328.a 2329.b 2330.c 2331.b 2332.a

2333.c 2334.b 2335.b 2336.a 2337.c 2338.b 2339.a 2340.c 2341.c

2342.a 2343.a 2344.a 2345.b 2346.c 2347.a 2348.c 2349.b 2350.b

2351.c 2352.a 2353.a 2354.b 2355.b 2356.c 2357.a 2358.b 2359.a

2360.c 2361.b 2362.b 2363.a 2364.c 2365.a 2366.b 2367.b 2368.c

2369.b 2370.b 2371.a 2372.c 2373.c 2374.b 2375.a 2376.a 2377.b

2378.c 2379.b 2380.c 2381.c 2382.b 2383.a 2384.c 2385.a 2386.b

2387.c 2388.a 2389.b 2390.c 2391.a 2392.a 2393.b 2394.c 2395.c

2396.a 2397.b 2398.a 2399.b 2400.c 2401.a 2402.b 2403.b 2404.c

2405.b 2406.a 2407.b 2408.a 2409.c 2410.b 2411.b 2412.b 2413.a

2414.c 2415.a 2416.a 2417.a 2418.b 2419.c 2420.c 2421.a 2422.b

2423.a 2424.c 2425.c 2426.a 2427.b 2428.c 2429.a 2430.b 2431.b

2432.c 2433.a 2434.c 2435.b 2436.a 2437.c 2438.b 2439.a 2440.b

2441.c 2442.b 2443.a 2444.c 2445.c 2446.a 2447.b 2448.a 2449.c

2450.a 2451.c 2452.a 2453.b 2454.b 2455.a 2456.c 2457.b 2458.b

2459.c 2460.b 2461.b 2462.a 2463.c 2464.b 2465.b 2466.c 2467.a

2468.a 2469.b 2470.a 2471.b 2472.c 2473.b 2474.a 2475.b 2476.c

2477.a 2478.c 2479.a 2480.b 2481.a 2482.c 2483.c 2484.c 2485.a

2486.b 2487.a 2488.c 2489.a 2490.b 2491.a 2492.b 2493.c 2494.a

2495.b 2496.b 2497.a 2498.c 2499.a 2500.b 2501.c 2502.a 2503.b

2504.b 2505.b 2506.c 2507.a 2508.c 2509.a 2510.b 2511.c 2512.a

2513.b 2514.c 2515.a 2516.b 2517.b 2518.c 2519.c 2520.a 2521.b

2522.c 2523.a 2524.b 2525.b 2526.c 2527.a 2528.c 2529.c 2530.b

2531.b 2532.c 2533.a 2534.c 2535.b 2536.a 2537.a 2538.b 2539.a

2540.c 2541.b 2542.b 2543.c 2544.a 2545.a 2546.c 2547.a 2548.b

2549.c 2550.c 2551.b 2552.a 2553.c 2554.a 2555.b 2556.a 2557.b

2558.a 2559.c 2560.b 2561.c 2562.c 2563.a 2564.a 2565.a 2566.b

2567.b 2568.c 2569.a 2570.b 2571.c 2572.a 2573.b 2574.b 2575.b

2576.c 2577.a 2578.a 2579.b 2580.b 2581.a 2582.b 2583.c 2584.a

2585.c 2586.a 2587.b 2588.a 2589.b 2590.b 2591.a 2592.c 2593.b

2594.c 2595.b 2596.a 2597.c 2598.c 2599.a 2600.b 2601.b 2602.c

2603.b 2604.c 2605.b 2606.a 2607.c 2608.b 2609.a 2610.c 2611.c

2612.b 2613.a 2614.a 2615.b 2616.c 2617.b 2618.c 2619.a 2620.b

2621.c 2622.b 2623.b 2624.a 2625.a 2626.b 2627.c 2628.c 2629.b

2630.a 2631.c 2632.b 2633.a 2634.c 2635.b 2636.a 2637.c 2638.b

2639.a 2640.b 2641.c 2642.a 2643.b 2644.b 2645.c 2646.c 2647.a

2648.a 2649.c 2650.b 2651.b 2652.a 2653.c 2654.a 2655.c 2656.b

2657.c 2658.c 2659.a 2660.c 2661.c 2662.a 2663.b 2664.b 2665.a

2666.c 2667.b 2668.b 2669.c 2670.a 2671.c 2672.b 2673.c 2674.a

2675.b 2676.c 2677.a 2678.b 2679.a 2680.a 2681.c 2682.c 2683.a

2684.b 2685.c 2686.a 2687.b 2688.b 2689.c 2690.a 2691.c 2692.b

2693.b 2694.c 2695.a 2696.b 2697.b 2698.a 2699.c 2700.b 2701.b

2702.c 2703.a 2704.c 2705.a 2706.b 2707.c 2708.a 2709.c 2710.b

2711.a 2712.b 2713.c 2714.a 2715.c 2716.b 2717.a 2718.c 2719.b

2720.c 2721.b 2722.a 2723.c 2724.a 2725.b 2726.b 2727.a 2728.c

2729.c 2730.b 2731.a 2732.c 2733.b 2734.b 2735.a 2736.b 2737.b

2738.c 2739.a 2740.b 2741.c 2742.a 2743.c 2744.b 2745.a 2746.c

2747.c 2748.c 2749.b 2750.a 2751.b 2752.a 2753.c 2754.b 2755.a

2756.c 2757.b 2758.a 2759.c 2760.a 2761.b 2762.c 2763.b 2764.b

2765.a 2766.c 2767.b 2768.a 2769.b 2770.b 2771.c 2772.b 2773.b

2774.a 2775.b 2776.b 2777.c 2778.c 2779.a 2780.a 2781.b 2782.c

2783.b 2784.c 2785.a 2786.a 2787.b 2788.c 2789.a 2790.a 2791.b

2792.c 2793.b 2794.a 2795.b 2796.b 2797.a 2798.c 2799.b 2800.b

2801.a 2802.c 2803.a 2804.c 2805.c 2806.b 2807.a 2808.b 2809.c

2810.a 2811.c 2812.b 2813.b 2814.c 2815.a 2816.b 2817.b 2818.c

2819.b 2820.a 2821.c 2822.b 2823.a 2824.b 2825.b 2826.b 2827.a

2828.b 2829.c 2830.a 2831.b 2832.a 2833.c 2834.c 2835.a 2836.b

2837.c 2838.a 2839.c 2840.b 2841.a 2842.a 2843.c 2844.a 2845.b

2846.a 2847.a 2848.c 2849.b 2850.a 2851.c 2852.a 2853.b 2854.a

2855.a 2856.c 2857.b 2858.a 2859.b 2860.c 2861.a 2862.c 2863.c

2864.b 2865.a 2866.a 2867.c 2868.a 2869.b 2870.a 2871.b 2872.a

2873.c 2874.b 2875.b 2876.b 2877.a 2878.c 2879.c 2880.a 2881.a

2882.b 2883.c 2884.b 2885.c 2886.a 2887.b 2888.c 2889.b 2890.a

2891.b 2892.b 2893.c 2894.b 2895.a 2896.a 2897.b 2898.a 2899.b

2900.c 2901.a 2902.b 2903.a 2904.c 2905.c 2906.c 2907.b 2908.a

2909.c 2910.b 2911.b 2912.b 2913.a 2914.c 2915.a 2916.b 2917.a

2918.c 2919.a 2920.b 2921.a 2922.c 2923.b 2924.a 2925.b 2926.c

2927.b 2928.b 2929.a 2930.c 2931.b 2932.a 2933.a 2934.c 2935.a

2936.b 2937.c 2938.b 2939.b 2940.b 2941.c 2942.a 2943.b 2944.b

2945.a 2946.c 2947.b 2948.a 2949.c 2950.b 2951.c 2952.b 2953.a

2954.b 2955.c 2956.a 2957.b 2958.c 2959.a 2960.b 2961.b 2962.a

2963.c 2964.a 2965.c 2966.a 2967.a 2968.b 2969.a 2970.c 2971.b

2972.a 2973.b 2974.a 2975.a 2976.c 2977.a 2978.c 2979.b 2980.a

2981.c 2982.a 2983.a 2984.b 2985.a 2986.b 2987.c 2988.b 2989.c

2990.b 2991.a 2992.b 2993.a 2994.b 2995.c 2996.b 2997.a 2998.c

2999.a 3000.c 3001.c 3002.a 3003.b 3004.b 3005.a 3006.c 3007.a

3008.c 3009.a 3010.b 3011.c 3012.a 3013.b 3014.c 3015.a 3016.c

3017.b 3018.b 3019.c 3020.a 3021.c 3022.b 3023.a 3024.c 3025.b

3026.a 3027.c 3028.a 3029.c 3030.b 3031.c 3032.a
3033.c 3034.b
3035.c 3036.a 3037.b 3038.a 3039.b 3040.c 3041.b
3042.a 3043.b
3044.b 3045.c 3046.b 3047.a 3048.b 3049.a 3050.c
3051.b 3052.c
3053.a 3054.b 3055.c 3056.c 3057.b 3058.a 3059.b
3060.a 3061.b
3062.c 3063.a 3064.b 3065.b 3066.a 3067.c 3068.a
3069.c 3070.c
3071.b 3072.c 3073.b 3074.b 3075.c 3076.b 3077.a
3078.b 3079.c
3080.b 3081.a 3082.b 3083.b 3084.c 3085.a 3086.b
3087.a 3088.a
3089.c 3090.b 3091.b 3092.b 3093.a 3094.c 3095.a
3096.b 3097.a
3098.b 3099.b 3100.c 3101.b 3102.c 3103.a 3104.b
3105.a 3106.b
3107.c 3108.b 3109.a 3110.c 3111.a 3112.b 3113.c
3114.b 3115.a
3116.b 3117.b 3118.b 3119.a 3120.c 3121.a 3122.b
3123.c 3124.b
3125.a 3126.b 3127.b 3128.b 3129.c 3130.b 3131.a
3132.c 3133.b
3134.c 3135.a 3136.b 3137.a 3138.b 3139.b 3140.a
3141.c 3142.b
3143.b 3144.c 3145.c 3146.a 3147.c 3148.c 3149.a
3150.b 3151.b
3152.a 3153.c 3154.b 3155.b 3156.a 3157.c 3158.b
3159.a 3160.a
3161.b 3162.c 3163.a 3164.a 3165.b 3166.a 3167.c
3168.b 3169.b
3170.a 3171.c 3172.a 3173.b 3174.a 3175.c 3176.b
3177.b 3178.a
3179.a 3180.a 3181.c 3182.b 3183.c 3184.a 3185.b
3186.c 3187.b
3188.a 3189.b 3190.c 3191.a 3192.b 3193.a 3194.b
3195.c 3196.b

3197.c 3198.a 3199.a 3200.b 3201.b 3202.a 3203.c
3204.c 3205.b
3206.a 3207.b 3208.a 3209.c 3210.c 3211.c 3212.b
3213.a 3214.b
3215.a 3216.b 3217.b 3218.c 3219.b 3220.c 3221.a
3222.c 3223.a
3224.b 3225.a 3226.b 3227.c 3228.a 3229.b 3230.b
3231.c 3232.a

3233.c 3234.a 3235.b 3236.a 3237.b 3238.c 3239.b
3240.a 3241.a
3242.c 3243.a 3244.b 3245.b 3246.b 3247.c 3248.a
3249.c 3250.b
3251.b 3252.b 3253.a 3254.c 3255.c 3256.a 3257.b
3258.b 3259.a
3260.c 3261.b 3262.b 3263.a 3264.c 3265.c 3266.a
3267.b 3268.c
3269.a 3270.b 3271.c 3272.a 3273.a 3274.b 3275.b
3276.c 3277.a
3278.c 3279.b 3280.a 3281.c 3282.b 3283.c 3284.a
3285.a 3286.b
3287.c 3288.a 3289.a 3290.b 3291.a 3292.c 3293.b
3294.a 3295.c
3296.b 3297.a 3298.a 3299.b 3300.c 3301.a 3302.c
3303.a 3304.b
3305.c 3306.b 3307.a 3308.b 3309.a 3310.c 3311.a
3312.c 3313.b
3314.b 3315.a 3316.a 3317.a 3318.b 3319.c 3320.b
3321.a 3322.c
3323.b 3324.c 3325.c 3326.b 3327.a 3328.c 3329.a
3330.a 3331.c
3332.a 3333.b 3334.a 3335.b 3336.a 3337.c 3338.a
3339.c 3340.a
3341.b 3342.b 3343.b 3344.a 3345.c 3346.a 3347.c
3348.a 3349.b
3350.c 3351.a 3352.c 3353.b 3354.b 3355.a 3356.b
3357.c 3358.a
3359.b 3360.a 3361.b 3362.c 3363.a 3364.a 3365.b
3366.c 3367.a
3368.b 3369.c 3370.a 3371.b 3372.c 3373.c 3374.a
3375.a 3376.a
3377.b 3378.c 3379.a 3380.a 3381.b 3382.b 3383.c
3384.a 3385.c
3386.b 3387.b 3388.c 3389.a 3390.c 3391.b 3392.a
3393.c 3394.a
3395.b 3396.c 3397.c 3398.b 3399.c 3400.a

***.